BIOPOETICS
Evolutionary Explorations in the Arts

Edited by

Brett Cooke and Frederick Turner

An ICUS Book
Lexington, Kentucky USA

Published by the
International Conference on the Unity of the Sciences
147 Goodrich Avenue
Lexington, Kentucky 40503 USA

The International Conference on the Unity of the Sciences (ICUS), a project of ICF, convenes distinguished scientists and scholars worldwide from every field of study, to pursue academic discussion of theoretical and practical concerns. ICUS seeks an integrated worldview based on absolute values generated through multidisciplinary, academic dialogue.

Library of Congress Cataloging-in-Publication Data
Biopoetics: evolutionary exploration in the arts / edited by Brett Cooke and Frederick Turner.

466 pages

Based on individual essays, previously published materials in journals, and two conferences held in 1990 and 1995.

Includes bibliographical references.

ISBN 0-89226-204-4 (cloth: alkaline paper). – 0-89226-205-2 (pbk.: alkaline paper).

1. Aesthetics. 2. Art–Psychology. 3. Human behavior. 4. Behavior evolution. I. Cooke, Brett. II. Turner, Frederick, 1943-

BH39.B54 1999 98-51505
111'.85–dc21 CIP

Contents

To my daughter Sasha, who first brought me to sociobiology.
As usual, it is all your fault.

L.B.C.

In memory of Victor Turner

F.T.

Acknowledgments

We have drawn on many sources to assemble this anthology: individual essays, previously published materials and, especially, the findings of two remarkable conferences. The first was the Conference on the Fantastic in New Critical Theories, which took place at Texas A&M University in 1990. We are grateful to the Texas A&M College of Liberal Arts and the Department of Modern and Classical Languages for making this gathering possible. The second major source was the Twentieth International Conference on the Unity of the Sciences, held in Seoul, Korea, in 1995, sponsored by the International Cultural Foundation and organized by Tor Ragnar Gerholm, conference chair; Neil Salonen, president of the International Cultural Foundation; Gregory Breland, executive director of ICUS; and Brian Wijeratne, associate chair of the panel on the biological functions of beauty. In preparing our collection for publication, it has been a particular joy to work with Gregory Breland, who both directed the project and was quick to come to our assistance on many occasions, and Rebecca Salonen, who thoughtfully copyedited the entire manuscript.

We are grateful to the following journals and publishers for permission to reprint materials which have gained the status of classics in biopoetics: Harvard University Press for extracts from Edward O. Wilson's books; the *Journal of Social and Evolutionary Structures* for Kathryn Coe's "Art, the Replicable Unit"; *Foundation* for Eric S. Rabkin's "Imagination and Survival"; Southern Illinois University Press for Eric Rabkin's "The Descent of Fantasy"; and *Stuttgarter Arbeiten zur Germanistik* for Daniel Rancour-Laferriere's, "Preliminary Remarks on Literary Memetics."

We are also grateful to The State Hermitage Museum in St. Petersburg, Russia for permission to use the curled panther on the cover. The coiling of the animal's body is a convention that occurs earlier in China than in Siberia or the Black Sea region, where it becomes a characteristic Scythian design. The animal in this instance may be a snow leopard, native to Siberia. The image is a piece of ancient Greek gold art executed for a wild Scythian client. Appropriately for this volume it is neatly balanced between primitive and civilized art. A curled-up panther made almost into a circle, it also ambivalently expresses both the natural and what Ellen Dissanayake terms "made special," by a human hand. As a beast of prey made symmetrical, beautiful, it exerts a push and a pull on us at the same time.

Part I

Overview and Origins

Biopoetics: The New Synthesis

Brett Cooke

Darwinian theory appears to leave no room for compromise. With evolution, it is all or nothing, take it or leave it, all of it or none of it. If natural selection did not shape any vital feature of a single living species, then, as Charles Darwin once argued, it does not pertain to any of us. But if it can be demonstrated to have shaped just one species, we will be hard pressed to determine where its enormous sway is bounded, if at all.[1] This includes the development of our own species, our behavior, our social organization—and our art. To be sure, neither hypothesis—evolution pertains to our behavior or it does not—seems subject to full proof, but the evidence is steadily mounting that if we wish to understand our profound and long-standing impulse to create and enjoy art we are well advised to attend to our evolutionary heritage.

In this volume we undertake to explore the implications—and the extraordinary promise—that the concept of evolution holds for art. In the years following the publication in 1975 of Edward O. Wilson's *Sociobiology: The New Synthesis*, scientists and philosophers debated whether various social behaviors could be traced to genetic influences. Perhaps because of its very complexity, art was pretty much left out of this discussion. But the question of art's place in evolution had to be raised: How could it be ignored by a theory that was gradually accommodating most other behaviors? As our annotated bibliography makes clear, it has been only recently that a growing number of scholars have tried to apply the tenets of evolution to various art forms to see what insight this new paradigm lends to such classic issues as originality, aesthetic pleasure, empathy, and morality in art. We may never settle on a singular evolutionary psychology of art, but it seems inevitable that we can use the newly available tools of sociobiology to dramatically increase our understanding of the centrality and persistence of the arts in human experience.

So we are mounting a new study of a subject that has resisted the pronouncements of critics, historians, and philosophers. Although our work is at a relatively early stage, the general features of this novel approach are taking shape. As with general sociobiology, which is now subsumed by evolutionary psychology, our endeavor proposes a new synthesis. To begin with, we regard the different arts, however fascinating their variety, as parts of one general human activity, the better to perceive their common features, often by means of crosscultural comparisons. John Tooby, Leda Cosmides, and Jerome Barkow predict that tenets of the new Darwinism will improve our perception; thanks to books like *The Adapted Mind* (1992), we are able to see what has been taken for granted or neglected—in effect, hidden in plain view. This volume is proof of what we are now able to see in the arts, thanks to these new cognitive tools. Furthermore, we can use principles of evolution to connect art firmly to all human issues. Even if art is for art's sake, it follows that we seriously consider what *that* purpose means in Darwinian terms. Not for nothing, we assume, as have many before us, is art found in every society, living or dead. The same importance is indicated by the sheer space, resources, time, and on occasion risk devoted to its production, performance, and consumption. This leads to the most important point. *Evolutionary psychology offers the arts demonstrable proof of their necessity*, explaining that art is one of the products of natural selection because it is, at least in toto and over time, adaptive.[2] What greater argument can we make for supporting art than to show that it is essential to our long-term health, i. e., fitness? There is already much to indicate a close relationship between aesthetics and selective advantage, between beauty and viability, between the arts and life.

As evolutionary psychology contributes to an expanded view of the arts, so art extends the range of evolutionary psychology. Art provides evolutionary psychology a virtual science of feelings. Artists are masters both of depicting emotions, as in a tone poem or a dramatic character, and of eliciting them in an audience. Additionally, as a true human "universal" with an array of "international languages" as apparently dissimilar as music and weaving, art constitutes what is close to being a single and profound perspective on our many cultures, focusing on issues that we deem to be of the greatest interest. If this were not so, artists, participants, and viewers would not bother with art. Art's ability to strike a common chord, to attract attention and contain value, despite its apparent lack of utility, invites intensive examination. Lastly, art offers us an extensive record of our species' common emotional experiences, those which are still able to hold us in their grasp over a span of hundreds, even thousands of years. Here history really can influence the present, in that extremely ancient works often are able to condition our consciousness with ever-fresh strength. Art and evolutionary psychology make available to each other an immense array of highly useful data, of lived facts and reactions to them. But, more than that, art constitutes the most comprehensive index of our common heritage, our deepest point of access into what may turn out to be our shared human nature.

Many of these thoughts, it will be admitted, have been uttered before. Nancy E. Aiken's history of earlier evolutionary approaches to art shows how evolutionists took an extensive interest in art during the latter half of the last century and the first decades of our own. And for good reason. The predecessors of sociobiology readily appreciated what Darwin's findings meant for art. They also sensed that art could not be left out of the new paradigm. Nevertheless, the general inquiry lapsed, although study of our physiological capacities continued, largely divorced from the notion of art's biological utility. A variety of reasons can be advanced for the ensuing neglect. One may well have been the dramatic growth of the social sciences and the prevailing success of culturalist explanations. Field workers emphasized the varieties of human activity, not the commonalities. (Both perspectives are correct; it just depends through which end of the telescope you choose to look.) Aestheticians, in line with the advent of what is now called modernism in the arts, raised art beyond the reach of most people, though it can be regarded more accurately as an everyday activity that involves just about everyone. Last, political, even racist, insensitivities compounded misconceptions and suspicions about evolutionary approaches to human questions.

Now, however, we seek artistic universals and features that reflect our common humanity. The heritage that interests us as the wellspring of art greatly predates the differentiation of our species. Some aesthetic proclivities, for example, appear to be held by a number of other animals, including a few quite distant from our own hominid lineage. It may well be that they share some of the same needs for art as we do, though such functions as mate attraction amount to but a fraction of the adaptive benefits human beings reap from aesthetic creativity.

Perhaps the greatest obstacle to the evolutionary study of art was that this nascent field had no common term or place in the library. People who were interested in the evolution of art worked in isolation, assuming they were the only such specialists in the world; there was no way to find one another. Now we know better. The time has come to endow this new approach with a name. "Evolutionary aesthetics" and "bioaesthetics" are often used to consider not just art but also the undeniable beauty of living things. Our mission is a narrower one in that we intend to study the creative arts, human-made beauty. I propose that we add the prefix "bio" to the Aristotelian root "poetics," a word which describes the science of at least one art—there is no English term for the study of *all* the arts. Derived from the Greek verb for *making*, "poetic" also refers to our impulse to create beauty. We then nominate the term "biopoetics."

The turning point for biopoetics came in the 1960s with refinements in evolutionary theory. With thinkers like W. D. Hamilton, R. L. Trivers, Richard Dawkins, Richard Alexander, and E. O. Wilson addressing the problems posed by altruism, the focus shifted to the gene as the unit of evolution. Now it was apparent that the nonreproductive individual could contribute to the future, if not via his or her offspring, then through nieces and nephews, cousins, and so on, by way of a widening, albeit diluted influence. Nor did this transmission have to be immediate or conscious. The animal kingdom is obedient to the same laws of natural selection, without "knowing" an iota of Darwinism. Concepts like reciprocity, replication, and deception yielded much new insight into the increasingly complicated but ever more rational picture of the whole of life. According to natural selection, our behavior is influenced by a very large number of genetic forces or, as Wilson terms them, epigenetic rules. The core of each of these is rational, but they can be counterpoised against one another. This produces a much greater potential variety in our activities, but we should not lose sight of the underlying commonalities. Adding further complication, Dawkins' meme and other proposed units of intellectual replication enable us to cope with such bewildering and fast-moving phenomena as we find in modern artistic culture. Artists have the additional option of replicating themselves into posterity directly via their works. Once again, the hunt was on as sociobiology, in its new guise of evolutionary psychology, suddenly reached into many fields, eventually including art, and what we now propose to call biopoetics came into being.

Thanks to these handy concepts, this volume constitutes another sort of synthesis in that it gathers contributors who have come to this one intersection from many different fields. A cursory review of the contents of the book will reveal that its findings derive from such diverse spheres as aesthetics, ethology, neuropsychology, entomology, psychoanalysis, biochemistry, folklore, narratology, archaeology, classical literature, science fiction, developmental psychology, sociology, ethnography, anthropology, critical theory, and philosophy. Some of the entries listed in our annotated bibliography also incorporate mathematics, botany, and astronomy via chaos theory. However, the relevant concepts are close to our everyday experience; the reader will see that our findings generally accord with common sense. Though the starting points are very diverse, the authors' conclusions often agree, constituting, perhaps, a form of scientific repeatability. For one, Kathryn Coe looks to archaeology to develop her notion that one of the basic aims of art is to attract attention; this compares well with Eric S. Rabkin's comments on fantasy literature about the benefits of holding the "storyteller's advantage." Coe's insistence on the conservative aims of art is borne out by my study of how daemon-lover tales constrain sexuality. Frederick Turner's introduction of chaos theory beautifully matches E. O. Wilson's observations on our special regard for the serpent. Indeed, some of the best indices to non-linear phenomena are emotional reactions which are incommensurate with their initial cause. Turner's "neurocharms" anticipate John Tooby and Leda Cosmides' theory of domain-specific modes of cognition. Nancy Easterlin's probing of how far anti-narrative can go and remain viable literature dovetails with Gary Westfahl's lament that conventional science fiction is so much more popular than what is truly novel. As a result, our efforts in common transcend what could be the findings of any single scholar, yet the conclusions consistently support evolutionary approaches to art.

The essays here represent just a small fraction of the intellectual spheres that we believe will both contribute to biopoetics and, eventually, rest on it. One reason is that evolutionary psychology enjoys great ease of access. The fundamental tenets are simple, and the issues are close to home, as we have discovered in the classroom. Biopoetic critics have the satisfaction of knowing that their work is supported by well-tested principles of experimental and observational science. Meanwhile, we are not working out towards some arcane fringe where the only people we can address are ourselves; rather, we are moving our diverse interests into the center, to issues that concern everyone all the time. That the same limited repertory of themes appears so repeatedly in the arts should be taken as vital evidence of the inexhaustible interest that the underlying biological principles elicit. How many times, for example, have we read boy-meets-girl stories—and will the repetition ever be enough to satisfy a species that reproduces the way we do? There is a moral fervor as well. Not only does biopoetics demonstrate the usefulness of art, it does so in a manner which emphasizes humankind's common heritage.

Part of the problem with recognizing the nature of art lies in modern conventions that make it out to be far more rare than it is. The production and consumption of art is truly an everyday activity for everyone. Ellen Dissanayake has demonstrated that there is a concrete basis for biopoetics in the form of "making special," now acknowledged to be a human universal in that our proclivity to refine our experience into something of greater value can be discerned in the arts of all cultures—indeed, in all media and levels of artistic behavior. She suggests that one difficulty in discussing art evolutionarily (i.e., positing its utility or selective value) lies in our confusion about what the word "art" refers to. We are conditioned by Western notions about art's exclusivity and non-utility, and by the specialized profession of artist. In pre-modern cultures, everyone engages in artful activity, and art is such an everyday behavior that there is often no word for it. "Making special" imparts a qualitative distinction to the otherwise quotidian. In this conception, art as making special incorporates many of the characteristics of play and ritual, areas where quality breeds social success, and, we should expect, likely reproductive success—i. e., a selective advantage both for the individual and for his group. Indeed, Dissanayake adduces many other sources of utility for these faculties, creating a synergy of adaptive forces sufficient for the evolutionary scenario she offers, one that goes back hundreds of thousands of years. Evidently, the arts are not a new hyperphenomenon but, rather, a deep human tendency that has always been worth the enormous expenditure of time and resources poured into them.

Dissanayake's singular insight opens the way for a remarkable diversity of approaches. Her various studies on "making special," here presented in brief, amount to the most plausible and comprehensive hypothesis produced so far regarding universal features of art which are arguably the result of our evolutionary heritage. Given evolution's all-encompassing character, being either entirely acceptable or totally discardable, her demonstration of a human universal closely associated with art, if not its very essence, establishes the basis for further biopoetic perspectives. This emboldens further inquiry into the other selective qualities of art. As a result, we expect that biopoetics will take many different forms, given, for one reason, the vast range of important aspects of art. Dissanayake's seminal concept readily leads us to questions, to begin with, of what, when, by whom, for whom, and why the chosen objects of art are "made special." We should not look forward to a single theory of art but, more fruitfully, only a common paradigm of perspectives. Life, nature, and art are not that simple. Besides, we have only just begun our sociobiologically inspired explorations in art.

So as to provide a firm foundation for future ventures, we have reissued in Part I some important statements which first appeared in obscure places. Eric S. Rabkin's "Descent of Fantasy" outlines the essentially social nature of both our species and our art, suggesting how art socializes us, especially by marking out borders, enforcing control, and issuing cautionary tales like the story of Little Red Riding Hood. Art does not necessarily represent life; in this case it enriches our experience with an impermissible inversion, telling us what must not be. Rabkin points out how human society is a many-stranded web of reciprocal relationships that must be based on trust, wherein our shared language is our greatest survival aid if only because it enables us greatly to widen our experience at no more cost than the pleasure of listening to a storyteller. Pleasure, Rabkin reminds us, is significant; our feelings are naturally shaped indicators of whether our behavior is adaptive. There is, then, little wonder that we enjoy creating order in society or in narrative. Furthermore, social rewards come not so much in statements of love as in the form of such highly adaptive practices as food sharing—and its derivative, storytelling.

In one of the very earliest biopoetic essays, Daniel Rancour-Laferriere takes us to what is still the periphery of the field to examine what is or is not a meme. His thoughtful distinctions, nevertheless, challenge contemporary thinking on units of cultural evolution comparable to genes. More importantly, Rancour-Laferriere points out that memes often entail a relationship between genetic affinity and intellectual affiliation. Rabkin's "storyteller's advantage" gains a new feature here in the concern artists feel for their productions and the care they take to perpetuate them, often speaking of them as if they were their children. Of course, it stands to reason that if we put more effort into our art, we are more likely to reap a selective advantage from it. Rancour-Laferriere notes both the Freudian qualities of this association and how much of our artistic behavior derives from confused or redirected attitudes to emotion-charged phenomena, like art. Art, in the best sense, is a child that never grows up, much like the notoriously neotenous species that produces it. Not only do we never lose our sense of play, our nurture of writing grows out of our inclination for parental behavior: both require large amounts of usually unreciprocated altruism. As with many of the traditional schools of artistic criticism, psychoanalysis here gains a more rational ground in evolutionary psychology. Rancour-Laferriere's example of the dedication of Nadezhda Mandelstam, who preserved her husband's poetry solely in her memory, reminds us of dissidents in Ray Bradbury's *Fahrenheit 451* who preserve whole books by memorizing them. But, after all, this was the common practice in our ancestral past, when the entirety of folklore was maintained only in people's minds.

Rancour-Laferriere's viral simile of the contagious meme certainly works for the contributors to this volume. All of us are largely applying statements by Edward O. Wilson and his colleagues to the creative arts. However, few of us are aware of what these first sociobiologists, especially Wilson, themselves had to say on the subject. Edward O. Wilson's contributions to what we can now call biopoetics were ignored as such, partly because he published them almost too openly—that is, in his ground-breaking books on sociobiology, which were largely addressed to specialists in other fields—and partly because they were scattered amid assorted other subjects. To bring Wilson's contributions into greater relief, we have extracted his various remarks on art, and I have added a parallel commentary. For instance, rereading his essays from a biopoetic perspective, we can see that Wilson was among the first to seize on the phenomenon of differential interest: this is to say that, thanks to learning curves which proceed at various rates, we are quicker to react to some things than to others—and the former are likely to hold our attention for a significantly longer span. These are essential issues for any survey of artistic themes, and indeed Wilson's observations on serpent imagery should be recognized as a classic statement on the ontology of myths. Elsewhere, Wilson points out the neurophysical dimension of the emotions that the arts are so good at eliciting. He outlines the benefits of play in terms of developing and expanding one's range of adaptive behaviors, and, discussing religion, he ponders our species-wide propensity to harbor deep beliefs in that which, from an objective standpoint, is unlikely. Indeed, Wilson observes in the arts the potential for exaggeration, anticipating Frederick Turner's and Alexander Argyros' notions of non-linearity as being a key characteristic of artistic behavior. Wilson's is a sophisticated perspective. He both acknowledges the co-evolutionary structure of art, play, and ritual, and notes that art is not necessarily adaptive in the immediate sense. Like Dawkins, Wilson observes that we may be gulled into being parasitized by ideologies which serve larger purposes, as in the case of personal sacrifices made in the name of religion. Biopoetics, admittedly, sees art as an amoral paradigm wherein the ends often justify the means, at least in terms of increased genetic potential. On the other hand, the arts have typically been the vehicle for the codification and, especially, the dissemination of moral systems.

In a concise presentation of his famous theory of "natural classicism," Frederick Turner traces the roots of art very far back into our evolutionary history, possibly back to the very beginning of the cosmos. Turner advances the daring thesis that our aesthetic sensitivities evolved as an index of the actual patterns of the universe. The adaptive significance and evolutionary history of this capacity are clear. Aesthetics are an essential element in most behaviors; the pleasure of beauty is a reward for value-rich forms of activity and attention. It follows that a feedback loop is created leading us to more successful actions, to become better adapted to our environment, whether natural or human. Turner revives the Keatsian equation of beauty with truth, simply because accurate perception and knowledge incline us to greater viability. His notion of "neurocharms" posits aesthetics as a more inclusive and in some respects superior form of cognition, one that allows us to grasp a situation with greater efficiency. As a result, a few lines in a fine novel suffice for us to imagine an entire fictional world. It is worth noting in this regard that the arts often serve a pedagogical function by imparting greater sensitivity and creativity. For very good reason they have traditionally been part of educational programs. Indeed, our findings in this volume should be taken to suggest that the arts be restored to their former prominence both in the classroom and in our wider social discourse. With ease and pleasure they train us in a variety of valuable cognitive skills, such as analogy, analysis, and synthesis. Certainly Turner's neurocharms constitute an aid to memory; they play a large role in oral—i. e., memorized—culture and, as a result, enable the arts to shape a group's behavior through time, helping them stay on a traditional course and or think out novel situations in the light of previous experience. My essay on dead-bridegroom folktales in widely separated societies offers illustrative support of Turner's thesis that common plot motifs are rooted in our genes.

Turner's dictum that the fundamental theme or tendency of the universe is feedback or reflexivity bears comparison to Richard Dawkins' posited law of self-replication and to Koen DePryck's conception of self-organizing systems. With the laws of physics thus working through the fleshly medium of genetics, either structure can plausibly generate familiar conditions, including a larger context for the arts, firmly situated in a new perspective of empirical causality. Turner extends his observation of nested complexity, a basic characteristic of the universe, to the medium of language, which has recently been a focus of poststructuralist thought. Since we are connected to everything else in so many ways, Turner draws no unnecessary dividing line cutting off "textuality" and "discourse" from the non-linear phenomena that constitute the physical realm. He sketches, in effect, a self-organizing model which would encompass various levels of lexical meaning, self-generating and -replicating memes and—just perhaps—a perfectly empirical equivalent of the soul.

Turner's view of beauty, like DePryck's, takes in the entire universe, and in a sense biopoetics has to be similarly expansive, a potential umbrella field for the many schools of both literary criticism and aesthetics. The marriage of criticism and aesthetics will not be easy, for a number of perspectives abhor the kind of objective demonstration and concrete empiricism that biopoetics calls for. Prominent scholars working in biopoetics, including Turner, Robert Storey, Joseph Carroll, and Dissanayake, have utilized findings in evolutionary studies to point out the groundlessness of contemporary deconstructionist and postmodernist "theory." Indeed, biopoetics can readily be seen as an antidote to views that the arts are useless and meaningless, which is the prevailing received opinion today. The very universality of the arts, surely not a pure accident, by itself argues strongly for the opposite position—namely, that the arts perform some sort of vital role in determining our evolutionary fate.

Although, as Carroll and Dissanayake have pointed out, much contemporary "theory" disavows the kind of inquiry promised by biopoetics, our new paradigm offers a solid, empirical ground for a number of contemporary perspectives. Whereas the deconstructionists seize upon various linguistic gaps and inconsistencies, Tooby and Cosmides have propounded a theory that the adapted mind is composed of separable "domain-specific" capacities; as a result, we get not a single all-purpose mentality, but a consciousness with discernible seams in it. While sociobiology explains our strong propensity to align ourselves in to social groups, it frustrates the utopian impulses so dear to Marxism. As Wilson once suggested (1978), one could argue that Marxism agrees with sociobiology's insight into the various circles of self-interested behavior, whether that involves self, family, or social class. However, Marxist theory would need to be informed by very same genetic biology that it abhors. Meanwhile, evolutionary psychology sets the irrational psyche posited by Freud and his followers into an eminently logical realm by showing how our emotional responses serve to set us in the direction of adaptive behavior. Although Joseph Carroll properly criticizes Freudianism as being outmoded, especially as an all-encompassing paradigm, many of Freud's findings are supported by evolutionist research. As Rancour-Laferriere (1985) has made clear, psychoanalysis provides insights into emotions that Darwinians view as mechanisms for making narrow choices in matters of family politics. Indeed, it may well be that genetic factors "prime" us to respond strongly to precisely those features of infantile experience that concern psychoanalysis. For example, the competing demands of eliciting kin altruism, as in the case of mother love, and avoiding incest help account for Oedipal ambivalence. Freudian insights, like natural selection, make the most of what is at hand. We are prone to use our parents as models of adult behavior, and much of our future character develops out of the primary stages of infantile experience. Finally, among the schools described by Carroll, pragmatic criticism finds unique insights in literary classics—which we would expect to be true of masterpieces in the other arts—such as are essential to a biological perspective. We need to take seriously the notion that artistic creativity encourages a level and perhaps type of cognition superior in some respects to other ways of thinking, that there may be some kernel of truth in the common perception that great artists are in their own ways wise. After all, if the arts did not provide cognitive benefits otherwise unavailable, we could hardly expect them to be found literally in every society.

As Carroll points out, biopoetics not only promises to connect the humanities with the scientific world—an ironic development, given that so much of postmodernism has been devoted to cutting them off—but also to impose scientific methods and standards of proof on arts scholarship. In effect, what is required is an intellectual rigor that has not been seen since the Russian formalists. Carroll touches on many of the problems which stand in the way of a scientific study of literature. It would not be enough, for example, to scan literary themes without taking into account the manner of their presentation. Indeed, the overriding problem posed by the arts is that of irony, which has the potential for overturning conclusions arrived at by literalistic means. The same problems and more are only to be expected when we extend Carroll's principles to the other arts. The studies which compose the rest of this volume constitute a variety of approaches to the challenges laid down by Carroll, in that they are informed by scientific knowledge, focus on issues which could produce a biologically significant advantage, and may be subjected to crosscultural comparisons.

Part II presents new perspectives on many of the basic features of art. It is surprising, if not disconcerting, how established criticism has paid so little attention to such central elements as novelty, tradition, constraint, liberation, empathy, attraction, and—especially—rapture. Perhaps it is because earlier perspectives took them for granted. However, nothing may be taken for granted in biology, where it is presumed that all life phenomena exist for reasons of natural selection. As a result, biopoetics prompts us to take a new look at the fundamentals of not only the arts, but also of so much else in human experience. Wayne E. Allen shows just how special "making special" can be. While Dissanayake emphasizes that art is a behavior, as opposed to an object, Allen focuses our attention on the internal states elicited by it. His position is that art, whether at its distant origins in the Pleistocene or in the present, makes use of a complex of factors and need not be the product of any single function or adaptation. But the experience conveys ecstasy, the element of emotional transport that we find essential to a viable piece of art, if not the principal reason we are attracted to it. Allen then shows how biochemical systems are essential to aesthetics: they cannot be taken for granted, for they process all sensation and mentation. According to his thesis, aesthetic experiences as we know them were partly evolved as a byproduct of our adaptation to marginal food sources, including hallucinogenic fungi. He also revives Darwin's notion that art derives from sexual attraction. Extreme experiences of both are in many ways similar, leading Allen to suggest that our aesthetic feelings are developed from our capacity for sensual pleasure.

This notion illustrates Turner's concept of nested complexity, where structures derive from underlying structures, indeed, emulate them; verily, as King Lear observes, nothing comes from nothing. Memes, for example, resemble the genes that gave rise to them in being particulate, replicable, and, quite possibly, as the unit of cultural selection, self-motivated. Meanwhile, art helps people to manipulate one another; an advantage probably outweighing the significant costs of art. Some aesthetic experiences verge on altered states of consciousness; these, it would seem, would entail some significant risks. Shamanism, for example, promotes both sociality and a sense of being oriented in one's environment, which are issues of clear adaptive significance. Allen's remarks about the special abilities of shamans to experience and express their experience of ecstacy and altered states of consciousness can hardly fail to remind the modern observer of the outlandish behavior of many contemporary artists. He adduces an adaptive benefit to being able to successfully imitate hallucinogenic experiences. If nothing else, this would serve to gain attention, possibly in the form of Rabkin's "storyteller's advantage." After all, it usually pays to attract the interest of others; otherwise, quite certainly, manipulation of others is difficult. Allen's is also a distinctly down-to-earth perspective reminding us that our internal experience is rooted in our physical responses to a great variety of biochemicals, strongly supporting the monist hypothesis that body and mind are united.

The emotions released by the arts are not spent uselessly but in most cases are directed to ends which are or once were biologically significant. For example, my own essay on sexual property expands on Eric S. Rabkin's concept of the "cautionary tale." I conduct a close comparison of fantasies involving the sexual constraint of widows, one by Pushkin, from Russia, the other an oral narrative from the highlands of New Guinea. If people in widely separated societies are thinking along the same lines, then it is likely their concerns reflect deep-set human proclivities, especially if the areas of agreement involve such matters of adaptive significance as, in this case, paternal certainty (knowing the parentage of their offspring) and the assurance of kin altruism. To exclude the possibility of cultural contamination, I invoke a "five continent rule" by identifying similar tales from a wide sample of other countries. At the same time, I establish a vertical perspective by studying Pushkin's *Snowstorm* in depth, examining both the drafts for the tale and the author's other works. A retrograde side to art is thus revealed. Some of the universal subjects it treats are predicated on inequalities in our personal relationships, such as the infamous "double standard." Biology is not necessarily fair; tenets of evolutionary psychology quite readily predict a strong tendency for greater controls to be placed on women, as we see in many societies. Second, in the light of evolutionary psychology, art provides us an archaeology of the mind; the ideologies we reveal may reflect ancient environments while being anachronistic in our own. This important qualifier expresses a distinction between sociobiology and evolutionary psychology. Thanks to the greatly differing rates of genetic and cultural evolution, we can now be said to be maladapted to modern conditions simply due to the speed of environmental change. True, in recent times art has often served the cause of liberation. Nevertheless, at the same time it often works to constrain us, to lay the structures for "internalized oppression." The "double standard" had its reasons in the past; it is increasingly hard to justify in the present. Judging by the relative success of countries which recognize women's rights, it seems to now be maladaptive. Third and perhaps most striking, objective analysis of a well-accepted artistic "classic" often reveals a substructure which we could hardly embrace when viewing it rationally. The point here is that art, with all of its affective properties, much as Carroll asserts, may work to augment some forms of cognition, particularly those needed in the environment of evolutionary adaptiveness (EEA), at a necessary cost to other faculties such as reason and an ethical sense.

Similar thinking underlies Lee Cronk's study of how human societies, fictional as well as actual, do not reflect even a small fraction, let alone the full range, of possible forms. In effect, our social imagination is limited. Cronk attributes this cognitive myopia to our innate tendency to spontaneously prefer those groups which foster family life, an essential ingredient in all viable societies. This is not to dispute our potential for thinking about virtually anything we set our minds to, but it raises the question of what we are actually likely to do. Mathematical extrapolation and the theoretical range of science fiction may appear to be almost boundless, but we rarely push the boundaries of thought evidenced by popular fiction. In effect, Cronk's study of family structures illustrates Charles Lumsden and Edward O. Wilson's assertion that what we often think of as the virtual infinity of human variety is, nevertheless, bounded; thereby it excludes an even larger range of theoretical possibilities. Cronk's choice of George Murdock's *Ethnographic Atlas* provides us a benchmark for measuring the active imagination. Often in academic inquiry one neglects missing evidence of what is, after all, nonexistent, but here Cronk uses the dark matter of ethnographic space to suggest that whatever we are, we are for discernible reasons. This is not to say that biology wields some sort of iron hand over our freedom of choice. John Tooby and Leda Cosmides (1992) argue that all behavior is equally co-evolved, that it will show the same degree of genetic influence. On the other hand, Cronk predicts that the closer we come to behaviors essential to evolutionary psychology, such as reproduction, the more universal features we should expect to find. Fantasy narratives, for example, are filled with love stories. Furthermore, Cronk looks at the actual ethnography of family patterns for evidence of how we may occasionally try out behavioral innovations but how, over the long run, we are likely to stay close to deep-set tendencies. His examples also suggest the kind of messy findings we should expect in the arts, namely, that every instance is individual and inevitably will wander from the norm, if only due to local conditions, but that, depending on the range of one's perspective, not many individuals can buck inbred tendencies for long and stay viable.

Our spontaneous biases seem to follow the lines of our reproductive interest. Gary Westfahl tests this idea by closely examining three classics of science fiction. Because this genre so readily outruns our normal experience, it typically probes the limits of human interest. Thanks to the grossly differing pace of genetic and cultural evolution, the range of our attention span is considerably less than it might be or, if we look at our present adaptive needs, should be. Stories which gratify our fantasies by appealing to our archaic heritage often prove to be much more popular than those which provide a more accurate picture of the universe in which we now live. On the other hand, the mere existence of a genre Westfahl bemoans as too mildly alien with regard to old sensibilities should enable us to make the opposite argument. The innovation we find in some works leads us to suggest that the arts also incline us to expand our horizons, to liberate ourselves from traditional styles of thought, and to accelerate our cultural evolution, the better to suit the universe which, as Westfahl puts it, we actually live in. Tales of exploration are, as we have come to master our planet, replaced by probing of the past and the future. Since so much of our evolutionary conditioning took place when we were foraging peoples, it only makes sense that we should continually be on the lookout for new resources and possibly profitable adventures.

There also seems to be a stretching of the innate limitations in methods employed by art, at least in terms of our ability to respond to new aesthetic forms. These are not matters of mere stylistic change but, rather, reflect our very grasp of the universe we inhabit. Nancy Easterlin surveys recent literary experiments with anti-narratives, noting how unusual perceptual structures in postmodernist novels frustrate our natural proclivity for causal thinking. Narrativity, after all, helps us to reconstruct and recall the past, to anticipate the near future as well as, probably most important, the actions of our fellow human beings; it is our most common means of making connections between phenomena, of understanding, and constitutes a skill of great adaptive significance. By setting us cognitive tasks, novel novels work to stretch our capabilities. Art often takes on the form of a double-edged sword. On the one hand, it establishes an ethnic boundary and enforces conformity. On the other, it prods our flexibility, thereby enabling us to take advantage of new situations. Indeed, it is very likely that we seek out novelty in the arts so as to practice our cognitive abilities to adapt, thereby contributing to our inclusive fitness. This gives further illustration of Westfahl's model for cultural evolution in that, thanks to intraspecific competition, the reader gets more and more adept at reading the normally unreadable; more will be required to give him or her the necessary challenge. An acceleration of stylistic change is the likely result. Easterlin demonstrates this by studying modern elite fiction that would likely appeal to only a small literary subculture—notably a group that is especially well adapted to the present cultural milieu. Art, like literature, is now hardly a monolith. Our aesthetic sensibilities are highly contingent on the degree to which we have adapted our capabilities to cope with our new and now rapidly changing environment. Art, Easterlin reminds us, is composed of a very large number of different elements, each of which would seem to be derived by natural selection, much like the innumerable features of our physiology. Furthermore, the different elements of the arts all are likely to influence each other, yielding an ever more complex picture, though still one we can subject to objective and perfectly rational analysis. Lastly, Easterlin's examination of several recent novels suggests how our so-called genetic "hard-wiring" can account for the extraordinary range of behavioral freedom that we enjoy.

Kathryn Coe questions our present-day over-valuation of innovation in art. The archaeological record dictates an extremely gradual rate of stylistic change in the past, one that she attributes to a socially dictated conformism. Considering what is likely the first form of art, decoration of our own bodies, Coe argues that practices like scarification could have served sexual attraction. The person who subjected himself to this painful process thereby made a public display of his conformity to the group's values. It was a sign of likely success, a distant echo of patrons today who use art to show off their wealth. Like Robert Joyce (1975), Coe uses evidence of the high costs of art in terms of time and materials, the adaptive *disadvantages* of such sacrifices, self-mutilation, and personal suffering as powerful arguments that, despite contemporary critics, art obviously serves a vital function. Coe finds one universal we can identify in all art, namely, that it serves to attract attention, somewhat in the mode of Dissanayake's "making special" and Rancour-Laferriere's statement that "literary value is appeal." Art may thus serve to help disseminate the agenda of the text, symbol, or, in this case, the person wearing it.

Eric S. Rabkin offers another study that considers the survival value of fantastic art for constructing possible scenarios and helping us rehearse contingency plans, much in agreement with Alexander Argyros' (1991) notion that art is a society's means of selecting its future. But there is a danger here both to society and to its artists. Neophilia contends with neophobia; Rabkin notes how often free use of the imagination is suppressed as a threat to the norm. Indeed, a number of societies, real and imagined, attempt to banish it. Artists were often associated in ancient societies with ritual and magic; as we come closer to the modern period there is a whiff of evil to their activities, a sensation revealing our own suspicions. Yet we need to keep our capacity for breaking perceptual sets and envisioning what else might be up our sleeve, if nowhere else. Fantastic art persists because, Rabkin suggests, it provides a socially acceptable haven for our genius, keeping it in store for times when it is needed. This helps us understand why the fantasy culture of highly traditional and, in their own way, regimented societies so often produces such wildly contrary-to-fact narratives. In such fictive disguise, art allows us to be at the same time both liberal and conservative with regard to the imagination.

Due to the many often incompatible innate forces which pull on us, our art, like our behavior, sometimes takes the character of a tug-of-war—only we are drawn in many more directions than two. Though there is the powerful drag of cultural inertia, there is also a contrasting impetus for exploration. Joseph Miller traces our need for novelty in science fiction, perhaps the quintessential genre for innovation, to matters of neuropsychology. Neophilia, born of the numbing brought on by sensory repetition and our drive to avoid boredom, is posited as one of our drive-states—one which, Miller says, cannot be traced to an immediate tissue need but which, like sex, clearly contributes to our adaptive fitness. We are impelled to seek out the new, to notice the novel element, to be curious and thereby maintain our behavioral flexibility. At least we need to keep our eyes open. Neophilia prompts us to randomize our behavior, to produce things which on the surface seem to be produced for their own sake. This activity in the end gives us a greater range of choices. Miller traces how the development of spoken language, then writing, and now recent technological media, has been fueled by competition between meme vectoring systems, especially including science. Yet he, too, sees the need for holding a leash on inquiry. Miller notes how science fiction also provides us an "early warning system" by allowing us to vicariously live in a society before we taken on the investment of building it.

According to Alexander Argyros, we have little choice but to maintain a metaphysical flexibility of sorts. He traces the common association of love with death, truly a major narrative theme, to the ancient invention of sex, which was accompanied by individual mortality. As a result of this connection between mortality and reproductive success, an evolved consciousness is poised between an awareness of its great potential and knowledge of its inevitable limitations in time and influence. Argyros shows how chaos theory offers each of us a chance, to exert influence on the world well out of proportion to our actual initiative. A single aesthetic idea may yield far-reaching fame, and art magnifies our minuscule odds in this endeavor. Argyros thus offers us a wonderful example of the interest generated by negotiability, our imperfect ability to handle an impending condition. In his view, art presents us a means for coping with an increasingly complicated world. Inasmuch as anyone can become a star, artists and other would-be cultural heroes attract our interest—as a wealth of myths and tales the world over makes clear. Argyros' insight into the nonlinear nature of both our biological domain and human culture is pertinent to the development of artistic history. Much as our distant forebears—that is, at a distance of two billion years—gave up the security of asexual reproduction for the opportunities and risks of sex, artists are increasingly leaving the anonymous safety and assured audiences of traditional art styles to take their chances at the big game, trying to carve out a place for themselves with increasing degrees of formalistic and thematic individuality.

An essential ingredient in our expanding interest is empathy. We can widen our lived experience with vicarious adventures better if we care about the personalities involved. Sociobiologists like Robert Trivers and Nicholas Humphrey have noted the competitive advantages of taking an interest in others. Since our major selection pressure comes from fellow human beings, this interpersonal advantage soon brings about competition in expression, deception, empathy, and skepticism. Brian Hansen shows here how we add to our store of knowledge by sympathetic identification with the characters involved. This underlies what he usefully calls the "performance contract." If demonstration is a teacher superior to mere explanation, it is considerably improved if we participate emotionally. Hansen demonstrates this with a speculative prehistory of theater. Theater requires (1) personal encounter, (2) a panhuman capacity for enactment, something shared with few animals, (3) an ability to distinguish self from non-self, and (4) a capacity to discern when inappropriate behavior is intentional, such as when animals put on a "play-face." As a result, Rabkin's "storyteller's advantage" is reversed; Hansen ponders the benefits of involved listening. As members of the audience, we can rapidly and cheaply add to our store of experiences with the likely result that we become better adapted to our cultural milieu. Since this contributes to our inclusive fitness, it is surely significant that theater draws on activities which we find naturally pleasurable, much as we saw with Rabkin's comments on storytelling.

According to Hansen, this "performance contract" began tens, possibly hundreds of thousands of years ago. We can also say that it begins in infancy, yet another illustration of how ontogeny repeats phylogeny. Ellen Dissanayake suggests that music originated in human evolution from our earliest affective interaction—that between mothers and infants. Utilizing the gestures, facial expressions, and rich prosody of "babytalk," a caretaker engages a baby's interest in a patterned dynamic interaction that provides significant developmental gains for the infant. Here is a wonderful example of Argyros' notion of extreme sensitivity to initial conditions, inasmuch as mother love put into practice may yield massive benefits for her child in later life. This, too, is a self-organizing activity, for it has been demonstrated that mothers learn mothering from their mothers and so on, more often than not producing greater inclusive fitness. The interaction is pleasurable for both participants, prompting them to carry on their conversation spontaneously. Because the mother-child bond is a fundamental relationship, human rituals of affiliation and congruence use similar temporal and structural means to synchronize, coordinate, and enculturate their participants, just as affiliative rituals (of courtship and appeasement) in birds and other mammals utilize behavioral elements drawn from parental prototypes. Though human rituals are cultural creations and animal rituals are biologically evolved, the analogy is a provocative if unorthodox one and suggests a plausible biological precedent for a complex cultural behavior.

One of the major problems for biopoetics is that of tracing relatively trivial features in the arts to natural selection's dire struggle for survival of the fittest. (Admittedly, this contest is usually overdramatized; we can readily adduce less rigidly deterministic forms of differential reproduction sufficient to drive evolution.) Koen DePryck offers another approach with a renewed look at sexual selection. He argues that, as Frederick Turner reminds us, we are the genetic product our forebears' mate selection: in effect, the sum of what they found to be beautiful. DePryck contends that the complexity and interdependence of the universe is such that for complex systems there is no single deterministic outcome at any given moment. How, then, does the physical universe itself choose its next state? His daring answer is that the basis of this choice is analogous to our own capacity for aesthetic judgment. Or rather, our capacity for aesthetic judgment is only the most complex and advanced form of a spontaneity required by any complex nonlinear system, from symmetry-breaking as the early universe cooled, to speciation in biological evolution. Our aesthetic sense gives us a holistic grasp of such complex phenomena; quite obviously, it is a function that yields significant adaptive benefit and should be understood as one of the supreme cognitive faculties, one still well beyond the grasp of clinical psychology. Although some of our studies have focused on distinct features of the arts for perfectly understandable reasons, we must remember that artworks themselves constitute phenomena by definition beyond the envelope of full rational explanation. All the more reason that DePryck sets forth a many-faceted cognitive model for our prospective biopoetics. If evolution took place, then all of our prior perspectives on the arts, if not on the nature of perception itself, will have to be reconsidered in our new evolutionary paradigm.

As a guide for further reading, Nancy Aiken and I have provided an annotated bibliography of those published studies which attempt to identify selective qualities of art. No assurance can be given of its completeness. New contributions are appearing at an accelerating rate, and we continue to find previously undiscovered works. Soon compiling such a list will approach impossibility. Biopoetics now has the character of an explosion as our endeavor reaches critical mass.

Works Cited

Argyros, Alexander J.

1991 *A Blessed Rage for Order: Deconstruction, Evolution, and Chaos*. Ann Arbor: University of Michigan Press.

Barkow, Jerome, Leda Cosmides, and John Tooby, eds.

1992 *The Adapted Mind: Evolutionary Psychology and the Generation of Culture*. New York: Oxford University Press.

Dennett, Daniel C.

1995 *Darwin's Dangerous Idea: Evolution and the Meanings of Life*. New York: Simon and Schuster.

Joyce, Robert

1975 *The Esthetic Animal: Man, the Art-Created Art Creator*. Hicksville, New York: Exposition Press.

Rancour-Laferriere, Daniel

1985 *Signs of the Flesh: An Essay on Hominid Sexuality*. Berlin: Methuen.

Tooby, John, and Leda Cosmides

1992 "The Psychological Foundations of Culture." In Barkow, Cosmides, and Tooby, eds., *The Adapted Mind*, pp. 19-136.

Wilson, Edward O.

1975 *Sociobiology: The New Synthesis*. Cambridge, MA.: Harvard University Press.

1978 *On Human Nature*. Cambridge, MA.: Harvard University Press.

Notes

1. This is the point of Daniel C. Dennett's aptly titled *Darwin's Dangerous Idea: Evolution and the Meanings of Life* (1995). Dennett considers the concept of natural selection as a veritable universal acid which, once

released into the intellectual environment, inevitably undermines other explanations of behavior.

2. Genetics affects our behavior not in the form of mechanical certitudes but as statistical tendencies, so the linkage is somewhat blurred. Because there will always be exceptions, a consideration also adducible to natural selection, evolutionary psychology can best be seen in action with larger populations.

"Making Special": An Undescribed Human Universal and the Core of a Behavior of Art

Ellen Dissanayake

To the casual observer, the arts appear to be products of culture, not biology. Their forms differ widely from society to society, and societies vary in the value they attach to individual arts. Yet the fact that every society displays at least one of the practices that we commonly think of as art suggests that underlying the individual manifestations of different societies' arts may be a broader biologically endowed adaptive behavioral proclivity. Tooby and Cosmides (1990, 396) usefully distinguish between adaptations (such as aggression or infant attachment) and their manifestations, which may vary from context to context. Perhaps "art," properly understood, is a biological adaptation with different manifestations appearing in different contexts or cultures.

To date, however, the treatment of art by evolutionary theorists, even on the rare occasions when they acknowledge it as a noteworthy human activity, has been almost uniformly unsatisfying.[1] While many ignore art altogether, others (e.g., Harris 1989, xi) admit outright that art and music are "difficult to explain in terms of evolutionary processes."

The few behavioral theorists who have discussed art invariably consider it as associated with or arising from other behavioral or mental features, such as communication, play, display, exploration and curiosity, amusement and pleasure, creativity and innovation, transformation, the joy of recognition and discovery, the satisfaction of a need for order and unity, the resolution of tension, the emotion of wonder, the urge to explain, and the instinct for workmanship.

While each of these human proclivities no doubt shares some or all of its features with one or another specific instance of artistic behavior, I find each one inadequate to explain the human impulse to make and value the arts. None characterizes all instances of art and thus cannot be used as a common denominator. What is more, each proclivity is found in other *non*artistic manifestations, so that one is still led to ask what makes "artistic" communication, play, display, and so forth different from *non*artistic communication, play, display, and exploration.[2] The usual evolutionary explanations of art at worst suggest that it has no reality in itself but is merely an offshoot or epiphenomenon of one or more antecedents;[3] at best, they still leave us wondering what is artistic about art.

Mistaken Emphases in Previous Evolutionary Explanations

The confusion inherent in the treatment (or lack of treatment) of art by evolutionary scientists derives, I believe, from tacit adherence to two erroneous or limited preconceptions.

"Art" As Fine and Rare

The first arises from the peculiar and anomalous concept of art that is held in the modern West, where, unlike in other societies, art is a superordinate category that may include visual art, music, dance—"the arts"—but characterizes only some works (some paintings, dances, poems) and not others. Also, uniquely in modern Western culture, art is considered to be inherently nonutilitarian, apprehended and appreciated apart from its use-value—in the terms of philosophy of art, by a special "disinterested faculty" (Osborne 1970).[4] In this view, art making (and even its recognition and appreciation) is confined to only an exclusive few, and it is abundantly evident that many people get along very well without it. While admitting that great works of art are in a mysterious way of obvious, even "necessary" significance and appeal, it remains "difficult" (as Harris noted) to find an evolutionary origin and function for something that—being made and revered by the few—is rare, elite, and by its own insistence removed from practical utility.

Although this view of art is entrenched, if tacitly, in most Westerners' thought, it is being increasingly challenged and shown to arise from features that characterize the historical socioeconomic and political configuration known as "modernity"—e.g., economic specialization, individualism, secularization, commodification, an emphasis on rationality (objectivity and analysis), efficiency, utility, and so forth. It is not applicable to premodern and traditional societies, where there is seldom if ever a concept or even a word "art" that remotely resembles the Western view. The sociohistorical circumstances that gave rise to "art" in the Western sense certainly do not pertain to the environment in which hominids evolved the behavioral traits that characterize human species nature.

Once we recognize the limited and limiting status of the Western concept of art, we can look anew at its possible evolutionary origin and function. For while "fine art" in the Western sense is notably lacking in many non-Western societies (and, for that matter, in the lives of most Westerners), every human society engages in the practice and valuing of activities that seem in some way—even if that way seems initially difficult to define with precision—"art-like," *different from ordinary behavior*. While "art" as a word or concept may not exist outside the modern West, there are most certainly arts: making visual ornament and decoration, shaping and embellishing the environment, speaking poetically, engaging in song, music, dance, and performance. Indeed, while a few human groups may be relatively impoverished with regard to some or even most of these activities,[5] far more human societies willingly, even persistently, invest in them a remarkable amount of time, energy, and other resources. Western modernity might view the arts as "useless," but biologists, using the evolutionarily salient criteria of universality, energy investment, and pleasure, would have to concede that engaging with the arts—like eating, sleeping, sex, socializing, and parenting—is a fundamental and essential part of human nature.

Self-Interest as the Prime Evolutionary Determinant

The second reason I believe evolutionary theorists have treated the subject of art's origin and function inadequately arises from their too-exclusive adherence to the sociobiological theorem that individual self-interest is the driving force behind all human behavior—hence the assumption that the arts are *primarily* avenues for competitive display and that they evolved for this purpose.[6] While the arts can no doubt be used for competitive display (as can swimming, spitting, and logsplitting), there is no need to assume that this was their origin or is their sole function. Acceptance of the "bottom line" of self-interest need not preclude accepting that some behaviors have been selected for their contribution to cooperation, which may of course ultimately serve self-interest (e.g., Eibl-Eibesfeldt 1989a, 102).

If evolutionary theorists look anew at the evolutionary value and purpose of art, using different assumptions about the nature of art itself and questioning the pervasive primacy of self-interest in all evolutionary explanations, I believe they will better appreciate art's enduring importance in human individual and species life.

"Making Special"As the Core of a Behavior of Art: The Relationship with Play and Ritual

Evolutionary scientists have had as difficult a time as philosophers of art in trying to contrive a viable comprehensive yet usable definition of art. They usually reduce it to or equate it with other behaviors and consciously or unconsciously founder on the problem of showing how, say, artistic order or play is different from nonartistic order or play.

My studies of art in crosscultural and evolutionary perspective (Dissanayake 1988, 1992) have led me to identify what I believe is a distinctive universal human behavior that remains undescribed or inadequately acknowledged in the literature and that can serve as a meaningful common denominator of art in all times and places. I have termed this behavior "making special." Making special refers to the fact that humans, unlike other animals, intentionally shape, embellish, and otherwise fashion aspects of their world to make these more than ordinary.

Each of the arts can be viewed as ordinary behavior made special (or extra-ordinary). This is easy to see in dance, poetry, and song. In dance, ordinary bodily movements of everyday life are exaggerated, patterned, embellished, repeated—made special. In poetry, the usual syntactic and semantic aspects of everyday spoken language are patterned (by means of rhythmic meter, rhyme, alliteration, and assonance), inverted, exaggerated (using special vocabulary and unusual metaphorical analogies), and repeated (e.g., in refrains)—made special. In song, the prosodic (intonational and emotional) aspects of everyday language—the ups and downs of pitch, pauses or rests, stresses or accents, crescendos and diminuendos of dynamics, accelerandos and rallentandos of tempo—are exaggerated (lengthened and otherwise emphasized), patterned, repeated, varied, and so forth—made special. In the visual arts, ordinary objects like the human body, the natural surroundings, and common artifacts are made special by cultural shaping and elaboration to make them more than ordinary.

It may at first seem as if making special has no more claim to serve as the core of a behavior of art than the other behaviors or mental predispositions that are usually suggested, such as those listed at the beginning of this essay. Yet there are several reasons why I find it to be an improvement.

1. Even though not all instances of making special may be art, all art is an instance of making special. This cannot be said about the other characteristics that evolutionists associate with art—i.e., not all art is a kind or instance of play, display, or scenario-building; neither is all art communicative, pleasurable, creative, transformational, ordered and unified, or tension-resolving; nor is it always the result of skilled workmanship, exploration, explanation, discovery, or wonder.
2. Making special, as I see it, characterizes only two other kinds of human behavior: play and ritual. These, like art, have seemed to lie outside the explanatory pale of functional behaviors such as courtship, mating, parenting, subsistence acquisition, aggression, and so forth.

Resemblances between play and art or ritual and art have often been noted. Like play, art often is characterized by novelty and unpredictability, surprise, ambiguity, fantasy, and make-believe; both are self-rewarding, performed for their own sake. Like ritual, art provides a form for feelings; it is generally compelling, capturing attention and arousing strong emotion; both ritual and art may condense or conflate several meanings in one feature or symbol. Yet despite these similarities, and while the line may be sometimes hard to draw, I do not believe that art can be reduced to either play or ritual as some have suggested.[7] The important ingredient that all three behaviors share (and which gives them a family resemblance) is their being outside ordinary behavior or ordinary life. In this extra-ordinary realm, events or objects are recognized as being special or are deliberately made special.

Both play and ritual, it has been found, have utility and give reproductive advantage. Play allows young animals in a protected or "not for real" arena to develop practical and social skills that can be used later, in adulthood; ritualized behaviors formalize, stylize, and emphasize ordinary attributes that thereby acquire a secondary communicative function and smooth the conduct of social life. Insofar as art shares features with play and ritual, similar selective value has been suggested for it.[8]

"Making Special" As Message-Reinforcement in Humans and Other Animals

I propose that the ability to recognize specialness and deliberately to make special is a human universal that has not heretofore been described.[9] I do not believe that it can be reduced to other proposed human universals such as, for example, Morris's (1967) "neophilia," Wilson's (1978) "mythopoetic drive," Lopreato's (1984) "desire for new experience" or "creative impetus," or Alexander's (1989) "scenario-building." Nor do I believe that it can be equated solely, as many have done, with what appear to be art-like phenomena in nonhuman animals—e.g., play, display, or ritualization.

The usual selective advantage posited for art-like behavior in animals and, by extension, art in humans boils down to what has been called "enhancement of communication" (Alland 1977; Eibl-Eibesfeldt 1989a, 1989b; Tiger and Fox 1971; Wilson 1978), display (Eibl-Eibesfeldt 1989a, Harris 1990), or, more specifically, "message reinforcement" (Coe 1992; Eibl-Eibesfeldt 1989a, 1989b; Geist 1978)—drawing or guiding attention to features that advertise or promote individual fitness: "See how desirable I am; how vital, strong, potent, comely, wealthy"; "See how tough I am: Don't mess with me"; "See what a powerful clan I belong to"; "See my irresistible childbearing and nurturing equipment." It is not to be denied that in every human society individuals make themselves and their possessions special in order to transmit just such messages.

In other animals, also, body and behavior made special are important features of ritualized displays that directly serve individual reproductive interests: they advertise territory and the command of other resources; they attract and persuade sexual partners; they facilitate and synchronize mating. The melodic elaboration of bird song, the courtship dances of sandhill cranes, the decorated bowers of bowerbirds, the astonishing visual displays of birds of paradise or peacocks are all analogous to human behaviors that involve the arts.[10]

Hence it is wholly understandable that evolutionary scientists, beginning with Darwin, have attributed the selective value of the arts directly to reproductive advantage.[11] This is fine, as far as it goes, but I claim it is only part of the story. Deliberate "making special" (as opposed to instinctively decorating a bower or warbling an inherited species courtship or territorial song) is a specifically human behavior, and I will argue that in addition to contributing to the competitive reproductive advantages of individuals as in other animal species, the selective advantage of making special resides in and reflects specifically human species characteristics. The messages that are reinforced by the arts, and the tendency to reinforce or make special these messages, promote communality and one-heartedness, and this has, I claim, given them additional human selective value.

Making Special As a Primary Not Secondary Behavior

To make my case, I will next describe how making special as the core of a behavior of art could have arisen and persisted, not as an epiphenomenon of other behavior but as a positive and primary motivation in its own right.

Earlier I described making special as intentional shaping, embellishing, and otherwise fashioning aspects of the world to make these more than ordinary, and I pointed out that in play and ritual a "special" realm is acknowledged that is outside the everyday strictures of functional subsistence behaviors (eating, mating, parenting, and so forth).

Other animals, of course, play and exhibit ritualized behaviors. One can certainly see in animal play and ritualizations elements of the behavioral proclivity in humans that I call making special—the ritualized behaviors of cranes, bowerbirds, and others described earlier come quickly to mind, as does the playing with painting materials that apes and even captive elephants or dolphins have been found to enjoy and to do without extrinsic reward (Morris 1962, Gucwa and Ehmann 1985, Henley 1992, Lenain 1990). Other animals also can distinguish between the ordinary and extra-ordinary (in the sense of what is normal and abnormal, neutral and extreme, requiring alertness or at least attention).

One can assume that early hominids, like other primates, engaged in play and ritualized behaviors and like other animals could distinguish between the ordinary and extra-ordinary. As early as 250,000 B.P. we find exotic fossils and minerals in human occupation sites, brought there from far away presumably because they appeared striking or unusual.[12] This collecting of artifacts may be not unlike the activities of jackdaws and packrats who accumulate or pick up shiny or otherwise attractive objects.

However, at some point, one can assume deliberate aesthetic use of natural materials—e.g. the application of red ochre and other pigments, even if initially used for utilitarian tanning,[13] surely began to be used for making bodies and objects special. The early Aurignacian use of beads made from exotic and rare shells and stones (White 1989a, 1989b) attests to making special as in necklaces and decorated garments at least from 35,000 B.P. We can only conjecture that the making special of body movements, language, and vocal intonation in dance, poetry, and song developed at least along with body decoration and probably appeared earlier.[14]

An awareness of extra-ordinariness or "specialness" would have been potentially available to serve a co-evolving human behavioral tendency, which I will call, along with Joseph Lopreato, an "imperative to act."[15] In circumstances of anxiety or periods of transition between one state and another, humans, unlike other animals (who simply fight, flee, or freeze), have a tendency to *do something*. The greater powers of human memory and foresight permit deliberate and intentional attempts to affect the outcome of uncertain or troubling circumstances.

I suggest that we can trace the motivation for a behavior of making special to the very appropriation from nature of the material conditions of life—food, drink, shelter—what Marx called the "means of subsistence." Handaxes, spearthrowers, digging sticks, fire, and clothing were products of the earliest technology, the cultural tools that enabled humans to better control the aspects of nature on which material production depended, so that they could survive. In the traditional materialist view of Marx, Marvin Harris, and others, art—along with religion, science, and politics—is assigned to the "structure" or "superstructure" that is dependent on the material subsistence base or "infrastructure."

However, I suggest on the basis of knowledge of premodern groups that we can observe today that at some point in human evolution making special itself became part of the technology of appropriation—that is, means of *enhancement* (making special) were allied to the means of production *in order to make them work more effectively.*[16] For example, procuring food is not taken lightly. Group members have strong feelings about the success of their venture so that in hunting societies, "behavior made special" is as much a part of preparation for a hunt as readying spears or arrows. Before a hunt, hunters may fast, pray, bathe, and obey food or sex taboos; they may wear special adornment; they may perform special rites concerning their tools or weapons, or mark these with special symbols in addition to sharpening them or treating them with poison. This control of behavior and emotions mimics the control necessary to achieve a desired goal. Special practices such as spells or use of charms may also be carried out during the hunt, as well as concluding rites after success, such as propitiation and appeasement of the prey animal's spirit.

In other words, the appropriation from nature of the means of subsistence often includes psychological along with technological components; the "nature" that requires cultural control includes human behavior and feeling as well as the physical environment (Dissanayake 1992). Where materialist thought is inadequate, I believe, is in its failure to acknowledge that *means of enhancement* (i.e., the control of human behavior and emotion outlined above) are frequently if not always intrinsic to the control of the means of production.

The means of enhancement do not necessarily have to be "aesthetic." For example, fasting, observing taboos, or sacrificing are certainly "special" or extra-ordinary behaviors even though they are not inherently artistic. Yet as extra-ordinary behaviors meant to serve important ends, they tend to be the occasion for ritual and artistic control and elaboration in word, gesture, and visual presentation.

Indeed, the artifices and practices that may arise from the human creature's imperative to act—its inherent efforts to deal with (to control) the uncertainties of its world[17]—tend also to be inherently and frequently what we call "aesthetic" or artistic. Divining rods are incised with a pattern; childbirth or burial is attended with chanting, special sounds and words, or rhythmic body movement. These events may be enhanced with special personal adornment or use of objects that are themselves decorated and applied in formally shaped ways. Again, that is to say, humans not only recognize the special but deliberately set out to make things special.

Not surprisingly, to an evolutionist, the desire or need to make special has been throughout human history primarily expressed in the service of abiding human concerns—ones that engage our feelings in the most profound ways.[18] The principal evolutionary context for the origin and the development of the arts (the individual manifestations of the adaptive behavioral complex of making special, as per Tooby and Cosmides, see above) appears to have been in activities concerned with survival: objects and activities that were part of ceremonies having to do with important material and social transitions such as birth, puberty, courtship, marriage, and death; finding food, securing abundance, ensuring fertility of women and of the earth, curing the sick, going to war or resolving conflict, and so forth.

I see the selective value of making special, then, as residing in several effects of particular value to humans (in addition to the oft-noted reproductive advantages to individuals of competitive display of their comeliness, vigor, wealth, and status to others).

1. The control inherent in making special is therapeutic to individuals in that it provides something to do in uncertain or troubling circumstances and gives the psychological illusion, if not always the actual reality, of coping (Kalma 1986).
2. Making special those objects and activities (e.g., tools, weapons, ceremonies) that have abiding human concern leads to their being treated with care and consideration, thus helping to ensure that they will be successfully achieved. As psychologically effective ways of enhancing the means of production, they promote actual success. Groups and individuals who do not bother to enhance the probability of achieving their serious and important goals will not prosper as well as those that do.
3. Of equal selective importance, the arts are everywhere used in multimedia group events or ritual ceremonies, themselves "something

special to do," which confer benefits to the social group as a whole and mean that any individual member in such a group will similarly prosper.[19] During human evolution, ceremonies made group knowledge more impressive and hence more compelling and memorable, helping to transmit vital information over generations (Pfeiffer 1982; Dissanayake 1988, 1992). The arts, particularly music, generally including synchronized movement and song, tend to unite people.

4. Additionally, insofar as ceremonies inculcate group values and promote agreement, cooperation, cohesiveness, and confidence, they also enhance survival. Working harmoniously in a common cause ensures as much as any other human attribute the welfare of individuals.

Aesthetic Making Special

In these two behavioral tendencies—the imperative to act and the ability not only to recognize specialness but to set out deliberately to make things special—humans differ from other animals. It is the behavioral tendency to make special that is, I claim, the human universal, rather than instances of displaying "art" as it is usually thought of by evolutionists influenced by modern Western intellectual culture.

Yet, as I have shown, making special frequently is what we would call aesthetic, and it is useful to try to distinguish aesthetic making special (or art) from nonaesthetic making special.

In ourselves, in our children, and presumably in early humans one can identify responses to protoaesthetic elements, features that inherently give perceptual, emotional, and cognitive pleasure and satisfaction in their own right. The reason that they are inherently pleasing and satisfying is probably because they indicate that something is wholesome and good—e.g., visual signs of health, youth, and vitality such as smoothness, glossiness, warm or true colors, cleanness, fineness, lack of blemish; vigor, precision, and comeliness of movement; sounds that are resonant, vivid, and powerful. In any modality, repetition, pattern, continuity, clarity, dexterity, elaboration or variation on a theme, contrast, balance, and proportion are appealing, presumably because they engage and satisfy cognitive faculties, indicating comprehension and mastery, hence security.[20]

When things are made special by means of the intentional and considered use of these protoaesthetic elements that provide sensuous notice and gratification, one can speak of aesthetic making special,[21] that is, of "art."

It is evident that my notion of making special departs from previous bioevolutionary explanations of art which tend to emphasize the importance of the message that is artfully conveyed (i.e., the content). Rather, I emphasize the artfulness, the inherent appeal, of the means used—the package. Usually people have chosen important messages to be made special, but these need not be enhanced; also there need be no content (symbolic or other) at all. The concept of making special, making artful or artfully making, allows us to regard "art" as a behavior rather than as the results (the objects, message, or content) of that behavior.[22]

Works Cited

Alexander, Richard D.

1987 *The Biology of Moral Systems*. New York: Aldine de Gruyter.

1989 "The Evolution of the Human Psyche." In Paul Mellars and Chris Stringer, eds., *The Human Revolution: Behavioral and Biological Perspectives on the Origins of Modern Humans*. Princeton: Princeton University Press, pp. 455-513.

Alland, Alexander, Jr.

1977 *The Artistic Animal: An Inquiry into the Biological Roots of Art*. Garden City, NY: Anchor.

Anderson, Richard L.

1990 *Calliope's Sisters: A Comparative Study of Philosophies of Art*. Englewood Cliffs, NJ: Prentice Hall.

Coe, Kathryn.

1992 "Art: the Replicable Unit—An Inquiry into the Possible Origin of Art As a Social Behavior." *Journal of Social and Evolutionary Systems* 15 (2): 217-34. Republished in this volume.

Deacon, H. J.

1989 "Late Pleistocene Palaeontology and Archaeology in the Southern Cape, South Africa." In Paul Mellars and Chris Stringer, eds., *The Human Revolution: Behavioral and Biological Perspectives on the Origins of Modern Humans*. Princeton: Princeton University Press, pp. 547-64.

Diamond, Jared

1991 "Art of the Wild." *Discover* (February), pp. 78-85.

Dissanayake, Ellen

1988 *What Is Art For?* Seattle: University of Washington Press.

1992 *Homo Aestheticus: Where Art Comes From and Why*. New York: Free Press.

Dubois, Cora

1944 *The People of Alor*. Minneapolis: University of Minnesota Press.

Eibl-Eibesfeldt, Irenäus

1989a *Human Ethology*. New York: Aldine de Gruyter.

1989b "The Biological Foundations of Aesthetics." In I. Rentschler, B. Herzberger, and D. Epstein, eds., *Beauty and the Brain: Biological Aspects of Aesthetics*. Basel, Switzerland: Birkhauser, pp. 29-68.

Festinger, Leon

1983 *The Human Legacy*. New York: Columbia University Press.

Freud, Sigmund

1959 "The Relation of the Poet to Daydreaming." In *Collected Papers*, Vol. 4, pp. 173-83. New York: Basic Books.

Geist, Valerius

1978 *Life Strategies, Human Evolution, Environmental Design*. New York: Springer.

Gucwa, David, and James Ehmann

1985 *To Whom It May Concern: An Investigation of the Art of Elephants*. New York: Norton.

Harris, Marvin

1989 *Our Kind: Who We Are, Where We Came From, Where We Are Going*. New York: Harper and Row.

Harrold, Francis B.

1989 "Mousterian, Châtelperronian, and Early Aurignacian in Western Europe: Continuity or Discontinuity?" In Paul Mellars and Chris Stringer, eds., *The Human Revolution: Behavioral and Biological Perspectives on the Origins of Modern Humans*. Princeton: Princeton University Press, pp. 677-713.

Hayden, Brian

1990 "The Right Rub: Hide Working in High-Ranking Households." In B. Graslund, ed., *The Interpretive Possibilities of Microwear Studies*. Uppsala, Sweden: Societas Archaeologia Upsaliensis, pp. 89-102.

1993 "The Cultural Capacities of Neanderthals: A Review and Re-evaluation." *Journal of Human Evolution* 24(January): 113-46.

Heider, Karl G.

1979 *Grand Valley Dani: Peaceful Warriors*. New York: Holt, Rinehart and Winston.

Henley, David R.

1992 "Facilitating Artistic Expression in Captive Mammals: Implications for Art Therapy and Art Empathicism." *Art Therapy* 9:4, 178-92.

Huizinga, Johan

1949. *Homo Ludens*. London: Routledge and Kegan Paul.

Jones, Rhys

1989 "East of Wallace's Line: Issues and Problems in the Colonisation of the Australian Continent." In Paul Mellars and Chris Stringer, eds., *The Human Revolution: Behavioral and Biological Perspectives on the Origins of Modern Humans*. Princeton: Princeton University Press, pp. 743-82.

Kalma, Akko

1986 "Uncertainty Reduction: A Fundamental Concept in Understanding a Number of Psychological Theories." In Jan Wind and Vernon Reynolds, eds., *Essays in Human Sociobiology*. Brussels: V.U.B. Study Series, 26:213-41.

Lenain, Thierry

1990 *La Peinture des Singes: histoire et esthetique*. Paris: Syros-Alternatives.

Lopreato, Joseph

1984 *Human Nature and Biocultural Evolution*. Boston: Allen and Unwin.

Low, Bobbi S.

1979 "Sexual Selection and Human Ornamentation." In Napoleon A. Chagnon and William Irons, eds., *Evolutionary Biology and Human Social Behavior: An Anthropological Perspective*. North Scituate, MA: Duxbury Press.

Lumsden, Charles J.

1991 "Aesthetics," In Mary Maxwell, ed., *The Sociobiological Imagination*. Albany: State University of New York Press, pp. 253-68.

Malinowski, Bronislaw

1944 *A Scientific Theory of Culture*. Chapel Hill: University of North Carolina Press.

Mellars, Paul, and Chris Stringer, eds.

1989 *The Human Revolution: Behavioral and Biological Perspectives on the Origins of Modern Humans*. Princeton: Princeton University Press.

Morris, Desmond

1962 *The Biology of Art*. New York: Knopf.

1967 *The Naked Ape*. New York: McGraw Hill.

Osborne, Harold

1970 *Aesthetics and Art Theory*. New York: E. P. Dutton.

Pareto, Vilfredo

1935 *The Mind and Society: A Treatise on General Sociology*. New York: Harcourt, Brace. (Original work published 1916.)

Pfeiffer, John

1982 *The Creative Explosion*. New York: Harper and Row.

Pitcairn, Thomas, and Margret Schleidt

1976 "Dance and Decision: An Analysis of a Courtship Dance of the Medlpa, New Guinea." *Behaviour* 58:298-316.

Rubin, Arnold

1989 *Art As Technology*. Beverly Hills, CA.: Hillcrest Press.

Schiller, Friedrich

1967 "Fourteenth Letter." In E. H. Wilkinson and L. A. Willoughby, eds., *Letters on the Aesthetic Education of Man*. Oxford: Oxford University Press. (Original work published 1795.)

Spencer, Herbert

1880-2 "The Aesthetic Sentiments." In *Principles of Psychology*, vol. 2:2. London: Williams and Norgate.

Tiger, Lionel, and Robin Fox

1971 *The Imperial Animal*. New York: Holt, Rinehart and Winston.

Tooby, John, and Leda Cosmides

1990 "The Past Explains the Present: Emotional Adaptations and the Structure of Ancestral Environments." *Ethology and Sociobiology* 2(4-5):375-424.

Trinkaus, E.

1983 *The Shanidar Neanderthals*. New York: Academic Press.

Turner, Frederick

1991 *Beauty: The Value of Values*. Charlottesville: University Press of Virginia.

Turner, Victor

1983 "Body, Brain and Culture." *Zygon* 18:221-45.

White, Randall

1989a "Production Complexity and Standardization in Early Aurignacian Bead and Pendant Manufacture: Evolutionary Implications." In Paul Mellars and Chris Stringer, eds., *The Human Revolution: Behavioral and Biological Perspectives on the Origins of Modern Humans*. Princeton: Princeton University Press, pp. 366-90.

1989b "Visual Thinking in the Ice Age." *Scientific American* (July) pp. 92-9.

Wilson, E. O.

1978 *On Human Nature*. Cambridge: Harvard University Press.

1984 *Biophilia*. Cambridge: Harvard University Press.

Young, J. Z.

1978 *Programs of the Brain*. Oxford: Oxford University Press.

Notes

1. Twenty-four important books on human behavior and evolution written or edited by professional academic evolutionary scientists, one-third did not treat art or the arts at all and another third mentioned them only tangentially, in connection with other activities such as religion, entertainment, or symbol use. Only seven books (by five authors) expressly set out to address a possible selective value for art (Dissanayake, 1992, 9, 227-28).
2. For example, Wilson (1984, 75) notes that art “explores the unknown reaches of the mind.” But so do science, philosophy, and shamanism. What is different about artistic exploration?
3. Festinger (1983) states outright that art is an “evolutionary peculiarity,” a spinoff of other behaviors that promoted creativity.
4. Lumsden (1991) has even attempted to suggest a function for disinterested aesthetic appreciation, apparently unaware that such a faculty is not universal and has been proposed and accepted by only a minority in the West since the late eighteenth century.
5. Hunter-gatherers and other nomadic people who cannot carry large artifacts about with them often have highly developed poetic and dramatic traditions (Anderson 1990). Heider (1979, 45), speaking of the Dani of Papua New Guinea, remarks that they “rarely expend energy to add beauty to a thing,” and Dubois (1944, 12) says of the people of Alor that their ceremonial practices are “slight and slovenly.” Yet it is evident from their ethnographies that the Alor practice gong-playing, versification, and dancing with respect to the important social area of financial reciprocity, and the Dani engage in personal ornamentation, group dancing, and singing associated with the important social practice of ritualized warfare. In modern America the fine arts are also devalued—music and art are the first subjects to be dropped from schools when funding is precarious. In a bottom-line, efficiency-oriented society that values rationality and practicality, art (as elaboration and ornament) is a liability. At best, art in contemporary America is a commodity to be made for sale and acquisition: this is far from its original function.

6. Theorists who have found the arts to be a means of individual display include Eibl-Eibesfeldt (1989a, 1989b), Geist (1978), Harris (1989), and Wilson (1978). Diamond (1991), Low (1979), and Eibl-Eibesfeldt (1989a, 1989b) mention its role in sexual selection.
7. Play theories of art are commonly associated with Schiller (1795/1967), Spencer (1880-82), Freud (1908/1959), and Huizinga (1949), as well as being proposed by Morris (1962). Ritual is frequently posited as the origin of art by prehistorians and anthropologists insofar as they see art as arising as a sort of symbolmaking for the purpose of religious ritual. They do not of course consider human ritual ethologically (i.e., as it resembles animal ritualized behavior). However, see V. Turner 1983.
8. The same holds for Alexander's (1989) notion of scenario▴building, which may have characteristics in common with some art, so that art is viewed by him within the broader category of scenario-building. However, unlike play and ritual, scenario▴building may not involve specialness at all. Moreover, making special does not inevitably build a scenario (e.g., collecting unusual stones or fossils, putting flowers in one's hair, filing one's teeth, or otherwise sculpting one's body).
9. Geist (1979) mentions the attraction of rarity, novelty, and the extraordinary in attention fixation and guidance as in ungulate-coat color-patterns and notes that human visual artists use similar means in their work. Eibl-Eibesfeldt (1989a, 701) mentions "the need to form super signs." However neither expands the notion to the level of a human universal behavior of making special.
10. Pitcairn and Schleidt (1976) describe a dance/courtship ritual in the Medlpa of Mount Hagen, Papua New Guinea, where pair synchronization is achieved.
11. Darwin noted the association between *beauty* in the animal world and sexual selection. However, beauty is not, strictly speaking, the same thing as making special, and no longer is it deemed essential to a thing's being "art," as it was in Darwin's day, when the words were almost interchangeable.
12. In *What Is Art For?* (p. 96) I show an example of a piece of fossil coral which was transported to an occupation site by an early *sapiens* ca. 250,000 B.P. Examples from Neanderthal sites of other transported

curios (such as fossils, concretions, and pyrites) are described by Harrold (1989) and Hayden (1993).

13. Pieces of red ochre or hematite are found in human dwelling sites from 300,000 B.P. It has been suggested that these substances could have been used initially for the utilitarian purpose of tanning hides, but by 100,000 B.P. shaped ochre pencils indicate drawing or marking (Deacon 1989), and by the Upper Paleolithic the use of ochres and other pigments had increased dramatically. See also Hayden (1990, 1993). Additionally, there are many examples of tools, being made from exotic materials even though naturally occurring flint was more abundant and easier to work—e.g., flaked tools made from transported natural glass in 11,000-24,000 B.P. in Tasmania (Jones 1989).
14. Coe (1992) mentions deliberate cranial deformation occurring from 70,000 B.P. and intentional toothfiling and ablation during the Upper Paleolithic (see Trinkaus 1983 and others cited by Coe). When tattooing, scarification, and other mutilation (or sculpting) of the flesh began is of course not knowable.
15. See Lopreato (1984, 299), who claims that the impulse to do something about our innate needs is overwhelming, and that we express any strong emotion by action. Pareto (1935, 1089) writes: "Powerful sentiments are for the most part accompanied by certain acts that may have no direct relation to the sentiments but do satisfy a need for action," and Malinowski (1948, 60) says essentially the same thing.
16. Arnold Rubin (1989) viewed art as part of technology; his untimely death, before his ideas became widely known, is regrettable. Henry Mercer, the architect, polymath, and collector of American preindustrial tools, also considered the arts and religion as secondary "tools," by means of which human existence was made possible (see display at Mercer Museum, Doylestown, PA, USA). J. Z. Young (1978, 38) has claimed that the activities of religion, art, and music "are even *more important*, in the literal practical sense, than the more mundane ones that are the concern of politics, business, and industry." See also Malinowski (1949, 98-99): "An object, whether a cooking pot or a digging stick, a plate or a fireplace, has to be skillfully, lawfully, and reverently manipulated, since it is very often effective not merely by

technology, but also by customary or ethical regulation." While Malinowski does not specifically mention artistic shaping and elaboration, this may be implied.

17. The fundamental evolutionary importance for humans and other animals of reducing environmental uncertainty is well described by Kalma (1986).
18. It is only recently in the modern West that "artists" have felt that they can make "anything" or "everything" special.
19. See Ligon (1991) for examples of cooperation and reciprocity in birds and mammals.
20. Geist (1978, 236) recognizes that a sensation of "beauty" is a guide to value and is attributed to the removal of disorder and confusion. Eibl-Eibesfeldt (1989a) derives aesthetics from perceptual biases (inherent in higher vertebrates) for Gestalts and prototypes. Frederick Turner (1991), in a fascinating essay, goes so far as to claim that beauty is an objective reality in the universe and that the human aesthetic sense is an adaptive response to this inherent feature of the cosmos.
21. Biologists do not consider mind and body to be separate; "sensuous" notice and gratification implies perception, cognition, and emotion acting together as a unity.
22. It has not been usual in Western aesthetics to think of art as a behavior but, rather, as an object or instantiation of a "work" (a statue, a poem, a musical or dance performance), or an essence (the X-factor that makes something "true art," such as harmony, originality, taste, unity-in-variety, significant form, and so forth). Biologists and many psychologists tend to be concerned with the content that the work conveys.

The Descent of Fantasy

Eric S. Rabkin

"All art," according to Oscar Wilde, in his preface to *The Picture of Dorian Gray* (1891) "is quite useless."[1] Indeed, all the qualities especially associated with verbal art are customarily dismissed as insignificant: specious arguments are just rhetoric, popular misconceptions are only myths, and impossible longings are mere fantasies. Nonetheless, we all acknowledge the universal occurrence of stories in general and of fantasies in particular: as the ancients knew, all leadership involves force of rhetoric; every culture founds itself on its own creation myth; and fantasies include both the socializing tales of insubstantial Faery and the breathless visions of humankind's highest hopes. In the face of such ubiquity, I reaffirm the utility of art and wish to uncover at least part of what that utility might be. This subject, of course, is vast, and as various as the forms of art and the myriad arenas of artistic production and consumption. And yet, if a phenomenon is universal, one supposes either parallel evolution of an extraordinary kind or descent from a common source or condition. This essay into what might be called semiobiology[2] is my initial attempt to sketch the first stages in the descent of fantasy. My speculations here are trials, attempts to lay out lines of inquiry and articulate areas of investigation without at this point marshaling the full data from those areas. Like Freud's primal myth, this cartoon is offered in the hope that it will draw forth debate and help in the posing of useful questions. I begin with the notion that if this fantastic story has use, as in eliciting useful questions, then other fantasies may have a use in common with it and that the telling of the story may suggest reasons why the story, and stories the world over, need to be told.

The first use of anything, or perhaps its last, is survival. The cacophony of modern biology opens every strain with random variations and ends each tune with a funeral dirge. Those of us who survive, dance to whatever tune the piper plays. In social beasts such as we, the piper's music symbolizes our most powerful tool for survival: sociality. Bees find pollen by communicating with bees, deer protect their young from lions by grazing in herds, and men defend their safe territories by pledging allegiance to a flag. While the young of sea turtles hatch alone and march wobbly-legged to the sea, the offspring of primates cling to their parents and gaze into their eyes. Among the competing hordes of our ancestors, those races with the chance capacity to employ more signals more subtly held their territory best, hunted the most efficiently, and beat or starved other hordes into extinction. The roaring lion coordinates the movements of his pride and holds sway over resources otherwise more easily run to ground by the swift but often solitary cheetah; the yapping canines flourish in far greater numbers—and biomass—than the stealthy felines; and the *Homo sapiens* who teaches his offspring to wield a club and circle in on prey to the sound of a beating drum defeats them all. Men, in number and in biomass, overgrow every other single species. Our groups are the most efficient groups, the largest groups, the most stable and subtle and adaptable groups, and we rule the world. The making of groups, the bringing of young into effective roles within groups, and the continual trimming of the life courses of individuals in groups makes our potent sociality possible. The single most flexible tool for the creation, adjustment, and use of human groups is language. To be capable of language is to have a survival advantage; to be incapable of language is to abandon this particular field. The gorilla withdraws to ever smaller plots of African forest while our species hurls itself at the stars.

No human infant dropped into the most equable clime could survive alone. While this is also true of some other animals, such as most primates, the interdependency of humans extends throughout life. Even the atavistic Natty Bumppo circulates about the fringes of society, tied to the rest of humanity by his need for shot and powder and, more important, his needs for companionship and sharing of values. To have been raised to human adulthood means to have been socialized, to have heard the stories of the sacrifice of one's own deity and the tales of origin of the plants one eats, to have acknowledged authority in the persons claiming your parentage, and to have chosen to take on your human mantle by speaking the formulaic words. The liar is cast out; the hypocrite is demoted; the tongue-tied are ignored; and the autistic do not reproduce at all. The greatest survival mechanism evolved by our species is sociality itself, and the greatest tool evolved by our species for sociality is language.

Virtually all human functions necessary for survival are beyond much conscious control. Although we can choose one sort of food over another, few of us, in the presence of food, could or would starve to death; none of us could hold our breath to the point of death. Almost all of us feel strong and frequent urges toward activity that results in tending the body and reproducing it. Most people, most of the time, succumb to these urges. In fact, human happiness seems to arise from the satisfaction of these urges to eat, to exercise, to rest, and even to tell and hear stories. I propose that such happiness is our reward for cooperating with the urges evolution has built into us. When we are tired, sleep feels good; when we are hungry, food feels good; when we are grappling with problems of understanding, storytelling and -listening feels good. I am glad to be able to tell this story to you.

In larger or smaller degree, those functions crucial to our group survival, which of course include functions that preserve the individual members of the group, all employ processes of exchange among members of the group. No human being could survive long, and certainly could not reproduce and raise young, outside a functioning human economy. You feed the child while I gather the berries; you draw the water while I hunt for meat; you stand guard while I sleep, and in turn I will later guard you. Safety is not only in numbers but in communication used to organize the relations among separate members. We will exchange your child-rearing services for my berry-gathering services, your water for my meat, our guardianship for each other's. Thus through exchange is sociality reinforced repeatedly and pleasurably in the daily necessities of human life.

In fairy tales, as Max Luthi points out in *Once Upon a Time* (1970), no one ever says “I love you”; instead, food is given and taken. Luthi was referring to mother love, as when Red Riding Hood's mother gives her cake and wine. But something is amiss in that story since the food is to be passed not to the child but by the child to the grandmother, that is, to the mother of the food provider. That social deformity manifests itself in Red Riding Hood's own desire to receive pleasure; she readily gives in to the wolf's suggestions that she stop and enjoy the woods. The girl's disobedience to her mother's instruction not to tarry compounds the social disorder. As the story proceeds, the consequences of this deformity grow: the girl is unsafe even in her own grandmother's house. Now the consequences of wishing oneself out of maternal control are traumatically clear; instead of eating the cakes and wine the mother gave her, the girl is in turn eaten. But social order is strong. The huntsman passes by and divines the difficulty. He slices open the wolf's belly and the girl gets the chance to be born again, this time much more obedient. In the Grimm brothers' version, "Little Red-cap said to herself that she would never stray about in the wood alone, but would mind what her mother told her."

This small story has much to tell us. Note first that it ends in obedience, that is, in the delineation of the exchange relations between parent and child: I give you food, you give me service. This obedience is established, or more properly reestablished, against expectable pressures. Mothers do sometimes show love to others than their own children; children sometimes have desires of their own. It is normal for some human affairs to tend against obedience. This is dangerous and wrong, the story seems to say to its little child listener, but, despite initial appearances, not necessarily fatal. One can easily imagine a grandmother lulling a granddaughter to sleep with this story, assuaging the child's guilt on a day that included some signal but understandable childish act of self-motivated desire. The story itself becomes a good for exchange: through the telling at the bedside, the grandmother is providing psychological pleasure in this story of heightened and then ameliorated fear; she is also providing the occasion to attend the child as sleep comes on, performing her grandmaternal guardianship. In return, the child is drawing the psychological sustenance that perhaps earlier it had been denied or feared it might lose as Red Riding Hood had to carry but not eat the cake and wine. In drawing this sustenance, the child listener is given one more opportunity at the end of the busy day to perform the required obedience. It can fall off to sleep now secure in the knowledge that it has been good and that the big people will therefore protect it. Society and its children rest secure on a base of known relationships.

This fairy tale is hardly unique. The relationship between mother love and food exchange is common. Witches are anti-mothers and known to be witches, as in "Hansel and Gretel," by their desire not to feed children but to eat them. When Snow White's evil stepmother can express her hate and envy no other way, she feeds the girl a poisoned apple. Cinderella's role in her stepmother's house is obviously topsy-turvy since it is the child who must do the cooking for the adult. Fortunately, the fairy godmother, doubtless the spirit of the dead true mother, provides help, just as other god figures in all cultures demonstrate their parental care by providing loaves and fishes or manna or cargo or, through their own ultimate sacrifices, the seasonal renewal that is life itself, a sacrifice in which we participate by retelling the god's story, by performing again the rituals of painful initiation, by taking the host into our own mouths and consuming the god in obedience to him. By this exchange, performed often with the help of such powerful tale-bearers as educated priests or epileptic shamans, human sociality is extended to the fullness of the awesome universe engulfing us. Thus the realm of the overpowering is made the realm of our parents, and our right relation to it is defined. Through the story, we become able to sleep in comparative peace.

There are kinds of love other than mother love. Cinderella dances in the embrace of the prince; Sleeping Beauty is awakened with a kiss; Rapunzel bears her lover twins. Put bluntly but truly, the phrase "I love you" is omitted from these stories not to be replaced by an exchange of food but by an exchange of physical contact. Seen most oppressively, the exchange of genital contact defines, at least for Susan Brownmiller (1975), a social order dependent on constant rape. I will give you my daughter if you will give me her bride-price. Seen less oppressively, the ordering of allowable exchanges of genital contact is not only the concern of these stories but of marriage rites, law, and courtship rituals—including a young couple's self-revelation through presentation of autobiographical narratives. Exchange of genital contact, like the exchange of food and guardianship, is crucial for the survival of our species and is, in our species, accomplished with and through the enjoyment of language in general and stories in particular.

Language can be used for many purposes. Each phrase made and attended to participates in the continual jostling within the web of sociality that maintains and develops our human groups. Aggressive competition, strongly suggestive of territorial posturing, plays out the social drama through the weapons of promise and threat. Promises and threats are made of language , and are exchange items. Social relations may be revealed in part by discovering whose threats have sway with whom, whose promises are relied on by whom, the nature of the reciprocity or asymmetry of those relations, and so on. The king's promise and threat are the law of the land;

he need rely on no one's word. The serf extends all promises of loyalty if required to do so, including the acknowledgment of the droit du seigneur, relying on the promise of protection and believing the threat of dissociation from the human economy by sanction or by death. Thus the hierarchy of feudal society comes into focus. Tristan is bound by his oath. Nowadays the exchange of food that means "I love you" (or is it the other way around?) does not go only from female to male, and the exchange of protection marked by the marriage ring does not go only from male to female. Women often pay for men's food at restaurants, and men often wear wedding rings. Tristan and Isolde each drank the magic love potion and created a symmetrical social order between themselves that was insupportable in the inevitable and overwhelming network of the hierarchical society they both more generally inhabited. The result was death. Tristan had no offspring.

Language obviously has exchange value. It is worth more to some people to have the right person say, "I dub thee knight," "He is my friend," or "You may now kiss the bride." Unlike money or cowrie shells, however, language does not have only exchange value. The exchanges of language may be used to warn, cajole, or coordinate. All of these activities, done by us to each other, keep producing our social world.

What world do we inhabit? My world, to take an example with which I am acquainted, floats tiny in the emptiness of space. Yet this was true of no one's world until 1643, the year in which Evangelista Torricelli deduced by experiment that the air around us was a local phenomenon and that most of the distance to the moon must be truly empty. How did he deduce this? I can only say by telling you what he did: He took a tube, sealed it at one end and filled with mercury, and inverted it into a bath of mercury. The mercury began to flow out of the tube but then stopped, producing at the top of the tube a partial vacuum and suggesting to the early physicist that air had weight. Given this hint, he quickly discerned that the weight of air necessary to hold up the column of mercury, what we now call barometric pressure, would be produced by a column no more than five miles tall if the air did not attenuate. And the moon was known to be a quarter of a million miles away. Suddenly nature preferred a vacuum. Outer space was discovered.

This little story, like the tale of Red Riding Hood, also has, I think, much to tell us. First, it has human interest, the happy conjunction of accident and genius, the satisfactory correction of error. Second, it must once have—in fact, did—reshaped people's beliefs about the nature of their world. Aristotle's assertion that nature abhors a vacuum was dealt a hard blow. This story is the current basis for my own belief in the vacuum of space although I did not know the story until many years after I had already been taught about the vacuum. I believed my teachers and they believed their teachers, or so I suppose, back to Torricelli. This story about Torricelli explains their belief, at least to my satisfaction, and thus my sense of the world conforms to the story. Yet I must admit that I have never felt or seen the vacuum of space, nor have I ever seen Torricelli's experiment performed. My belief rests on the reliance I place on the tale and on the plausibility of the tale given all else I have come to accept. It is true that so-called scientific facts take their places within a web of observations and assertions which have implications for each other, and so no single experiment need be personally experienced in order for us to assent to science. Yet it is equally true that the vast majority of what we know, we know only by report, relying on a few tests' having proved true and thus having established the probable believability of individuals. When scientists are found to have distorted their results, they are fired and ostracized. Believability is not simply a matter of the truth of one's assertions but of one's place in the social fabric, a place defined by one's own experience and attested to by one's own life story. When you apply for an academic job, you send your vita—the summary of your life—before you. I did a few experiments in school, and many of them worked out much as the books said they would, but my belief in outer space really rests on my belief in the social order, a continuous and evolving thing that extends back over three centuries to Torricelli and over the eons to our mute ancestors on the ancient plains.

All explanations, I would suggest, are at bottom narrative. Not only does scientific explanation require faith in the telling, but all matters of human fact are established by testimony and history. Not only will the sun rise because it has always risen, but the sacred symbol will lead us to victory because it has always done so. The most immutable narratives, the explanations for the most profound aspects of our world, are told in a time out of time, the time of ever-repeatable scientific experiment and the time of myth and fairy-land; the time, in short, of permanent reality and of untouchable fantasy. We learn by conditioning: once bitten, twice shy. For a social animal, there is an obvious survival advantage in being able to understand and believe someone else's experience. Events happen to us all. Language can report these events. Narrative is the exchange of the report of events. A full theory of narrative would clearly need to ask who exchanges what sorts of reports, of what sorts of events, with whom, in what contexts, for what purposes. That is a massive project. Let us focus in this first effort on the story at hand.

My telling the story of Torricelli does have exchange value. It may, for example, by its oddity, perhaps, or its satisfactory resolution, strike you as a good story and hence one you are glad to have heard. That would make me, in consequence, a bit more of an individual whom you might credit, to whom you might extend believability. In addition to simple exchange value (I'll tell you a joke for five dollars), a storytelling performs other social functions. The telling may well help define the status of the teller and of the hearer in the sociality, the nature of the world-beliefs they may share, and may give happiness or in some other way cooperate with some fundamental urge. The fundamental urges we might observe operating in the telling of this story are several: curiosity has survival value, and so does its exercise; its assuagement by this narrative ought to give some pleasure. Order and regularity are well worth perceiving for they help us predict future conditions and hence prepare for them; stories with perceivable form assuage the desire for order. But once we have come to the idea of stories serving us by their very order, we have come to the point of suggesting that part of the true use of a story is its aesthetic value. I would suggest that the telling of proper tales, well-made and rhetorically interesting tales, in a social world so dominated by language exchange as ours, signals social success and the likelihood of social position. He who can produce good language has a constant supply of items for social exchange. Just as grebes delight potential mates with displays of plumage and acrobatics, we delight our potential mates, or curry our employers, or dominate our inferiors, by displays of language. The development of an aesthetic sense has survival value, and one ought to wonder little that, in varying degrees, all humans share it.

The most brutal narratives simply assert social order on the basis of that order: "Do this because I am your father" or "The law is the law." In other words, there are other words, older words that recount earlier events, such as intercourse or legislation, and these earlier events are to be taken to institute and explain our world. Yet it is not events which institute our world but our belief in the report of the events. This belief comes in part from our experience in social exchange. We know teachers and doctors and patients are trustworthy by experience and by failure to disconfirm our earlier belief in them. This belief also comes in part from our capacity to test some of the reports against our own experience, and this belief finally comes in part from our aesthetic sense. To tell a well-made story is to move up in the social scale. Priests and poets have often dominated soldiers and stone cutters. The pen, we have all said, is mightier than the sword. For a species for which the question of the well-madeness of language is and should be central to survival and reproduction, an aesthetic sense is a tool for survival. How shall we exercise that aesthetic sense?

Narratives are but one class of language that might be tested aesthetically, but they are a significant class. Some utterances are primarily adjunct to accomplishing physical deeds. We warn people to duck a flying object, command platoons into battle in the most deadly manner, and teach apprentices how to wield their tools. These utterances are judged in part by their well-madeness, but mostly they are judged by their effect. A vulgar, mispronounced order that nonetheless carried the day was a good order. In narratives, different sorts of events may be reported. Some of those events, such as what happened when Torricelli did what to which, are testable and may be judged good or bad according to their accuracy. Such tales, however, fit less completely into the realm of physical consequence of military commands and more into the social fabric of believability. The tale might be better or worse told. Narratives that are the least susceptible to physical test must be judged most by their well-madeness. There is minimal specifiable content to the great assertions of religion like "God is love," and there is minimal testable report in the great narratives of creation. The same is true of fairy tales. But these tales are great despite their untestability because they satisfy, in a broad and powerful way, our aesthetic sense. While the theories of caloric and phlogiston are no more, the story of the Fall still touches us. In part this is so because the content accords with something in our own lives, of course, but in part because the story handles that something in ways to create potent order, aesthetic order. The more the particular, realistic content in a narrative, the more susceptible it is to disconfirmation; the less the particular, realistic content, the more its value rests on aesthetic considerations. Fantasies are special narratives made of unfalsifiable events, in part so that the reports of these events can be exchanged long after particular reality changes. The exchanging of reports of fantastic events shapes the world of *Homo sapiens*. And it is by well-made fantasy that *Homo sapiens* shapes the world. Put another way, displaced as they are from our time and our world, fantasies are the richest field for the growth and display of the human aesthetic urge, an urge inherited through the accidents of survival and competition and remaining with us as a crucial capacity for our group struggle on toward the future. The descent of fantasy mirrors the descent of man.

Works Cited

Brownmiller, Susan.
1975 *Against Our Will: Men, Women, and Rape*. New York : Simon and Schuster.

Luthi, Max
1970 *Once Upon a Time: On the Nature of Fairy Tales*. New York, F. Ungar.

Notes

1. This study was first published in George E. Slusser, Eric S. Rabkin, and Robert Scholes, eds., *Coordinates: Placing Science Fiction and Fantasy* (Carbondale, IL: Southern Illinois University Press), pp. 14-22.
2. The term "semiobiology" was suggested by Wladyslaw Godzich at the Conference on Theories of Narrative held in Bloomington, Indiana, 24-26 October 1980, under the auspices of the Department of English of Indiana University and the Society for Critical Exchange. It was at that

conference that I first began to organize diverse ideas into a form that led to this essay. I wish to thank many people for their stimulation and comment at that conference, especially David Bleich, Ralph Cohen, Jonathan Culler, Paul Hernadi, Mary Louise Pratt, Gerald Prince, Leroy Searle, and James Sosnoski. In addition, much of my thinking about evolution in particular and science in general has been stimulated by conversations with colleagues at the University of Michigan and in particular with Richard Alexander, Gordon Kane, Matthew Kluger, and Roy Rappaport. I thank them all.

Preliminary Remarks on Literary Memetics

Daniel Rancour-Laferriere

Books, the children of the brain.

Jonathan Swift, *A Tale of a Tub*

In 1937 Freud wrote in a letter to Marie Bonaparte, "The moment one inquires about the sense or value of life one is sick, since objectively neither of them has any existence" (Jones 1957, 3: 465).[1]

It would be hard to find a more pessimistic statement about value. True, thinkers as different as Ludwig Wittgenstein and E. M. Forster have also told us there is no such thing as objective value in the world, but Freud made us really squirm, really resist the thought of life without value. And he resisted too, judging from his many years of fighting the cancer that eventually killed him.

What made Freud *value* his work enough to continue it even as he was dying? What makes any writer—scientific, literary, or of whatever variety—value the written object even in the knowledge that death will have us anyway?

Take the literary artist, supposed to be one of the most sensitive creatures on the planet, one of the apexes of human potential. Why does this creature not just commit suicide? Sylvia Plath and Vladimir Mayakovsky seem to be exceptions. Of all people, it is the literary artist who should be most capable of meditating *to the end* on the vanity of leaving literary progeny. But there, I think, is the answer: literary *progeny.* The literary artist will not, as Horace said, die completely. It is true that in the future lies certain death, so why not get it over with? But also in the future are one's progeny, so why not wait? The question of literary value is a question of the future.

But there is more to it than that. There is a very special feeling about progeny of any kind. The writer does not despair of writing in the same way that the mature human adult does not despair of having and nurturing children. One's writings are one's children. This is a commonplace among literary artists. Zamyatin once said, for example, that he had no children other than his books.

We care for our children. Over the eons, naturally selected genes have shaped our limbic and hypothalamic centers to *make* us care for our children. The writer generates and cares for literary progeny through the action of the same dumb genetic mechanism that forces most of us to generate and care for merely biological progeny. The *same* mechanism. Writers are sometimes even more parental in their behavior toward their literary works than toward their (real) children. Solzhenitsyn declared, for example, that he had resolved to let the Soviet secret police keep his children as hostages rather than stop the publication of *The Gulag Archipelago*.

But now there is a difference. Most parents bring up their children, and that is the end of it. However, the literary artist, after the literary child is ready, expects others to adopt this child, to become foster parents. The trick is to make the child so appealing that generation after generation of readers will continue to parent it. The ideal literary work is a child that never grows up.

"Don't you just *love* them at that age!" say all the parents who have ever fussed over their little children. The successful writer keeps his child perpetually at "that age." Literary value resides in this appeal. Literary value *is* appeal. Sartre once said: "L'oeuvre d'art est valeur parce qu'elle est appel" (1948, 62).[2] But surely the appeal of the child and the appeal of the literary work are merely analogous things. Surely the reader is more sensible, less passionate, less literal—than the writer.

I am not so sure. All the critical fuss about the "work itself" reveals that we readers personify the child of the writer's brain as much as the adoring mother her child. The Structuralists of the Left Bank like to tell us that literary language "speaks," that writing "writes," that myths "think" (Laferriere 1979, 311). Roland Barthes even gives the literary text erotic appeal: "Le texte que vous ecrivez doit me donner la preuve *qu'il me desire*" (1973, 13).[3] One could even do a linguistic study of the similarities between baby talk and Parisian mumbo-jumbo.

But still, is there not a limit to how far one may carry an analogy? Perhaps there is, but I am not going to look for it here. To do so would require a detailed comparison of all the signals which make us altruistic toward a child with all the signals which make us altruistic toward a literary text. By "altruistic" I mean contributing to the survival of the other, possibly at the expense of the self. When certain neotenous features of the child's physiognomy make us perceive the child as "cute" or "cuddly," for example, then the child has already begun to elicit altruistic behavior from us. These features have been catalogued by ethologists (e. g., Eibl-Eibesfeldt 1971, 21).

What is there about the literary work of art that elicits our altruism? What does it mean to be altruistic to the child of the writer's brain? What is the appeal which makes us attach value to the work?

A biologist (e. g., Mayr 1976, ch. 26; Wilson 1975, 23) would call these questions of proximate cause because the answers must be relatively nearby in geologic time. What is operating at the moment of literary response to make the response altruistic? What is the proximate mechanism which induces us to continue reading the work we have started, to read the work more than once, to advise others to read the work, to encourage publishers to print and reprint the work, to do literary analyses of the work, or to require the work for college courses? In short, what makes us do the things that insure the *survival* of the work? Clearly this question is vast in scope, judging from the plethora of theories of literary evaluation that exist—sociological, Marxist, psychoanalytic, hermeneutic, structuralist, semiotic, and reception theoretical among others.

Even vaster, however, is the question of ultimate cause: what is there in the long view in literary history which caused receivers to be altruistic toward some works and not toward others? One could conceivably ask an even "more ultimate" question: what is there in the late development of the hominid line which caused receivers to be altruistic toward literary works at all?

It is my impression that literary theory has not made much progress toward answering the questions of either proximate or ultimate cause. There have been some admirable first steps, but basically literary theory is in as primitive a state as biology before Darwin or Mendel. It has neither a developed concept of selection nor a genetics.

Perhaps the lessons learned by biologists can be of help to literary theoreticians. Perhaps at least some questions of definition can be raised, even if the big theoretical questions of proximate and ultimate cause are still out of reach. Assume, for example, that literary evolution, like the evolution of organisms, is based on the survival of the fittest. A question of definition that would then have to be asked is, survival of the fittest *what*? Precisely what are the literary units that endure from century to century? Or, from the axiological viewpoint, what are the literary units that we endow with value, and thus permit to survive?

Lest the reader react with horror to so biological a metaphor as "the survival of the fittest," let me point out that this phrase is neither particularly biological nor even a metaphor. In the first place, Darwin borrowed it from Spencer, who happened to use it for purposes of sociological theorizing before Darwin used it for purposes of biological theorizing (Ghiselin 1974, 219; Edel 1978). In the second place, "survival of the fittest" cannot be a metaphor unless it is implicitly understood what biologists had in mind that survived. In fact, biologists have been quite fickle about specifying just what survives. Nowadays in sociobiology it is survival of the fittest gene or allele of a gene (e. g., Dawkins 1976) or the fittest individual (e. g., Trivers 1971, 48), whereas it used to be the fittest social group or fittest species. In any case, if the literary scholar is going to make any use of the concept "survival of the fittest," then that scholar will, like the biologist, have to tackle the problem of determining what exactly is "fit" or "not fit," or "more fit" versus "less fit."

For starters, I would like to suggest that we follow the lead of Richard Dawkins, who has already begun to study the parallels between biological and cultural (including literary) evolution. In his highly readable book, *The Selfish Gene* (1976), Dawkins proposes that the unit of cultural survival is something called the *meme*.

> We need a name for the new replicator, a noun which conveys the idea of a unit of cultural transmission, or a unit of *imitation*. "Mimeme" comes from a suitable Greek root, but I want a monosyllable that sounds a bit like "gene." I hope my classicist friends will forgive me if I abbreviate mimeme to meme. If it is any consolation, it could alternatively be thought of as being related to "memory," or to the French word même. It should be pronounced to rhyme with "cream."

> Examples of memes are tunes, ideas, catch-phrases, clothes, fashions, ways of making pots or of building arches. Just as genes propagate themselves in the gene pool by leaping from body to body via sperms or eggs, so memes propagate themselves in the meme pool by leaping from brain to brain via a process which, in the broad sense, can be called imitation. (Dawkins 1976, 206)

As is obvious, Dawkins' now famous notion of meme is rather broadly and loosely defined. The range of human behaviors which may be termed imitative is enormous,[4] but the underlying notion is quite straightforward: if it is a cultural entity and if it replicates, then it is a meme. The replication may take place within the central nervous system, as in an idea or concept passed on from person to person, or the replication may involve an external object of culture, as in the reproduction of a painting by photographic means. Various scholars have noted that there is this dichotomy in cultural replication (e.g., Cloak 1975, 168; Rancour-Laferriere 1979, 183-84; Mundinger 1980, 198).

Dawkins gives the Robert Burns poem "Auld Lang Syne" as an example of a literary meme. The poem can be replicated in a number of ways. It can be memorized, i.e., stored in a concatenation of neural traces of some kind. It can be printed on paper. It can be recorded on electronic tape. Of these methods of memetic replication, the covert neural one seems to be basic, the one closest to what genes have programmed us to do. The neural meme is, furthermore, very much like a brain parasite. It *is* a parasite.

> Memes should be regarded as living structures, not just metaphorically but technically. When you plant a fertile meme in my mind you literally parasitize my brain, turning it into a vehicle for the meme's propagation in just the way that a virus may parasitize the genetic mechanism of a host cell. (Dawkins 1976, 207, quoting a comment by N. K. Humphrey)

It has been said that making metaphors can be very creative, but here is another example of an insight that can be achieved by being literal. I wonder whether Tolstoy was being metaphorical or literal when he said something similar long before sociobiology was invented.

> Art is a human activity in which one person . . . transmits to others, by means of external signs, sensations felt by him, and those others are infected [*zarazhayutsya*] by those feelings and relive them. (Zholkovsky and Shcheglov 1976, 8)

The host of the memetic parasite is the central nervous system, the vector is the sign ("*vneshnimi znakami*"—"by means of external signs," says Tolstoy). What an opportunity there is here for the cooperation of biologists and semioticians.

Like biological evolution, literary evolution must be a process of differential selection from alternative choices. Some memes are selected for, others are selected against. This analogue of natural selection Mundinger calls psychological selection.

> Natural selection is differential replication of alternative alleles. Psychological selection is differential selection of alternative memes. The agents of natural selection, such as differential mortality, differential natality, and so on, are all associated with the reproductive process in one way or another. . . .The agents of psychological selection are totally different, but they too are associated with replication, in this case with the psychology of imitative learning. (Mundinger 1980, 200)

Mundinger mentions differential teaching and differential learning predisposition and possible determinants of the psychological selection of memes. Here again I will leave open the question of what might be the differential agents selecting some literary memes over others, and will focus instead on the question of just what the selected memetic units might be.

Dawkins seems to assume that the meme appropriate to literary evolution is the literary work. There are some other methods of replication, however. Allusion is an example. In alluding to a previous work (sometimes to the extent of direct quotation), a given work is replicating some portion of the previous work. Or to use a term common in Slavic literary criticism, a *subtext*,[5] insofar as it is the target of allusion by a later text (or texts), would be an example of a literary meme. Thus some of the poetry of Horace is memetically replicated when Pushkin alludes to it in *Eugene Onegin*.

Another candidate for literary meme is the conventionalized *genre*. The genre of the sonnet, for example, further replicates every time a new sonnet is invented, regardless of the content. A genre that endures is a memetic lineage, a lineage that is not so personally tied to an author as an individual literary work or a subtext.

Yet another type of meme is to be found among the linguistic and rhetorical devices (*priemy*—Shklovsky) of a work. For example, the printed device of "stepped form" in Russian Futurist poetry is continued fifty years after Mayakovsky and others by such poets as Voznesensky and Evtushenko. The original template for the current meme is the observed Futurist model.

It would not make sense, however, to regard all literary devices as memes. Take the well-known and many-faceted device of parallelism (*parallelismus membrorum*) in poetry. Jakobson observed this device in many of the world's literatures—ancient Hebrew poetry, Chinese verse, the Indic Veda, Finnish folk poetry, the Russian epos (Jakobson 1966). Obviously, the extant varieties and tokens of parallelism (or more broadly, automorphic structures—Laferriere 1976) did not all "descend" from a single instance of parallelism in one particular ancient literature. Rather, parallelistic verbal structure has spontaneously and independently arisen in the literatures of widely scattered languages, most likely because of a universal human affinity for such structures. In biology there is a similar phenomenon called convergent evolution. A great variety of organisms have, for example, organs which detect light, but this does not mean that all such organs are necessarily genetically related. The eye of the octopus is amazingly similar to the eye of a man yet arose independently in evolution. A syntactic parallelism in a Yeats poem may be remarkably similar to a syntactic parallelism in a poem by Lorca, but that does not mean the parallelisms are memetically related.

Given that some literary devices are memes and others are not (or are, only in a trivial sense), then we are confronted with the task of distinguishing between the two. However, this may not be as difficult a task as it sounds. Intuitively, it would seem that most devices are not memes at all. If one thumbs through a dictionary of poetics, the majority of devices listed there will not be limited to one particular tradition in literary history. In Lausberg's standard *Handbuch der literarischen Rhetorik*, for example, we find items such as metaphor, metonymy, catachresis, paranomasia, and ellipsis—all of which can be exemplified by passages from Pynchon just as well as by passages from Quintillian. These devices cannot possibly be memes. Or rather, the devices per se cannot be memes. The content of such devices may in fact be memetic, as when Robert Burns extends a long tradition of "rose metaphors" by saying, "My love is like a red, red rose." But the device in itself in this famous line is no meme. The device of metaphor (here more strictly a simile) serves rather as a kind of skeleton through which fragile memetic traditions may pass. If some catastrophe (extinction) were to befall the literary rose meme, the device of metaphor, a basic mechanism of language itself, would still survive. Only some other meme—the periwinkle, say—would be harnessed by this device. The different "flowers" which might compete to enter the device would thus be rather like the different alleles which compete with one another on the genetic level. The fittest "flower meme" would survive to live on in further floral metaphors.

Devices are not the only things which do not change much in the course of literary evolution. A psychoanalyst would argue, for example, that certain basic unconscious fantasies are activated by the literatures of all historical periods. An Oedipal conflict can just as much occur in a Joyce novel as in Sophocles, but the one that occurs in Joyce does not replicate the one that occurs in Sophocles. Most of the entities studied by psychoanalytic critics are not likely to be memes.

Basic plot structures (what Chatman 1978 calls "narrative macrostructures") are probably not memes either. Nor are a variety of other narrative structures and techniques. The device of flashback (analepsis), for example, is probably not a meme. I think it would be difficult to argue that the use of flashbacks in Arthur Miller's *Death of a Salesman* is memetically related to the use of flashbacks in Solzhenitsyn's *Cancer Ward*. However, some narrative techniques are clearly memetic in nature. The Russian tradition of *skaz* (use of a fictional narrator with certain substandard speech characteristics) is an example. What the narrator of Zoshchenko's *Stories of Nazar Il'ich Mister Bluebelly* does is memetically related to what the narrator of Gogol's *Evenings on a Farm Near Dikanka* did a century earlier. At least most of my Slavist colleagues would probably agree that the two are related, while non-Slavists are likely to know only about the Gogol collection. This brings up the problem of determining just where memetic lineages are located. The *skaz* meme, for example, is replicated in quite a variety of places: the casual reader of Russian literature (who may have heard only of Gogol, but not of Zoshchenko), the serious reader of Russian literature, the critic of Russian literature, and the writer of Russian literature. Each of these creatures possesses what I would like to call a different phenotype in his or her brain of the underlying, basic memotype known as *skaz*. A Russian reader of the first half of the nineteenth century, for example, might have possessed only the Pushkin phenotype or the Gogol phenotype of *skaz*. A poorly educated Soviet citizen of the 1930s might have carried only the Zoshchenko phenotype. Zoshchenko himself must have carried at least the Pushkin, Gogol, and Leskov phenotypes in his memory, and they influenced his production of the mutant, Zoshchenko phenotype.

Among the various candidates for literary meme which I have so far proposed—the literary work, the subtext, the genre, and certain kinds of linguistic, rhetorical, and narrative devices (this must only be a partial list)—it is the literary work (or a portion of it) to which we are most likely to attach value. I am not saying *why* we value one work more highly than another, but that we tend to evaluate works. We are not as likely to evaluate genres, for example. A sonnet is not in any significant sense "better" than a short story. Differing genres may be competing memes in certain stages of history, as when, for example, the long novel gained ascendency over the short lyric during the second half of the nineteenth century in Russia. But a Tolstoy novel is not "better" than a Pushkin lyric. A Pushkin lyric *is* "better" than a lyric by Sasha Cherny (as evidenced by the fact that most of us have probably never heard of Cherny). A sonnet by Shakespeare *is* more likely to be highly valued than a sonnet by some poet we have never heard of before.

To put it another way: some value may rub off on a genre because of certain works written in that genre, but in the long run practically no value accrues to a work just because of its genre. At a particular point in literary history, for example, the ode may be more highly valued than the epistle, but that is a temporary thing, and centuries later preferences may be different. In the meantime, what is valued has survived, regardless of the temporary preferences. It is Horace's *works* that are valued, not his odes per se or his epistles per se.

Another way to argue that it is works that tend to be valued, as opposed to other literary memes, is to consider how far people will go in order to either preserve or extinguish works. Again I will resort to a Russian example. Today we are able to read many of the great poems of Osip Mandelstam only because Nadezhda Mandelstam memorized them. For a long time during the Stalin period these poems existed in just one memetic copy, in the brain of the poet's wife. Had this woman not physically survived the Stalin years—if she had written down some of the poems and the Soviet secret police had discovered them—then the expansive diffusion of Mandelstam memes ("meme flow") among post-Stalin devotees of Russian poetry could never have occurred.

I began by quoting Freud to the effect that life has no value. If the basis of life is genes, then it is genes that have no value. Value comes only as a result of genes which program us to *evaluate* the world. Nowadays (as opposed to the more than 99 percent of the time of human evolution spent at hunting and gathering) a part of the world is literature, i.e., is literary memes. It is not as if we were not already evaluating things before there was literature, and it seems unlikely that so recent a thing as literature or literary evaluation should have a special genetic basis. My guess is that some other, long-entrenched evaluative process was a *preadaptation* for evaluating literature. Above I suggested that the preadaptive basis for our literary evaluative behavior is our genetically determined proclivity to evaluate persons, especially children. In saving the children of Osip's brain, Nadezhda Mandelstam was making an intensely positive evaluation of a person. Someone, not just something, survived as a result of her altruism. The personified meme is the meme with a future. In Russian, by the way, *Nadezhda* means "hope."

Works Cited

Barthes, Roland

1973 *Le Plaisir du texte*. Paris: Editions du Seuil.

Chatman, Seymour

1978 *Story and Discourse: Narrative Structure in Fiction and Film.* Ithaca: Cornell University Press.

Cloak, F. T., Jr.

1975 "Is a Cultural Ethology Possible?" *Human Ethology* 3:161-82.

Dawkins, Richard

1976 *The Selfish Gene.* New York: Oxford University Press.

Edel, Abraham

1978 "Attempts to Derive Definitive Moral Patterns from Biology." In A. L. Caplan, ed., *The Sociobiology Debate*. New York: Harper and Row, pp. 111-16.

Eibl-Eibesfeldt, Irenaus

1971 *Love and Hate: On the Natural History of Basic Behavior Patterns*. Translated by G. Strachan. London: Methuen.

Ghiselin, Michael T.

1974 *The Economy of Nature and the Evolution of Sex*. Berkeley: University of California Press.

Hamilton, W. D.

1977 "The Play by Nature." *Science* 196:757-59.

Jakobson, Roman

1966 "Grammatical Parallelism and Its Russian Facet." *Language* 42:399-429.

Jones, Ernest

1953-7 *The Life and Work of Sigmund Freud.* New York: Basic Books.

Laferriere, Daniel

1976 "Automorphic Structures in the Poem's Grammatical Space." *Semiotica* 10:333-50.

1979 "Structuralism and Quasi-Semiotics." *Semiotica* 25: 307-318.

Mayr, Ernst

1976 *Evolution and the Diversity of Life*. Cambridge: Harvard University Press.

Mundinger, Paul C.

1980 "Animal Cultures and a General Theory of Cultural Evolution." *Ethology and Sociobiology* 1:183-223.

Rancour-Laferriere, Daniel

1979 "Speculations on the Origin of Visual Iconicity in Culture." Ars *Semeiotica* 2:173-85.

1980 "Semiotics, Psychoanalysis, and Science: Some Selected Intersections." *Ars Semeiotica* 3:181-240.

1981a "Sociobiology and Psychoanalysis: Interdisciplinary Remarks on the Most Imitative Animal." *Psychoanalysis and Contemporary Thought* 4:435-526.

1981b "On Subtexts in Russian Literature." *Wiener Slavistischer Almanach* 7:289-96.

Sartre, Jean-Paul

1948 *Qu'est-ce que la littérature?* Paris: Gallimard.

Trivers, Robert L.

1971 "The Evolution of Reciprocal Altruism." *Quarterly Review of Biology* 46:35-57.

Wilson, E. O.

1975 *Sociobiology: The New Synthesis*. Cambridge, MA: Harvard University Press.

Yando, Regina, Victoria Seitz, and Edward Zigler

1978 *Imitation: A Developmental Perspective*. Hillsdale, N.J.: Erlbaum.

Zholkovsky, A. K., and Yu. K. Shcheglov

1976 *Matematika i iskusstvo (poètika vyrazitel'nosti)*. Moscow: Znanie.

Notes

1. An earlier version of this essay was published in Karl Menges and Daniel Rancour-Laferriere, eds., *Axia: Davis Symposium on Literary Evaluation* (Stuttgart: Akademischer Verlag Hans-Dieter Heinz, 1981). Pp. 77-87.
2. Translation, "The work of art is of value because it has appeal."
3. Translation, "The text which you write should prove *that is desires me*."
4. See Yando et al. 1978, Rancour-Laferriere 1981a.
5. Cf. Rancour-Laferriere 1981b.

On Art

Edward O. Wilson

From *Sociobiology: The New Synthesis,* abridged edition (Cambridge, MA: Harvard University Press, 1980).

Page 3

1. The biologist, who is concerned with questions of physiology and evolutionary history, realizes that self-knowledge is constrained and shaped by the emotional control centers in the hypothalamus and limbic system of the brain. These centers flood our consciousness with all the emotions—hate, love, guilt, fear, and others—that are consulted by ethical philosophers who wish to intuit the standards of good and evil. What, we are then compelled to ask, made the hypothalamus and limbic system? They are evolved by natural selection.

Pages 288-89

2. Artistic impulses are by no means limited to man. In 1962, when Desmond Morris reviewed the subject in *The Biology of Art*, 32 individual nonhuman primates had produced drawings and paintings in captivity. Twenty-three were chimpanzees, 2 were gorillas, 3 were orangutans, and 4 were capuchin monkeys. None received special training or anything more than access to the necessary equipment. In fact, attempts to guide the efforts of the animals by inducing imitation were always unsuccessful. The drive to use the painting and drawing equipment was powerful, requiring no reinforcement from the human observers. Both young and old animals became so engrossed with the activity that they preferred it to being fed and sometimes threw temper tantrums when stopped. Two of the chimpanzees studied extensively were highly productive. "Alpha" produced over 200 pictures, while the famous "Congo," who deserves to be called the Picasso of the great apes, was responsible for nearly 400. Although most of the efforts consisted of scribbling, the patterns were far from random. Lines and smudges were spread over a blank page outward from a centrally located figure. When a drawing was started on one side of a blank page, the chimpanzee usually shifted to the opposite side to offset it. With time the calligraphy became bolder, starting with simple lines and progressing to more complicated multiple scribbles. Congo's patterns progressed along approximately the same developmental path as those of very young human children, yielding fan-shaped diagrams and even complete circles.

3. The artistic activity of chimpanzees may well be a special manifestation of their tool-using behavior. Members of the species display a total of about ten techniques, all of which require manual skill. Probably all are improved through practice, while at least a few are passed as traditions from one generation to the next. The chimpanzees have a considerable facility for inventing new techniques, such as the use of sticks to pull objects through cage bars and to pry open boxes. Thus the tendency to manipulate objects and to explore their uses appears to have an adaptive advantage for chimpanzees.

4. The same reasoning applies a fortiori to the origin of art in man. As Washburn (1970) pointed out, human beings have been hunter-gatherers for over 99 percent of their history, during which time each man made his own tools. The appraisal of form and skill in execution were necessary for survival, and they probably brought social approval as well. Both forms of success paid off in greater genetic fitness. If the chimpanzee Congo could reach the stage of elementary diagrams, it is not too hard to imagine primitive man progressing to representational figures. Once that stage was reached, the transition to the use of art in sympathetic magic and ritual must have followed quickly. Art might then have played a reciprocally reinforcing role in the development of culture and mental capacity. In the end, writing emerged as the ideographic representation of language.

5. Music of a kind is also produced by some animals. Human beings consider the elaborate courtship and territorial songs of birds to be beautiful, and probably ultimately for the same reason they are of use to the birds. With clarity and precision they identify the species, the physiological condition, and the mental set of the singer. Richness of information and precise transmission of mood are no less the standards of excellence in human music. Singing and dancing serve to draw groups together, direct the emotions of the people, and prepare them for joint action. The carnival displays of chimpanzees described in earlier chapters are remarkably like human celebrations in this respect. The apes run, leap, pound the trunks of trees in drumming motions, and call loudly back and forth. These actions serve at least in part to assemble groups at common feeding grounds. They may resemble the ceremonies of earliest man. Nevertheless, fundamental differences appeared in subsequent human evolution. Human music has been liberated from iconic representation in the same way that true language has departed from the elementary ritualization characterizing the communication of animals. Music has the capacity for unlimited and arbitrary symbolization, and it employs rules of phrasing and order that serve the same function as syntax.

From *On Human Nature* (Cambridge, MA: Harvard University Press, 1978).

Pages 187-88

6. The sacred rituals are the most human [rituals]. Their elementary forms are concerned with magic, the active attempt to manipulate nature and the gods. Upper Paleolithic art from the caves of Western Europe indicates a preoccupation with game animals. There are many scenes showing spears and arrows embedded in the bodies of the prey. Other drawings depict men dancing in animal disguises or standing with heads bowed in front of animals. Probably the function was sympathetic magic, derived from the notion that what is done with an image will come to pass with the real thing. The anticipatory action is comparable to the intention movements of animals, which in the course of evolution have often been ritualized into communicative signals. ... Magic was, and still is in some societies, practiced by special people variously called shamans, sorcerers, or medicine men. They alone were believed to have the secret knowledge and power to deal with the supernatural forces of nature, and as such their influence sometimes exceeded that of the tribal headmen.

7. sacred rites mobilize and display primitive societies in ways that appear to be directly and biologically advantageous.

Page 191

8. This extreme form of certification is granted to the practices and dogmas that serve the vital interests of the group. The individual is prepared by the sacred rituals for supreme efforts and self-sacrifice. Overwhelmed by shibboleths, special costumes, and sacred dancing and music accurately keyed to his emotive centers, he is transformed by a religious experience. The votary is ready to reassert allegiance to his tribe and family, perform charities, consecrate his life, leave for the hunt, join the battle, die for God and country.

Pages 197-98

9. Finally there is myth: the narratives by which the tribe's special place in the world is explained in rational terms consistent with the listener's understanding of the physical world. Preliterate hunter-gatherers tell believable sacred stories about the creation of the world. Human beings and animals with supernatural powers and a special relationship to the tribe fight, eat, and beget offspring. Their actions explain a little bit of how nature works and why the tribe has a favored position on earth. The complexity of the myths increases with that of societies. They duplicate the essential structure in more fantastic forms. Tribes of demigods and heroes, warring for kingship and possession of territory, allocate dominion over different parts of the lives of mortal men. Over and again the myths strike the Manichaean theme of two supernal forces struggling for control of the world of man. For some of the Amerinds of the Amazon-Orinoco forests, for example, the contenders are two brothers representing the sun and the moon, one a benevolent creator, the other a trickster. In the later Hindu myths Brahma, benevolent lord of the universe, creates Night. She gives birth to the

rakshasas, who try to eat Brahma and to destroy mortal men. Another recurrent theme in the more elaborate mythologies is the apocalypse and millenium, wherein it is forecast that the struggles will cease when a god descends to end the existing world and to create a new order.

Pages 213-14

10. I ... do not envision scientific generalization as a substitute for art or as anything more than a nourishing symbiont of art. The artist, including the creative writer, communicates his most personal experience and vision in a direct manner chosen to commit his audience emotionally to that perception. Science can hope to explain artists, and artistic genius, and even art, and it will increasingly use art to investigate human behavior, but it is not designed to transmit experience on a personal level or to reconstitute the full richness of the experience from the laws and principles which are its first concern by definition.

From *Biophilia* (Cambridge, MA: Harvard University Press, 1984)

Pages 60-61

11. Elegance is more a product of the human mind than of external reality. The brain depends upon elegance to compensate for its own small size and short lifetime. As the cerebral cortex grew from apish dimensions through hundreds of thousands of years of evolution, it was forced to rely on tricks to enlarge memory and speed computation. The mind therefore specializes on analogy and metaphor, on a sweeping together of chaotic sensory experience into workable categories labeled by words and stacked into hierarchies for quick recovery. To a considerable degree science consists in originating the maximum amount of information with the minimum expenditure of energy. Beauty is the cleanness of line in such formulations, along with symmetry, surprise, and congruence with other prevailing beliefs. This widely accepted definition is why P. A. M. Dirac (1963), after working out the behavior of electrons, could say that physical theories with some physical beauty are also the ones most likely to be correct, and why Hermann

Weyl (1956), the perfecter of quantum and relativity theory, made an even franker confession: "My work has always tried to unite the true with the beautiful; but when I had to choose one or the other, I usually chose the beautiful."

12. Einstein offered the following solution to the dilemma of truth versus beauty: "God does not care about our mathematical difficulties. He integrates empirically." In other words, a mind with infinite memory store and calculating ability could compute any system as the sum of all its parts. Mathematics and beauty are devices by which human beings get through life with the limited intellectual capacity inherited by the species. Like a discerning palate and sexual appetite, these esthetic contrivances give pleasure. Put in more mechanistic terms, they play upon the circuitry of the brain's limbic system in a way that ultimately promotes survival and reproduction. They lead the scientist adventitiously into the unexplored fractions of space and time, from which he returns to reports his findings and fulfill his social role. Riemannian geometry is declared beautiful no less than the bird of paradise, because the mind is innately prepared to receive its symmetry and power. Pleasure is shared, triumph ceremonies held, and the communal hunt resumed.

Pages 62-64

13. Scientific innovation sometimes sounds like poetry, and I would claim that it is, at least in the earliest stages. The ideal scientist can be said to think like a poet, work like a clerk, and write like a journalist. The ideal poet thinks, works, and writes like a poet. The two vocations draw from the same subconscious wellsprings and depend upon similar primal stories and images. But where scientists aim for a generalizing formula to which special cases are obedient, seeking unifying natural laws, artists invent special cases immediately. They transmit forms of knowledge in which the knower himself is revealed. Their works are lit by a personal flame and above all else they identify, in Roger Shattuck's expression, "the individual as the accountable agent of his action and as the potential seat of human greatness" (1974).

14. The aim of art is not to show how or why an effect is produced (that would be science) but literally to produce it. And not just any cry from the heart—it requires mental discipline no less than in science. In poetry, T. S. Eliot explained, the often-quoted criterion of sublimity misses the mark. What counts is not the greatness of the emotion but the intensity of the artistic process, the pressure under which the fusion takes place (1919). The great artist touches others in surgical manner with the generating impulse, transferring feeling precisely. His work is personal in style but general in effect.

15. Ideally art is powerful enough to cross cultures; it reads the code of human nature. Octavio Paz's poem "The Broken Waterjar" (*El cantaro roto*) accomplishes this result with splendid effectiveness. Paz is torn by the contradiction in the Mexican experience. He says that the minds of his people are capable of long flights of imagination and visions of piercing beauty. The people look at the sky and add torches, wings, and "bracelets of flaming islands." But they also look down to a desiccated landscape, symbolizing physical and spiritual poverty. A potentially great nation had been divided by the Conquest and stifled by oppression.

> Bare hills, a cold volcano, stone and a sound of panting
> under such splendor, and drouth, the taste of dust,
> the rustle of bare feet in the dust, and one tall tree in the
> middle of the field like a petrified fountain! (1973)

The resolution is not offered in the form of practical advice, which might easily prove wrong, but in the poet's vision of unity in a search back through time, "mas alla de las aguas del bautismo," to a more secure metaphysical truth, and Paz says,

> vida y muerte no son mundos contrarios, somos un solo
> tallo con dos flores gemelas

Mexico is a single stem with twin flowers, united by the continuity of time.

16. The essence of art, no less than of science, is synedoche. A carefully chosen part serves for the whole. Some features of the subject directly perceived or implied by analogy transmits precisely the quality intended. The listener is moved by a single, surprising image. In "The Broken Waterjar" the rustle of bare feet in the dust conveys the pauperization of Mexico. The artist knows which sensibilities shared by his audience will permit the desired impact.

17. Picasso defined art as the lie that helps us to see the truth. The aphorism fits both art and science, since each in its own way seeks power through elegance. But this inspired distortion is only a technique of thinking and communication. There is a still more basic similarity: both are enterprises of discovery. And the binding force lies in our biology and in our relationship to other organisms. In art, the workings of the mind are explored, whereas in science the domain is the world at large and now, increasingly, the workings of the mind as well. Of equal importance, both rely on similar forms of metaphor and analogy, because they share the brain's strict and peculiar limitations in the processing of information.

Page 67

18. We have now come to the common, human origin of science and art. The innovator searches for comparisons that no one else has made. He scrambles to tighten his extension by argument, example, and experiment. Important science is not just any similarity glimpsed for the first time. It offers analogies that map the gateways to unexplored terrain. The comparisons meet the criterion of principal metaphor used by art critics: one commanding image synthesized from several units, such that a single complex idea is attained not by analysis but by the sudden perception of an objective relation.

Pages 74-81

19. At the moment the spark ignites, when intuition and metaphor are all-important, the artist most closely resembles the scientist. But he does not then press on toward natural law and self-dissolution within the big picture. All his skills are aimed at the instant transference of images and control of emotions in others. For purposes of craft, he carefully avoids exact definitions or the display of inner logic.

20. In 1753 Bishop Lowth made the correct diagnosis in *Lectures on the Sacred Poetry of the Hebrews*: the poetic mind is not satisfied with a plain and exact description but seeks to heighten sensation. "For the passions are naturally inclined to amplifications; they wonderfully magnify and exaggerate whatever dwells upon the mind, and labour to express it in animated, bold, and magnificent terms" (cited in Abrams 1953).

21. The essential quality can be rephrased in more modern terms. The mind is biologically prone to discursive communication that expands thought. Mankind, in Richard Rorty's expression, is the poetic species (1982). The symbols of art, music, and language freight power well beyond their outward and literal meanings. So each one also condenses large quantities of information. Just as mathematical equations allow us to move swiftly across large amounts of knowledge and spring into the unknown, the symbols of art gather human experience into novel forms in order to evoke a more intense perception in others. Human beings live—literally live, if life is equated with the mind—by symbols, particularly words, because the brain is constructed to process information almost exclusively in their terms.

22. I have spoken of art as a device for exploration and discovery. Its practitioners and expert observers, whose authority is beyond question, have stressed other functions as well. In Samuel Johnson's definition, to instruct by pleasing. According to Keats, to uplift by the refinement of shared feelings. No—moral, the role of art is moral, according to D. H. Lawrence. A spell against death, to create and preserve the self, in the formulation of Richard Eberhart. For the more prosaic cultural anthropologists, art above all else expresses the purposes of a society. Indeed, affirmation may have been the original evolutionary driving force behind Paleolithic cave art. It was certainly served by the early oral poets of Europe, including the illiterate Homeric bards who recited the *Iliad* and *Odyssey* at festivals and thus transmitted the central myths and legends of ancient Greece. When this cohesive functions fails, and tradition and taste fragment as part of culture's advance, criticism becomes a necessary and honored profession. Then we also witness revolutionary art, which goes beyond innovation to promote a different society and culture.

23. All these functions are variously filled according to circumstances. Nevertheless, art generally considered to be important appears to be marked by one consistent quality: it explores the unknown reaches of the mind. The departure is both calculated and tentative, as in science. The poet focuses on the inward search itself and attracts us to his distant constructions. Something moves on the edge of the field of vision, a new connection is glimpsed, holds for a moment. Words pour in and around, and the image takes substantial form, at first believed familiar, then seen as strikingly new. It is something, as in Thomas Kinsella's "Midsummer,"

> that for this long year
> Had hid and halted like a deer
> Turned marvelous,
> Parted the tragic grass, tame,
> Lifted its perfect head and came
> To welcome us. (1973)

24. But the poet refuses to take us any farther. If he goes on the precise image will melt into abstract descriptions; light and beauty will congeal into rows of formulas. In this essential way art differs from science. The world of interest is the mind, not the physical universe on which mental process feeds. Richard Eberhart, a keen observer of nature, listened to the same New England birds that led Robert MacArthur to mathematical theories of ecology, and I daresay that the first swirl of imagery, the first tensile pleasures were the same, but the two then diverged, the poet inward and the scientist outward into separate existences:

> No, may the thrush among our high pine trees
> Be ambiguous still, elusive in true song,

Never or seldom seen, and if never seen
May it to my imperious memory belong. (1976)

He holds back, on himself and on us, in order to cast his spell. Again we see that the dilemma of the machine-in-the-garden exists in the rain forests of the mind as surely as it does in the American continent. Our intrinsic emotions drive us to search for fresh habitats, to cross unexplored terrain, but we still crave the sense of a mysterious world stretching infinitely beyond. The free-living birds (thrush, nightingale, bird of paradise), being rulers of the blank spaces on the map and negligent of human existence, are worthy symbols of both art and science.

25. I have emphasized the expansive role of poetry to argue that, whereas art and science are basically different in execution, they are convergent in what they might eventually disclose about human nature.

Pages 78-81

26. *They must be true*: ... can be said of outstanding achievements in literature and the arts, which pull the rest of us along until the construction becomes self-evident. Eliot wrote that "unless we have those few men who combine an exceptional sensibility with an exceptional power over words, our own ability, not merely to express, but even to feel any but the crudest emotions, will degenerate" (1975). The difference in power is one of degree rather than kind, but it crosses a threshold to create a qualitative new result in the same way that a critical speed lifts a glider off the ground into flight.

27. Research on cognitive development has shown that in the course of its growth the mind probes certain channels much more readily than others. Some of the responses are automatic and can be measured by physiological changes of which the individual is mostly or entirely unaware. For example, using electroencephalograms in the study of response to graphic designs, the Belgian psychologist Gerda Smets found that maximal arousal (measured by the blockage of the alpha wave) occurs when the figure contains about 20 percent redundancy (1973). That is the amount present in a spiral with two or three turns, or a relatively simple maze, or a neat cluster of ten or so triangles. Less arousal occurs when the figure consists of only one triangle or square, or when the design is more complicated than the optimum—as in a difficult maze or an irregular scattering of twenty rectangles. The data are not the result of a chance biochemical quirk. When selecting symbols and abstract art, people actually gravitate to about the levels of complexity observed in Smet's experiments. Furthermore, the preference has its roots in early life. Newborn infants gaze longest at visual designs containing between five and twenty angles. During the next three months their preference shifts toward the adult pattern measured with electroencephalograms. Nor is there anything foreordained or otherwise trivial in the aesthetic optimum of human beings. It is easy to imagine the evolution of some other intelligent species in another time or on some other planet, possessing different eyes, optic nerves, and brain—and thus distinct optimal complexity and artistic standards.

28. We can reasonably suppose that the compositions of artists play upon the rules of mental development that are now beginning to receive the objective attention of experimental psychology. The distinction between science and art can be understood more clearly from this different perspective. The abstracted qualities of the developmental rules of the mind are the principal concern of science. In contrast, the node-link structures [of long-term memory] themselves, their emotional color, tone, cadence, fidelity to personal experience, and the images they fleetingly reveal, are more the domain of art. Of equal importance to both enterprises are the symbols and myths that evoke the mental structures in compelling fashion. Certain great myths—the origin of the world, cataclysm and rebirth, the struggle between the powers of light and darkness, Earth Mother, and a few others—recur dependably in cultures around the world. Lesser, more personal myths appear in crisis poems and romantic tales, where they blend imperceptibly into legend and history. Through the deep pleasures they naturally excite, and the ease with which they are passed from one person to another, these stories invade the developing mind more readily than others, and they tend to converge to form the commonalities of human nature. Yeats in his 1900 essay on Shelley distinguished between the theoretician who seeks abstract truth and the naturalist-poet who celebrates detail. In the universe of the mind, Yeats said, no symbol tells all its meanings to any generation. Only by discovering the ancient symbols can the artist express meanings that cross generations and open the full abundance of nature.

29. We need not worry about the extravagances of visionary artists, so long as they reveal the deeper channels of their minds in a manner that gives meaning to our own. Each human mindscape is idiosyncratic and yet ultimately obedient to biological law. Like the forest of some newly discovered island, it possesses unique contours and previously undescribed forms of life, treasures to be valued for their own sake, but the genetic process that spawned them is the same as elsewhere. Continuity is essential for comprehension; the imagery chosen by the artist must draw on common experience and values, however tortuous the manner of presentation. Thus in 1919 the American modernist Joseph Stella created "Tree of My Life" to translate his own vaulting optimism into a physical paradise within the mind. Bright tropical plants and animals served as the symbols. He described his feelings that led to the painting:

> And one clear morning in April I found myself in the midst of joyous singing and delicious scent—the singing and the scent of the birds and flowers ready to celebrate the baptism of my new art, the birds and the flowers already enjewelling the tender foliage of the new-born tree of my hopes. (cited in Sweeney 1977)

30. We are in the fullest sense a biological species and will find little ultimate meaning apart from the remainder of life. The fiery circle of disciplines will be closed if science looks at the inward journey of the artist's mind, making art and culture objects of study in the biological mode, and if the artist and critic are informed of the workings of the mind and the natural world as illuminated by the scientific method. In principle at least, nothing can be denied to the humanities, nothing to science.

Pages 83-86

31. Science and the humanities, biology and culture, are bridged in a dramatic manner by the phenomenon of the serpent. The snake's image enters the conscious mind with ease during dreams and reveries, fabricated from symbols and bearing portents of magic. It appears without warning and departs abruptly, leaving behind not the perception of any real snake but the vague memory of a more powerful creature, the serpent, surrounded by a mist of fear and wonderment.

32. The snake and the serpent, flesh-and-blood reptile and demonic dream-image, reveal the complexity of our relation to nature and the fascination and beauty inherent in all forms of organisms. Even the deadliest and most repugnant creatures bring an endowment of magic to the human mind. Human beings have an innate fear of snakes or, more precisely, they have an innate propensity to learn such fear quickly and easily past the age of five. The images they build out of this peculiar mental set are both powerful and ambivalent, ranging from terror-stricken flight to the experience of power and male sexuality. As a consequence the serpent has become an important part of cultures around the world.

33. There is a principle of many ramifications to consider here, which extends well beyond the ordinary concerns of psychoanalytic reasoning about sexual symbols. Life of any kind is infinitely more interesting than almost any conceivable variety of inanimate matter. The latter is valued chiefly to the extent that it can be metabolized into live tissue, accidentally resembles it, or can be fashioned into a useful and properly animated artifact. No one in his right mind looks at a pile of dead leaves in preference to the tree from which they fell.

34. What is it exactly that binds us so closely to living things? The biologist will tell you that life is the self-replication of giant molecules from lesser chemical fragments, resulting in the assembly of complex organic structures, the transfer of large amounts of molecular information, ingestion, growth, movement of an outwardly purposeful nature, and the proliferation of closely similar organisms. The poet-in-biologist will add that life is an exceedingly improbable state, metastable, open to other systems, thus ephemeral—and worth any price to keep.

35. Certain organisms have still more to offer because of their special impact on mental development. I have suggested that the urge to affiliate with other forms of life is to some degree innate, hence deserves to be called biophilia. The evidence for the proposition is not strong in a formal scientific sense: the subject has not been studied enough in the scientific manner of hypothesis, deduction, and experimentation to let us be certain about it one way or the other. The biophilic tendency is nevertheless so clearly evinced in daily life and widely distributed as to deserve serious attention. It unfolds in the predictable fantasies and responses of individuals from early childhood onward. It cascades into repetitive patterns of culture across most or all societies, a consistency often noted in the literature of anthropology. These processes appear to be part of the programs of the brain. They are marked by the quickness and decisiveness with which we learn particular things about certain kinds of plants and animals. They are too consistent to be dismissed as the result of purely historical events working on a mental blank slate.

36. Perhaps the most bizarre of the biophilic traits is awe and veneration of the serpent. The dreams from which the dominant images arise are known to exist in all those societies where systematic studies have been conducted on mental life. At least 5 percent of the people at any given time remember experiencing them, while many more would probably do so if they recorded their waking impressions over a period of several months. The images described by urban New Yorkers are as detailed and emotional as those of Australian aboriginals and Zulus. In all cultures the serpents are prone to be mystically transfigured. The Hopi know Palulukon, the water serpent, a benevolent but frightening godlike being. The Kwakiutl fear the *sisiutl*, a kind of three-headed serpent with both human and reptile faces, whose appearance in dreams presages insanity or death. The Sharanahua of Peru summon reptile spirits by taking hallucinogenic drugs and stroking the severed tongues of snakes over their faces. They are rewarded with dreams of brightly colored boas, venomous snakes, and lakes teeming with caimans and anacondas.

37. These cultural manifestations may seem at first detached and mysterious, but there is a simple reality behind the ophidian archetype that lies within the experience of ordinary people. The mind is primed to react emotionally to the sight of snakes, not just to fear them but to be aroused and absorbed in their details, to weave stories about them.

Pages 92-101

38. What is there in snakes anyway that makes them so repellent and fascinating? The answer in retrospect is deceptively simple: their ability to remain hidden, the power in their sinuous limbless bodies, and the threat from venom injected hypodermically through sharp hollow teeth. It pays in elementary survival to be interested in snakes and to respond emotionally to their generalized image, to go beyond ordinary caution and fear. The rule built into the brain of a learning bias is: become alert quickly to any object with the serpentine gestalt. *Overlearn* this particular response in order to keep safe.

39. Other primates have evolved similar rules. When guenons and vervets, the common monkeys of the African forest, see a python, cobra, or puff adder, they emit a distinctive chuttering call that rouses other members in the group. (Different calls are used to designate eagles and leopards.) Some of the adults then follow the intruding snake at a safe distance until it leaves the area. The monkeys in effect broadcast a dangerous-snake alert, which serves to protect the entire group and not solely the individual who encountered the danger. The most remarkable fact is that the alarm is evoked most strongly by the kinds of snakes that can harm them. Somehow, apparently through the routes of instinct, the guenons and vervets have become competent herpetologists.

40. The idea that snake aversion on the part of man's relatives can be an inborn trait is supported by other studies on rhesus monkeys, the large brown monkeys of India and surrounding Asian countries. When adults see a snake of any kind, they react with the generalized fear response of their species. They variously back off and stare (or turn away), crouch, shield their faces, bark, screech, and twist their faces into the fear grimace, in which the lips are retracted, the teeth are bared, and the ears are flattened against the head. Monkeys raised in the laboratory without previous exposure to snakes show the same response to them as those brought in from the wild, although in weaker form. During control experiments designed to test the specificity of the response, the rhesus failed to react to other, nonsinuous objects placed in their cages. It is the form of the snake and perhaps also its distinctive movements that contain the key stimuli to which the monkeys are innately tuned.

41. Grant for the moment that snake aversion does have a hereditary basis in at least some kinds of nonhuman primates. The possibility that immediately follows is that the trait is evolved by natural selection. In other words, individuals who respond leave more offspring than those who do not, and as a result the propensity to learn fear quickly spreads through the population—or, if it was already present, is maintained there at a high level.

42. How can biologists test such a proposition about the origin of behavior? They turn natural history upside down. They search for species historically free of forces in the environment believed to favor the evolutionary change, to see if in fact the organisms do *not* possess the trait. The lemurs, primitive relatives of the monkeys, offer such an inverted opportunity. They are the indigenous inhabitants of Madagascar, where no large or poisonous snakes exist to threaten them. Sure enough, lemurs presented with snakes in captivity fail to display anything resembling the automatic fear responses of the African and Asian monkeys. Is this adequate proof? In the chaste idiom of scientific discourse, we are permitted to conclude only that the evidence is consistent with the proposal. Neither this nor any comparable hypothesis can be settled by a single case. Only further examples can raise confidence in it to a level beyond the reach of determined skeptics.

43. Another line of evidence comes from studies of the chimpanzee, a species thought to have shared a common ancestor with prehumans as recently as five million years ago. Chimps raised in the laboratory become apprehensive in the presence of snakes, even if they have had no previous experience. They back off to a safe distance and follow the intruder with a fixed stare while altering companions with the *Wah!* warning call. More important, the response becomes gradually more marked during adolescence.

44. This last quality is especially interesting because human beings pass through approximately the same developmental sequence. Children under five years of age feel no special anxiety over snakes, but later they grow increasingly wary. Just one or two mildly bad experiences, such as a garter snake seem writhing away in the grass, a playmate thrusting a rubber model at them, or a counselor telling scary stories at the campfire, can make children deeply and permanently fearful. Other common fears, notably of the dark, strangers, and loud noises, start to wane after seven years of age. In contrast, the tendency to avoid snakes grows stronger with time. It is possible to turn the mind in the opposite direction, to learn to handle snakes without apprehension or even to like them in some special way, as I did—but the adaptation takes a special effort and is usually a little forced and self-conscious. The special sensitivity will just as likely lead to full-blown ophidiophobia, the pathological extreme in which the mere appearance of a snake brings on a feeling of panic, cold sweat, and waves of nausea.

45. Why should serpents have such a strong influence during mental development? The direct and simple answer is that throughout the history of mankind a few kinds have been a major cause of sickness and death. Every continent except Antarctica has poisonous snakes. Over large stretches of Asia and Africa the known death rate from snake bite is 5 persons per 100,000 each year, or higher. The local record is held by a province in Burma, with 36.8 deaths per 100,000 a year. Australia had an exceptional abundance of deadly snakes, a majority of which are relatives of the cobras. Among them the tiger snake is especially feared for its large size and tendency to strike without warning. In South and Central America live the bushmaster, fer-de-lance, and jaracara, among the largest and most aggressive of the pit vipers. With back colored like rotting leaves and fangs long enough to pass through a human hand, they lie in ambush on the floor of the tropical forest for the small warm-blooded animals that form their major prey. Few people realize that a complex of dangerous snakes, the "true" vipers, are still relatively abundant throughout Europe. The common adder *Viperus berus* ranges to the Arctic Circle. The number of people bitten in such improbable places as Switzerland and Finland is still high enough, running into the hundreds annually, to keep outdoorsmen on a sort of yellow alert. Even Ireland, one of the few countries in the world lacking snakes altogether (thanks to the last Pleistocene glaciation and not Saint Patrick), has imported the key ophidian symbols and traditions from other European cultures and preserved the fear of serpents in art and literature.

46. Here, then, is the sequence by which the agents of nature appear to have been translated into the symbols of culture. For hundred of thousands of years, time enough for the appropriate genetic changes to occur in the brain, poisonous snakes have been a significant source of injury and death to human beings. The response to the threat is not simply to avoid it, in the way that certain berries are recognized as poisonous through a process of trial and error. People also display the mixture of apprehension and morbid fascination characterizing the nonhuman primates. They inherit a strong tendency to acquire the aversion during early childhood and to add to it progressively, like our closest phylogenetic relatives, the chimpanzees. The mind then adds a great deal more that is distinctively human. It feeds upon the emotions to enrich culture. The tendency of the serpent to appear suddenly in dreams, its sinuous form, and its power and mystery are the natural ingredients of myth and religion.

47. Consider how sensation and emotional states are elaborated into stories during dreams. The dreamer hears a distant thunderclap and changes an ongoing episode to end with the slamming of a door. He feels a general anxiety and is transported to a schoolhouse corridor, where he searches for a classroom he does not know in order to take an examination for which he is unprepared. As the sleeping brain enters its regular dream periods, marked by rapid eye movement beneath closed eyelids, giant fibers in the lower brainstem fire upward into the cortex. The awakened mind responds by retrieving memories and fabricating stories around the sources of physical and emotional discomfort. It hastens to recreate the elements of past real experience, often in a jumbled and antic form. And from time to time the serpent appears as the embodiment of one or more of these feelings. The direct and literal fear of snakes is foremost among them, but the dream-image can also be summoned by sexual desire, a craving for dominance and power, and the apprehension of violent death.

48. We need not turn to Freudian theory in order to explain our special relationship to snakes. The serpent did not originate as the vehicle of dreams and symbols. The relation appears to be precisely the other way around and correspondingly easier to study and understand. Humanity's concrete experience with poisonous snakes gave rise to the Freudian phenomena after it was assimilated by genetic evolution into the brain's structure. The mind has to create symbols and fantasies from something. It leans toward the most powerful preexistent images or at least follows the learning rules that create the images, including that of the serpent. For most of this century, perhaps overly enchanted by psychoanalysis, we have confused the dream with the reality and its psychic effect with the ultimate cause rooted in nature.

49. Among prescientific people, whose dreams are conduits to the spirit world and snakes a part of ordinary experience, the serpent has played a central role in the building of culture. There are magic incantations for simple protection as in the hymns of the Atharva Veda:

> With my eye do I slay thy eye, with poison do I slay thy poison. O Serpent, die, do not live; back upon thee shall thy poison turn.

50. "Indra slew thy first ancestors, O Serpent," the chant continues, "and since they are crushed, what strength forsooth can be theirs?" And so the power can be controlled and even diverted to human use through iatromancy and the casting of magic spells. Two serpents entwine the caduceus, which was first the winged staff of Mercury as messenger of the gods, then the safe-conduct pass of ambassadors and heralds, and finally the universal emblem of the medical profession.

51. Balaji Mundkur (1983) has shown how the inborn awe of snakes matured into rich productions of art and religion around the world. Serpentine forms wind across stone carvings from paleolithic Europe and are scratched into mammoth teeth found in Siberia. They are the emblems of power and ceremony for the shamans of the Kwakiutl, the Siberian Yakut and Yenisei Ostyak, and many of the tribes of Australian aboriginals. Stylized snakes have often served as the talismans of the gods and spirits who bestow fertility: Ashtoreth of the Canaanites, the demons Fu-Hsi and Nu-kua of the Han Chinese, and the powerful goddesses Mudamma and Manasa of Hindu India. The ancient Egyptians venerated at least thirteen ophidian deities ministering to various combinations of health, fecundity, and vegetation. Prominent among them was the triple-headed giant Nehebku who travelled widely to inspect every part of the river kingdom. Amulets in gold inscribed with the sign of a cobra were placed in the wrappings of Tutankhamen's mummy. Even the scorpion goddess Selket bore the title "mother of serpents." Like her offspring, she prevailed simultaneously as a source of evil, power, and goodness.

52. The Aztec pantheon was a phantasmagoria of monstrous forms among whom serpents were given pride of place. The calendrical symbols included the ophidian *olin_nahi* and *cipactli*, the earth crocodile that possessed a forked tongue and rattlesnake's tail. The rain god Tlaloc consisted in part of two coiled rattlesnakes whose heads met to form the god's upper lip. *Coatl*, serpent, is the dominant phrase in the names of the divinities. Coatlicue was the a threatening chimera of snake and human parts, Cihuacoatl the goddess of childbirth and mother of the human race, and Xiuhcoatl the fire serpent over whose body fire was rekindled every fifty-two years to mark a major division in the religious calendar. Quetzacoatl, the plumed serpent with the human head, reigned as god of the morning and evening star and thus of death and resurrection. As inventor of the calendar, deity of books and learning, and patron of the priesthood, he was revered in the schools where nobles and priests were taught. His reported departure over the eastern horizon upon a raft of snakes must have been the occasion of consternation for the intellectuals of the day, something like the folding of the Guggenheim Foundation.

53. A contradiction of ophidian images was a feature of Greek religion as well. Among the early forms of Zeus was the serpent Meilikhios, god of love, gentle and responsive to supplication, and god of vengeance, whose sacrifice was a holocaust offered at night. Another great serpent protected the lustral waters at the spring of Ares. He coexisted with the Erinyes, demons of the underworld so horrible they could not be pictured in early mythology. They were given the form of serpents when brought to the stage by Euripides in the *Iphigeneia in Tauris*: "Dost see her, her the Hades-snake who gapes / To slay me, with dread vipers, open-mouthed?"

54. Slyness, deception, malevolence, betrayal, the implicit threat of a forked tongue flicking in and out of the masklike head, all qualities tinged with miraculous powers to heal and guide, forecast and empower, became the serpent's prevailing image in western cultures. The serpent in the Garden of Eden, appearing as in a dream to serve as Judaism's evil Prometheus, gave humankind knowledge of good and evil and with it the burden of original sin, for which God repaid in kind:

> I will put enmity between you and the woman,
> between your brood and hers.
> They shall strike at your head,
> and you shall strike at their heel.

55. To summarize the relation between man and snake: life gathers human meaning to become part of us. Culture transforms the snake into the serpent, a far more potent creation than the literal reptile. Culture in turn is a product of the mind, which can be interpreted as an image-making machine that recreates the outside world through symbols arranged into maps and stories. But the mind does not have an instant capacity to grasp reality in its full chaotic richness; nor does the body last long enough for the brain to process information piece by piece like an all-purpose computer. Rather, consciousness races ahead to master certain kinds of information with enough efficiency to survive. it submits to a few biases easily while automatically avoiding others. A great deal of evidence has accumulated in genetics and physiology to show that the controlling devices are biological in nature, built into the sensory apparatus and brain by particularities in cellular architecture.

56. The combined biases are what we call human nature. The central tendencies, exemplified so strikingly in fear and veneration of the serpent, are the wellsprings of culture. Hence simple perceptions yield an unending abundance of images with special meaning while remaining true to the forces of natural selection that created them.

57. How could it be otherwise? The brain evolved into its present form over a period of about two million years, from the time of *Homo habilis* to the late stone age of *Homo sapiens*, during which people existed in hunter-gatherer bands in intimate contact with the natural environment. Snakes mattered. The smell of water, the hum of a bee, the directional bend of a plant stalk mattered. The naturalist's trance was adaptive: the glimpse of one small animal hidden in the grass could make the difference between eating and going hungry in the evening. And a sweet sense of horror, the shivery fascination with monsters and creeping forms that so delights us today even in the sterile hearts of cities, could see you through to the next morning. Organisms are the natural stuff of metaphor and ritual. Although the evidence is far from all in, the brain appears to have kept its old capacities, its channeled quickness. We stay alert and alive in the vanished forests of the world.

From Jeffrey Saver, "An Interview with E. O. Wilson on Sociobiology and Religion," ***Free Inquiry*** **5 (1985): 15-22**

Page 19

58. People do have a strong tendency to appreciate and love life. I use the word *biophilia* to stress this natural human impulse to affiliate with and even to love living things. It's no coincidence, for example, that most science fiction entails life, either at the fairly crude level of a transference of human life, politics, or social existence to some distant imagined place, or at the more speculative level of envisioning contact with other forms of life. Very little sci-fi entails the real substance of physics and chemistry. How compelling is it in the end to know what lies one kilometer below the surface of Jupiter? But people become truly excited when writers start talking about the prospect of making contact with extraterrestrial life. Then unlimited possibilities seem to open.

From *The Diversity of Life* (Cambridge, MA: Harvard University Press, 1992).

Page 350

59. The favored living place of most peoples is a prominence near water from which parkland can be viewed. On such heights are found the abodes of the powerful and rich, tombs of the great, temples, parliaments, and monuments commemorating tribal glory. The location is today an aesthetic choice and, by the implied freedom to settle there, a symbol of status. In ancient, more practical times the topography provided a place to retreat and a sweeping prospect from which to spot the distant approach of storms and enemy forces. Every animal species selects a habitat in which its members gain a favorable mix of security and food. For most of deep history, human beings lived in tropical and subtropical savanna in East Africa, open country sprinkled with streams and lakes, trees and copses. In similar topography modern peoples choose their residences and design their parks and gardens, if given a free choice. They simulate neither dense jungles, toward which gibbons are drawn, nor dry grasslands, preferred by hamadryas baboons. In their gardens they plant trees that resemble the acacias, sterculias, and other native trees of the African savannas. The ideal tree crown sought is consistently wider than tall, with spreading lowermost branches close enough to the ground to touch and climb, clothed with compound or needle-shaped leaves.

Works Cited

Abrams, M. H.
1953 *The Mirror and the Lamp*. New York: Oxford University Press.
Dirac, P. A. M.
1963 "The Evolution of the Physicist's Picture of Nature." *Scientific American* 208 (May): 45-53.
Dyson, Freeman J.
1956 Obituary for Hermann Weyl. *Nature* 177: 457-58.
Eberhart, Richard
1976 "Ultimate Song." In *Collected Poems, 1930-1976*. New York: Oxford University Press.
Eliot, T. S.
1975 "Tradition and the Individual Talent" (1919). In *Selected Prose of T. S. Eliot*. New York: Harcourt Brace Jovanovich.
Kinsella, Thomas
1973 "Midsummer." In *Selected Poems, 1956-1968*. Dublin: Dolmen Press.
Morris, Desmond
1962 *The Biology of Art*. New York: Knopf.
Mundkur, Balaji
1983 *The Cult of the Serpent: An Interdisciplinary Survey of Its manifestations and Origins*. Albany: State University of New York Press.
Paz, Octavio
1973 "The Broken Waterjar." Translated by Lysander Kemp in *Paz, Early Poems, 1935-1955*. New York: New Directions.
Rorty, Richard
1982 "Mind as Ineffable." In R. Q. Elvee, ed., *Mind in Nature*. New York: Harper and Row, pp. 60-95.
Shattuck, Roger
1974 "Humanizing the Humanities." *Change* (November): 4-5.
Smets, Gerda
1973 *Aesthetic Judgment and Arousal: An Experimental Contribution to Psycho-physics*. Leuven, Belgium: Leuven University Press.

Sweeney, J. Gray
1977 *Themes in American Painting*. Grand Rapids, MI: Grand Rapids Art Museum.

Washburn, S. L.
1970 Comment on "A Possible Evolutionary Basis for Aesthetic Appreciation in Men and Apes." *Evolution* 24 (4): 824-25.

Edward O. Wilson on Art

Brett Cooke

During the early spring of 1994, members of the Human Behavior and Evolution Society (HBES) suddenly took up the issue whether sociobiology should be used to study literature. A number of subscribers soon entered the discussion by e-mail and a furious debate ensued for the next six weeks, with several postings often being exchanged each day. Classic themes were readily seen to correlate with biosocial tenets, but from the very start participants expressed concern that sociobiologists avoid the kinds of biased and sloppy research methods generally attributed to literary critics and their various schools. Contributors insisted that standards of scientific rigor be applied to this new enterprise, that hypotheses be advanced that are falsifiable, and that data be collected on a crosscultural if not worldwide scale.

E-mail polemics are a sort of ephemera; they happen and generally disappear without a trace. Though advice and bibliographical citations are solicited and given, no records are kept. There is little point in taking such messages seriously. Comments are barely screened, and little rigor is required in this activity. Just the same, we should take the very occurrence of the debate as a further sign of the urgent need for bringing the arts into the evolutionary paradigm. After all, where would any general set of theories regarding our species be if it ignored so long-standing and universal a portion of our behavior? It was clear to all in the e-mail debate that the issues proffered by the arts are vital. Indeed, the examples discussed, mostly involving romance fiction, quickly attracted the attention of other members. Second, that the participants from other fields were able to provide so much of interest in such a brief period with little effort should be understood as a token of the enormous and immediate potential for a biopoetics. The debaters also sensed that the arts offer an immense storehouse of information about our own kind, readily available as close as the nearest library, and a few research projects were suggested. The very quality of these—unfortunately not publishable—comments constitutes a challenge to conventional criticism. These ethologists readily made considerable progress in arts scholarship. In effect, they accomplished tasks that mainstream critics should be undertaking—a consideration which points out the uselessness of much contemporary study of the arts.

Yet another striking feature of the discussion was that it was conducted in almost complete ignorance of earlier findings. Indeed, the participants were hardly the first evolutionists to look at the arts, liberated not deterred by the traditional critics they were neglecting. Richard Dawkins, for example, makes various comments in passing on science fiction in *The Selfish Gene* and *The Blind Watchmaker*.[1] Martin Daly and Margo Wilson illustrate their *Homicide* with references to fairy tales.[2] But most glaring of all is our common failure to recognize that the most accomplished critic working in sociobiology was none other than the man most often acknowledged as its founder, Edward O. Wilson.

It needs to be said that Wilson has advanced no claims to expertise as a critic. Nor, prior to the tenth chapter of his recent *Consilience: The Unity of Knowledge* (1998), has he written anything intended as arts scholarship. This is by no means to Wilson's discredit, given all that he has done to help formulate and establish sociobiology, to create biogeography, to add immensely to our understanding of the social insects, and to lead the recent effort to maintain biological diversity. Nevertheless, in the course of his famous writings, Wilson often refers to the arts for illustrations. He commonly interlaces his books with citations from poetry and mythology collected from around the world. One can readily detect a growing confidence in this manner, tracing a steeply rising curve from his cautious and derivative statements on art in *Sociobiology* to his daring and extended extemporizing in *Biophilia* and *Consilience*. No doubt he was responding to the same intellectual challenges and opportunities that the HBES members felt, only much more so, given his evident affection for the arts.

America's most famous scientist and one of its greatest writers surely needs no introduction, except, perhaps, as an authority on the arts. We propose to set excerpts from his works in a new context, first by selecting just those which focus on the arts and then by offering, as it were, a one-sided and informal conversation intended to outline how they pertain to this new field. We decided to separate the two texts so that the reader can peruse Wilson's statements on art directly, with my commentary serving as an optional supplement. My commentary pretty much follows the order of the excerpts from Wilson's work, which I numbered so as to permit easy reference. Since *Consilience* appeared too close to our press time to permit the inclusion of Wilson's chapter on the arts in these pages, we will simply refer the reader to that volume. The following remarks are inspired by Wilson's statements but, of course, express my own opinions.

The evolution of aesthetics figures prominently in Wilson's early public statements on sociobiology. Although his paradigm-setting *Sociobiology: The New Synthesis* was primarily addressed to social scientists and philosophers, he mentions the powerful role of emotions in effecting behavior in his opening paragraph (1). The latent significance of aesthetics in our apprehension of all actions may pertain to "ethical philosophers," but they are yet more relevant to those of us who study the arts, where they perform an even more vital role. That feelings, both those mentioned ("hate, love, guilt, fear") and those covered by "and others," are often expressed in narrative and lyric in an exaggerated form should demonstrate the great potential for arts scholarship in the new biology of human behavior. This is especially the case when we consider that the creative artist can choreograph these sentiments so as to manipulate both performers and audience, as well as himself. Indeed, he can do so on a repeatable basis, and to a large extent he does so for no better reason.

Wilson's introduction also serves to remind us that at some level the arts are founded, with our emotions as a necessary interface, on our physiology. The question is, when does it make a difference? Perhaps it does not matter. All proximate causes, such as local culture, ideology, immediate history of the genre, and, at a somewhat greater distance, psychology, are rooted in ultimate origins. These include genetics and, going a bit further, chaos theory and Richard Dawkins's postulated universal law of replication. Nevertheless, if the biosocial critic wishes to produce dramatic findings, he is well advised to focus on those rare phenomena where proximate explanations do not suffice.

Later, in the highly controversial final chapter of *Sociobiology*, when Wilson brought his new paradigm to our own species, he covered the arts in a fairly perfunctory manner.[3] Wilson's long citation of information (2) from Morris's *Biology of Art* reminds us of just how undeveloped biopoetics was in 1962, at the time of Morris's book, in 1975, when *Sociobiology* came out, and indeed until the past few years. Wilson literally had no other major authority to turn to, save perhaps Morris Peckham. He then developed this new perspective on his own. Many of the insights Wilson subsequently produced on art cannot be traced to outside sources.

Clearly, we all sensed there was much more to be done, to mention only the follow-up questions one might wish to pose about chimpanzee artists and their work. The parallels between chimpanzee art and the development of our children's art is especially enticing when we consider that the ape experiment was cut off when the animals were still relatively young, as typically happens with chimpanzee language-learning. The sheer speed of Congo's development demonstrates both the attractive nature of artistic activity and its peculiar quality of accelerating learning. This is another regard in which chimpanzees unsettlingly come to resemble us, indeed testing the limits of the so-called "humanities." In recent years, similar proclivities have been found with more distant animal relations, including elephants, porpoises, and ostriches, which would indicate that the potential for art greatly predates the hominid line (see Diamond 1989).

Wilson's argument (3) begs for some extension. If chimpanzees improve their manipulative abilities by means of activities related to art, then their aesthetic potential reflects some adaptive advantages. So, nullifying humankind's exclusive dominion over art with one hand, Wilson offers the arts an immense opportunity with the other. What assertion could convey more political advantage to the arts than to prove that they are adaptive, that they are not merely the product of culture? Surely their very ubiquity suggests, as others have noted, that they somehow promote our biological interests.

One angle of approach is to note the pedagogical nature of the arts. Much of children's schooling, especially in early years, is occupied with art education and activities. Like play, art performs a vital role in development of the young, while sharpening the wits of those of us who intend never to grow old. Typically, exposure to art causes us to explore relationships in space, pattern, sound, and texture, thereby widening our experience and tolerance of new states and processes. There is then little wonder that artistic greatness generally tends to be associated with states enjoying political power and/or economic prosperity, such as Periclean Athens, Renaissance

Italy, China under the Ming dynasty, the Mongol empire, and northwestern Europe at the end of the nineteenth century.

Wilson goes on in the next paragraph (4) to trace, per S. L. Washburn, how this might have worked with our early ancestors. It should be noted that frequently there was an aesthetic element to hand-made tools and that they appear to have been crafted from materials not conducive to manipulation, suggesting a very powerful aesthetic impulse (Joyce 1975). Stone implements survived, while, we presume, more perishable instruments have disappeared. Very likely the arts provided a useful way to kill time without deadening one's faculties. Our own kind characteristically sleeps a smaller portion of the diurnal clock than most other animals, indeed a shorter span than the hours of darkness for much of the year. Is this what kept us up at night? All the better that we imbue the activity with a larger-than-life purpose, if only to make better artifacts. The development of artistic craft, sympathetic magic, and representation may well have been co-evolutionary. From the point of view of the original producers and consumers, sympathetic magic, then the equivalent of science, was a means of making tools more effective. Much as one might hone a handaxe, one might add a religious symbol.

Human beings have, of course, made aesthetic objects of both bird songs and birds, an abiding interest exhibited in innumerable examples (5). One can only exploit what is available. We are at the same time adept at identifying, finding, often hunting, and sometimes fleeing various species because to do so is biologically advantageous (57). In *Consilience*, Wilson describes how hunter-gatherers spend much time discussing their most challenging and desired prey, commonly in the form of stories. Trying to better understand these beasts, the hunters often mythologize and endow them with supernatural powers (1998, 233ff.). The great potential for a sociobiological perspective on the arts is that notions of biological adaptiveness promise to explain the phenomenon of interest. Furthermore, differing degrees of adaptiveness may account for differential interest, given that not everything is equally salient to our genetic futures. Another aspect of art's adaptive quality is its use as a socializer for organizing cooperative behavior. Certainly this has been noted of love songs, workers' chants, and battle hymns. A chimp carnival reminds us of the arts' function, much like that of dreams, for relieving tensions, and possibly to make communal life more livable. Wilson ends his first substantial statement on art with the notion that it has achieved a kind of environmental release and in so doing has accelerated our mental development. Art subsequently became a kind of basic research program in that it now generates an immense variety of ways to think about our common world.[4]

The very ubiquity of mythologies, their unlikely and at the same time stereotyped contents, would seem to indicate a common biological heritage. While noting such commonalities (9), Wilson and other sociobiologists bemoan the tendency for most anthropologists to focus on the great variety of differences among such traditions. Another question continues to be raised: why is it that so many people believe in phenomena which could not possibly be true or have never been part of their actual experience? That these tall tales are, nevertheless, so readily believed forces us to ponder whether there might be not only a "universal" need for explanations but also a panhuman impetus to accept them.

Wilson's entire discussion of religion in *On Human Nature* (6-9) pertains to art. Indeed, it is usually difficult to distinguish the two when it comes to our early ancestors. Art, like the religion it serves, has the effect of enabling magic, in the sense that it incurs a willingness to believe, to be swayed, and thereby aids the ends of religion. Narrative art, especially in its modern form, fiction, clearly benefits from this same tendency of humans to be gullible, to suspend our disbelief. Certainly I am not the first to suggest that our artists are the modern variants of the primeval shamans.

But there is another point to be made, in which sociobiology is potentially better suited than other perspectives to cope with the facts of our art. Put simply, what matters in nature is not the means but the ends. It matters little how replication is achieved, only that the task is accomplished, over and over again. There is no necessary reason for natural selection to make us more intelligent, when sometimes our very propensity for fantasy and belief serves its real "ends" of continuance far better. Another consequence of this notion is that there need be little similarity among the vast array of artistic behaviors, so long as the same "ends," such as cognitive development, socializing, and so on, are achieved.

What extreme forms the "means" may take is evident from Wilson's list (8) of what religion and religious art can motivate a person to do, all at a likely cost to his immediate self-interest but for his own genetic good via that of his family and community. What other theory so effectively accounts for the self-sacrificing behavior involved? That this is vital to society is indicated by the sheer cost of ceremonies. This reminds of us of the wide variety of forms that indoctrination can take and how often the arts will be called on to contribute. It is only in recent secular art that this behavior has been split off from these purposes, but the same or at least similar effects can be viewed at an effective aesthetic performance. We go to a concert or a film, above all else, to be *moved*, albeit not to any particular action. Admittedly, exceptions abound. No less an authority in coercion than Joseph Stalin pronounced the artist to be "the engineer of human souls."

Wilson often comments on the important features which set the arts off from the sciences, how the jobs of artists and scientists are essentially different, and how one may never replace the other. His statement (10) of future collusion is predictive, inasmuch as science is increasingly being brought to the task of interpreting the arts. Though this has long been the case with psychological, especially psychoanalytical, approaches, the other studies included in this volume represent just a small fraction of the fields now adopting tenets of sociobiology (also see the annotated bibliography). And there are other new scientific perspectives in the offing. The work of Alexander Argyros and Frederick Turner are representative of the fascinating attempts to discern the phenomena of chaos theory in the arts, namely, spontaneous and stable forms of non-random order. Lastly, science is more frequently exploiting the arts both for illustration as Wilson often does in *On Human Nature*, which, for example, closes with an extended citation from Aeschylus' *Prometheus* and as a convenient data base. Wide samples of art and literature are used to settle issues having little to do with art (Alvarez 1990, Grusser 1983, Ellis and Symons 1990). Furthermore, each art work stands not just for its creator but also for the sometimes vast audience which accepts it as effective art. In effect, this yields larger numbers for statisticians to scan. Elsewhere in *On Human Nature* (pp. 210-12), Wilson chides "intellectuals" for their ignorance of modern science and calls for the two fields to be bridged, with sociobiology serving "as a kind of antidiscipline to the humanities."

Certainly Wilson has done as much as anyone to bring science and the humanities together. He pointed out the artistic qualities of science while at the same time noting how the sciences point out beauty and provide inspiration to the arts. Wilson finds a biological utility for our preference for elegance, a common quality in both fields, if only for reasons of cognitive economy (1-2 and 1998, 219). His views have recently been extrapolated by Frederick Turner as an essential law of life. In *Beauty: The Value of Values*, Turner describes our recognition of beauty as a feedback system which helps us better glimpse the true nature of the universe (1991). But Wilson goes further, adding a "drive for discovery," saying that our sheer curiosity, our impulse to explore and bring a wide range of phenomena under at least our intellectual control, suits the hunter-gatherers we used to be. Put these two drives together and there is an even greater need for compact information-processing and -storage.

Wilson productively compares the experience of scientists with those of artists and other humanists. He highlights (13-17) the analytical achievement of artists and the creativity, the often sheer inspiration, of his own kind. However, we do not have to agree with everything Wilson says about art. For example, he suggests later that artists tend to depict individual items which are somehow representative of much else; landscape painting, for example, often expresses an attitude about the nature of the universe. We might object that, first, little proof is produced as to its being truly representative and, second, that the relationship may be ironic, such as when artists depict the unusual or exotic. In deriving a universal law, no scientist is able to examine more than a small fraction of the total relevant data. Here there is a greater need to demonstrate the representative qualities of any data sample, but the same issue applies.

Meanwhile, it is worth pondering how art gives us a vicarious experience that resembles living experience itself. This goes well beyond Wilson's statement that the artist creates special cases, produces effects, and transfers feelings. The syncretic thought characteristic of art suffices to create a vicarious experience; clearly one form of consciousness is grafted from another. One clue, as Wilson illustrates (15) with Paz's "Broken Waterjar," is that the best art manages this with but a few select details. Part of the reason for art's effectiveness lies in our being so primed to respond to it that little is necessary to set the process into motion. Of course, one reason we find meaning in poems like Paz's is because we seek it. The writer depends on the reader's readiness to participate in a game of code, synecdoche, and representation. This quality is crucial to our impulse for discovery. The estimate that mankind has had 100,000 religions (Anthony F. C. Wallace, cited in *On Human Nature*, 176) suffices to show how often we have anxiously sought solutions to important questions and have come away satisfied with erroneous answers. Great discipline is required to avoid projective reading because we are so eager to believe in what we want to believe.

Second, meaning is not limited, say, to Paz's fellow Mexicans but potentially includes all who can read the poem. In *Consilience* Wilson notes how Hollywood films sell in Singapore and Nobel prizes for literature are given to non-Western writers (1998, 229). Wilson's statement that art crosses cultural boundaries because it can read the code of human nature imports wide ramifications, namely, that there is a human nature and that art has the potential for revealing that code. That art is, somehow, a distillate of the human spirit has often been taken for granted and given lip service; sociobiology can get us beyond mere cliches in this regard, both by studying nature and by comparing humans to other species.

What Wilson says for originality in science (18) also pertains to art, which is increasingly obsessed with an emphasis on novelty. Furthermore, much as the scientist must stick to the facts, art is also constrained by an indefinite but extant sense of "artistic truth." Artistic innovation must be validated by a demonstration of its appropriateness, that the new combination or observation or whatever suits the general work, that in some sense of the word it is "true." Taken in addition to Wilson's many comparisons between the two fields, it should be recalled that art and science were once, along with religion, one enterprise.

Wilson rightly discerns a drive for discovery (19-25) in both fields; tantamount to Joseph Miller's neophilia, it needs to be tempered by a countervailing force, a virtual neophobia. Not all of us become explorers of one sort or another; many prefer the familiar, to stick close to home. After all, science, art ,and everything else that is new typically meet with resistance. This is to say that our human nature must comprise a cross-matrix of often contrary forces. The advantage to this is that it compares well with what we know of the genetics of physiology, wherein more than one gene influences certain features like pigmentation. The coexistence of opposing forces also permits a similar manifold expansion of the variety of possible attitudes. People may be born equal, but we are certainly not all alike, thanks to the shifting process of nature, one that permits many subtle degrees of differentiation from which nature selects. These countervailing forces may reflect the various periods and environmental needs we experienced during our long and ongoing process of evolution.

The cross-matrix also applies to the words (21) we use, especially including the artistic word, which is determined according to many factors. In a sense, so is every aesthetic element or scientific fact. A great multitude of factors affects each phenomenon and action. The mind is shaped to cope with this state of things; for example, it is able to use words, sorting out and weighing all of their likely meanings according to the context in which they fall. Sociobiology and with it biopoetics not only promises to contribute to the cross-matrix sciences concerned with our behavior, it is best equipped to account for the structure of the matrix itself, thanks to the particulate manner of genetic and, possibly as well, memetic transmission.

That we can readily cope with the far more "overdetermined" language of art suggests that it is more suited for the mind, and the mind shaped to suit it, than is science. We generally grasp an artistic notion immediately, albeit never wholly, with the benefit of little or no training. As a case in point, consider how quickly we discern a false note or sense an artistic *non sequitur*.

Wilson (22) cites a number of "functions" which have been adduced to art. He thus provides further evidence of art's complex structure, that it can address so many needs at once. But we should go further and state that art simply *is*, that it is an essential part of us. Imagine how hard it would be to live completely without it, especially if we understand art as an everyday behavior performed by virtually everyone, as Ellen Dissanayake would have it. What measures of restraint would be required to abstain from art, given that it is so natural, so spontaneous (1988, 1992)?[5] Indeed, practicing art is a proclivity always readily available to do more or less whatever we need.

Even to call it a form of self-expression falls short; it is an essential part of self.

Meanwhile, can we not extend Wilson's parallels between art and science a bit further? Art does not go only inward. It is also a means of outward reach. Try to describe or paint something you do not understand and you will feel how great a degree of interpretive penetration is required. Many scientists were important artists and vice versa for good reason. Furthermore, art is frequently described as a kind of *Gedankenexperiment*, a means of testing ideas. A good example is literary utopia, wherein idealists try to fully imagine what it would be like to live in an ideologically planned society. In mainstream fiction, Tolstoy wrote *War and Peace* to reform our conception of the historical process. He did this by trying to render honest and fulsome depictions of battles. Then Tolstoy wrote *Anna Karenina* to think out his understanding of personal morality, learning in the course of the book that he had more sympathy for an adulteress than he had suspected. In a sense, this is true of each and every ambitious artwork.

But then there is the very capacity to explore, which we cannot take for granted. Like science, art serves to expand our faculties of perception. Charles Ives believed that music should "stretch" our ears. Its pedagogical qualities endure, keeping us cognitively, albeit not physically, flexible well into old age. Hopefully, we, the ever neotenous species, never outgrow our ability to play at art, and to learn.

Wilson next adds to the matrix his view that mental receptors were shaped by natural selection so as to allow us to take interest in and learn certain phenomena more readily than others. This, of course, is the well-spring of differential interest, one of the major features our behavior laid bare by the cognitive devices offered by sociobiology, as Wilson later illustrates with his essay on serpent mythology. Our perception and cognition, it must be admitted, fall far short of ideal and absolute as if our minds are not boggled already by what is before our eyes! What we are able to do and likely to do, both the propensities and the constraints, we do for a variety of reasons. There has to be an effect on art, if not on everything else as well. This goes beyond the pointlessness of painting in the ultraviolet or composing at pitches above our hearing or writing books without syntax though similar attempts to extend the formal range of art have been tried.

Innate learning potentials also have to do with what we are inclined to put our attention to. This has manifold consequences for the content of art. How mental proclivities lead to universal myths, a striking example of differential interest not adducible to chance or cultural exchange, is the major underexplored potential for biopoetics. In the furious competition for our limited span of attention, itself a form of memetic selection, some themes have a natural advantage in that they so easily interest us. Tax forms and life insurance, items of great adaptive significance today, have a rough row to hoe; but, as everyone knows, sex sells, even among those of us long happily married. On the other hand, consider what an evolutionary push the arts, especially fiction, require to be able to compete on an equal footing all this despite their formal difficulty of access and relative lack of utilitarian application. Such ideas have to be competitive and dense with meaning for us. Significantly, when the society that produced them is gone, artworks are often all that remains, if only because they can speak also to us.

Wilson's comment on the differing ease of passage (28) for some ideas raises yet another consideration, namely, that the history of culture involves not just transmission but also reception, subjecting ideas to the constraints of our attention span. When Wilson then describes ideas as if they have a will of their own, saying that certain mythic "stories invade the developing mind more readily than others," we are reminded of Richard Dawkins's meme, the intellectual equivalent of the self-interested or "selfish" gene, which behaves as if its own replication mattered (1976). Wilson and Charles J. Lumsden soon developed their own version, that of the "culturgen," describing them in *Genes, Mind and Culture* (1981) and *Promethean Fire* (1983) as exhibiting many of the qualities of biological phenomena, a vision that we can best test in art. Whatever might possibly be the biological basis of the meme or the culturgen, our intellectual experience at least gives them some plausibility. Consider the case of fictional characters who, according to the testimony of innumerable authors, "take on a life of their own," or advertising jingles, which, like the viruses that plague computers, prove extremely difficult to expunge from the mind.

But for now we need to consider again the downside to our evolutionary heritage. Though we take notice of some objects and events with dispatch, we are slow to observe and may even totally ignore many others. If "the mind probes certain channels much more readily than others" (27), what of the paths not taken? While they might have been insignificant in archaic environments, they may well be vital today. There is thus a propensity for blindness and distortion in our perception, much as the deconstructionists have claimed.[6] Art, as Wilson puts it, "play[s] upon the rules of mental development" (28); it reflects and exploits our innate strengths and weaknesses. Since the living mind can never be a vacuum, what we neglect will be replaced in our consciousness with something that is not necessarily as significant as we imagine it, or even real; our propensity for gullibility typically will call for an exchange between reality and fantasy. Science, on the other hand, has a duty to be objective, therefore to rationally get beyond our biases. It is not easy.

Nevertheless, we do not have to accept the gloomy verdict of the deconstructionists as the last word on the supposed meaninglessness of art. The half-empty glass is also half full. This is not to deny de Man, Derrida, and their colleagues their due for revealing the real gaps in artistic communication, if not in all discourse. Indeed, their insights help us perceive the real conduct of artistic intercourse. Perhaps in applying ourselves to these activities we are not doing anything effective or worthwhile. Art, then, could not perform any utilitarian task unless there is some benefit in convincing us that it has value. Would it not, then, be more truly fascinating that so many of us persist in trying to do what the critics now declare to be impossible? Surely, there must be a reason for this mass delusion.

Wilson's chapter "The Serpent" (31-57) is his most extensive study of mythology. It also serves as the best introduction to biosemiotics. In the diction of semiotics, the serpent is highly marked. It can be positive or negative but is always decidedly one or the other, never in between. As Wilson notes (57), we are conditioned to look at snakes; it is highly maladaptive to ignore them. As a result, snakes are never boring, no matter how little they may do. Nor do we perceive them as weak, whatever the facts may be. Their potential for injury suffices to grab our attention. Wilson's examples of the serpent image (43, 50-53) are easily broken down into the very evil and the very good. None is trivial.

There is no problem accounting for the malign category on a biological basis, but how can we explain the powerful attraction that snakes exude?

Here we have to return to our earlier notion of ideas competing for our attention. In this regard, snakes and serpents constitute trump cards. People also compete for each other's attention, a common struggle with clear selective advantages, given that it usually pays to be noticed and hurts to be ignored. While snake and serpent images can be used to warn of danger, a symbol recognized in our own culture, they also imbue the holder with power and serve as sign of importance, even magic (50-53). This explains the common association of snakes with shamans.

Semiotics also introduces an essential ingredient of "slippage." We do not react to objects, animals, and other persons, for these are ultimately unknowable; this is basic epistemology. All that we ever can experience are the images of objects. In effect, nature works by means of signs, yielding the potential for us to be affected not only by snakes but also by snake-like images, i. e., signs. And signs readily deceive. Nature is replete with camouflage, with deceptive images. We are therefore susceptible to being gulled into inappropriate reactions, a weakness narrative is quick to exploit with legions of odious villains, cold-blooded killers, and distinctly reptilian extraterrestrials. Why is it that knights slay dragons while spacemen contend with Dracs, if these are not further extrapolations of the serpent? As these examples suggest, the serpent and its immense semiotic force extends well beyond snakes, to anyone or anything exhibiting any of a serpent's features such as the clammy, the scaly, the squint-eyed, and those who slither or lie quietly in the grass.

Wilson then (38-57) outlines the necessary developmental stages from biological origin to an effective symbol or image. The biopoetic critic should try to attend to each step if he is to link ultimate cause to contemporary behavior. For this reason, I summarize Wilson's points. First of all, there must be a significant selection pressure, e. g., danger or reproductive opportunity (45, 57). We should assume that the beginnings are rarely inconsequential. Then a sufficient period of exposure is required (46). Our symbols proceed from long-standing experience, although they may take disguises of temporary derivation. Put simply, our reactions to such artistic phenomena is inappropriate often precisely because they are anachronistic. As cardiologists tell us, we are hunter-gatherers who wear suits and are susceptible to stress. We have developed an innate propensity for hysteria, for overreacting, that is incommensurate with immediate causes (47). Our hysteria may be aversion or attraction, or, in the case of morbid fascination, an admixture of both. Growing up in perfectly snakeless Hawaii, I developed at about five years old precisely the ophidiophobia Wilson described (44). Not only did I have recurring nightmares about snakes, but I would not even touch a picture of one. I still will not. But I love to read about snakes, as in Wilson's account of his childhood experiences with them in the panhandle of Florida, which he recounts in "The Serpent." Snakes energize a story.

Human culture then adds the next stage, environmental release (55). We no longer need the snake, now that we can use its image or sign. For example, the modern writer captures the snake in words and on paper; he does not need the real animal. From this stage, all our reactions are hysterical, inappropriate all the better for an artist to manipulate his audience.

A case in point is the common sign of the middle finger variants are popular in other countries which refers to lovemaking but expresses hate. Could this not be a distant relative of animals' genital display, intended to ward off evil and/or enemies?[7] Here we can tie in the Freudian connection between snakes and phalli, indeed suggest how this volatile association originated (48). What makes genital display an effective form of territorial defense for monkeys may be that it reminds intruders of snakes.[8] This would explain the brightly colored markings in the genital area of some primates, all the better to attract the interloper's attention. Need we add that the phallus must be erect if the sign is to do its job? The mounting behavior observed among male apes or the "pecking order" maintained by our own, establishes a hierarchy of dominance; it conveys not so much sexual impulse, although that undeniably is involved, as the exercise of force, hence eliciting fear. As a result of these developmental stages, we end up with the infamous "bird," which conveys all that Wilson associates with the serpent, "sexual desire, a craving for dominance and power, and the apprehension of violent death" (47). Whether delivered as manual gesture or verbal abuse, it may be expressed again and again and again, with a great variety of meanings. Repetition does not matter, for the sign always retains the same ever-renewing biosemiotic force.

Wilson, it turns out, has outlined an entire research methodology for the biology of symbols. It is just that we have to turn it around and begin by looking for incommensurate reactions, for hysteria, or for statistical anomalies such as the serpentine forms which teem throughout Celtic art. Anything illogical will do, especially if it eludes proximate explanations. Next, look for the same behavior in other cultures. Then work backwards for the ultimate causes though always exercising the rigor called for by our e-mail correspondents. What Wilson has done with the serpent can be repeated with a great variety of phenomena. There are many more strands to the cross-matrix of human nature (56). Anyone interested in spiders?

Inanimate things can also give rise to symbols and myths, especially if they convey more adaptive significance than trivial living things (58). In *On Human Nature* Wilson talks about the selective advantage of developing phobias for heights and close spaces (1978, 70). These, not incidentally, elicit interest and attract Freudian associations. The same goes for gold, whereas only a biologist is likely to be obsessed with microscopic life. The phenomenon has to be noticeable, to exhibit a sign, or at least a dramatic effect, as in the case of plagues. On the other hand, Wilson's biophilia accords with our common practice of anthropomorphizing not only animals but objects as well. Many of us give personal names to animals, ships, homes, and computers. In effect, we personalize them because, as Daniel Rancour-Laferriere recently argued (1993, vii), we are so primed to deal with personalities that we may be entertained by a literary character, never composed of more than an extremely limited number of words.

Sometimes an immediate selective advantage is not even necessary. As Wilson points out (59) in various places, we feel most comfortable in environments which somewhat resemble the attractive features of ancient and long-standing habitats. This line of thinking pertains to crafted gardens and shopping malls, replete with fountains; it also holds for the artificial flowers some apartment dwellers use for ornamentation. If these plastic imitations cannot even give off an attractive scent, what function could they possibly serve, other than to remind us of our ancestral home? But they have been anticipated by the landscape paintings and *nature morte* depictions Europeans have long used to brighten up their living spaces. Not that we are such homebodies that we turn a blind eye to the undeniable attractions of *terra incognita*. Given our heritage as hunter-gatherers, we have an impulse to explore the unknown, to seek new resources to exploit. Hence the arts serve to enchant us (1998, 227), to beckon us with their mystique to inquire into what might never be truly known.

With the ink on *Consilience* barely dry as we write this, it is perhaps premature to assess Wilson's latest contribution to biopoetics and its likely influence on future work. Yet it is immediately clear that he calls us in several new and promising directions. One involves his observation of how the arts, however much a necessary keystone in his grand unification of academic fields, remain in many ways incommodious with science. Thanks to the subjective element recognized by Wilson as so crucial to good interpretation as well as the arts' role of imparting experience, not explanation, Wilson declares, "the arts are the antithesis of science" (1998, 218). He persists, however, in attempting this seemingly impossible linkage, pointing out how both fields seek an economy of description (219) and express the common human drive to exercise control over the universe. Wilson's depictions of early humans and present-day hunter-gatherers raises the possibility that their arts should also be regarded as a primitive form of science. Cave paintings, tribal myths, and other traditional practices help to train attention to important factors in the environment, sharpen perception, and maintain a record of what the group has observed, creating a social memory that has proved, on balance, more of an advantage than not.

By pointing out how artists do not think like scientists, Wilson also seems to raise the possibility that they engage in what we might term artistic cognition. Wilson's chapter "The Arts and Their Interpretation" provides inviting evidence of the efficacy of artists in terms of productive thought. He repeatedly stresses that artistic classics convey near-universals of behavior which bear comparison with tenets of sociobiology; he posits that "the greatest works of art might be understood fundamentally with knowledge of the biologically evolved epigenetic rules that guided them" (213). Thematic and formal universals or near-universals exist because artists repeatedly discover the same limited range of means to entertain audiences the world over. In effect, they confirm each other's findings. If students of biopoetics follow Wilson's lead, then another form of demonstration is at hand, for perceiving the ubiquitous presence of the epigenetic rules in a significant portion of international masterworks would truly bring scientific observations into accord with artistic visions. In a sense, only now are scientists coming to learn what artists, so it seems, have always known. Sociobiology could be said to be the science of intuition, that elusive faculty of the mind which, on balance, has allowed humans and other species to prosper without science.

However, this is not to say that the arts contain only scientific truths or that artists and audiences are always able to distinguish the actual from the unreal. While science may be a construct intended to keep people from lying to themselves which is difficult to achieve the arts possess myriad means of self-deception. Certainly traditional and classical arts the world over convey a wealth of myths which are patently false, at least to the educated eye. Surely only the Bushmen Wilson depicts near the end of his chapter actually believe that some beasts of prey protect themselves by magic from arrows and eagles can foresee the outcome of a hunt (235-36). Due to such an obvious dollop of fiction, the arts would seem to be maladaptive, if it were not for the sense of confidence they, rightly or wrongly, impart to people like Wilson's hunters. Whether one's tradition involves carving "magical" images on a weapon or participating in a pre-hunt ritual, the hunter must surely benefit from his faith that he has a better handle on his own fate. "In a bewildering and threatening world, people reach out for power by any means they can find" (228). The mere illusion of gaining power probably will improve performance. Modern people are not as dissimilar in this regard as we might think. Nowadays American athletes keep plush dolls in their lockers, refuse to shave or change their sweater during a winning streak, or pray, in hopes that God will help them hit a home run. We are reminded here of Ellen Dissanayake's (1992, 126, 129) apt observation that the arts require both control and self-control, certainly valuable faculties in an otherwise uncontrolled environment.

Wilson ends his latest contribution to biopoetics with no giddy impression that fitting the keystone in his "*fiery circle of the arts and science*" will be an easy matter (237). Earlier he noted how the arts and their interpretation have been subjected to pendulum swings between seemingly irreconcilable poles of romanticism and neoclassicism, personal and impersonal, passion and reason. Perhaps in vain he hopes that a scientific grasp of human nature will establish some equilibrium (216). He is on solid ground in noting significant inroads into the neuropsychology of aesthetics, such as optimal design configurations or contours of female facial beauty (221, 230), and it would be fruitful to compare his sample list of thematic archetypes (223-24) with both international folklore motifs and the plot lines of literary classics. His suggestion that the phenomenon of supernormal stimulus, whereby some animals are attracted to unreal but harmless ideal images of mates, pertains to the exaggeration so often characteristic of the arts simply begs for formal investigation (231). Achieving the kind of fusion that Wilson envisions will require us to venture into a wilderness, but with findings like those he offers it is not wholly unknown territory. There are signs that the outing will lead us somewhere and, besides, it is in our human nature to accept his invitation to sally forth. Such is the future of biopoetics, which now lies before us, thanks in large part to Edward O. Wilson.

Works Cited

Alvarez, Gonzalo

1990 "Child-Holding Patterns and Hemispheric Bias: Evidence from Pre-Columbian American Art." *Ethology and Sociobiology* 11:75-82.

Argyros, Alexander J.

1989 "Learning from the Stock Market: Literature As Cultural Investment." *Mosaic* 22 (3):101-116.

1991 *A Blessed Rage for Order: Deconstruction, Evolution, and Chaos.* Ann Arbor: University of Michigan Press.

Cooke, Brett

1996 "The Biopoetics of Immortality: A Darwinist Perspective on Science Fiction." In George Slusser, Gary Westfahl, and Eric S. Rabkin, eds., *Immortal Engines: Life Extension and Immortality in Science Fiction and Fantasy*. Athens, GA: University of Georgia Press, pp. 90-101.

Daly, Martin, and Margo Wilson

1988 *Homicide*. New York: Aldine de Gruyter.

Dawkins, Richard

1976 *The Selfish Gene*. Oxford: Oxford University Press.

1986 *The Blind Watchmaker*. Harlow: Longman.

Diamond, Jared

1991 "Art of the Wild." *Discover* 12 (February):78-80, 82, 84-85.

Dissanayake, Ellen

1988 *What Is Art For?* Seattle: University of Washington Press.

1992 *Homo Aestheticus: Where Art Comes from and Why*. New York: Free Press.

Ellis, Bruce J., and Donald Symons

1990 "Sex Differences in Sexual Fantasy: An Evolutionary Psychological Approach." *Journal of Sex Research* 27:527-55.

Grusser, Otto-Joachim

1983 "Mother-Child Holding Patterns in Western Art: A Developmental Study." *Ethology and Sociobiology* 4:89-94.

Joyce, Robert

1975 *The Esthetic Animal: Man, the Art-Created Art Creator*. Hicksville, NY: Exposition Press.

Kernan, Alvin B., Peter Brooks, and J. Michael Holquist

1971 *Man and His Fictions: An Introduction to Fiction-Making, Its Forms and Uses*. New York: Harcourt Brace Jovanovich.

Lumsden, Charles J., and Edward O. Wilson

1981 *Genes, Mind and Culture*. Cambridge: Harvard University Press.

1983 *Promethean Fire: Reflections on the Origin of Mind*. Cambridge: Harvard University Press.

Peckham, Morse

1965 *Man's Rage for Chaos*. Philadelphia: Chilton.

Rancour-Laferriere, Daniel

1985 *Signs of the Flesh: An Essay on Hominid Sexuality*. Berlin: Mouton de Gruyter.

1993 *Tolstoy's Pierre Bezukhov: A Psychoanalytic Study*. London: Bristol Classical Press.

Sutterlin, Christa

1987 "Mittelalterliche Kirchen-Skulptur als Beispiel universaler Abwehrsymbolik." In Johann Georg Prin von Hohenzollern and Max

Liedtke, eds., *Vom Kritzeln zur Kunst*. Bad Heilbrunn: Verlag Julius Klinkhardt, pp. 82-100.

1989 "Universals in Apotropaic Symbolism: A Behavioral and Comparative Approach to Some Medieval Sculptures." *Leonardo* 22 (1):65-74.

Turner, Frederick

1991 *Beauty: The Value of Values*. Charlottesville: University of Virginia Press.

Wilson, Edward O.

1998 *Consilience: The Unity of Knowledge*. New York: Alfred A. Knopf.

Notes

1. These are examined in my article on Dawkins's meme in space colonization stories, Cooke 1996.
2. Their paper at the 1990 HBES conference, "'Deconstructing' Symbolic Interpretations of Cruel Stepparent Stories," noted the international prevalence of this theme. Daly and Wilson sharply criticized psychoanalytic and feminist scholars for ignoring the significant fact that the villains so often are *step*parents, not genetic parents, a distinction highly meaningful for sociobiology.
3. Ellen Dissanayake complains of this neglect by the major ethologists (1992, 8-11, 227-28).
4. Alexander Argyros has subsequently developed this notion of art as a means of conceiving models of the world, useful for offering a society a wider range of possible futures from which to choose. See Argyros 1989 and 1991.
5. Alvin B. Kernan, Peter Brooks and J. Michael Holquist make a similar argument, noting that a large portion of our day is occupied by fictions, including dreams, planning, and speculation, along with the usual entertainments (1971, 4-6).
6. For an extensive study of the possible biological basis for deconstruction, see Argyros 1991.

Indeed, medieval European churches often display precisely this form of defense in their decorations. See Sutterlin 1987 and 1989.

8. Phallic display may have been a behavior adaptation that exploited the already extant ophidiophobia in primates. See Rancour-Laferriere 1985, 271.

An Ecopoetics of Beauty and Meaning

Frederick Turner

In this essay I wish to refound the traditional humanistic concepts of beauty and meaning on a sound scientific basis, and thus secure them from the assault of recent postmodern criticism. I shall begin by summarizing the evolutionary and neurobiological descriptions of the function and experience of beauty, as it is developed in earlier works of mine (Turner 1986, 1991a, 1991b, 1995). Building on this conceptual foundation, I shall attempt a neurobiological description of linguistic meaning, claiming that such a description dispels many of the traditional philosophical problems of reference that have served poststructuralist theorists as a justification for semantic skepticism.

All human societies possess the concept of beauty, often with a very precise vocabulary and a tradition of argument about it. People see (hear, touch, taste, smell) the beautiful, and recognize it by a natural intuition and a natural pleasure. Even animals do: antiphonal birdsong, the brilliant shapes and colors of flowers (what more precise record could there be of the aesthetic preferences of bees?), and the gorgeous ritual mating garments of tropical fishes and birds of paradise, all attest to a more-than-utilitarian attraction in certain forms of organization.

This “natural intuition” is for us human beings activated, sensitized, and deepened by culture; that is, a natural capacity of the nervous system now incorporates a cultural feedback loop, and also uses the physical world, through art and science, as part of its own hardware. The theory of such a training or sensitization, the incorporation of this cultural feedback loop, the plugging of it in to the prepared places in our brains, is what I call “natural classicism.” The foundation of the natural classical perspective is that the universe, and we, evolved. This fact entails two truths about beauty: a special evolutionary truth and a general evolutionary truth.

The special evolutionary truth is that our capacity to perceive and create beauty is a characteristic of an animal that evolved. Beauty is thus in some way a biological adaptation and a physiological reality: the experience of beauty can be connected to the activity of actual neurotransmitters in the brain, endorphins and enkephalins. When we become addicted to a drug such as heroin or cocaine we do so because its molecular structure resembles that of the chemistries of joy that the brain feeds to itself.

What is the function of pleasure from an evolutionary point of view? The pleasure of eating is clearly a reward for the labor of getting ourselves something to eat. Certainly few would go to the extraordinary metabolic expense and aggravation of finding a willing member of the opposite sex and reproducing with him or her unless there were a very powerful inducement to do so. We are presented with this very great pleasure of beauty, for which artists will starve in garrets and for whose mimicked substitutes rats and addicts will happily neglect food and sex. What is it a reward for? What adaptive function does beauty serve that is so much more important than immediate nourishment and even the immediate opportunity to reproduce the species?

To answer this question we need to know a little about the timing of human evolution, as it is becoming clear from the work of paleoanthropologists, paleolinguists, archaeologists, and paleogeneticists. The crucial point is that there is a peculiar overlap between the last phases of human biological evolution and the beginnings of human cultural evolution, an overlap of one to five million years, depending on how the terms are defined. In any case, there was a long period during which human culture could exert a powerful, indeed dominant, selective pressure upon the genetic material of the species and thus upon the final form it has taken (if ours is the final form).

For over a million years the major genetic determinant in the environment of our genus was our own culture. A creature that is living under cultural constraints is a creature that is undergoing an intensive process of domestication. Consider wheat, dogs, apple trees, pigeons: how swiftly and how dramatically they have been changed by human selective breeding! But we domesticated ourselves as well. Imagine a mating ritual, which directly affects the reproductive success of the individuals within a species. Those who are neurologically capable and adept at the complex nuances of the ritual would have a much better chance of getting a mate and leaving offspring. Now imagine that this ritual is being handed down from generation to generation not just by genetic inheritance, but also, increasingly, by cultural transmission: imitation, instruction, eventually language (did it evolve in order to facilitate this transmission?).

Genetic inheritance is the way in which an entire species learns about its environment and about itself. But it is a very slow process: the learning is being done at the genetic level, not at the social or mental level. However, in the thought-experiment that we have commenced, changes in the ritual can be handed down very quickly, in only one generation; and so the faster system of transmission will tend to drive and direct the slower system of transmission. That is, cultural modifications in the ritual will tend to confer a decisive selective advantage upon those members of the species that are genetically endowed with greater neural complexity, a superior capacity for learning the inner principles of the ritual which remain the same when its surface changes, for following and extending the ritual's subtleties, and for recognizing and embodying the values that the ritual creates. Cultural evolution will drive biological evolution. This species, of course, is ourselves: perhaps what created us as human beings was an improved love song. In the beginning, indeed, was the word.

In this scenario the idea of beauty clearly has a central place. The capacity for recognizing and creating beauty is a competence that we possess, a competence that was selected for by biocultural coevolution: it is both a power that the "mating ritual" of human and prehuman culture demanded and sharpened, and a value generated by that ritual that it was in our reproductive interest to be able to recognize and embody. To be, and to be able to recognize, a beautiful human being, and to desire to mix one's seed with his or hers, might be a survival strategy that drove the flowering of *Homo sapiens*.

What are the results of this coevolution in the neurobiology of aesthetic experience? Simply to be able to ask this question—that it should be reasonable, indeed predicted by a solid theory, for beauty to have a pancultural neurobiological base—overturns modernist and most postmodernist aesthetics. The evolutionary perspective suggests that we have inherited a number of related natural-classical genres or systems by which we generate, recognize, and appreciate beauty. What are these genres?

The experimental neuropsychologist Ernst Pöppel and I have investigated one of them in some detail—poetic meter, or what we have called the "neural lyre." All over the world human beings compose and recite poetry in poetic meter; all over the world the meter has a line-length of about three seconds, tuned to the three-second acoustic information-processing pulse in the human brain. Our acoustic present is three seconds long—we remember echoically and completely three seconds' worth of acoustic information, before it is passed on to a longer-term memory system, where it is drastically edited, organized for significant content, and pushed down to a less immediate level of consciousness.

If a natural brain rhythm, like the ten-cycle-per-second alpha rhythm—or the three-second informational present—is "driven" or amplified by an external rhythmic stimulus, the result can be large changes in brain state and brain chemistry, and consequently in the amount and kind of information that the brain can absorb, and in the kind of higher-level processing it can put to work. But poetry, unlike ritual chant or political slogan, does not just give us a repeated rhythmic line; instead, it establishes a steady meter but then elaborates upon it. The difference between the expected rhythm and the actual rhythm carries information, as a tune does or as a line does in a drawing; and that information is processed and understood not with the linguistic left brain but with the musical and spatial right brain. Thus, unlike ordinary language, poetic language comes to us in a "stereo" neural mode, so to speak, and is capable of conveying feelings and ideas that are usually labeled nonverbal; the genre itself is a biocultural feedback loop that makes us able to use much more of our brains than we normally can.

We need not go into this kind of detail with the other genres, but they show the same kind of fascinating interplay between inherited biological and learned cultural factors. Let us just list a few of them.

1. The significant spacemaker. This operator creates architecture, diagrams, emblems, and ideographs, and finally results in writing.
2. The metrical "operator" of music, which is related to but different from the poetic metrical operator, and which also connects with dance. It is very highly developed in African drum rhythms.
3. The reflexive or dramatic operator, by which we are able to simulate other people's consciousness and points of view in imaginative models

(containing miniature models of the other person's model of us, and so on), and set them into coherent theatrical interaction.

4. The narrative operator, that genre by which we give time a complex tense-structure, full of might-have-beens and should-be's, conditionals, subjunctives, branches, hopes, and memories. Fundamentally, the narrative operation constructs a series of events which have the curious property of being retrodictable (each one seems inevitable once it has happened) but not predictable (before it happens, we have no sound basis on which to foretell it)—which is why we want to know what happens next. This operator comes with a large collection of archetypal myths and stories, such as *The Swan Princess*, which are fundamentally identical all over the world because their seeds are in our genes.

5. The color-combination preferences that are associated with the so-called color wheel.

6. A similar visual detail-frequency preference system, which makes us prefer pictures and scenes with a complexly balanced hierarchy of high-frequency information (dense textures and small details) ranging through to low-frequency information (large general shapes and compositions). Consider, for instance, Japanese prints, or the arcadian landscape paintings of Poussin and Claude.

7. A representational operator (unique to human beings), whereby we can reverse the process of visual perception and use our motor system to represent what we see by drawing, painting, or sculpting.

8. Musical tonality and the inexhaustible language it opens up, from Chinese classical music, through Balinese gamelan, to the fugues and canons of Bach.

And many more. Researchers of great boldness and brilliance are working to clarify the neuropsychology and anthropology of these systems; their results so far are described in a recent book entitled *Beauty and the Brain* (Rentschler, Herzberger, and Epstein, eds. 1989).

The forms of the arts are not arbitrary but are rooted in our biological inheritance. To say this is not to imply that the natural classical genres are constraints or limits upon the expressive powers of the arts. Quite the reverse; these systems, which incorporate a cultural feedback loop into the brain's processing, can enormously deepen and broaden its powers. Language itself may be one of the most comprehensive and earliest of them. They are not constraints any more than the possession of a hammer or a screwdriver is a constraint upon our carpentry, but their use must be learned. An aesthetic education that assumes that genres are obstacles to creativity, and which thus does not bother to teach the old ones, deprives our children of their inheritance.

So much for the special evolutionary truth about beauty. Without the general evolutionary truth, it would be meaningful only in a practical sense. It would leave out that tremble of philosophical insight that we associate with beauty, and would ignore the beauty that we find in nature and in the laws of science. It is not enough, from an evolutionary point of view, that individuals within a species should be endowed with a species-specific sense of beauty related to cooperation and sexual selection, even if the selection favors big brains, sensitivity, and artistic grace. The whole species must benefit from possessing a sense of beauty. This could only be the case if beauty is a real characteristic of the universe, one that it would be useful—adaptive—to know. How might this be?

I want to suggest that the experience of beauty is a recognition of the deepest tendency or theme of the universe as a whole. This may seem a very strange thing to say; but there is a gathering movement across many of the sciences that indicates that the universe does have a deep theme or tendency, a leitmotif which we can begin very tentatively to describe, if not fully understand.

Let us play with an idea of Kant's and see where we get if we treat the aesthetic as something analogous to perception. Imagine dropping a rock on the floor. The rock reacts by bouncing and by making a noise, and perhaps undergoes some slight internal change; we would not imagine that it felt anything approaching a sensation.

Now imagine that you drop a worm on the floor; the impact might cause it to squirm, as well as to bounce and produce a sound of impact. The worm, we would say, feels a sensation; but from the worm's point of view it is not a sensation of anything in particular; the worm does not construct, with its primitive nerve ganglia, anything as complex as an external world filled with objects like floors and experimenters.

Next imagine that you drop a guinea pig. Clearly it would react, as the rock does, and also feel sensations, as the worm does. But we would say in addition that it perceives the floor, the large dangerous animal that has just released it, and the dark place under the table where it may be safe. Perception is as much beyond sensation as sensation is beyond mere physical reaction. Perception constructs a precise, individuated world of solid objects "out there," endowed with color, shape, smell, and acoustic and tactile properties. It is generous to the outside world, giving it properties it did not necessarily possess until some advanced vertebrate was able, through its marvelously parsimonious cortical world-construction system, to provide them. Perception is both more global, more holistic, than sensation—because it takes into account an entire outside world—and more exact, more particular, because it recognizes individual objects and parts of objects.

Now if you were a dancer and the creature that you dropped were a human being, a yet more astonishing capacity would come into play. One could write a novel about how the dance-partners experience this drop, this gesture. Whole detailed worlds of implication, of past and future, of interpretive frames, come into being; and the table and the dancing-floor do not lose any of the guinea pig's reality, but instead take on richnesses, subtleties, significant details, held as they are within a context both vaster and more clearly understood. What is this awareness that is to perception what perception is to sensation, and sensation to reaction? The answer is: aesthetic experience. Aesthetic experience is as much more constructive, as much more generous to the outside world, as much more holistic, and as much more exact and particularizing than ordinary perception, as ordinary perception is than mere sensation. Thus by ratios we may ascend from the known to the very essence of the knower. Aesthetic perception is not vague and "touchy-feely" relative to ordinary perception; quite the reverse. This is why, given an infinite number of theories that will logically explain the facts, scientists will sensibly always choose the most beautiful theory. For good reason: this is the way the world works.

Beauty in this view is the highest integrative level of understanding and the most comprehensive capacity for effective action. It enables us to go with, rather than against, the deepest tendency or theme of the universe, to be able to model what will happen and adapt to or change it.

This line of investigation has clearly brought us to a question which it seems audacious to ask in this anti-metaphysical age. Let us ask it anyway: what is the deepest tendency or theme of the universe?

To begin to answer, let us make another list, a list of descriptions or characteristics of that theme or tendency. We can always adjust or change the list if we want.

1. Unity in multiplicity: The universe does seem to be one, though it is full of an enormous variety and quantity of things. Our best knowledge about its beginning, if it had one, is that everything in the universe was contracted into a single hot, dense atom.
2. Complexity within simplicity: The universe is very complicated, yet it was generated by very simple physical laws like the laws of thermodynamics.
3. Generativeness and creativity: The universe generates a new moment every moment, and each moment has genuine novelties. Its tendency or theme is that it should not just stop. As it cooled, it produced all the laws of chemistry, all the new species of animals and plants, and finally ourselves and our history.
4. Rhythmicity: The universe can be described as a gigantic, self-nested scale of vibrations, from the highest-frequency particles, which oscillate with an energy of ten million trillion giga-electron volts, to the slowest conceivable frequency (or deepest of all musical notes), which vibrates over a period sufficient for a single wave to cross the entire universe and return. Out of these vibrations, often in the most delicate and elaborate mixtures or harmonies of tone, everything is made.
5. Symmetry: Shapes and forms are repeated or mirrored in all physical structures, whether at the subatomic, the atomic, the crystalline, the chemical, the biological, or the anthropological levels of reality. The more complex and delicate the symmetry, the more opportunities it presents for symmetry-breaking, the readjustment of the system toward a new equilibrium, and thus adaptation toward even more comprehensive symmetries.

> 6. Hierarchical organization: Big pieces of the universe contain, control, and depend on smaller pieces, and smaller pieces on smaller pieces still, and so on.
> 7. Self-similarity: Related to the hierarchical property is a marvelous property now being investigated by chaos theorists and fractal mathematicians—the smaller parts of the universe often resemble in shape and structure the larger parts of which they are components, and those larger parts in turn resemble the still larger systems that contain them.

Like Dante's *Divine Comedy*, in which the three-line stanza of its microcosm is echoed in the trinitarian theology of its middle-level organization and in the tripartite structure of the whole poem, so the universe tends to echo its themes in different scales but with variations and interferences that give life to the whole. If you look at the branches of a tree you can see how the length of a twig stands in a similar—but not quite the same—relation to the length of the small branches as the small branches stand to the large branches, and the large branches to the trunk. You can find this pattern in all kinds of phenomena—electrical discharges, frost-flowers, the annual patterns of rise and decline in competing animal populations, stock market fluctuations, weather formations and clouds, the bronchi of the lungs, corals, turbulent waters, and so on. This harmonious yet dynamic relation of small to large is beautiful.

Now these descriptions would be immediately recognized by scientists in many fields as belonging to feedback processes and the structures that are generated by them. The fundamental tendency or theme of the universe, in short, is reflexivity or feedback. We are beginning to understand more and more clearly that the universe is a phenomenon of turbulence, the result of a nested set of feedback processes. Hence it is dynamic and open-ended: open-ended, moreover, precisely in and because of its continual attempt to come to closure, to fall to a stop. Moreover, as with any dynamic nonlinear open feedback process, the universe continually generates new frames and dimensions, new rules and constraints, and its future states are too complicated to be calculated by any conceivable computer made out of the universe as it is. It is retrodictable but not predictable, like a good—a beautiful—story.

The process of evolution itself is a prime example of a generative feedback process. Variation, selection, and heredity constitute a cycle, which when repeated over and over again produces out of this very simple algorithm the most extraordinarily complex and beautiful life forms. Variation is the novelty generator; selection is a set of alterable survival rules to choose certain products out of the novelty generator. Heredity, the conservative ratchet, preserves what is gained.

Evolution is only one of a class of processes that are characterized by various researchers in various ways: nonlinear, chaotic, dissipative, self-organizing. All such processes produce patterns with the familiar characteristics of branchiness, hierarchy, self-similarity, generativeness, unpredictability, and self-inclusiveness. To look at, they are like the lacy strands of sand and mud that Thoreau observed coming out of a melting sandbank in Walden; they are filled with lovely leaf designs, acanthus, chicory, ferns, or ivies; or like jacquard paisleys, the feathers of peacocks, the body-paint or tattoo designs of Maoris or Melanesians, the complexity of a great wine, the curlicues of Hiroshige seafoam, or Haida ornamentation, or seahorses, or Mozart melodies.

The iterative feedback principle which is at the heart of all these processes is the deep theme or tendency of all of nature—nature, the creator of forms. It is the logos and eros of nature; and it is what we feel and intuit when we recognize beauty. Our own evolution is at the same time an example of the principle at work, the source of our capacity to perceive it in beautiful things, the guarantee of its validity (if it were not valid we would not have survived), and the origin of a reflective consciousness that can take the process into new depths of self-awareness and self-reference. As the most complex and reflexive product of the process that we know of in the universe, we are, I believe, charged with its continuance; and the way that we continue it is art.

If beauty is a real property of things and, though fertile of free and unpredictable developments, rooted in the physical universe, then the whole body of contemporary critical theory and practice is deeply in error and should be revised. The postmodern avant garde founds its criticism upon the principle that beauty is a socially or individually constructed illusion that can be reduced to the glamour of economic interest and mimetic desire, the sadistic shudder of power, and the sickly jouissance of repressed sex. Out of these assumptions have come the radical forms of environmentalist, feminist, and multiculturalist criticism. These ideologies, however, could only begin to flourish once the meanings and values of literature and the other arts had been discredited. The critical movement known as deconstruction was the agent of that discrediting. Having dissected the living body of the cultural tradition, deconstruction left a vacuum where its central content had been; and into that vacuum rushed the enthusiasms of political reduction.

A vital criticism is essential to a vital art; thus in the hopeful rebuilding of our culture that I propose, a new system of critical theory is essential. What must that theory do to be successful? One way of answering this question is in terms of healing: the rejoining of broken wholes, the reuniting of false dichotomies, the bringing together of cultural energies vitiated by their division. Our theory, then, must rejoin artist with public, beauty with morality, high art with low, art with craft, passion with intelligence, art with science, and past with future.

However, before we can begin any new project in critical theory it will be necessary to correct certain central and crucial mistakes in postmodern linguistic philosophy and semiotics—and thus to restore a view of language itself in which meaning is possible. The core mistake, from which grow the simplifications of Derrida and all the sad reductions of contemporary political reading, concerns the problem of reference and representation. In a way the issue is really the peculiar reflexiveness of the prefix "re" in these words. To what does "refer" refer? What can a representation represent except the absence of what is represented? A whole tradition, running from Kant to Mach to Wittgenstein to Derrida, questioned the meaning of meaning and the value of value. Kant envisioned the categories of perception as standing between us and the thing in itself. Mach questioned the reality of scientific "abstractions" such as the atom. (What would he have made of contemporary tunnelling-electron photographs of atoms?). Wittgenstein pointed out, with the brilliance of obviousness, that we must be silent about that of which we cannot speak—the limits of our language being the limits of our world. (Of course in saying this Wittgenstein is, precisely, speaking about that of which we cannot speak, so that it is not unspeakable any more.)

Derrida generalizes the problem of reference to all words, since all words tacitly claim to be referring, and thus all words deconstruct themselves, confess their necessary difference from, and deferral of delivery upon, the meaning that they claim. Wittgenstein had pointed out that the whole (speakable) world was apportioned among our various language-games; Derrida extends this idea, both into a radical skepticism about any natural forerunner of those games, and into a critique of any text for its slippage between those games, its inability to maintain its purity as belonging to one or another. Derrida is all very ingenious, but it becomes clear when his own smoke screen of language is blown away that this emperor has no clothes. For all he is saying, after all, is that a word is not the same thing as what it refers to. The "new clothes" show up as nonexistent the moment we reflect that perhaps words never claimed to be the same thing as what they referred to, but that they might very well be related in very solid ways with their referents, for instance as whole to part, as pattern to element, as harmonic to tone or wave, as enactment to intention (as Wittgenstein hinted), or as container to contained. Nor need we be intimidated by the multifariousness of meaning-strategies. Wittgenstein's idea of language as a toolbox, containing many different ways of meaning, is instructive here; but we do not need to infer from his idea, as have many critics of meaning, that there is no such thing as meaning. Rather, we might seek out a semantic theory which identifies various ways of meaning within a larger evolutionary picture, as species with common roots within a shared ecosystem of signification: and this would be the beginnings of an ecopoetics. The toolbox, after all, is a toolbox.

Derrida insists on breaking language down to its elements—what he calls "morceaux" or "traces"—and, like a physicist who has discovered the indeterminacy of a subatomic particle, proclaims that those elements cannot be pinned down in a precise way. However, the conclusion he draws from this truth is faulty and reveals a reductiveness he inherits, as have so many cultural critics of our century, from outdated Victorian philosophy of science: that because the parts of a text are indeterminate, the whole must be also; and that because a text can be broken down, it is only a mass of fugitive and disseminated fragments. The very analogy of the quantum scientist and the indeterminate particle gives the game away: for an ensemble of those particles can generate robust harmonics that have all the solidity, durability, and efficacy of traditional matter. As Wittgenstein said, a distinction that makes no difference is no distinction. If it looks like a duck, and quacks like a duck—if it weighs like matter and bounces like matter—if it reads like a coherent text and means like a coherent text—then it is a duck, a piece of matter, a meaningful text. If it fails to pass some test of its elements, some criterion of direct linkage with ultimate being that Derrida believes would qualify it to be what he thinks it claims to be, that is Derrida's problem. Derrida should not let his anger at an absolute transcendent divine being for not existing defile the rather promising, if amateurish, achievements of this actual evolving universe in the pursuit of being and meaningfulness.

What would an evolutionary theory of value and meaning look like? Value evolved slowly in the universe, increasing with each access of reflexivity and level of feedback, complex entities conferring value upon each other and upon the less complex by sensitively registering their presence, perceiving, eating, mating with, desiring, or loving them; and conferring value upon themselves by their increasingly intentional and planned attempts to survive and reproduce. More intense and more universal values evolved with increasing ecological interdependence, whether among whole populations of species or in those fantastically complex and swiftly evolving inner ecologies, the nervous systems of higher animals. Human beings represent the most elaborated and reflexive stage of this process of which we are aware.

Given this view of the universe, various candidates for a good definition of such terms as meaning, reference, representation, and value emerge without strain.

It is clear that a word occupies the last and most temporally complex milieu in the evolutionary series I have described—the human—and that later and more advanced milieux embrace and include earlier ones, though with all the tragic strains, paradoxes, and existential tensions they have accrued in the process. Thus we could well define the relationship of reference or representation, for the kind of word that refers to a non-human object, as constituting one of containment or inclusion—even if the containment is not entirely successful and the inclusion is procrustean in the ways characteristic of a temporal universe. The fact that the operation of reference or meaning is not always successful—Priestley's word "phlogiston" is not as good at including and exemplifying its chemical ancestors as the word "oxygen" that supplanted it—does not mean that the operation itself is intellectually incoherent or so compromised by internal contradiction as to be infinitely deconstructable.

In this analysis we will find again and again that the claims of the poststructuralists, exciting and apocalyptic as they sound at first, are really rather wild and hysterical—perhaps because they originated in the overheated atmosphere of denied shame, opportunistic ambition, and intellectual and sexual display that was characteristic of postwar Paris. It is only if utterly unrealistic claims of perfection are attributed to human language that words will fail the test of referring, fairly reliably, to a real world in which they themselves have an existence no less real. We should not allow ourselves to be confused by the relationship of containment, as humanistic intellectuals often are. Local indeterminacy can coexist in a perfectly rational way with global coherence; and the fact that an element of something—a discourse, a text, a society, a human body, a world—requires a context should not be cause for astonishment or skepticism about their reality. They themselves help to create their context, and contexts are the more robust and substantial, the more inclusive they are. Nor should this idea lead us to conclude that society alone, being the "largest" context, has the exclusive power to construct reality. For society, as we have seen, only imperfectly contains its individual members; and it is not, in any case, the largest context, since it itself exists, as the environmentalists remind us, within a much larger context of natural history and ecology. Society will only come to include that context to the extent that we come to understand the universe through science—so that larger parts of nature get the vote, so to speak—and to the extent that scientific knowledge really becomes disseminated through the population, including its scientifically illiterate cultural critics.

We can picture the relationship of containment that is proposed here for certain kinds of signification, in terms of those remarkable fractal images that are now being generated by the iterative self-including algorithms of the new mathematicians. A word is like the radiant snowman of the Mandelbrot set, the flying scud of the logistical equation, the twisted butterfly of the

Lorenz attractor—which, when blown up to show its inner detail, reveals miniature, simpler versions of itself at an infinite variety of scales. A word's meaning is the inner structure of a highly complex feedback system involving a human nervous system and some part of the rest of the physical universe.

Meaning is the relationship of strange attractors to the physical processes in which they inhere. Any nonlinear dynamical system, when triggered by a stimulus, will generate a sequence of unpredictable events, but those events will nevertheless be limited to their attractor, and further iteration will fill out the attractor in more and more detail. The brain itself holds memories in the form of such attractors, the dynamical feedback system in this case being circuits of Hebb cells. Thus we can picture the relationship of a word to its meaning as the relationship of a given trigger to the attractor that is traced out by the feedback process it initiates. When the word "refers" to a perceived object—say, a smell or a sight—that object is one which can trigger a subset of the full attractor, as a Julia set is a subset of the Mandelbrot set. Thus a single word can trigger a "meaning-attractor," sections of whose fine detail can also be triggered by various sensory stimuli. This description rather nicely matches with our Proustian experience of connotation and poetic evocation, and with the logical form of generalization. It accords with the results of linguistic experiments concerning the relative strength by which a given example—say, a duck, an ostrich, or a sparrow—is recognized by a speaker as belonging to the meaning of a word ("bird"). It also explains the difference between ideas and impressions that exercised the philosophical imaginations of Locke and Hume: the richly detailed subset evoked by the sight of an object would certainly make the general sketch of the whole set evoked by the word look somewhat pale by comparison.

Since the trigger—whether the word or the sensory stimulus—is itself part of the feedback system, it is encompassed by its description, which is the attractor proper to it when it is allowed to iterate its effects upon a complex neural network. Thus the represented, the representation, and the experiencer of the representation are all part of the same physical system. The usual critique of physical descriptions of representation—for instance, John Searle's Chinese room analogy for artificial intelligence—is that however a given object is represented inside the physical system, it requires a smaller system inside the system to see it and know it, or, as John Eccles believes, a detachable non-physical soul. The chaotic-attractor theory of meaning holds out the promise of an intelligible physical description of meaning that does not require an inner homunculus or the intervention of a metaphysical deus ex machina, with further attendant problems of infinite regress—how does the god in the machine perceive and know the representation?—to make it work. One way of putting this is that the issue of reflexiveness, of self-reference or self-inclusion, has been transferred from the metaphysical level, where it can only be interpreted as a barren infinite regress or reductio ad absurdum, to the physical realm, where it can be studied as we study turbulences of other kinds, with its own emergent properties and self-generated orderliness. The reflexiveness, we feel intuitively, should be there in any account of meaning; the trick is to keep it from messing up our own thinking about it, and place it where it belongs, in the operation of the brain itself.

It remains to suggest how this "attractor theory" of signification might work itself out in the etymological history of a language, and express itself in terms of phonology, morphology, and metaphor. Here the idea of sacrificial commutation may be of use. Every sacrifice was an expiation of the crime of a previous sacrifice, though with the penalty commuted, refined, and abstracted. Sacrifice itself is necessary in order to render the shame of our condition as evolved and self-reflexive animals over into the epiphany of beauty. It is related to the whole history of the universe as a cumulative and nested set of contradictions solved at each higher level at the cost of new, emergent contradictions. Those existential tensions express themselves at the physical level in the turbulences and bifurcations of nonlinear dynamical systems, and at the psychological level as shame, the fear of death, and beauty. The commutative history of sacrifice recapitulates this recursive and tragic process. I suggest that human signification itself might have developed through the commutation of sacrificial cost.

In other words, the social and cultural dimension of language, like the neurosensory dimension, has the form of a nonlinear dynamical system with strange attractors pulling it toward certain "archetypal" forms. Those forms could be seen in the odd "targetedness" of the great sound-shifts that periodically convulse a language; they can also be observed in the way that metaphorization will take parallel paths in different languages, so that when a colorful idiom from another language is presented to us, we can almost always find an equivalent in our own. Thus the words "spirit" in English and "Atman" in Sanskrit have identical metaphoric histories, as do the words "kind," "nature," and "genus," all of which came together again in English, having led separate lives in Germanic, Latin, Greek, and other tongues for thousands of years after their common root in Indo-European. Metaphorization and sound-changes are every new human generation's way of committing a sacrificial impiety against the tongue of its ancestors, an impiety that commutatively atones for the crime of the ancestors themselves in similarly appropriating the language for themselves from their own mothers and fathers. And since meaning dies the moment it ceases to cut slightly against all previous usage—another valuable if overemphasized and not entirely original contribution of deconstruction—it is *constituted* by this continual low-level feedback between the language and the world it contains.

Such might be the rudiments of a new, evolutionary poetics and a new nonlinear theory of meaning and representation. Obviously I have only scratched the surface. We do not need to sit helplessly in the morass of late poststructuralist despair and misologism; there are still worlds for the literary humanities to conquer.

There are also practical implications of this model of meaning. (By now such phrases as "model of meaning," with their invitations to further reflexive iteration, should hold no terrors for us, since we hold a clue to the labyrinth, a clue whose own windings are equal to the windings of that dark place we would discover.) One implication is that many of the characteristics of the relationship of word to meaning are already present in the relationship between a percept and the experience of it. If a sense-perception can generate a sort of "Julia set" in the firing-circuits of brain neurons, then in a way a sense perception is like a word. That is, we share with other higher animals the elements of a sensory language which preexisted the more encompassing kind of language that uses words. Or we could put it the other way around and say that language is just a larger kind of sensing, using internal triggers to evoke larger attractor-sets than any percept could. Obviously we have here a further reason for exploring our relationship with our animal friends: it is a way of understanding the fundamentals of our own language, of discovering that ur-language we share with other parts of nature than ourselves. One huge advantage of that ur-language is that it is not riven by the linguistic boundaries that divide the more fully human languages like English and French from each other; and if we learn to speak it better, we may find more common ground with cultural Others as well as with biological Others.

In one sense, of course, we already possess such ur-languages, in the shared imagery of the visual arts and in the "universal language" of music. But the theory of meaning proposed here suggests that there is something analogous to music and visual imagery that underlies language itself, obscured by its more recent evolutionary achievements, to be neglected only at the cost of a vitiation and graying of our expression and understanding. I came to this conclusion by an entirely different route a few years ago, while translating the poetry of Miklos Radnoti with my colleague Zsuzsanna Ozsvath (Radnoti 1992). Suffice it to say here that poetic meter turns out to be a sure road to the ur-language, or, to change the metaphor, meter is the lyre or golden bough or magic flute that enables us to enter the underworld of that language and to return with intelligible gifts for the community. Meter, like music and visual imagery, is an ancient psychic technology by which human nature and human culture are bridged; appropriately, and as we might imagine from our discussion of the fractal harmonics of Hebb-cell circuitry, meter is a rhythmic and harmonic system in itself, a way of inducing the wave functions of the brain. The lyre through which Rilke traces Orpheus in the *Sonnets to Orpheus* is the poetic form of the sonnet itself.

If the words of a poet can induce in one brain the same strange attractor that they proceeded from in the poet's brain, an extraordinary possibility presents itself. This possibility is that when those harmonics are in our heads we are actually sharing the thoughts, and indeed the subjectivity, of the poet, even if he or she is dead. The poet lives again when his or her attractors arise in another brain. Poetry, then, is a kind of artificial intelligence program that springs into being when booted correctly into any good human meat-computer. Thus poetry is indeed a journey to the land of the dead. This view of reading is profoundly different from that of deconstruction and reader-response theory, as the present reader can surely see.

We need a new kind of poetics, which we might call ecopoetics. The word is, I believe, the coinage of the scholar and literary biographer Tim

Redman, who applies it primarily in the economic sense of "eco"; I believe it is a valuable term and can be expanded to cover some important new ground. Though this approach applies to all the arts, I shall specifically address literature. Essentially I am calling for the abandonment of a good part of the present activities of the literary academy and the beginning of a new literature, a new poetics, and a new criticism based upon the evolving universe and our own leading part in it.

Works Cited

Radnoti, Miklos

1992 *Foamy Sky: The Major Poems of Miklos Radnoti*. Translated by Frederick Turner and Zsuzsanna Ozsvath. Princeton: Princeton University Press.

Rentschler, I., B. Herzberger, and D. Epstein, eds.

1989 *Beauty and the Brain: Biological Aspects of Aesthetics*. Basel: Birkhauser Verlag.

Turner, Frederick

1986 *Natural Classicism: Essays on Literature and Science*. New York: Paragon House.

1991a *Beauty: The Value of Values*. Charlottesville: University Press of Virginia.

1991b *Rebirth of Value: Meditations on Beauty, Ecology, Religion, and Education*. Albany: SUNY Press.

1995 *The Culture of Hope: A New Birth of the Classical Spirit*. New York: Free Press.

"Theory," Anti-Theory, and Empirical Criticism

Joseph Carroll

People who could be described as evolutionary literary critics presuppose the validity of a scientific understanding of the world, and they believe that the biological study of human beings is the necessary basis for a scientifically valid understanding of literature. These assumptions separate them from most of their colleagues in literature departments, but the assumptions do not go very far toward identifying an actual program of research. In what follows, I shall characterize the two main parties that currently control the field of literary studies—the dominant postmodern party and the traditionalist opposition—contrast them both with critical study that orients itself to a biological understanding of human nature, and then pose a question: what should evolutionary literary critics do? This one large question contains several smaller questions. Where should we start? What guidelines should we follow? What should be the range of our activity? What kind of knowledge can we expect to produce? Is it possible to integrate literary study with empirical social science? What challenges and difficulties do we face in trying to reach this goal?

About thirty years ago, a specific complex of ideological and literary ideas began to emerge on the continent, and in the past twenty years this complex has achieved dominance in Anglo-American academic literary study. There are three central components of the complex: deconstructive linguistic philosophy, Marxist social theory, and Freudian psychology. In their combined scope, these three theories offer a comprehensive account of certain crucial areas of reality: Deconstructive philosophy informs us that the ultimate nature of reality is linguistic or rhetorical in character, and it stipulates that this rhetorical order is both self-enclosed and self-subversive, forbidding us access to any realm outside a chain of constantly displaced signifiers. Marxism provides a comprehensive model of social and economic life, including the historical development of social orders; and Freudianism takes in the whole field of individual psychology, sexual relations, and family dynamics. In isolation, each of these three theories has a certain totalizing and self-insulating quality. Moreover, the most cosmically inclusive of the theories, deconstruction, affirms the autonomy of all rhetorical constructs, and it thus covers the whole complex with a defensive force-field that renders it impervious to empirical criticism. As Foucault explains in "What Is an Author?" Freudianism and Marxism must be conceived not as empirical disciplines that are susceptible to disproof but rather as "discursive practices" that transcend all critical categories (132). In this respect, the elements of the poststructuralist synthesis are similar in ontological status to the categories of pure reason analyzed by Kant in the *Critique of Pure Reason*. They are the conditions of possibility of critical thought, the categories without which thinking could not take place.

The comprehensiveness of scope and the self-insulating and self-affirming character of contemporary literary theory can help us to understand one of the striking peculiarities in the attitude of contemporary literary academics. In its positive aspect, as seen from the inside, one might characterize this attitude as one of poise and self-assurance, a stance reflecting a mature and sophisticated intellectual development. From the outside, as seen by practitioners in other disciplines, one might characterize it as arrogance, a certain narrow and overweening vanity, a provincial complacency that is protected by the general laxity of intellectual standards in the humanities.

The attitude I have in mind is apparent in the way critics have become habituated to using the word "theory" itself. More often than not, one hears the word theory used with no limiting adjective. It is not "literary" theory or "postmodern" theory or "current" theory. It is just "theory" *tout court.* Now, since literature is only one of many fields of knowledge, and since efforts to construct theories of literature and of criticism are at least as old as Plato and Aristotle, this usage has quite specific implications. The usage implies that no theory worthy of the name existed before this current theory; and that the current theory is therefore in some way quintessentially and uniquely theoretical. It is not just one among other possible, competing theories; rather, it partakes of some hitherto inaccessible essence of theory, an almost numinous theoreticity or theoriness of theory, something like the thingness or *Dinglichkeit* a phenomenologist seeks to intuit within any actual Thing. The use of the word *theory* without limiting adjective implies, further, that other fields of knowledge—fields like history, particle physics, and psychology—fall outside or below the range of "theory." Whatever virtues such disciplines might possess as systematized fields of inquiry, with their own special procedures and vocabularies, and however successful they might be in explaining or manipulating the world, they still lack some special quality of rhetorical or linguistic self-reflexiveness, some savvy, insider sensitivity to the theoreticity of theory.

Such claims often resonate tacitly in the very intonation with which the word "theory" is pronounced, but the claims for a quite particular supremacy in the world of intellect have not of course remained merely latent or tacit. One of the fastest-growing fields in literary studies over the past ten or fifteen years has been the cultural study of science, and it is precisely the motive of this field to extend the province of postmodern theory over the whole realm of scientific knowledge. The confident expansionism of the field has taken a few rude shocks of late, first by the quite unexpected counter-blast given by Paul R. Gross and Norman Levitt in their book *Higher Superstition: The Academic Left and Its Quarrels with Science*, and then by what will surely rank as one of the great literary hoaxes of all time, Alan Sokal's parody of postmodern science study, "Transgressing the Boundaries: Toward a Transformative Hermeneutics of Quantum Gravity." At gatherings such as the annual conference for the Society for Literature and Science, one now hears a new note of caution, defensiveness, and even of propitiation; but these notes are as yet only the reflexive gestures of pained surprise and flustered embarrassment. No substantive changes in theoretical orientation have as yet taken place.

There can hardly be any doubt about the dominance of the postmodern paradigm in current literary studies, but there is a party of opposition. This party consists largely of senior members of the profession who are still committed to more traditional forms of study, and it now has something of an institutional home, the Association of Literary Scholars and Critics, an offshoot of the intellectually conservative academic organization, the National Association of Scholars. As a member, a reader of the Newsletter, and an eavesdropper on the e-mail discussion list, I think it safe to say that the members of the organization would have a very difficult time formulating a consensus view of the positive principles that bind them into a party. They are firm in their dislike of the prevailing paradigm; indeed, they are quite certain of its flagrant iniquity, but they are also haunted by a vague apprehension that their opposition is largely negative and reactive.

Some members of the organization are still affiliated with the New Criticism, and would thus affirm the virtually autonomous centrality and primacy of individual literary texts. They thus dislike the deconstructive notion of dissolving texts into the amorphous mass of textuality, and they dislike as well the New Historicist extension of textuality to social context. Other members of the organization make more allowance for traditional contextual study—the study of biographical and social influences on texts. Those with a biographical bent dislike the postmodern excision of the author as an originative force, and those with a social bent are made uneasy by the notion that texts only passively reflect larger historical epistemes and do not thus achieve the dignity of critical, reflective power. A good many members are personally committed to a religious view of the world, and they tend to regard literature as a medium for the play of spirit and as a secular vindication for their own sense of a transcendent power embodied in the human imagination. Scholars with this religious bent are deeply alienated by the spirit of nihilistic persiflage that animates much postmodern rhetoric.

Are there any common ideological or methodological elements here? I think there are. The common ideological element is a residual Arnoldian humanism, that is, a conviction that the canonical texts of Western culture embody a normative set of values and imaginative experiences. Postmodern critics either take literature itself as a subversive agent or regard it as implicated in the hegemonic power structures of the larger culture, and they believe that the function of criticism is to demystify such structures. All the parties within the traditionalist reaction, despite their large differences, are united in their revulsion against the subversive or anti-normative spirit of the postmodern paradigm. Whatever else they might think about literature and how one ought to study it, they feel strongly that one ought to approach it with a respect bordering on reverence. The business of criticism is not to demystify or subvert but to appreciate and affirm. Criticism should illuminate and explain, to be sure, but it should also serve as the archival medium through which a precious heritage is kept alive and transmitted to future generations.

The common methodological element in the traditionalist reaction can be identified, in one of its central guises, as "pragmatic" or "practical" criticism. Pragmatic criticism rejects the subordination of literary texts to "theory." Since "theory" now generally means postmodern theory, in rejecting "theory-controlled" readings, pragmatic critics naturally tend to focus on the kind of theory that currently prevails; but the rejection of "theory-controlled" reading is broader and more fundamental than a rejection of any specific theory or complex of theories. Even among postmodern critics, there are many scholars who wear their theory lightly, accepting it as an unavoidable lingua franca of current academic discourse but protecting themselves from any coercive influence it might exercise by not taking it altogether seriously. It is taken, instead, as a set of fragmentary and ad hoc heuristic terms, part of the eclectic body of critical terms available for local descriptive and analytic purposes. In the most practical, down-to-earth sort of critical work, the mundane business of discussing literary works in classrooms with students, most critics probably fall back on some not too dissimilar set of traditional and common-language terms, blurring the boundaries of coherent doctrine for the sake of speaking more or less sensibly with student readers. What distinguishes pragmatic critics as a distinct theoretical group, to put it sympathetically but fairly, is that they feel the need to make their theory coincide with the practice I have just described.

In what, then, does the theory of pragmatic criticism consist? In answering this question, I shall be characterizing views that I myself held just a few years ago. Pragmatic criticism consists in the belief that literary texts have a rich complexity of qualitative meaning that transcends or exceeds any specific theoretical reduction. A pragmatic critic has an intuitive conviction that the psychology in Dickens' depictions of character is more subtle and true than any Freudian premise. He or she believes that George Eliot's depictions of social life display a unique and supreme kind of insight, an understanding by the side of which Marxist analysis is merely a clumsy, hopelessly crude framework for analysis. And he or she feels that the poetic insights of Yeats or Wallace Stevens exhibit an intimate familiarity with the living power of language in comparison to which deconstructive analysis can provide at best a feeble and distorted illumination. Pragmatic critics reject theory-controlled reading precisely because they believe that the theory implicit in canonical literary texts is a much more complete and adequate "criticism of life," to use Matthew Arnold's humanistic phrase, than the ideas available in any of standard versions of the social sciences that have been available for humanistic study ("Literature and Science," 10: 68). In this respect, then, the common methodological element of pragmatic criticism is integrally connected with its common ideological element. Pragmatic critics believe that canonical literary texts have a central normative value in good part because they believe that these texts embody the best intelligence of their civilization. The great books are, again in Arnold's phrase, repositories of "the best that is known and thought in the world" ("The Function of Criticism at the Present Time," 3: 282).

These are, again, views I once formulated as my own, and I shall now briefly try to analyze the conditions and characteristics of literary study that led me to these conclusions, these conditions and characteristics which are partly historical and partly inherent in the nature of literature and of criticism. I shall begin with literature itself, and with its historical situation. Until very recently, up to the past century or so, there was no social science. The kind of ethical and social philosophy that dealt with the problems of human behavior and human value operated within the range of common knowledge and more or less inspired speculation. This is the same intellectual range in which literature operates. The ideas about psychology, social life, and nature that are contained in literature, as specifically formulated theses, are roughly concordant with those available in the larger culture in which any given text is written. Philosophy or essayistic commentary is more systematic, but it is thus also more liable to false reductions, to the angularities of single ideas. Literature tends to work with the total lexicon of common language and thus to be more flexible and subtle in its depiction of personal and social life.

In depicting personal and social life, literature has an advantage in its very nature and purpose. The function of philosophy and science is to reduce phenomena to valid elementary principles. It is abstract and cerebral. Literature can also engage in philosophical generalization, but it has other purposes as well. It seeks to evoke subjective states of mind, register and stimulate emotional response, and give aesthetic shape to experience. It is thus much closer to the phenomenal surface of life, to life as it is commonly observed and experienced.

The same historical considerations that pertain to literature pertain to criticism. A curious adolescent who is seeking a broad familiarity with human behavior and human circumstances might well feel that literature offers a more valuable guide than any systematic philosophy and most history. Moreover, given the very large overlap between imaginative literature and essayistic belles-lettres, students of literature almost inevitably expand the range of their studies to include philosophy and social and psychological commentary. They regard these subjects, understandably enough, as forms of "literature." The result is that critics tend to get absorbed into their subject. They have no standpoint outside of it. They have no Archimedean point of critical leverage. To analyze and explain literature, they can only use the general humanistic knowledge that is generated and limited by literature.

The tendency for critics to become absorbed into their subjects is exacerbated by the peculiarly dual nature of critical study. Critics are both connoisseurs and scholars. As connoisseurs, they share in the subjective aspects of what they study. Unlike physicists, geologists, or biologists, they do not merely try to see the object as in itself it really is; they also deploy a sensitive receptivity to the personal qualities of literary works—to their aesthetic and emotional and moral qualities. As scholars, however, critics are responsible to the same general standards of objective validity that apply to all knowledge: they seek to produce explanations that integrate empirical observations with valid elementary principles. This is a difficult balancing act. The great critics have performed it well within the limits allowed by the inspired amateurism to which they have been historically limited.

In the modern world, as more and more territory is colonized by systematic and progressive empirical science, the productions of inspired amateurism have taken on an ever more problematic cast. Many of us in the humanities have long lived with a half-suppressed sense of uneasiness at the hodge-podge hit-and-miss character of our inquiries. We have ourselves suspected that we could be judged from the kind of perspective taken by Edward O. Wilson in his book of 1978, *On Human Nature*. Wilson is a distinguished biologist and a pioneer in the field of sociobiology, that is, the effort to extend biological understanding to include the social life of animals, including human beings. He believes all knowledge should be assessed by universal standards of empirical validity and that it should be integral with contiguous disciplines. Applying this standard to the finest literary journal articles of the time, he observes that they consist "largely of historical anecdotes, diachronic collating of outdated, verbalized theories of human behavior, and judgments of current events according to personal ideology—all enlivened by the pleasant but frustrating techniques of effervescence" (203). We should note that this chilling assessment falls, chronologically, in the period of transition between old-fashioned humanism and the postmodern synthesis, and that it is broad enough, as a methodological description, so that it can be applied to both.

There are at least three possible responses to the kind of criticism formulated by Wilson. One, the traditionalists' response, is to reject out of hand the standard he uses. The humanities, we are told, are fundamentally and irreconcilably different in nature from the hard sciences, or even the social sciences. There is nothing wrong with the way we have been going about humanistic study, and there is no legitimate alternative to it. We just have to get rid of the postmodern deviations and go back to the old ways. The postmodern response is not to declare the humanities a separate and distinct area but rather to declare that the sciences themselves fall within the province of rhetorical inquiry. The postmodern strategy is to encircle and deconstruct the standard by which Wilson would assess humanistic study. The third response, my own and that of a few other scattered proponents of a sociobiologically oriented criticism, is to accept the criticism as a historically accurate diagnosis of a crucial intellectual failure. Those who adopt this position believe that we are in a historically novel situation and that we now have before us the potential to create an empirically valid study of literature, a kind of study that would be integral with the social sciences that are themselves grounded in biology.

If we adopt this third position, we might well feel like Milton's Adam and Eve leaving the garden of Eden. "The world was all before them"—a daunting wilderness to be explored and settled (1060). What direction do we take? Where do we begin? I shall suggest three basic guidelines. First, we need to identify the elementary concepts that hold good from biology across the social sciences to the humanities. Second, we have to hold these concepts not loosely but empirically, understanding that they are only our best approximations and will almost certainly need to be qualified, and at times even discarded, as our empirical understanding progresses. On this issue, the attitude of empirical science should merge with the prudential skepticism of a traditional humanism that weighs all reductions against a flexible, intuitive, common-level understanding. Third, we must firmly grasp the principle that all subjects of study have their own specific forms of organization, and that the study of literature will thus have to have its own categories and structures embedded within the larger general principles of biology and social science. (Even the social sciences must find mid-level principles that resist premature reduction to elemental biological principles of fitness maximization.)

Let me give one example of what I have in mind when I recommend formulating ideas that are integral across the disciplines but that have their own specific applications and structures within a literary context. One idea that is basic to biological thinking is the idea of organisms and environments. Phenotypes, the observed characteristics of organisms, are the product of interactions between innate characteristics and environmental influences. For the social sciences to advance as sciences, it is necessary that they adopt this principle and thus abandon any exclusive fixation on social or environmental causation. Despite the massive ideological resistance to the idea of innate characteristics, this kind of advance is virtually inevitable. There is now a constantly increasing flood of hard data on genetic and developmental characteristics. Psychologists and other social scientists who ignore this information are condemning themselves to irrelevance. In the literary field, very briefly, the idea of organism and environment has at least two fundamental applications. The first application is to the situations depicted in literary works. These situations involve, as primary components, the interactions of organisms with their environments, including their social environments. To stipulate this much is to affirm that the traditional categories of characters and settings are in fact fundamental categories of analysis. And to affirm even so simple a proposition as this provides us with one basic common point of reference. To possess such points is an indispensable condition for making cumulative contributions to an empirical body of knowledge. The second application is to authors and readers as producers and consumers of literary works. Both authors and readers are organisms in environments. Hence, if we are to understand how literary meaning is produced and received, we have to acquire adequate information about the human personality and the way that personality interacts in varying environmental conditions. One primary task for evolutionary criticism is to assimilate that kind of information from biology and the social sciences, including linguistics and cognitive psychology, and use these ideas in the elucidation of literary texts, both as an end in itself—to understand the texts—and as a means of testing and refining the ideas.

If literary studies are ever to satisfy the criteria for empirical validity, they will have to include a range of activities that can be located on a scale of empirical constraint, and these activities will have to be interdependent. At the lower end of the scale, with the least empirical constraint, we can locate most of what we now think of as literary criticism. A the upper end, with the greatest constraint, we can locate the kinds of experimental study—in psychology and linguistics—that are already being conducted but that have not often been expanded to include literature. As a behavioral science, experimental literary study would affiliate itself closely with observational disciplines like ethology and cultural anthropology. Such disciplinary connections would make it possible to pose and answer empirical questions about how art functions in social groups, what kinds of social needs it satisfies, and how it interacts with other social factors. The results of such study would supply us with the basic facts for the statistical generalizations that are indispensable for causal explanations of cultural and literary history.

To engage in empirical study, we must be able to propose alternative hypotheses, conduct experiments, confirm or fail to confirm predictions, and thus falsify propositions. So far, even the most conscientious evolutionary criticism has failed to establish any method for testing its theoretical or interpretive hypotheses. The most we have done is to assimilate and integrate the findings of social science, applying them in a speculative way to specific texts or to literature in general. As an illustrative instance, consider a book that has just been published, Robert Storey's *Mimesis and the Human Animal: On the Biogenetic Foundations of Literary Representation*. Storey goes further than anyone else yet has in assimilating empirical study from fields like cognitive psychology, ethology, and personality theory. He integrates these findings with specifically literary forms of meaning in narrative theory, genre theory,and audience psychology, and he applies his theoretical constructs to practical criticism. His work thus exemplifies the kind of program I have been proposing here. The one main thing Storey's book does not do is to propose any means by which the correlations he identifies could be tested and either validated or falsified. In this respect, his work reflects the one central methodological limitation to which interpretive literary study has been subject.

So far, our only constraints are those we impose on ourselves by virtue of our own sense of what seems reasonable. To impose even these constraints within the framework of evolutionary understanding is an immense step forward from interpretive caprice within the framework of obsolete social and psychological doctrines like those of Marx and Freud, but it is not enough to shield us from the legitimate reservations of those who take seriously the criteria of validity in the empirical sciences. How would we even begin to overcome this limitation? We need to restrict the possible range of plausible disagreement, and in order to do this we need to start accumulating experimental findings about the production and reception of meaning in literary texts.

In a paper delivered at an annual meeting of the Human Behavior and Evolution Society, the biologist D. S. Wilson has provided one striking example of experimental literary study. Wilson gave personality tests to experimental subjects, determined their position on a scale of Machiavellianism, and had them write short stories that were then analyzed for content that was correlated with their scores. Apart from the considerable interest of the specific findings, this experiment is important simply because it shows that this one crucial thing can be done: that is, experiments relating to the production of literary meaning can be conducted. Moreover, at this point, when so little is firmly established, almost any specific finding is going to offer us important implications. The results of Wilson's experiment, for example, give evidence in support of the contention that individual psychological differences influence the action of a story they write. Here is a specific instance in which a finding can provide support for a basic working hypothesis in interpretive criticism.

Generalizing from this example, we can say that virtually any psychological test that can be given to people, and any description of general traits for a given group of people, can be correlated with the blood-flow changes under specific stimuli. It is not, I think, extravagant to suggest that such stimuli could eventually include the reading of literary texts. We can identify a whole array of mental and emotional characteristics in experimental subjects. We can track mental responses to given stimuli. Could we not then also identify specific literary forms, hypothesize connections between these forms and measurable forms of mental and emotional reaction, and test these hypotheses in experimental subjects? Could we, for instance, take the opening chapter of Jane Austen's novel *Pride and Prejudice*, have an experimental subject read it while under a scanning machine, and find out something about the way comedy actually alters the brain? By correlating the responses of individual people with other data on the same people—psychological and social profiles, for example—and by comparing such correlations across individuals and groups of individuals, we could begin to formulate precise empirical propositions about the conditions under which audience response varies. At the moment, this scenario sounds like science fiction. The technical limitations of scanning do not yet allow for such large-scale study, and progress will probably come through an accumulation of more minute findings, but I see no reason, in principle, that we cannot begin to produce empirical results in interpretive criticism.

Most of the people who concern themselves with evolutionary criticism are engaged in the practice of interpreting literary texts. Such interpretations have characteristically consisted of analyses of plot and character designed to demonstrate that the stories being told illustrate the kind of behavior evolutionary psychology teaches us to expect. One main form of study that has been envisioned for evolutionary criticism is to accumulate large aggregates of such analyses. Examples would include content analyses of plots for the purpose of identifying the frequency of certain sociobiological themes, such as mate choice, parent-child conflict, kin selection, or group-affiliation behavior. One could imagine plot summaries of, say, 5,000 famous novels and plays, broken down into categories common to evolutionary psychology and anthropology, with variations graphed historically, and correlated with cultural and socioeconomic variables or variables in the author and audience—variables such as age, sex, and social status. All of this seems to me eminently worth doing. It would give us a substantial set of provisionally stable points of factual reference. I would certainly not urge that we stop doing this, but I shall suggest two reservations or cautions about it.

The first reservation is that we need to be aware of one large and problematic assumption built into the procedure: the assumption that literary authors represent human behavior in ways that correspond to our current understanding of evolutionary psychology. To a remarkable extent, I think authors in fact do this. Beneath and apart from their structure of conscious beliefs, authors, like people in general, are instinctively attuned to evolutionary psychology. It is the psychology by which they actually operate. If people behave in ways that illustrate evolutionary psychology, and if authors offer reasonably realistic portrayals of human behavior, then no matter what the authors' own belief systems might be, the stories they tell would tend to illustrate evolutionary psychology. But at times they do not, and the deviations are at least as interesting as the normative instances. In examining the represented content of stories, we need to take account of how personal and cultural factors influence the representation of human behavior. To give a few examples, sentimental idealism, cynicism, utopian fantasy, sexual deviance, and other forms of psychological idiosyncrasy can be shown to affect the kinds of actions that are represented in specific stories.

My second reservation expands on the first: represented actions are not the only factors to be considered in literary texts. The presence of the author as registered in tone, point of view, and style, is a crucial feature of meaning in most of the texts we read. Simple folk tales passed on in oral tradition are the closest thing to an exception to this rule, but even these tales reflect a collective cultural point of view. For literary authors in a culture with more highly developed forms of individuality, the interaction between the collective ethos and that of the author—very often an antagonistic, ironic interaction—becomes a central point of interest. I would suggest, then, that evolutionary criticism should not limit itself exclusively to the analysis of represented content of plot and character. We need to pose more fundamental questions about how meaning is produced in literary texts, and we need to take account of the individual psychology of authors and the way this psychology interacts with their particular set of cultural circumstances. To say this is not to step outside the range of repeatable elementary phenomena, which is the domain of science. It is rather to locate an evolutionary study of literature within the same range of historical sciences that includes biology and geology—sciences in which there are large general laws such as natural selection, but in which there are also unique historical phenomena such as speciation events.

In conclusion, I want to take a step back from the immediate problem of methodology and give a broader, behavioral context to the question, "What should evolutionary literary critics do?" Regarding my own case as fairly typical, I would argue that if our training has been primarily literary and humanistic, we need to engage in a long-range program of basic re-education. We need to learn more in technical detail about the common knowledge of contemporary physics, astronomy, genetics, and molecular biology, among other disciplines. Why? Partly because the truth of the modern scientific world view is in the detailed sense of an intricate and elaborately interconnected set of mechanisms. Our own sense of the world needs to be adjusted to this modern scientific world view. If it did nothing else, this sort of knowledge would give us a chastened sense of what counts as plausible propositions and worthwhile evidence. Yet further, basic scientific literacy is a precondition for engaging in any collaborative work with experimental scientists and even for making intelligent use of the findings from empirical science.

Our historical position presents special challenges. We are seeking to construct a theory of literature that would be integral with a total body of scientific and social-scientific knowledge, but this larger integrated context is itself only now beginning to take shape. While working as speculative theorists and as empiricists in our own practical criticism, we also have to work as polemicists and revolutionists, not only within our own almost wholly hostile discipline but within the much larger field of "the human sciences." At the widest level, then, we have to be reformers, agitating for a fundamental revision in the way we organize higher education. Even while worrying about how to provide minimal employment for our current generation of graduate students, we have to work toward restructuring the humanities curriculum so that future generations of students will be scientifically literate. They would then be much less likely to waste their professional lives in futile rhetorical gambits like those parodied by Alan Sokal, and they would be much more likely to make good on the promise of an empirical, evolutionary study of literature.

Works Cited

Arnold, Matthew

1962 *The Complete Prose Works of Matthew Arnold.* Edited by R. H. Super. Vol. 3, *Lectures and Essays in Criticism.* Ann Arbor: University of Michigan Press.

1974 *The Complete Prose Works of Matthew Arnold.* Edited by R. H. Super. Vol. 10, *Philistinism in England and America.* Ann Arbor: University of Michigan Press.

Foucault, Michel

1977 *Language, Counter-Memory, Practice: Selected Essays and Interviews.* Translated by Donald F. Bouchard and Sherry Simon. Edited by Donald F. Bouchard. Ithaca: Cornell University Press.

Gross, Paul R., and Norman Levitt

1994 *Higher Superstition: The Academic Left and Its Quarrels with Science.* Baltimore: The Johns Hopkins University Press.

Milton, John

1968 *The Poems of John Milton.* Edited by John Carey and Alastair Fowler. London: Longman.

Sokal, Alan D.

1996 "Transgressing the Boundaries: Toward a Transformative Hermeneutics of Quantum Gravity." *Social Text* 14: 217-52.

Storey, Robert

1996 *Mimesis and the Human Animal: On the Biogenetic Foundations of Literary Representation.* Evanston: Northwestern University Press.

Wilson, David Sloan

n.d. "The Deceptive Nature of Exploitative Social Strategies." Under submission.

Wilson, Edward O.
1978 *On Human Nature*. Cambridge, MA: Harvard University Press.

Part II

New Sociobiological Explorations in Art

Biochemicals and Brains: Natural Selection for Manipulators of Sexual Ecstasy and Fantasy

Wayne E. Allen

> Science can hope to explain artists, and artistic genius, and even art, and it will increasingly use art to investigate human behavior, but it is not designed to transmit experience on a personal level or to reconstitute the full richness of the experience from the laws and principles which are its first concern by definition.
>
> Edward O. Wilson

> Any learning ability makes possible—as an incidental effect, or by-product—the development of behaviors other than those for which it was designed by natural selection.
>
> Donald Symons

Throughout human history the communication of aesthetic emotion and ineffable experiences such as fantasies and ecstatic states has consistently been the endeavor of poets, artists, and the purveyors of myths. These highly subjective experiences could most effectively be viewed as psychological events with an intense emotional component adjunct to them. Such experiences in all probability had their origin in the genetic adaptations of the evolving phenotypes of sexually reproducing organisms.

The functions for which structures and behaviors evolve are not always the only functions that the structures and behaviors perform. For example, the human brain did not evolve to appreciate great works of art, nor did it evolve as a generalized information processor with the purpose of maximizing reproductive fitness. Rather, it evolved in specific environments with domain-specific functions that were distinct adaptations to distinct environments (see Williams 1966, 14-16; Symons 1979, 35-50, 1987, 1989, 1991; Daly and Wilson 1983, 258-61, 314-15, 1988, 3-9; Tooby and Cosmides 1989a and 1989b).

That the human brain functions to produce the human mind, which in turn performs many tasks that were not, and possibly are not, specifically adaptive, merely reflects what Williams (1966, 121) called "historical accident" or "historical contingency." Unlike most other species humans can internally generate, with their minds, psychological states that have enormous consequences for themselves and their environment. These psychological states are known as conceptualizations, and if other species have them there is not much evidence, other than that for our nearest primate relatives, the apes, that they act upon them. Human beings, on the other hand, conceptualize fantasies which not only impact upon psychological states of mind but can also have profound physiological and behavioral consequences (see Gazzaniga 1988).

It is important to note that in contemporary humans the experiences and formulations of aesthetic emotions, fantasies, and ecstatic states are internally generated mental phenomena—i. e., conceptualizations as opposed to percepts. As a consequence they are much more difficult to convey to conspecifics through the symbolic constructs of language, representational art, and mythology than are shared "objective" experiences such as somatic perceptions of the external environment. This situation is reflected in the evolution of communication mechanisms in animals, such as signs, calls, ritualizations, and displays, whose function is to convey information concerning externally generated somatic perceptions of the environment and reproductive potential. On the other hand, the closest thing in the animal kingdom to calls, signs, ritualizations, and displays' communication of internally generated mental phenomena would be moaning or crying, representing pain; cooing and purring, representing pleasure; or anomalous postures and behaviors, representing a pathology.

Historically it is the case that human beings systematically engage in, and manipulate, mentally generated conceptualizations for purposes ranging from self-gratification—e. g., daydreaming, brainstorming, and sexual fantasies—to the extrasomatic symbolic representation of these conceptualizations, oftentimes with the agenda, sometimes hidden, of manipulating the responses of conspecifics—e. g., love poems, plays, representational art, theater, propaganda, media advertising, and pornography.

The following hypothesis explores how such a manipulative capacity evolved, whether or not it is a specific adaptation, and whether or not it has implications for human beings' maximizing reproductive fitness through behaviors that exploit this capacity to generate, comprehend, and be impressed by symbolic constructs.

The Evolution of Biochemical Mechanisms

It was during the long eons of evolution that the specific physiological processes which underpin psychological and emotional mechanisms for sexual arousal and sexual gratification were selected because of their adaptive significance in reproduction. These arousal and gratification mechanisms functioned as behavioral reinforcers in sexually reproducing organisms with developing central nervous systems.

It is extremely likely that some of the adaptive psychophysiological mechanisms which would underlie later, more complex emotional attachments and experiences found in social mammals—specifically the primates—were

1. The ability to experience intense emotional attachment to a member of the opposite sex for the purpose of mating, which functions to establish and maintain social ties between non-related conspecifics;
2. The ability to experience intense sexual pleasure (ecstasy), which functioned as an operant reinforcer for completing the coital act (for a discussion of operant behavior in an ecological context see Jochim 1981, 22-31); and
3. The pleasures associated with parent/offspring bonding, which functioned as an adaptive mechanism assuring inclusive fitness.

In the evolution of mammals, natural selection operated upon specific genes, which produced the mammalian brain's capacity to experience the aforementioned pleasures. This was accomplished through a cybernetic physiological process whereby the production of hormones, neurotransmitters, and their amino-acid precursors had the effect of directing, altering, or intensifying the mental and emotional states of the organism. This biochemical feedback was accomplished by mechanical or chemical sexual stimuli triggering the production and massing of neurohormones at "nodal points" in the mammalian brain's limbic centers. The subsequent effects that were experienced by the mammalian individual as pleasurable functioned as behavioral reinforcers that facilitated adaptive reproductive and social behaviors such as sex and socializing.

The external stimuli for achieving these psychophysiological pleasure responses associated with mammalian sex and reproduction were, and still are, primarily either mechanical—sights, sounds, touch, taste—or chemical—smell (pheronomes). However, the internal process occurring in the brain of the organism is always biochemical.

In this context, then, it is questionable whether most mammals can subjectively, or psychologically, generate sexual arousal—i. e., just by thinking about it. It is reasonably apparent that most mammals require an external stimulus of a mechanical or chemical nature. Human beings, on the other hand, can and do arouse themselves through the means of internally generated stimuli. The implications for this evolutionary phenomenon, and the role it has played in human beings' manipulation of symbolic constructs, will become more apparent further below.

Evolution built upon the structural and functional foundation of biochemically based sexual arousal, attachment, and pleasure to produce a unique consequence in one family of the primates—the hominids. It was within the family Hominidae that natural selection and mutation were to create the mental capacity to subjectively perceive, conceptualize, and communicate psychological and emotional states through symbolic means. What was originally a physiological process with its origin in a reproductive adaptation later became one of the major contributing factors in complex human emotions.

This evolutionary event, or series of events, occurred during the "human environments of evolutionary adaptedness (EEA)" (Tooby and Cosmides 1989; Symons 1991), or the Pleistocene. It was then that the occurrence of hormonally based psycho-emotional mechanisms, a facultative phenotype with the psychological capacity to be subjectively aware of them, and the subsequent development of the psychophysiological and morphological mechanisms for complete communication had the effect of superseding straightforward genetic information transference.

Sometime during the Pleistocene, probably coinciding with the genus *Homo*, the symbolic conveyance of externally generated somatic perceptions of the environment combined with the communication of internally generated psychological and emotional experiences to produce the beginnings of that unique behavioral and social process that would come to be known as "culture." The formulation and symbolic representation of internally and externally generated mental states, i. e., concepts and percepts, would thereby function to enhance, and in some instances alter, what were heretofore biologically determined social relationships and social identities.

Later on, during the Upper Pleistocene and coinciding with the rise of the species *Homo sapiens*, shamans and shamanism in all likelihood represented the first concerted effort by individuals to systematically organize symbols in an extrasomatic manner for purposes other than specific subsistence or reproduction. The two primary reasons for this were the aforementioned need to communicate to kin and affines complex environmental information displaced in time and place, and also the uniquely hominid need to convey the subjective conceptualizations of psycho emotional experiences such as psychological fantasies, pleasures and pains; affective attachments to others; awe of the unknown; and aesthetic emotions.

One of the fundamental vehicles for such communication would have been mythic poems enacted in ritualized theatrical dramas, with items of representational art as accessories and backdrops. It is likely that these distinctly hominid behaviors were a complex modification of ancestral behaviors with a functional design—i. e., calls, signs, ritualizations, and displays. Such behaviors have evolved in numerous animal species, but among hominids they were to take on a qualitative difference of exponential proportions.

In the situation one finds among contemporary hunters and gatherers, who live in band- and tribal-level societies, the generalist shaman is the primary communicator of fantasy, ecstasy, and awe. Today in many complex societies this artistic/ritual role has been usurped by creative specialists such as actors, writers, painters, dancers, sculptors, priests, comedians, and numerous others. But it was sometime back in our ancestral past, during the

Pleistocene, that shamans became the masters of experiencing and communicating ecstasy, fantasy, aesthetic appreciation, and awe.

The archaeological record contains numerous items that have been interpreted as shamanic accouterments (see Dickson 1990). Along with these data the crosscultural ethnographic record reveals the universals of shamanic behavior—e. g., ecstatic trances or altered states of consciousness, heroic sagas, ritual drug use, a multitiered universe, the elevation of altruism to a moral standard, an Axis Mundi, a sacred/profane dichotomy, sacred marriages, soul flights and soul loss, and anthropomorphic/theriomorphic shape-changing (see Eliade 1964; Harner 1980; Halifax 1982; Kalweit 1988; Walsh 1990). Crosscultural ethnographic data concerning shamanism reveal the universal human tendency to construct complex cosmologies—i. e., conceptualizations about the nature of the universe.

By combining the archaeological data with the ethnographic data, one can see that the complex cosmologies of shamanism represent a universe that is accessed internally by entering a shamanic trance, perhaps more appropriately referred to as an altered state of consciousness. Like internally generated sexual fantasies, shamanic fantasies, if you will, are a unique feature of the human psyche. In fact, both Roger Walsh, a professor of psychiatry, and Richard Noll, a psychologist, have argued that "shamans are 'fantasy prone' personalities who are able to organize and learn from their intense images in ways that are both personally and socially beneficial. They may be particularly adept at creating and recognizing images" (Walsh 1990, 119).

When one looks at the intense emotional and psychological experiences of shamanic ecstasy, and the altered states of consciousness which characterize shamanism in the ethnographic literature, one frequently encounters mythic, poetic, and artistic metaphors that are sexual in nature used to describe these experiences. Upon further examination of the crosscultural ethnographic data, though, one finds that the vehicles frequently used by shamans for inducing ecstasy and altered states of consciousness are only occasionally sexual.

More often, the means to achieving the shaman's trance are either mechanical—as sonic driving through means of drumming or chanting, the manipulation of patterns of light for optic stimulation, pain induction, fasting, and/or sensory deprivation—or induced by the ingestion of plants, fungi, or animal byproducts that contain biochemical toxins. In both instances there is a biochemical effect that has the desired result of inducing an altered state of consciousness. In the one instance mechanical means stimulate the internal production of the biochemicals by the endocrine and central nervous systems of the shaman; and in the other there is the ingestion of a sacrament, usually a plant or a fungus but sometimes an animal byproduct such as ground-up toad skins or urine, that contains biochemical toxins.

The process is similar to that involved in sexual arousal—i. e., it is either mechanically or chemically induced. The parallels between the ecstatic pleasures of the two experiences were not lost on shamans. In fact, shamanic trances have often been viewed by humans as necessary for their own fertility as well as the fecundity of their economic resources (Eliade 1946, 79-81, 198-199, 503). Further, these intense psychological and emotional states—i. e., shamanic trances and sexual arousal—often subjectively expressed as profound emotional experiences with an aesthetic and poetic component in them, are always the result of an evolved physiological process that has similar biochemicals at its core.

What is unique about the human animal, though, is its ability to psychologically stimulate the production of these biochemicals—i. e., hormones, neurohormones, and neurotransmitters—through fantasy and thereby induce sexual arousal or a shamanic trance. The ability to manipulate fantasies for the purposes of pleasure is a distinctly human characteristic, and it may be one of the hallmark conditions necessary for the development of extrasomatic systems of symbolic representation and communication.

The biochemical toxins which are the active ingredients in most shamanic sacraments are of the indole alkaloid and phenylethylamine types—i. e., hallucinogenic drugs. These biochemical compounds have molecular structures that are nearly identical to those functional neurohormones which are utilized during sexual arousal and activity, as well as for a whole range of psychophysiological functions. In fact, when ingested, these biochemicals of the indole alkaloid and phenylethylamine types mass at the same receptor clusters, known as "nodal points," as do neurohormones associated with sexual activity and found in the brain's limbic system (see Jacobs 1987). The limbic system is oftentimes referred to as the brain's "pleasure center."

In this light it is very interesting that neurophysiologists have identified the biochemical responsible for feelings of "being in love" as phenylethylamine. People who are passionately in love secrete this chemical, which produces an "amphetamine-like high" (Gazzaniga 1988, 176). Chocolate contains large amounts of phenylethylamine. Isn't it appropriate that people frequently give chocolate to their prospective lovers?

Another example of a biochemical in the phenylethylamine class is mescaline, a hallucinogen found in the peyote cactus. The Huichol Indians of central Mexico annually make a three hundred-mile sacred trek to the mountains in the high desert, where they enter the mystical land of Wirikuta, home of Grandfather Deer/Peyote. The shaman and the peyote pilgrims hunt for peyote and deer, ingest them in their most sacred ritual, and harvest enough for the following year. The ethnographic literature reports that a strong sense of unity and affection is experienced by the pilgrims while in Wirikuta—in fact, this place is their mythic paradise, and one must be ritually clean to enter it.

On the way to Wirikuta the people stop to conduct a ritual in which they publicly confess their sins and the shaman ties knots in a cord to symbolically represent these sins. The only sins the Huichol recognize are those of sexual infidelity. While the sin is confessed, the person who has been affronted, and the person who participated with the sinner are usually present. It is said that no one holds back, because Grandfather Peyote would see and would be offended if anyone tried to take the peyote without being cleansed by confession. The knotted cord representing sins is then thrown into the fire, cleansing the sinner. Public confession and cleansing of illicit sexual ecstasy before one may enter into shamanic or religious ecstasy is an interesting phenomenon that is nearly universal. It may reveal something of the syncretic process that was at work in the EEA, where biochemical sacraments and their ecstatic states became public replacements for private sexual ecstasy.

Such a situation may have occurred because the biochemical compounds utilized by shamans to enter ecstatic trances fall into the two distinct classes of alkaloids mentioned earlier: tryptamine, or indole alkaloid, and phenylethylamine. These alkaloids are powerful hallucinogens that occur in very few structural types but are frequent throughout the plant, animal, and fungal kingdoms. What is even more interesting is the fact that they have a necessary and complex function in the brains of all warm-blooded animals (Schultes and Hofmann 1980, 25).

Hominid brains, like those of other mammals, evolved the capacity to utilize these same biochemical compounds for reproductive/psychophysiological functions. In fact Albert Hofmann has said, "The structural similarity between the most important hallucinogenic compounds of plant origin and neurohumors which play an essential role in the biochemistry of psychic functions is probably not accidental" (Schultes and Hofmann 1980, 27).

Tryptophan is the amino acid precursor for 5-hydroxytryptamine, or seratonin. Seratonin is the primary neurotransmitter that is enabling you to think about what you are reading right now. Seratonin is also found in elevated levels in the bloodstreams of sexually dominant primates (See Mcguire and Raleigh 1985, 1987). It is extremely interesting that most of the biochemical hallucinogens employed by shamans are seratonin-specific (see Jacobs 1987). For example, the "ebene" used by the Yanomano Indians of southern Venezuela contains as its active ingredient dimethyltryptamine (DMT), as do most of the hallucinogens employed by Indians in South America (Chagnon 1983, Schultes and Hofmann 1979, 1980).

These biochemical compounds, when they occur in the brains of warm-blooded animals, function as what Francis O. Schmitt calls "informational substances." They are produced by the endocrine system, and like all proteins they fold into three-dimensional shapes. They "plug into" receptors in the brain and on monocytic and macrophagic cells that act as messenger cells between the central nervous system and the lymphatic (immune) system, thus connecting three systems, endocrine, central nervous, and lymphatic, as one cybernetic system whose evolved function is to combat microscopic disease vectors.

Some researchers believe that these informational substances "may assemble into the intercellular equivalent of the genetic code and influence medicine in the 21st century the way that research on DNA has influenced

20th-century biology" (Hall 1989, 64). According to Candice Pert, "evolution has plucked certain serviceable molecules and used them again and again—not just in humans but all living creatures—to do what they do well. And what these molecules do well is regulate, modulate, and convey information" (Hall 1989, 68).[1]

Using radioactively tagged molecules, Pert and her associates have found that informational substances mass in dense clusters at "nodal points" in the brain's limbic system, parts of the brain long associated with emotional processes. According to Pert, "Nodal points mark junctions where information molecules commingle and influence behavior" (Hall 1989). Pert says, "Emotions are so important in regulating behavior, and regulating survival, that the very first successful evolution in that direction would be preserved. It would tend to be used over and over again. After all, the great pleasures of life—eating and sex—are both necessary for survival" (Hall 1989, 68).

When these biochemical compounds occur in plants and fungi, as well as in some animals, they are often there because they evolved as biochemical "barbs" in species lacking physical barbs (see Siegel 1989). These toxic barbs exist in many species to protect the organism from predation (Siegel 1989), but occasionally they function in exactly the opposite manner, where another species coevolves with them. Often coevolved species will have high tolerance levels for the endogenous toxins in the host species, thereby being able to use the toxic organism for a food source and gain an adaptive edge (Siegel 1989).

Similarly, hominids utilizing a foraging subsistence strategy that was omnivorous would have encountered high frequencies of exposure to biochemical toxins. It would certainly have been adaptive for hominids to have had tolerance levels that allowed them to forage on these food sources in times of scarcity. And how powerful would the operant conditioning have been for the ingestion by the hosts of these biochemicals if when ingested they stimulated intense pleasure responses, responses similar to sexual ecstasy?

We now know that these biochemicals do just that for humans and that humans universally express such experiences in sexual metaphors (Grof 1985, 221-31; Walsh 1990, 60-69; Reichel-Dolmotoff 1971, 1987). In fact, an historical example of this syncretism is to be found in the practices of witches in medieval Europe. These women were midwives and herbalists who made ointments out of "deadly nightshade (*Atropa belladonna*), henbane (*Hyoscyamus niger*), thorn-apple or jimson weed (*Datura stramonium*), and mandrake (*Mandragora officinarum*); sometimes animal ingredients were added, such as toad or salamander skin" (Grof 1985, 224). In preparation for their altered states of consciousness, these witches would smear the ointment on broomstick handles, insert the handles into their vaginas, where it would be topically absorbed, and "ride the broom into ecstasy" (see Harner 1973). This was done because the biochemicals in the herbs they were using were potentially deadly unless topically administered. There were two reasons for placing the ointment in the vagina: one, it was absorbed much more rapidly and thus one was in a state of ecstasy much sooner; and two, there was an obvious analogy between this act and sexual orgasm. The ritual was the embodiment of sympathetic magic, the symbolic association between similar objects or actions. No wonder an organization of celibate males and females condemned such witches to the stake.

We also know that these substances were, and are, frequently ingested in association with creative symbolic and ritual endeavors. In fact it may be the case that the very first expressions of representational art—the Paleolithic paintings in the caves in the Franco-Cantabrian region of southwestern Europe—were produced by artist-shamans who were in an altered state of consciousness induced by ingesting hallucinogenic plants and fungi (see Lewis-Williams and Dowson 1988; Dickson 1990, 129-37). What is remarkable is the plethora of sexual symbols found in these caves and in the artifacts found in association with them (Dickson 1990). These paintings are considered to represent a time when hominids first began to express that which really makes us human: culture.[2]

Adhering to Symons' warning at the beginning of this chapter, it is doubtful that humans evolved to be creative symbolic-users or shamanic trancers. Nor is it likely that either of these complexes of behaviors were selected for as generalized strategies for maximizing reproductive fitness. It is much more likely that these behaviors were byproducts of several specific adaptations. The initial function of these specific adaptations was in all likelihood the physiological demands and mechanisms for sexual attraction, arousal, and gratification. The fact that these psychophysiological mechanisms facilitated tolerances for potentially deleterious biochemical toxins was an additional advantageous adaptation.

It is an entirely plausible hypothesis that the exposure of hominids to mutagenic biochemical compounds in foods played a role in the evolutionary expansion of the neocortex. This would have occurred sometime during the Pleistocene. With hominid social structure organized around females who were practicing nomadic subsistence strategies, there would have been a high likelihood that individuals in these foraging bands would have experimented with plant and fungal species containing biochemical toxins. In the "boom and bust" cycles of ecosystems, such toxin-bearing foods may have been emergency foods in times of scarcity. Those individuals who could ingest the toxins with a tolerance level that allowed them to survive and reproduce would have enjoyed a selective advantage. Pregnant females in the first trimester would have either been forced to eat these toxic foods or chosen to do so because of the behavioral reinforcer of ecstatic pleasure. A random genetic mutation thereby could have been established. If such a mutation were established—i. e., one that increased the number and organization of neurons such that when toxins were ingested and amassed in the brain they did not flood it and overwhelm its basic survival functions —larger-brained individuals would have had a distinct adaptive edge. Females who were adept at conveying to their offspring resource identification and the conceptual experiences resultant from toxic ingestion would have had an adaptive edge that would certainly be somatic, and probably reproductive. Perceptual information about how to identify the host species for these toxins would have been combined with conceptual information about the subjective effects of such toxins in an informational matrix.

Similar scenarios have occurred in evolution. For example, chimpanzees, gibbons, and baboons systematically identify plants with toxins in them and use them to medicate or to intoxicate themselves. In the case of chimpanzees, the young apes learn from their mothers which plants to use, and likely when to use them (Siegel 1989, 90-92). Opium beetles and weevils, tobacco hawkmoths, and koalas are another small sample of animals that have coevolved with plant hosts that contain powerful toxins.[3]

When primates, and especially humans, ingest certain biochemicals they have hallucinations. In humans these hallucinations run the gamut from visual geometric patterns, swirls, whorls, colors, and auditory hallucinations to "seeing" theriomorphic and anthropomorphic figures (Lewis-Williams and Dowson 1988). These biochemically generated symbols—i. e., conceptualizations—appear as perceptions to the subject. Hallucinogenic compounds also can significantly alter the way somatic perceptions process information, often heightening the senses in human subjects (Siegel 1989, 60-73). Could it be that the symbolizing behavior that typifies humans is simply the by-product of a preadaptation to hallucinogenic biochemical toxins naturally occurring in the ambient environment and diets of early humans? People have historically, and most likely prehistorically, used powerful biochemicals which produce pronounced hallucinations of a symbolic nature. Is this of evolutionary significance for the human ability to generate abstract symbols?

The fact that larger, more complex brains imparted a selective advantage because of their ability to process greater amounts of information in new and innovative ways may not be precisely why they were selected. Their greater size and complexity may have simply evolved as an adaptation which facilitated the maintenance of survival functions in the face of toxin absorption. The fact that hallucinogenic toxins generate symbolic experiences may have been significant in the natural selection of manipulators of sexual ecstasy and fantasy.

An added feature contributing to the potential viability of this hypothesis is based upon the fact that the ingestion of these compounds radically alters the emotional and psychological state of the user by stimulating hallucinations of a highly metaphoric nature. Individuals who became expert at internally generating and manipulating fantasies may have enjoyed greater reproductive success. If they were able to show their conspecifics how to experience ecstasy though food as well as through sex it is easy to see how this would have been viewed as magical and profound. In fact, one of the main ways primates court mates is by grooming, sharing foods, and playing—in other words, imparting pleasure to the individual who is the object of the romantic intentions.

According to Walsh and Noll it was, and is, the case that shamans are adept fantasy manipulators (Noll 1985, Walsh 1990), and hominids enjoy fantasy. These same shamans reap status which can translate as productive and reproductive rewards for their shamanizing—i. e., their manipulation of fantasies and conspecifics confers benefits (Noll 1985, Walsh 1990, Lee 1984, Chagnon 1983, Eliade 1964, Halifax 1982).

The crosscultural data strongly attest to the fact that hunting and gathering peoples frequently engage in their most creative endeavors while in altered states of consciousness, either mechanically or biochemically induced. Much indigenous art represents visions obtained while in this state of consciousness. In fact, there is not a major artistic or religious institution that can claim its ultimate origins did not originate with someone who had a "vision."

People's ability to appreciate artistic creations—i. e., to experience aesthetic emotions—is based upon a physiological process involving biochemicals in their brains. After all what is an aesthetic emotion? It is likely the manipulation of a neurochemical that originally evolved to serve reproductive functions. It is probably a neurochemical high, like that of phenylethylamine, similar to "being in love."

Conclusion

The similarity between psychological and emotional states experienced during sexual arousal and orgasm, pair bonding, and parent/offspring bonding and those states experienced during shamanic trances facilitated by the ingestion of biochemical sacraments of an hallucinogenic nature may be, until fairly recently, one of the most overlooked phenomena in evolutionary biology, evolutionary ecology, Darwinian psychology, and Darwinian anthropology.

It is also interesting to note how similar an aesthetic emotion is to all other emotions, including those induced by ingesting a biochemical hallucinogen. The similarity between aesthetic emotions and other emotions is the reason why philosophers of art constantly engage in metaphor and simile to describe aesthetic experiences. The inability to pinpoint the experience is one of the classic laments of the philosophy of art.

Perhaps a Darwinian perspective will reveal that aesthetic emotions are so difficult to convey through language, because they are the by-product of other adaptations. A good analogy might be to try to describe exactly how you feel when you have a sexual orgasm. Like an aesthetic feeling, it is very hard to describe, but you know when you have had one.

The Darwinian scholar should at this point be asking several pertinent questions: Are creative endeavors that employ symbolizing behaviors representative of a set of psychological algorithms designed by natural selection for the purpose of maximizing reproductive fitness (as many Darwinian social scientists might contend)? Or are they simply psychological by-products of a preadaptation—i. e., something which was selected for in psychophysiological structures and functions that had nothing to do initially with the generation of symbols to represent and communicate concepts and percepts to kin and affines? Was the preadaptation sexual, biochemical, or both? Is it possible that the expanded neocortex, the basis of symbolizing behaviors, is an adaptation to naturally occurring biochemical toxins found in plants, fungi, and animals? Could such mutagenic compounds have played a selective role in the evolution of the hominid neocortex due to their ability to mimic neurohormones whose functional role was to induce states of psychological and emotional arousal selected for as a sexual adaptation? Whatever the evolutionary origins of our minds and their associated symbolic constructs, one should expect that we will continue to manipulate one another through fantasy and sexual ecstasy. And perhaps somewhere within this mystery lies the evolutionary answer to the art of being human.

Works Cited

Chagnon, Napoleon A.

1983 *Yanomano: The Fierce People*. New York: Holt, Rinehart and Winston.

Daly, Martin, and Margo Wilson,

1983 *Sex, Evolution and Behavior*. Belmont, CA: Wadworth.

1988 *Homicide*. New York: Aldine de Gruyter.

Dickson, D. Bruce

1990 *The Dawn of Belief: Religion in the Upper Paleolithic of Southwestern Europe*. Tucson: University of Arizona Press.

Eliade, Mircea

1964 *Shamanism: Archaic Techniques of Ecstasy*. New York: Pantheon.

Gazzaniga, Michael

1988 *Mind Matters: How Mind and Brain Interact to Create Our Consciousness*. Boston: Houghton Mifflin.

Grof, Stanislav

1985 *Beyond the Brain: Birth, Death and Transcendence in Psychotherapy*. Albany: State University of New York Press.

Halifax, Joan

1982 *Shaman: The Wounded Healer*. New York: Crossroad.

Hall, Stephen S.

1989 "A Molecular Code Links Emotions, Mind and Health." *Smithsonian* (June):62-71.

Harner, Michael

1980 *The Way of the Shaman: A Guide to Power and Healing*. New York: Harper and Row.

Jacobs, Barry

1987 "How Hallucinogenic Drugs Work." *American Scientist* 75:386-92.

Jochim, Michael A.

1981 *Strategies for Survival: Cultural Behavior in an Ecological Context*. New York: Academic Press.

Kalweit, Holger

1988 *Dreamtime and Inner Space: The World of the Shaman*. Boston: Shambhala.

Lee, Richard Borshay

1984 *The Dobe !Kung*. New York: Holt, Rinehart and Winston.

Lewis-Williams, J. D., and T. A. Dowson

1988 "The Signs of All Times: Entopic Phenomena in Upper Paleolithic Art." *Current Anthropology* 29 (2):201-45.

1979 *Plants of the Gods: Origins of Hallucinogenic Use*. New York: Alfred van der Marck Editions.

1980 *The Botany and Chemistry of Hallucinogens*. Springfield, IL: Chas. C. Thomas.

McGuire, M. T., and M. J. Raleigh

1985 "Serotonin-Behavior Interactions in Vervet Monkeys." *Psychopharmacology Bulletin* 21:458-63.

1987 "Serotonin, Behavior, and Aggression in Vervet Monkeys." In B. Oliver, J. Mos, and P. F. Brain, eds., *Ethnopharmacology of Agonistic Behavior in Animals and Humans*. Dornecht: Martinus Nijhoff.

Noll, R.

1985 "Mental Imagery Cultivation as a Cultural Phenomenon." *Current Anthropology* 26:443-51.

Siegel, Ronald K.

1989 *Intoxication: Life in Pursuit of Artificial Paradise*. New York: E. F. Dutton.

Symons, Donald

1979 *The Evolution of Human Sexuality*. Oxford: Oxford University Press.

1987 "If We're All Darwinians, What's the Fuss About?" In Crawford, Smith, and Crebs, eds., *Sociobiology and Psychology: Ideas, Issues, and Applications*. Hillsdale, NJ: Lawrence Erlbam Associates.

1989 "A Critique of Darwinian Anthropology." *Ethology and Sociobiology* 10:131-44.

1991 "On the Use and Misuse of Darwinism in the Study of Human Behavior." In John Tooby, Leda Cosmides, and J. H. Barkow, eds., *The Adapted Mind*. Oxford: Oxford University Press.

Tooby, John, and Leda Cosmides

1989a "Evolutionary Psychology and the Generation of Culture, Part I: Theoretical Considerations." *Ethology and Sociobiology* 10:29-49.

1989b "Evolutionary Psychology and the Generation of Culture, Part II: Case Study: A Computational Theory of Social Exchange." *Ethology and Sociobiology* 10:51-97.

Walsh, R. N.

1990 *The Spirit of Shamanism*. Los Angeles: Jeremy P. Tarcher.

Williams, George

1966 *Adaptation and Natural Selection: A Critique of Some Current Evolutionary Thought*. Princeton: Princeton University Press.

Notes

1. Candice Pert, of Johns Hopkins Medical School was the co-discoverer of the brain's opiate receptors in 1973, the first endogenous opiate in 1975, and since then has found about 50 peptide molecules in the brain which are formed by complex chains of amino acids. She is a leading researcher in a new branch of medicine known as "psychoneuroimmunology." This field has arisen as a response to the AIDS crisis, among other things.
2. For more information on the role of biochemical hallucinogens in cultural development, see Wasson 1969; Wasson et al. 1977; Weil 1986; Furst 1972, 1976, 1986; Metzner 1988; Schultes and Hofmann 1979, 1980; Szasz 1985; Siegel 1989.
3. For a more thorough review see Siegel 1989.

Sexual Property in Pushkin's "The Snowstorm": A Darwinist Perspective

Brett Cooke

By applying genetic theory to behavior, evolutionary psychology provides a rational underlying structure for the emotion-laden phenomena which motivate the writing and consumption of most of our best literature. This structure must in some fashion be or have been sufficiently adaptive at some time in our evolutionary history to motivate art works. By the same token, it does not have to accord with present-day values. The emotional responses elicited by an art work may have been shaped in an earlier and very different environment which required correspondingly different attitudes and behaviors. Without some awareness of such a diachronic perspective, we are likely to lose sight of this distinction, especially when enjoying a work of art. For when the curtain is drawn, other cognitive functions besides disbelief may be suspended as we experience a fictional narrative. Often, objective analysis is able to discern gaps and inconsistencies in a plot that do not disturb subjectively involved viewers. More seriously, scholars are frequently able to expose latent meanings in artworks which in contemporary society would be recognized as immoral. Indeed, the affective qualities of a narrative may persuade us to accept ideologies which, in the cold light of reason, we would normally oppose. As a result, art has the potential to condition us in a surreptitious and all the more pernicious manner. These processes are more likely to come into play when we have a hot-blooded theme like sex as the subject of the plot.

A case in point is Alexander Pushkin's (1799-1837) treatment of the various aspects of sexual property, the tacit control of and exclusive rights to the sexuality of another person, in "The Snowstorm," the second of his *Tales of Belkin*. This concept had great meaning for him. Not only did it powerfully influence his narrative works, it played a significant role in his life. Indeed, Russia's greatest poet died fighting to defend his claim that his wife was his sexual property. Of course, his fatal challenge to Georges D'Anthes-Heckeren came as the culmination of a number of factors which were increasing pressure on the beleaguered poet during the mid-1830s.

Nevertheless, the final straw that moved Pushkin to act so dramatically as to fire a shot at his wife's purported lover was neither these pressures, nor his wife's careless behavior, nor D'Anthes' unremitting pursuit, but rumors of cuckoldry. Pushkin regarded the protection of his honor as a husband—i.e., the appearance of his possessing sole sexual access to his wife, no matter what the actual condition of their marriage—to be an issue worth facing death for. We cannot justify the challenge on a rational cost/benefit basis, but, quite obviously, this was not the manner of Pushkin's thinking during the winter of 1836-37. Consider the best possible outcome, that the poet might kill D'Anthes and, no doubt, suffer some form of punishment. We already know the worst possible outcome, but to him death also might have been preferable to cuckoldry. Viewed in an objective light, Pushkin's violent intentions and irrational action are hard to reconcile with our affection for his works and for the poet himself. However, this same irrational quality invites biopoetic inquiry.

A modern person also recoils from the sexism implicit in Pushkin's challenge. His threat to D'Anthes is tantamount to a claim that his wife is his property, that she may not give her heart to another without risking her lover's death. Moreover, the husband's duty to protect his family's honor suffices to release him from his normal responsibilities of providing resources and security for his wife and their children. Pushkin risked and lost these necessities by dueling with D'Anthes.

True, this was the common practice for gentlemen in his social context, where few could live with the dishonor of cuckoldry. Yet Pushkin's behavior was not characteristic of only a specific society: men strive to avoid cuckoldry and to limit the sexuality of their women in virtually all social groups. The means of coercion may vary, but they commonly involve either violence or the threat of violence, whether against the woman or her lover. In some cases, adultery by the wife is punishable by law, while other laws frequently make allowances for violence committed by the "wronged" husband. British law in Pushkin's time considered the husband's murder of an unfaithful wife and/or her lover, if witnessed in flagrante delicto, to be manslaughter of only the lowest degree, because "there could not be a greater provocation."[1] Of course, one could easily think of greater provocations, if one took the trouble. Meanwhile, the obverse is largely ignored; few husbands are legally punished or suffer violence as a result of their infidelity, unless it is at the hands of another husband. Consider the following possibility: What if one of the various rumors proved true that Pushkin had himself been involved in some extramarital affairs, and his wife had heard about them? Would her society or any society, including ours, have expected her to try to kill her rival?[2] Very few women commit murder for reasons of their husband's infidelity, despite the much greater incidence of adultery by husbands. Nowhere is the lot of a cheated wife considered to be nearly as pitiable and ridiculous as that of a cuckold. Notably, there is no suitable female equivalent for "cuckold" in the major European languages (Rancour-Laferriere 1985, 94-95).[3]

To the extent that Pushkin was aware of traditional notions of sexual property, he, no doubt, regarded them as natural. In a number of his writings he extended a husband's exclusive possession of his wife to beyond the grave. This astonishing claim was first isolated by Anna Akhmatova in her study of *The Stone Guest*. She related the play's major plot elements, the return of a dead husband in the form of a statue to punish his wife's lover, to a letter which Pushkin wrote to his future mother-in-law on April 5, 1830, wherein the poet contemplated his possible early death:

> God is my witness that I am ready to die for her, but to die so as to leave her as a brilliant widow, free on the next day to choose a new husband for herself, this thought for me is hell. (14:76)[4]

Written on the eve of Pushkin's formal proposal to Natal'ya Goncharova, this passage amounts to a claim of sexual possession of his wife-to-be, one he apparently wished to maintain after his death. These were not fleeting sentiments, for Akhmatova found similar passages in his works. Pushkin titled his treatment of the Don Juan legend *The Stone Guest* and recast the title figure as Dona Anna's husband, not father, so that the statue's killing of "Don Guan" would enforce the dictum that, "A widow must remain faithful even to the grave" (7:164). More of the same is found in Eugene Onegin. There the narrator ironically notes how Lensky's "jealous shade" fails to respond when the poet's erstwhile fiancée, Ol'ga, "not faithful to her grief," marries an uhlan only shortly after he dies fighting a duel over her

(6:422, 142). Tat'yana culminates her refusal to abandon her husband for Onegin with the famous statement, "I always will be faithful to him" (6:188). Akhmatova found an even more striking example of posthumous fidelity in *Boris Godunov*, where Kseniya grieves for her dead fiancé and promises "I will be faithful to him, even in death"—a remarkable sentiment, considering Kseniya had never met her intended (7:42; Akhmatova 1977, 107-8).

Pushkin's contemplation of his impending marriage apparently prompted him to make yet another statement on what he regarded as a man's enduring exclusive possession of "his" woman. "The Snowstorm" also raises the theme of the faithful widow. It was composed during the fruitful autumn he spent in Boldino (1830) prior to his marriage, i.e., at about the same time as he wrote *The Stone Guest* and the last chapter of *Eugene Onegin*. Late in the story Mar'ya Gavrilovna impresses her neighbors with what they take to be her steadfast love for her deceased beau, Vladimir; they regard her as a "virginal Artemiza" (8:83). According to the context, one imagines that they have in mind Artemisia, the faithful widow who built one of the "Seven Wonders of the World" in memory of her husband, Mausoleus, king of Halicarnassus, in the fourth century B.C. However, Artemisa is also the name of Apollo's twin sister, a powerful and promiscuous goddess hostile to monogamy (Graves 1969, 1:225). This double entendre suits Pushkin's dramatic irony, for both Mar'ya Gavrilovna and the narrator withhold the information that she already was unwittingly married to Burmin, a total stranger who took her intended's place at their secret wedding. She may honor Vladimir's memory, but her chastity could be also motivated by her sense of duty to her unknown and possibly still living husband; despite the death of Vladimir, she is not a widow. Yet Pushkin insistently places the notion of the faithful/faithless widow in the reader's mind. Another reference to widow's fidelity consists of the epigraph taken from Zhukovsky's "Svetlana," an adaptation of Burger's "Leonore," which relates how a ghost returns from death in a distant battle to take his faithful fiancée to her death. Furthermore, on the eve of her elopement, Mar'ya Gavrilovna dreams of Vladimir being fatally wounded on the battlefield; he implores her to marry him before he dies. As various commentators have noted, these passages create false expectations of a plot in the manner of the Gothic ballad. Though her fiancé dies of his wounds sometime after the Battle of Borodino, no specter returns to haunt Mar'ya Gavrilovna, and the story ends with her happy marriage to another man (Bethea and Davydov 1981, Debreczeny 1983, Lednicki 1956).

Pushkin, then, builds his plot on false expectations, which are readily evoked in the reader's mind. To understand the effectiveness of this device one needs to consider Pushkin's folk materials. Although the likely sources for this motif were Zhukovsky's and Burger's ballads, as well as Washington Irving's ironic treatment of the same tradition in "The Specter Bridegroom," ghost husbands/fiancés bedevil widows, faithful and unfaithful, in many societies (Berkovsky 1962).[5] This theme is not only popular, it inspires belief, as we can see in the widespread traditions of ghost attacks on widows as well as in the many ritual behaviors intended either to drive away the hostile revenant or to keep the widow from remarrying. In all cases, the central issue is the limitation of a widow's sexuality. Although neither Zhukovsky's Svetlana or Burger's Leonore consider any other man for a husband, many folktales on the same theme involve the rivalry of spirit and second husband/fiancé over the living woman. In *The Fear of the Dead in Primitive Religion*, J. G. Frazer notes that "the ghosts of dead husbands and wives are commonly deemed very dangerous to their surviving spouses .... especially when the surviving partner has taken himself or herself a second wife or husband, for the ghost is *naturally* jealous of the second wife or husband" (1977, 199; emphasis added). He traces a great number of these beliefs amongst primitive and not-so-primitive peoples in New Guinea, the Philippines, Oceania, Africa, India, Asia, Siberia, Australia, and North America.[6]

A cursory review of these traditions readily shows that widows generally are much more exposed to forms of constraint than widowers. The protocols taken to limit their sexuality are often extreme, as in the case of suttee, wherein the husband's family will persuade or coerce the widow of a rich man to join him on the funeral pyre. Suttee was apparently practiced by the Mycenaeans; Robert Graves described the early Hellenic rite as a "patriarchal practice... which grew from the Indo-European custom which forbade widows to remarry," adding that it was "customary for women to commit suicide on the death of their husbands" (1969, 1:225, 245). Similar rituals are reported in a number of early accounts of the pre-Christian Slavs.[7]

Helena Znaniecka Lopata noted that in India suttee was not expected of pregnant women, of wives past their child-bearing years, or of women among the lower classes. Instead, their communities would forbid their remarriage, shave their heads, and force them to live a secluded, sheltered life. Mourning dress would further stigmatize them and put them beyond the pale of eligible men by making them unattractive. Most traditional societies prescribe harsher degrees of mourning appearance and behavior for women than for men. In some New Guinea societies a widow must confine herself to home and spread feces over her body (Berndt 1966). Irrespective of announced justifications, anthropologists understand suttee as a means of averting "the possible birth of offspring who could not be filiated with the [husband's] family line" (Lopata 1979, 14).[8] Similar considerations have been applied to social codes of female virginity and marital chastity, i.e., the sexual "double standard," whereby men enjoy significantly greater sexual freedom than women. Where remarriage is permitted, many traditional societies recognize various forms of ghost-marriage, wherein a member of the husband's family, usually his brother, will provide for the widow, both economically and sexually. The ghost-husband will be recognized as the father of all her children. In other societies, given the common preference for virgins, it is relatively more difficult for a widow to find another husband.

Gathering folklore in the eastern highlands of New Guinea, Catherine H. Berndt recorded a number of Kamano spoken narratives—*kinehera*—which describe the return of dead husbands to attack widows and their new husbands, all part of a tradition of ghosts who try to drag their living spouses, husbands as well as wives, with them. In one *kinehera*, "Girl Accompanies Ghost Husband to the Land of the Dead," a dead husband takes his young wife outside the tribe's area to a dark house, where, in a ghoulish scene, he forces her to eat disgusting things and then impregnates her. Here, as elsewhere, the story illustrates what is accepted to be true; such narratives are typically accompanied by a variety of ritual behaviors intended to ensure the constraint of female sexuality. For example, the Kamano believe that ghosts are likely to attack their surviving spouses, especially widows. The tribe may encourage a widow to commit suicide or may kill her so that she can "take the same road," that is, accompany her husband in death. The common assumption is that either she cannot endure without him or that the dead husband wants her company on the grounds that their marriage survives his death. One alternative is for a widow to continue her marriage by marrying one of her husband's relatives. After all, his family did pay a bridewealth for her; if she refuses their offer of marriage, they have the right to kill her (Berndt 1966, 248-49).

Similar, though less primitive, patterns of widow constraint may be traced among traditions found in the developed world and probably known to Pushkin. Mourning dress and periods are relaxed; it is easier for a woman to marry a second husband of her choice, although social restraints tend to be greater for her than for a widower, especially if she is a mother. It is common for a widow's children to resist her remarriage. Their fear of step-parents is partly justified by estate problems as well as by cases of child-abuse committed by stepfathers and maternal boyfriends. The same concern is reflected in the common fairy-tale treatment of stepparents.[9]

A number of the ballads Percy collected in the Scottish border region convey this motif of a ghost returning to his wife or fiancée. There is no evidence to indicate Pushkin knew of them, but they may well have served as sources for Burger's "Leonore."[10] In one ballad, "James Harris, the Daemon Lover," a ghost returns to reclaim his former fiancée seven years after his death at sea. Although she had waited for news of his fate for three years, she had finally married and become a mother. Nevertheless, she rides with her specter bridegroom to her doom, and her living husband hangs himself. In some versions, the "daemon lover" shows a cloven hoof; former husbands and lovers may constitute an equivalency class with the devil. The fidelity of the living widow/fiancée crops up in a number of other folk texts. After the murder of her lover in "Clerk Saunders," the heroine announces she will dress as a widow and observe such self-stigmatizing "austerities" as not combing her hair, "for [another] man shall never enjoy me" (Child 1956, 1:161). Her beloved returns to her a year later to lead her off to his grave. Many such narratives conclude with the death of the woman, i.e., with the spirit's "property rights" protected, as happens in "The Suffolk Miracle" and the many other versions of the dead-fiancé narrative which flourished throughout Europe and the Americas.[11]

The popularity of this motif in virtually all areas of the world leads us to look beyond cultural explanations and to ponder a much more ancient and profound derivation, namely, that it is a by-product of human evolution. As an actual belief, the ghost bridegroom tradition works to ensure paternal confidence and the maintenance of the father's genetic investment in his offspring by instilling fear in his widow, thereby constraining her future sexual activity.

The daemon-lover motif is not limited to folklore. Burger's "Leonore" and other similar narratives obviously struck a sympathetic chord throughout Europe. A large number of translations and imitations soon ensued; the motif crops up in works by Coleridge, Mickiewicz, Blake, and Heine; in Kuzmin's "The Trout Breaks through the Ice," Charlotte Bronte's *Wuthering Heights*, Hemingway's *A Farewell to Arms*, Dvořak's oratorio *The Spectre's Bride* (based on Bohemian folk-songs), de Falla's *El amor brujo*, and Kalatozov's classic film, *The Cranes Are Flying*.[12] Pushkin played with the same tradition in "K molodoy vdove" (To a young widow) in 1817, when he assured a young widow that the "cold sleep" of the grave was "undisturbed" and that no "infuriated jealous [husband]" or "envious shade" would haunt her (1:242). In *Eugene Onegin*, the narrator casts himself as the ghost bridegroom when he relates how his muse

> often, along the cliffs of the Caucasus,
> she, as Leonora, in the moonlight,
> rode with me on horseback! (6:166)

Besides having these folk and elite fictions, Europe and North America are rife with ghost-husband narratives believed by many people to be true. According to one study, more than 40 per cent of modern-day Welsh widows experience the presence of their dead husbands aurally, visually, and/or tactually, so strongly that they express no doubt about the visitation: "He's always with me," "Seems so close," "By my side" (Rees 1975, 67). Evidently these reports express the widows' emotional state; there is no objective reason to believe that the dead husband is expressing his own feelings. Hence, the widow's guilt over "infidelity" may result if she remarries. W. Dewi Rees and Lopata both note the tendency for widows to "sanctify" the memory of their late and now "idealized" spouses though they will overcome this somewhat when they set about remarrying and exchanging their past for a hopefully happier present (Rees 1975, 146; Lopata 1979, 124-25, 167-69). Notably, Mar'ya Gavrilovna begins to openly preserve mementos of Vladimir only after his death, whereupon she considers his memory "sacred." Previously, she had never spoken about him (8:83, 82). Nor is there any mention of him after Burmin reappears.

Pushkin built "The Snowstorm" on the basis of common patterns of emotional response, indeed, on a confluence of motives which are central to panhuman sexuality. Although these patterns were affected and transmitted by society, they and society are ultimately adducible to human evolution, whereby these behavioral protocols must have proved at one time or another to be adaptive. Social conventions usually do not make rational sense of these patterns; to do so one must turn to the wider context of biological adaptation. In the light of sociobiology, which examines the biocultural adaptation of social behaviors, we can better perceive the emotional logic of "The Snowstorm."

Sociobiology is the systematic study of the biological basis of behavior. It provides a rational and objective context for all individual facts and organizes them, ranging from microbiology to ethology and anthropology, in a single paradigm founded on the basic concept that genes will work to promote their own replication. After all, those that fail to reproduce soon will no longer be around to influence behavior. Genes may propagate themselves via related organisms which possess a large portion of the same genetic material, therefore providing the motivation for the preferential treatment of relatives, including one's own progeny.

With gendered species, the great differential between the reproductive investment made by the two sexes in their offspring influences differences in their behavior. The female generally has much less reproductive potential than the male, and she invests significantly more time and energy in each offspring. The male usually makes little investment and, theoretically, has a vast reproductive potential. It then follows that the female will carefully select her mate, so as to optimize her limited reproduction. Male of most species may, as one alternative, try to be as promiscuous as possible so as to have more offspring. Some of these differing strategies are expressed in human behavior, such as the common age differential between husbands and wives. To a varying degree in most societies, women are selected for signs of fertility and men for their potential as providers of material resources. Although nature often makes mistakes and much elaboration is necessary to account for the behavior of any species, these considerations also help explain why women are more safety-conscious, while men, especially unmarried young men, tend to take risks. This is reflected in literature. For example, in "The Snowstorm," Mar'ya Gavrilovna anticipates her elopement with great trepidation, while her intended groom, Vladimir, contentedly dines with neighbors.

Moreover, once men assure themselves of a reproductive resource—i.e., a wife or wives—they tend to become "responsible." The maturing of Burmin in "The Snowstorm" can be adduced to marriage as much as to age. Burmin is so carefree as an unmarried man that he is able to intrude on a wedding, marry another man's (Vladimir's) bride on an impulse, and then fall asleep in the sleigh after his risky adventure. Only much later can the full impact of his transgression and married state be sensed in his "interesting paleness" and taciturn manner (8:83). A similar change can be discerned in Pushkin during the fall of 1830, on the eve of his own marriage, when he was about to become a man of "sexual property," as the formerly self-styled Don Juan wrote *The Belkin Tales*, worrying about his future widow.

The reproductive differential between the sexes is somewhat muted for humans. Due to the greatly extended time necessary for the cranial and cognitive development of his child, a would-be father usually has to make a significant parental investment if he wants viable children. Therefore, he will demand some proof that his wife's children are also his own and that he is not investing in the offspring of a rival male. Thanks to concealed ovulation, he cannot be as confident of the paternity of his children as their mother. This consequent paternal uncertainty gives rise to the sexual double standard. There are many other precipitates which can be extrapolated, but already it is evident why men are much more concerned about adultery and at the same time more likely to "cheat" on their spouses. Female adultery is punished more severely than the male equivalent in most societies; in no society is the obverse true. Meanwhile, Pushkin did not seem to mind sharing women other than his wife with other men, as in the case of Anna Kern; not only was Kern a married woman, Pushkin approved of the affair she had previously had with the poet Arkady Rodzianko. Nor, prior to his marriage, did Pushkin see any need for placing constraints on widows. In 1825 Pushkin wrote to Kern about the possibility that her husband might die, which would make her "as free as the air" to continue her liaison with him (13:214). Darwinists note that female adultery is usually treated not as a sexual but a property offense against the husband's paternal confidence (van den Berghe 1979, 64, 104; Daly, Wilson, and Weghorst 1982, 12-14). This, in part, explains why Pushkin could be so tolerant of the escapades of one married woman and not of another, his own wife.

Evolutionist thinking on the double standard and other concerns can readily be extended to literature. The two fields share many points of tension, therefore interests. Biology is especially concerned with reproduction, much as narrative art tends to focus on themes closely related to reproduction: love, especially in the sense of mate selection, parental care, and reciprocity. These constitute many of the so-called cultural universals. The mere notion that certain concerns are "universal," i.e., panhuman, should lead us to suspect that they were derived by natural selection. The concept of a common biogramic influence on literary texts helps us to understand how we are capable of an emotional response, often a profound one, to works composed in distant places and cultural contexts.

Sociobiological research often begins by examining phenomena which are statistically non-random, such as the greater age of husbands over that of their wives, the huge disproportion between the numbers of polygynous and polyandrous societies, and the differing roles played by the two sexes. Literary scholars can begin by looking at these same phenomena and then by searching for their occurrences in fictive texts. It is rarely necessary to look far; first of all, if sociobiology pertains to one text, it should apply to all works. Second, literature tends to focus much more on reproduction-related issues than does our actual behavior. The reason is evident; narrative art not only reflects biological processes of adaptation, it is part of the process. In the book that founded the new discipline, *Sociobiology; The New Synthesis*, Edward O. Wilson envisions our emotions, tastes, and innate values as enabling mechanisms shaped by natural selection so as to cause certain adaptive behaviors (1975, 3). The arts are saturated with such enabling mechanisms, which tend to be associated with notions of truth, beauty, and morality.

This is not to say that all works of art texts express essentially the same things. With enabling mechanisms, the ends justify the means and a great variety of means may be employed; their utility is based on whether they bring about adaptive behaviors, i.e., behaviors more likely to result in (1) viable offspring or (2) altruism rendered to closely related individuals. Furthermore, an enabling mechanism need be only relatively successful to prosper. As a result, all are faulty in some respect, and some become anachronistic, thanks in part to the increasing pace of cultural development.

Evolutionary research often probes what we already take for granted. The common differential in age between spouses is a case in point which is usually attributed to culture. However, when a social convention is found in the great majority of societies, we should reexamine our premises, especially when the reproductive advantages for both genders is so apparent. Intuition and habit are not the same as objective knowledge, and the humanist would do well to carefully investigate their sources. Since the human biogram profoundly influences our notions of "common sense" and "decency," it is useful to consider logical alternatives. As we suggested above with Pushkin's fatal duel, this can be accomplished by switching the genders of the participants. Such alternatives may strike us as absurd, but they are not illogical. Rather, they contradict our expectations—that is, what we "take for granted," namely, in this case, that men are much more likely to use violence against a sexual rival.

Sociobiology must not be construed as a conscious or cultural influence. Biocultural adaptation affects in the same degree all individual organisms, animal and human, and among our conspecifics both those who are aware of Darwinian thought and the great mass who are not. The major difference is that humans, especially educated ones, will have a greater variety of behavioral protocols available. Nevertheless, we tend to act "as if we knew" how our behavior affects our reproductive futures, whether we do or not. Sometimes the texts which elicit enabling mechanisms will express biological truths, but much more often their overt statements will have little to do with them. All that matters is their ability to produce adaptive behaviors.

Nevertheless, this is not an all-powerful mechanism. An individual or group may buck the often obsolete trends of biological adaptation, but they usually will pay an emotional price for doing so. In "The Snowstorm," although Mar'ya Gavrilovna is eloping with her beloved, she castigates herself as a transgressor. At one point the narrator refers to her as a "criminal": her "crime" is that by marrying Vladimir, she is defying her parents and their customary control of a daughter's mate selection, as well as flouting the woman's typically more conservative behavior (8:79). In this case, hers is a particularly egregious transgression because Vladimir is hardly an ideal suitor—the kind of mate who can best maximize her limited reproductivity—and she probably senses that she might have done far better to have heeded her parents. According to Claude Levi-Strauss, all traditional marriage customs involve a financial transaction—or their ritual enactment—between two men, the bride's father and the groom (1969).[13] Defiance of this custom apparently causes Mar'ya Gavrilovna to have a guilt-ridden nightmare in which her angry father pulls her from the sleigh and throws her into a dark, "bottomless" hut (8:78). She punishes her impulse for sexual freedom with a vision of severe claustration. Many variants of the "ghost bridegroom" tradition include the theme of elopement; most depict the dead fiancé coming to the woman's house at night and enticing her to steal away with him. This is often explicitly interpreted as an offense against a male figure of authority, such as the father ("The Suffolk Miracle" and "Clerk Sanders"), a living husband ("James Harris, the Daemon Lover"), or God (Burger's "Leonore" and Zhukovsky's "Lyudmila"). Mar'ya Gavrilovna has a second nightmare in which Vladimir, mortally wounded on the battlefield, implores her to marry him before he dies. She overcomes these dream-imparted constraints and goes through with the elopement, but her emotional strain certainly contributes to the mis- (or bon-) adventure whereby she marries a stranger.

Humanists pay most attention to viable texts which, though produced by relatively few individuals, are read by masses. This is especially true of folklore, in that it is popularly composed as well as consumed. Given their popular and, hence, not idiosyncratic origin, it is to be expected that folklore narratives often constrain sexual behavior by warning against deviation from the norm. On the other hand, motifs like the "match made in heaven" point out desired ideals; the permanent pair-bond expressed by "happily ever after" endings admirably suits both paternal confidence and stable parental investment in children. Notably, both anachronistic motives, the ghost bridegroom and the fate-matched couple, play an important role in "The Snowstorm."[14]

The new Darwinist paradigm also helps us understand which issues are to be treated in literature, namely, which points of tension threaten subliminal notions of norm and decency, as in the case of promiscuous widows. This applies to comic treatments as well as serious, such as we find in "The Snowstorm." By raising age-old concerns over female chastity and remarriage, Pushkin manages to get the reader to think about and then misapply the motif of the daemon lover. Deprived of the essential information about what transpired at the church, both Mar'ya Gavrilovna's acquaintances and the reader treat her as a widow, albeit only of a dead and unofficial fiancé. Indeed, she lives up to our expectations by seeming to act like one.[15] But she is not a widow, and Pushkin's ironic device serves to expose our own deep-seated emotional propensities.

As David M. Bethea and Sergei Davydov demonstrated, one important parodic element of "The Snowstorm" is the extreme contrivance of its unlikely plot (1981, 12). Certainly the narrator, Miss K. I. T., overcomes incredible odds of probability with, first, Vladimir's getting lost in the blizzard while Mar'ya Gavrilovna marries Burmin and next, her reunion with her unknown husband in a different province, where they just happen to be neighboring landowners. This contrivance is clumsily covered over with standard cliches about fate. As every reader must have noted, the blizzard shows a knowing hand in rearranging the marital destinies of the protagonists; the wind hampers Mar'ya Gavrilovna efforts to go to the church, and it puts Vladimir off his path, while Burmin recalls how an "incomprehensible anxiety" overcame him and a mysterious "someone" pushed him out on his fateful midnight journey (8:85). There are other references to fate. Vladimir receives the news of how he has blundered "like a man sentenced to death" (8:80). This turns out to be true, but it has the nature of a self-fulfilling prophecy in that he rejoins the army with suicidal intentions. Mar'ya Gavrilovna's second nightmare, of Vladimir's dying in battle, may be somewhat prophetic, but the first nightmare is not. The same goes for her parents' deciding to accept Vladimir as a son-in-law on the basis of fate-saturated proverbs. These prove to be either untrue or misinterpreted; either conclusion serves to show up their process of decision-making.[16]

More serious are the faux pas in the plot committed by Miss K. I. T. or Belkin or Pushkin—it does not matter by whom, for the story does not fall apart, despite its contradictions. For example, why is it that neither the priest, the witnesses, nor Tereshka, Vladimir's coachman, see that Burmin is not Vladimir? The church may be dark, but this does not keep Burmin from seeing that Mar'ya Gavrilovna is attractive. Nor does Tereshka note how Burmin arrives in a coach with a driver, while Vladimir set out on his own (Bulgarin 1834, cited in V. V. Gippius, 1966, 35; Lednicki 1956; van der Eng 1968; Bethea and Davydov 1981; and Debreczeny 1983). Another contradiction creeps in later, when Mar'ya Gavrilovna maneuvers Burmin into a confession of his feelings for her. As far as the first-time reader knows, they are both eligible to be married; but the withheld information on their marriage changes the moral evaluation of their actions. Although her behavior would be permissible for a widow, which she is not, it hardly suits a married woman, which she is. During Burmin's narration of his wedding, Mar'ya Gavrilovna's own interjections suggest that she is about to admit to having the same obstacle to marrying Burmin; she says "I never could be your wife" (8:85). So, then, why does she elicit his declaration of love if it is to no useful purpose that she can anticipate? She does not suspect Burmin to be her husband. Of course, the same thinking goes for Burmin, who is similarly encumbered and, hence, not an eligible suitor.[17]

Sex-charged motives usually blind us to these inconsistencies and unlikelihoods, as generations of satisfied readers attest. What we take for granted may be related to the suspension of disbelief necessary for fictional narratives. Of course, the sheer improbability of such plots contributes to their narrative interest. Moreover, the various contrivances gratify the reader by working in so beneficent a manner. Consider other alternative plot variants which are at least as probable. One is that the priest and witnesses notice that Burmin is not Vladimir, and that Vladimir and Mar'ya Gavrilovna are able to elope on another occasion; as we might speculate, this would have led to an ill-begotten marriage, certainly not one which seems as promising as that of Mar'ya Gavrilovna to Burmin. Another variant would be for the misadventure in the church to occur as given in the story and then for Mar'ya Gavrilovna to fall in love with a hussar after the war, unfortunately, with someone who never passed by Zhadrino. Obviously, the happiness of the story's ending lies in our recognition that the snowstorm, the agency of a knowing fate, effected sexual justice by choosing a superior husband for Mar'ya Gavrilovna.

Because sociobiology has much to say about our innate notions of sexual justice and property, it helps us to account for many of the common yet illogical elements of the story as follows:

1. **The central cast of characters**. An attractive woman early in her child-bearing years and two eligible bachelors. This cast structure is characteristic of most narratives; two or more men contend over a single woman far more often than the obverse. For a single man to choose from a number of women is far too commonplace to have immediate narrative interest. Due to the human tendency toward forms of polygyny, male choice seems to be taken for granted. On the other hand, men are much more threatened by the possibility of a male rival. This not only makes for greater plot interest, it also demonstrates the generally male bias of most literature, as is often exposed by feminist scholars. A cursory glance at narrative plots, whether in literature, drama, film, or, especially, opera, makes the point clear that the audience does not want to be confused by a multiplicity of available women. We could derive the same conclusion by reversing the gender roles in a given plot, then considering its new aesthetic effect. What if it had been Mar'ya Gavrilovna who had gotten lost in the snowstorm and Vladimir had unwittingly married an unknown but impetuous woman? One might consider another case, that of Pushkin's *Ruslan and Lyudmila*: What if the sorcerer Chernomor had been a woman and had abducted not the newly wed Lyudmila but Ruslan, her groom? Would Prince Vladimir have sent out a number of Amazons to rescue him? Either reversed plot would cut against the grain of panhuman sexual norms in which men are "wooers" and pursuers, while women only occasionally are permitted to be "choosers."

2. **The selection of Mar'ya Gavrilovna's husband**. Fiction is obviously uncomfortable with a woman's right to choose her mate. This constitutes the major transgression which generates the plot and first elicits narrative

interest in "The Snowstorm." After all, it was Mar'ya Gavrilovna who, according to the narrator's diction—"the object [of her love] chosen by her"—first pursued Vladimir. What makes the misdeed more grave is that she does so for the wrong reasons; like Tat'yana Larina, who confesses her love to Eugene Onegin, she is influenced by her reading (8:77).[18] Both women are punished for trying to exercise their choice. Female initiative, particularly with regard to sexual behavior, is characteristically treated by classical writers as a negative attribute. This quality figures prominently in depictions of the *femme fatale* and other misogynist characterizations of women. The sexually liberated woman threatens the male ego, while the passive and faithful woman, like Tat'yana in the last chapter of *Eugene Onegin*, is regarded as a paragon of morality. From a sociobiological perspective, the former represents a perceived danger to the paternal confidence desired by a prospective husband.[19] This is reflected in social traditions regarding female chastity, including various forms of non-sexual "chaste" behavior. Mar'ya Gavrilovna is exalted by her neighbors for what can be described as her passivity; indeed, fate long since deprived her of the right to choose by having selected a husband for her.

The common narrative issue of "who gets the girl" is typically settled not by her sexual attraction to a particular contender but more likely by his demonstration of his greater potential as a provider. Few societies permit brides much say in the choice of their spouses. In fact, a number of modern plots, including *Ruslan and Lyudmila* and some of Wagner's operas, treat the woman as a prize to be given to the victor in a contest, irrespective of her own preferences. That the victor turns out to be her heart's desire merely expresses the confluence of two biological factors, sexual attraction and reproductive calculation; this typical fictional contrivance effects a sense of "sexual justice." The issue is more than a trite literary convention. A woman's choice or marital lot is crucial because her husband will have a major influence on her limited reproductive destiny. Due to the male constraint of female sexuality, which appears to be a crosscultural universal, a woman generally gets only one chance to maximize her direct genetic fitness by establishing a stable pair-bond (Daly, Wilson, and Weghorst 1982, 11). She is not likely to get a second husband and father for her children if she outlives the first. Indeed, the ghost bridegroom strives to deny her another man once she has had a fiancé or even a first love.

3. **Mar'ya Gavrilovna's age—seventeen at the beginning of the story.** Besides being the age of a typical debutante—and of Pushkin's fiancée in 1830—seventeen or thereabouts is a characteristic age for fictional heroines. Like most traditional societies, literature everywhere seems to pay the most attention to women at the time of their greatest reproductive potential. Beth Ann Bassein bemoans "the almost universal identification of women [in literature] with sex and the historical tendency to see sexuality as their main or only function" (1984, ix). As a result of this limitation to "those years of [a woman's] life when she is thought most appealing sexually, omitting almost all others," readers "rarely get a picture of her total life span or any notion of the variety that her life contains"; instead, such portraits "present only partial truths about women's lives, leaving the rest unvoiced or relegated to the unimportant" (Bassein 1984, 61, 69). This bias reflects the connection made by various scientists between fertility and female attractiveness, and it is reflected in the average age and typical appearance of Pushkin's heroines, to say nothing of Ivan Turgenev's. The literary imagination has little interest in more mature women, save for when they try to behave as if they were much younger, whereupon they become objects of horror, comedy, or—grotesquely—both, as in the case of the aged title character of Pushkin's *Queen of Spades*. This statistical imbalance is motivated by the crucial nature of a woman's marital destiny since, from society's viewpoint, that is the major and most controllable variable in the determination of the next generation. There is little wonder, then, that most societies take care to control the sexuality of young women. As we noted above, widow constraints are relaxed in many societies after menopause.

In this regard, we should note that all heroines of ghost-bridegroom tales are relatively young. Thus, it is their greater reproductive potential that hangs in the balance. The bride in the New Guinea tale is such a child that her parents do not permit her to live with her husband; she plays while her parents are at her husband's funeral feast. This consideration brings in the common motive of the fiancé's untimely death that makes her an especially *young* widow. His demise is considerably facilitated by another topos, the distant battle, like the one which claims Vladimir.

4. **Relative social status of the principal characters**. Mar'ya Gavrilovna's fortune adds considerably to her value as the prize which the male protagonists will contend over by finding their way through the storm. In other words, she is treated as a commodity, and her wealth adds considerably to the demand. We are told, "She was considered to be a rich bride and many intended her for themselves or for their sons" (8:77). She has no rivals. Pierre van den Berghe notes how an upper-class woman's wealth helps her to out-compete lower-class women (1979, 101). Raising the ante on Mar'ya Gavrilovna normally would serve to put her beyond Vladimir's reach. The common pattern is for a woman to marry a man equal or higher in social status. The pronounced tendency for female hypergamy is motivated by the bride's limited reproductive potential and her consequent need to find the mate most likely to enhance that potential by providing their offspring with material resources and social advantages. A poor subaltern who retired "while young," Vladimir fails on both accounts (8:77). Nor does he promise any better, given that his mental attributes give him little hope of rising in status, *other than by marrying Mar'ya Gavrilovna*. Vladimir has everything to gain, and she can only lose, by their marriage; characteristically, he suggests the elopement and, although blindly in love, she hesitates before agreeing and then is so emotionally distraught at her unjustified risk that she helps to botch the alliance.

Rich and socially advantaged, Burmin gets married as a joke. Although he underestimates the gravity of this action, a man's reproductive investment is considerably cheaper and much more revocable. Evolutionists note that men are much less choosy with regard to mates and are more interested in brief liaisons. This, apparently, is what Burmin has in mind when he decides to go through with the wedding; notably, he does this before he gets a glimpse of Mar'ya Gavrilovna and judges her "not bad" (8:86). Pierre van den Berghe points out how men will try to parasitize the reproductive resources of women without having to make a paternal investment—a threat which women will normally try to avoid, and one which is clearly present in the wedding scene (1979, 63). Burmin's behavior resembles that of a rapist in that he tries to take advantage of a situation where the risks, i.e., likely costs, are small. Notably, when the ruse is exposed, he flees (Thornhill and Thornhill 1983, 137-73).

The differential reproductive potential of the two sexes motivates the common parental constraint of daughters, as contrasted with sons. When a daughter marries beneath her social status, she reduces not only her own genetic fitness but also that of her parents. Mar'ya Gavrilovna's parents forbid her to consider Vladimir as a suitor. Claustration of women is significantly tighter with higher status. As with Tat'yana Larina, Mar'ya Gavrilovna's wealth makes her transgression all the more grave, at least in her own eyes. Later, when her love for Vladimir brings her to the brink of death, her parents change their minds, as if thinking it was better to have a poor son-in-law than none at all.

5. **Sexual fidelity**. Why does Mar'ya Gavrilovna remain faithful to Burmin, especially when he is a complete stranger to her? Adultery, or better, thanks to the brevity of their conjugal life having Mar'ya Gavrilovna simply ignore her vows must have occurred to Pushkin, since that is a real possibility in the last chapter of *Eugene Onegin*. The failure of a couple to consummate their marriage is often sufficient cause for an annulment and, given her highly unusual wedding, Mar'ya Gavrilovna certainly has a strong case for one. Nevertheless, it is interesting that she does not seem to consider this action.[20] Notably, in *Ruslan and Lyudmila*, when Chernomor abducts Lyudmila from the bridal chamber, apparently before her marriage to Ruslan is definitively consummated, Prince Vladimir tacitly annuls the marriage by offering the bride to the warrior who rescues her. But these logical alternatives do not satisfy the literary imagination. What if Rogday or Farlaf, and not Ruslan, brought Lyudmila back to Kiev? Obviously, the tale would have had a different emotional effect. In most narrative works, as in most traditional societies, a woman becomes the exclusive "sexual property" of her first husband. Interestingly, both narratives and most versions of the ghost-bridegroom tale do not deal with women who either have obviously healthy sexual relationships with their first husbands or who are mothers; "James Harris, the Daemon Lover" is one exception. This suggests that for such

contented wives, enduring "fidelity"—internalized sexual constraint—is taken for granted. Instead, the motif focuses on relationships which have not reached sexual consummation. Typically, the fiancé is taken off to war before the couple can get to church or they are separated immediately after their vows. As a result, the woman's fidelity cannot be assumed and the relationship is in doubt. It follows that, for example, New Guinea *kinehera* focus on the kinds of marital contracts which are most in question (Berndt 1966, 259). The common feature of all versions of the daemon-lover story is that the spirit insists on taking the bride off to a ghoulish "Brautbett," where consummation will make her eternally "his" in death.

In this regard, Mar'ya Gavrilovna's second nightmare possibly reveals her subliminal acknowledgment that she is incompatible with Vladimir. Here she is on the eve of their elopement, whereupon she presumably will become "his" for the rest of her days. His dying wish is to establish an enduring claim on her, for why else would a dying man want to marry? But here it is part of a *nightmare*.[21]

6. **The couple's reunion**. Waclaw Lednicki compared "The Snowstorm" to an ancient tradition of tales wherein a married couple is separated after their wedding and before consummation, whether by accident or due to their incompatibility (1956).[22] After an prolonged interval, they meet again as strangers and fall in love before recognizing one another. This, of course, is the same situation, a relationship in doubt, as we noted above. In each of these plots, the separation or incompatibility is resolved, leading to a happy and presumably consummated marriage. Lednicki also mentions Terence's *Hecyra*, a case of strange bedfellows, where a couple has failed to consummate their marriage due to incompatability. They do not know that, some time before their wedding, while drunk, the husband had raped the bride. He neither knew her identity at the time nor remembered her appearance. Their marital problems and his crime are both happily resolved when they later meet as strangers, fall in love as it were on a novel basis, then recognize one another. A similar tale is found in the Scottish ballad, "The Knight and the Shepherd's Daughter," wherein the man rapes the woman and later falls in love with her. The couple is considerably relieved to find that each is of the

same noble rank, a condition which facilitates their marriage. Both cases amount to rape rewarded.

The notion of a man's finding marital happiness by raping his future wife also pertains to "The Snowstorm." The unusual wedding and Burmin's hurried flight serve to raise anxieties about the couple's marital fate. That Burmin and Mar'ya Gavrilovna did not consummate their marriage in Zhadrino serves to put their alliance in doubt. He admits the crime—"my criminal prank"—in his irresponsible action, a crime tantamount to the traditional view of rape, in that he takes sexual possession of her (8:86). As a result of the wedding, Mar'ya Gavrilovna is no longer free to marry Vladimir. This not only places a constraint on her sexual choice, it results in the death of her erstwhile fiancé and her own near approach to the grave. These concerns are gratifyingly resolved by Burmin and Mar'ya Gavrilovna's falling in love before they recognize one another. Here, too, the man's crime serves to place his claim on the woman who will later make him happy. Indeed, if the ghost bridegroom shows up in the story, it is not Vladimir, who is pushed off the page in mid-paragraph and is heard from no more. Burmin's rash action prevented Vladimir from establishing his claim to Mar'ya Gavrilovna. Vladimir is "cuckolded" before he gets to the altar, for Burmin must have known that he was marrying another man's bride. Rather, it is the dimly remembered Burmin who most resembles the sexually possessive spirit; he comes back from a distant battlefield to claim the woman who, unwittingly, is demonstrably "his."

Pushkin's story may end with a happily concluded love match, but the actions of fate leave a bad taste in the mouth. Burmin's and Mar'ya Gavrilovna's joy are purchased at the price of Vladimir's misfortune and consequent suffering. As Richard Gregg reminds us, the reader does not "forget that cruel *quo* (the annihilation of Vladimir) which [fate] has demanded in exchange for Burmin's quid" (1977, 756). Berkovsky also is discomfited by "The Snowstorm." Given all of Burmin's advantages, Berkovsky suspects that his victory expresses Pushkin's approval of the class system (1962, 293). Gregg makes the same point in noting that storytellers prefer "to draw their protagonists from the ranks of the fortunate." Indeed, he attributes "Burmin's wild and wanton caprice of marrying an unknown bride without her consent" to "a touch or more of patrician presumption"; this "has nothing to do with virtue and is, at times, opposed to it" (1970, 748-49). Burmin's crime and the covert immorality of the tale seem all the more troubling because they remain latent.[23] One is bemused by this parody of sentimentalist prose without being troubled by its basic content, content which generally has been exposed only by recent objective readings. As a result, the inattentive reader, like the author, may be seduced into trivializing the serious transgression which lies at its heart.

The apparent struggle between evolutionary psychology and philosophy that characterized the early debate on sociobiology was ignited by Wilson's hypothesis that moral systems were primarily intuited from our biologically shaped emotions. It was evident that our ethics are also shaped by reason. Wilson and his colleague Charles Lumsden later went on to develop a theory of biocultural evolution. According to their model, culture is a biologically based device for greatly accelerating adaptation; obviously, rationality plays a central role in this enterprise (Wilson and Lumsden 1983). One inevitable consequence of this dualistic model is that genetically shaped behavioral propensities will often contrast sharply with products of cultural evolution. The double standard provides many salient examples of this common antinomy between relatively fixed and, hence, anachronistic traditional patterns on the one hand and recent adaptations, which typically are more rational in character, on the other. Both continue to be relevant to our behavior and to the enabling mechanisms for behavior, including our emotions. Furthermore, this clash of "old" and "new" figures prominently in fiction and the verdicts are often mixed. Storytellers typically choose plots where the tug-of-war is evenly balanced so as to create greater narrative interest. The old patterns of emotional response continue to gratify, however much they may offend us. New Guinea *kinehera*, for example, often end with morals that decry the actions of ghost husbands, but these lurid narratives by their very nature promulgate outdated systems of sexual dominance (Berndt 1966).

The moral danger of even so innocuous-seeming a story as "The Snowstorm" lies in the possibility that its array of rhetorical devices may lure us into accepting and being gratified by actions that, if encountered in an objective and/or rational light, we would reject. Disbelief is not the only cognitive function that is suspended in a typical reading experience. Pity, for example, is conspicuously missing in the many plots which do not shed tears over the losing party, like Vladimir in "The Snowstorm." There is, quite conspicuously, little of the "new" and morally opprobrious in the story, unless we choose to discern it in Pushkin's ironic tone. But, then, literature and philosophy derive from distinctly different cognitive processes, a point which rational analysis from a Darwinist perspective makes evident.

Works Cited

Arbesmann, Rudolf

1939 "The Bride of Hades." *Classical Bulletin* 15: 66-67.

1944 "The Dead-Bridegroom Motif in South American Folklore." *Thought* 19: 95-111.

Akhmatova, Anna

1977 *O Pushkine: Stat'i i zametki*. Leningrad: Sovetsky pisatel'.

Barash, David P.

1977 *Sociobiology and Behavior*. New York: Elsevier.

Bassein, Beth Ann

1984 *Women and Death: Linkages in Western Thought and Literature*. Westport, CT: Greenwood.

Berndt, Catherine H.

1966 "The Ghost Husband: Society and the Individual in New Guinea Myth." In Melville Jacobs and John Greenway, eds.,*The Anthropologist Looks at Myth*. Austin: University of Texas Press, pp. 244-77.

Bethea, David M., and Sergei Davydov

1981 "Pushkin's Saturnine Cupid: The Poetics of Parody in *The Tales of Belkin*." *PMLA* 96:8-21.

Berkovsky, N. Ya.

1962 *Stat'i o literature*. Moscow-Leningrad: Gosudarstvennoe izdatel'stvo khudozhestvennoy literatury.

Blackstone, W.

1803 *Commentaries on the Laws of England*. 4 Vols. edited by St. G. Tucker. Philadelphia: William Young Birch and Abraham Small.

Blair, Karin

1979 "Scripts for Feminine Consciousness in Child Ballads." *Southern Folklore Quarterly* 43:223-39.

Bulgarin, F. V.

1834 "Povesti, izdannye Aleksandrom Pushkinym." *Severnaya pchela* 192:765-66.

Chernaev, N.

1900 "Metel'." In *Kriticheskie stat'i i zametki o Pushkine*. Kharkov, pp. 233-92.

Child, Francis James, ed.

1956 *The English and Scottish Popular Ballads*. 5 Vols. New York: Folklore.

Clayton, J. Douglas

1987 "*Povesti Belkina* and the Commedia dell'arte: Callot, Hoffmann and Pushkin." Paper presented at the 1987 Pushkin in America Today Conference in Madison, Wisconsin.

Cooke, Brett

1992 "Pushkin and the *Femme Fatale*: Jealousy in *Tsygany*." *California Slavic Studies* 14: 99-126.

1995 "Acquaintance Rape in Kalatozov's *The Cranes Are Flying*." In Simon Karlinsky, James L. Rice, and Barry P. Scherr, eds., *O rus! Studia litteraria slavica in honorem Hugh McLean.* Berkeley: Berkeley Slavic Studies, pp. 69-80.

Daly, Martin, and Margo Wilson

1983 *Sex, Evolution and Behavior*. 2d. North Sciutate, MA.: Duxbury.

1990 "Deconstructing Symbolic Interpretations of Cruel Stepparent Stories." Paper presented at the Human Behavior and Evolution Society Conference in Los Angeles, California.

Daly, Martin, Margo Wilson, and Suzanne J. Weghorst

1982 "Male Sexual Jealousy." *Ethology and Sociobiology* 3:11-27.

Debreczeny, Paul

1983 *The Other Pushkin: A Study of Alexander Pushkin's Prose Fiction.* Stanford: Stanford University Press.

Frazer, James George

1977 *The Fear of the Dead in Primitive Religion*. New York: Arno.

Gippius, V. V.

1966 *Ot Pushkina do Bloka*. Moscow-Leningrad: Nauka.

Graves, Robert

1969 *The Greek Myths*. 2 Vols. Harmondsworth, England: Penguin.

Gregg, Richard

1970 "Tat'yana's Two Dreams: The Unwanted Spouse and the Demonic Lover." *Slavonic and East European Review* 48:492-505.

Peter D. Grudin

1987 *The Demon-Lover: The Theme of Demonality in English and Continental Fiction of the Late Eighteenth and Early Nineteenth Centuries*. New York: Garland.

Konick, Willis

1977 "Categorical Dreams and Compliant Reality: The Role of the Narrator in *The Tales of Belkin*." *Canadian-American Slavic Studies* 11:75-90.

Lednicki, Waclaw

1956 *Bits of Table Talk on Pushkin, Mickiewicz, Goethe, Turgenev and Sienkiewicz*. The Hague: Martinus Nijhoff.

Levy-Strauss, Claude

1969 *The Elementary Structures of Kinship*. Boston: Beacon.

Little, William A.

1974 *Gottfried August Burger*. New York: Twayne.

Lopata, Helena Znaniecka

1979 *Women as Widows: Support Systems*. New York: Elsevier.

Lumsden, Charles and Edward O. Wilson

1983 *Promethean Fire: Reflections on the Origin of Mind*. Cambridge, MA: Harvard University Press.

Millett, Kate

1970 *Sexual Politics*. Garden City, NY: Doubleday.

Rabkin, Eric S.

1983 "The Descent of Fantasy." In George E. Slusser, Eric S. Rabkin, and Robert Scholes, eds., *Coordinates: Placing Science Fiction and Fantasy*. Carbondale, IL: Southern Illinois University Press, pp. 14-22. Republished in this volume.

Rancour-Laferriere, Daniel

1985 *Signs of the Flesh: An Essay on the Evolution of Hominid Sexuality*. Berlin: Mouton de Gruyter.

1987 "Pushkin's Still Unravished Bride: A Psychoanalytic Study of Tat'jana's Dream." *Russian Literature* 25:215-58.

Reed, Toni

1988 *Demon-Lovers in British Fiction*. Lexington, KY: University of Kentucky Press.

Rees, W. Dewi

1975 "The Bereaved and Their Hallucinations." In Bernard Schoenberg, Irwin Gerber, Alfred Wiener, Austin H. Kutscher, David Peretz, and Arthur C. Carr, eds., *Bereavement: Its Psychosocial Aspects*. New York: Columbia University Press, pp. 66-71.

Semenko, Irina M.

1976 *Vasily Zhukovsky*. Boston: Twayne.

Shaw, J. Thomas

1977 "Pushkin's 'The Stationmaster' and the New Testament Parable." *Slavic and East European Journal* 21:3-29.

Thompson, Stith

1955-58 *Motif-Index of Folk-Literature*. 6 Vols. Bloomington: Indiana University Press.

Thornhill, Randy and Nancy Wilmsen Thornhill

1983 "Human Rape: An Evolutionary Analysis." *Ethology and Sociobiology* 4:137-73.

van den Berghe, Pierre L.

1979 *Human Family Systems: An Evolutionary View*. New York: Elsevier.

van der Eng, Jan.

1968 "*Les recits de Belkin*: Analogie des procedes de construction." In Jan van der Eng, A. G. F. van Holk, and Jan M. Meijer, eds., *The Tales of Belkin by A. S. Pushkin*. The Hague: Mouton, pp. 9-60.

Vernadsky, George, ed.

1972 *A Source Book for Russian History from Early Times to 1917*, 3 Vols.. New Haven, CT: Yale University Press.

Wilson, Edward O.

1975 *Sociobiology: The New Synthesis*. Cambridge, MA.: Harvard University Press.

Wollner, W.

1882 "Der Lenorenstoff in der slavischen Volkspoesie." *Archiv fur slavische Philologie* 6:239-69.

Notes

1. Blackstone 1803, 192. A similar position was outlined in *Dukh zhurnalov* in 1820; see my article (1992) on the sexual jealousy in Pushkin's *The Gypsies*.
2. Many societies expect a cuckold to take violent measures if he is to restore his "name." See Daly, Wilson, and Weghorst 1982, 20-24; and Millett 1970, 43.
3. David Barash notes how the tenets of sociobiology predict that the cuckold will feel shame and the cuckolder, quite possibly, pride; after all, the first loses "fitness" (genetic potential) by allowing his resources to be parasitized by the latter, who gains reproductive opportunity (1977, 296).
4. Further references to the "Jubilee" edition of Pushkin's complete works, Pushkin 1937-1949, will be provided by volume and page number only. All translations are my own.
5. J. Douglas Clayton (1987) suggests that an 1829 French translation of E.T.A. Hoffmann's "Der unheimliche Gast" ("Le Spectre fiancé") may have influenced Pushkin's "Snowstorm."
6. Other ethnographers have found similar traditions in many parts of the world not covered by Frazer. See Blair 1979; 223-39; Thompson 1955, 58; Wollner 1882, 239-69; Arbesmann 1939, 66-67; and Arbesmann 1944, 95-111. Irina M. Semenko cites traditions of the hostile dead fiancé in northern Russian folktales (1976, 95).
7. Cf. George Vernadsky 1972, 1: 9, 11.

8. Hence, there is no reason to subject postmenopausal widows to suttee. Meanwhile, by also saving pregnant widows, the deceased's offspring, i.e., the fetus, is preserved.
9. Martin Daly and Margo Wilson (1990) explicated the evolutionary psychology of this common fairytale motif.
10. Apparently a copy of Percy's *Reliques of Ancient Poetry* was available in the Göttingen Library when Burger wrote "Leonore". See Little 1974, 99; Child 1956, 5: 60n. Already the subject of scholarly controversy, the actual sources of Burger's "Leonore," Zhukovsky's "Svetlana," and Pushkin's "Snowstorm" are not so important to this study as the propensity of authors and their audiences to be interested in such narratives.
11. Francis James Child and Waclaw Lednicki both believed the story was Slavic in origin (Child 1956.5, 60; Lednicki 1956, 47n.).
12. See Grudin 1987, Reed 1988, and Cooke 1995.
13. J. Thomas Shaw notes how the "question of fatherly or parental blessing (or curse) on mating and marriage was very much on the mind of the mature Pushkin" during the late 1820s and 1830; this motif, as Shaw traces it, finds its way into *Poltava*, "The Stationmaster,'" and Pushkin's own request for his parents to bless his marriage to Natal'ya Goncharova (1977, 27-28n). Of course, this theme also appears in "The Snowstorm," when Mar'ya Gavrilovna's parents first forbid her to consider Vladimir as a suitor and, later, try to encourage their union.
14. Generally speaking, at a high level of cultural sophistication, elite texts will proffer more complex structures from the perspective of sociobiology; a modern author will throw one behavioral propensity shaped by natural selection against another. Instead of a choice between a norm and a heinous deviation, the reader may have to choose between two contradictory but equally viable protocols. Such is the stuff of tragedy or of mature endings, as in *Eugene Onegin* where Tat'yana chooses an uninteresting man of resources over an interesting man, one whom she loves but who does not promise stable material and social support.
15. One reason for Mar'ya Gavrilovna's mournful behavior is the death of her father shortly after her nocturnal escapade.

16. On the other hand, Pushkin introduces a bit of dramatic irony, visible only with a backward glance, when her neighbors speak about her projected marriage to Burmin as an "already accomplished fact"—which is literally true (8:84).
17. At some point, Pushkin considered and rejected the notion of introducing an additional and similar complication into the plot in the form of a rival for Burmin. Interestingly, to judge by the drafts of the story, this would have been the same young uhlan who was a witness at the wedding ceremony three years earlier (8:617-18). Given that he also knows that Mar'ya Gavrilovna is married, one wonders what he would be doing by paying court to her.
18. Their reading also influences Mar'ya Gavrilovna and Vladimir to pledge "eternal love"; in other versions of the ghost-bridegroom tradition, this action causes the dead groom to return for his bride (8:77).
19. For all the complications which derive from female sexual initiative, see Rancour-Laferriere 1985, 313-29.
20. Lednicki (1956, 60-86) examines how the theme of remaining true to one's wedding vows in the face of conjugal infidelity figures in Pushkin's "Dubrovsky" and Turgenev's *A Nest of Gentlefolk*.
21. One other reason for this dream is being a nightmare is that the combination of marriage and the groom's death, basic elements of the "ghost bridegroom" tradition, add up to fatal necrophilia, inevitably leading to the bride's death.
22. Also see Bethea and Davydov 1981, 19n.
23. N. Chernaev claimed the story was not only moral but also that it inspired "faith in Providence" and respect for the sanctity of legal marriage (1900: cited in Gippius 1966, 32).

Gethenian Nature, Human Nature, and the Nature of Reproduction: A Fantastic Flight through Ethnographic Hyperspace

Lee Cronk

In the late 1960s, thanks to the work of ethnographer O. T. Oppong, a fascinating people living in a little-explored place called Gethen were brought to light. Because today Gethen is nearly inaccessible and inhospitably cold, some researchers think it likely that the Gethenians' ancestors migrated there during a warm interglacial period tens of thousands of years ago. During their many millennia of isolation, the Gethenians developed a unique culture that has been the object of much study and speculation.

Gethenian social life is especially remarkable for the wide and unusual range of options it allows concerning sexual ties and familial organization. Sexual relations, called *kemmer*, are usually enjoyed by pairs, but promiscuous mating in communal homes, called *kemmerhouses*, is also very common and fully accepted. A third option is to "vow *kemmering*." Although this is essentially like monogamous marriage, vowing *kemmering* does not have any legal status in Gethen. Incest between generations is forbidden, as in almost all societies, but the Gethenians are unusual in that they do allow siblings to have sex.

Gethen is also notable for its extreme sexual egalitarianism. Unlike so many of the societies familiar to anthropologists, Gethen is not at all dominated by males. Gethenians call the mother "the parent of the flesh," and they place great stress on the tie between mother and offspring. The rule of descent is, accordingly, strictly matrilineal. Gethenians also do not have any sexual division of labor, apart from the fact that female Gethenians nurse their children for the first six to eight months. The idea that a person's gender would determine his or her role or status in society is unknown in Gethen. Some might find it tempting to argue that the lack of male control over Gethenian affairs explains the absence of warfare in Gethen, but it would be wrong to say that Gethenians are truly peaceful. Oppong reports that even though organized aggression is unknown, Gethenians are still quite competitive and even capable of violence: "They kill each other readily by ones and twos; seldom by tens and twenties; never by hundreds or thousands."

Cultural Diversity and Cultural Uniformity

So far, Gethen may sound rather exotic but not beyond the realm of ethnographic possibility. If not for the lousy weather, it might even make for an interesting visit. But the only place that you will find O. T. Oppong and the Gethenians is between the covers of Ursula K. Le Guin's *The Left Hand of Darkness* (1969). Le Guin's novel is a work of social science fiction, a sort of extraterrestrial ethnography that explores the relationships among sexuality, psyche, and society. Throughout the book, Le Guin demonstrates her trademark sociological inventiveness and cultural sensitivity, which anthropologists often like to think are attributable to her parentage. Her father, Alfred Kroeber, was a pioneer in American anthropology and founded the anthropology program at the University of California, while her mother, Theodora Kroeber, was the author of *Ishi in Two Worlds*, a biography of a California Indian (Kroeber 1961). While the Kroebers concentrated on societies that actually have existed, Le Guin has chosen instead to imagine new ones.

Gethen is just one imaginable society that has never existed. It is easy to think of many other combinations of social characteristics and cultural practices that may seem plausible but that we earthlings have somehow never invented. Although humanity's diversity has long been cultural anthropology's raison d'etre, in fact human societies and cultures also display a remarkable degree of uniformity. The tendency of cultures to stick to certain basic patterns suggests that social formations are not endlessly variable, bounded only by our imaginations. Rather, this tendency suggests that there are constraints acting on culture, channeling societies in certain directions and steering them away from others. By imagining such nonexistent societies as Gethen we may be better able to understand the forces that constrain cultural variability as well as the limits of those constraints. The uniformity of cultures has the potential to tell us as much about human nature—those fundamental characteristics and propensities that we all share as members of a single species—as can our societies' much advertised diversity.

Plotting Points in Ethnographic Hyperspace

Just how diverse or how uniform are human societies? One way to approach this question is to look at information about many different cultures. Such crosscultural data bases are often used to test ideas about societies and to look for patterns that occur across many cultures. For example, an anthropologist might ask if one type of family arrangement is more common among hunting people than among fishers, or if certain political systems are usually found in societies with castes. This approach was pioneered as long ago as the 1880s by the British social anthropologist E. B. Tylor (1889), but it was developed most successfully by the late George Peter Murdock, along with his colleagues and students, first at Yale University and later at the University of Pittsburgh. By the time of his death in 1985, Murdock had catalogued and coded information about more than twelve hundred different societies around the world and throughout recorded human history. The resulting files, which are still being modified, supplemented, and refined, are one of anthropology's most valuable resources and one of its finest contributions to comparative social science.

Although the emphasis in crosscultural research is, naturally, on societies that actually exist, this approach can also throw light on those that do not. One of Murdock's crosscultural samples, the *Ethnographic Atlas* (Murdock 1967), contains information on more than eight hundred different cultures, coded according to more than forty different variables that describe each society's economy, social system, political practices, religious beliefs, and even what games they play. Each variable has many different possible values, ranging from a handful to a hundred or more for complicated topics like marriage rules. In its totality, the *Ethnographic Atlas* describes a sort of ethnographic hyperspace, with each variable defining a dimension and each society occupying a single point whose location is described by the values of its variables. The vast majority of points in this space is not occupied by any known society, and probably never has been nor ever will be. For example, no hunting and gathering society has ever developed a state form of government. The rarity of occupied sites in the ethnographic hyperspace is easy to see by calculating the total number of possible combinations of the variables. If all of the variables in the *Ethnographic Atlas* are included, the number of imaginable societies is a figure consisting of twelve followed by fifty-two zeros. If we take a more conservative approach and consider only those variables that have to do with reproduction and family life, we still get a minimum of two hundred billion possible combinations.

A table of variables like the *Ethnographic Atlas* is, by definition, a bad place to look for uniformity. If all peoples did something exactly the same way, it would be silly to provide a variable for it, just on the slim chance that a place like Gethen might be discovered. However, occasionally anthropologists have imagined practices that seem like logical possibilities but have never been observed. By their very nonexistence such imaginary customs may suggest something about the constraints underlying cultural uniformity. For example, it is not uncommon for newly married couples to live with the husband's mother's brother. This practice, called avunculocality, is often found in matrilineal societies because it keeps matrilineally related males together. However, the opposite pattern, called amitalocality, in which the newlyweds live with the wife's father's sister's family, so far is known to exist only as an unoccupied point in ethnographic hyperspace, perhaps somewhere not far from Gethen (Murdock 1949, 71).

Although the reasons why amitalocality does not exist are still poorly understood, human cultures share other similarities that are more fundamental and revealing than the universal absence of this anthropological curiosity. Perhaps the most basic human constant is the family. Apart from a few largely unsuccessful utopian experiments that have tried to do away with the family as the basic social unit, all societies have had some form of family, whether nuclear, extended, polygamous, or monogamous. Why should this be? Indeed, why should there be any invariable features at all across cultures?

In Search of Culture's Great Attractor

To extend the analogy between ethnology and cosmology a bit further, the problem we face is a bit like that facing astronomers who want to know the locations and dimensions of dark matter in the universe. By definition such matter does not reveal itself through the emission of radiation. Black holes, for example, have such tremendous gravity that they let no light or other radiation escape. The presence of such objects can only be inferred by their effects on other, observable objects like stars and galaxies. The most dramatic example of the effects of such dark matter is the so-called Great Attractor, a mysterious object with the mass of tens of thousands of galaxies towards which the Milky Way and its neighboring galaxies are gravitating at speeds of up to seven hundred miles per second (Dressler 1989).

In short, we are in search of the Great Attractor of human culture. To find it, we need to examine the forces that shape cultural and social patterns, and ask which of them are sources of uniformity rather than diversity. There are several possibilities.

Our Limited Imaginations

The least flattering possibility is that although a variety of better, more beneficial and rewarding sociocultural arrangements is possible, we earthling humanoids simply do not have imaginations fertile enough to invent other possible social arrangements. Although by definition we are incapable of evaluating this possibility ourselves, I submit that this very discussion and its subject matter have provided ample evidence of the powers of the human imagination.

The Limited Size of Ethnographic Hyperspace

Another possibility is that even my conservative estimate of two hundred billion overstates the number of societies that are really plausible. This would be true if many of the variables in the crosscultural data files were highly correlated. If societies' inheritance practices always matched up with their marriage patterns, for example, then these should really be considered just one variable, not two. In fact, many such correlations among different variables are known to exist. Anthropologists Jack Sawyer and Robert Levine (1966) found that there were enough regularities in the relationships among some aspects of culture that just nine different variables were needed to describe a sample of more than five hundred societies from around the world. Only one variable was necessary to describe the variations in sociopolitical stratification, while subsistence practices and family organization each required just four variables. If we recalculate the total number of possible combinations using only these variables, there are still over one hundred million possible combinations. Although this is a small fraction of my earlier estimate of two hundred billion, it still suggests that only a tiny percentage of the points in the ethnographic hyperspace are occupied.

Cultural Inertia

Maybe the problem is that only certain pathways through the ethnographic hyperspace are actually possible. Once a society gets started on a path, it may not be able to leave it very easily, and changing directions or jumping to nonadjacent points may be difficult. A society's current form is obviously a product of the way it used to be, and it may be that history itself constrains culture. This is analogous to an idea in evolutionary biology called phylogenetic inertia, which states that the power of natural selection to change a species is limited by the range of variations that could plausibly appear in the species. In other words, just because we can imagine that a particular new trait would be helpful to an organism does not mean that it will ever appear. Baboons, for instance, might find wings extremely useful for flying away from leopards or for scouting out new food sources, but there is virtually no chance that they will sprout them any time soon. The necessary modifications in baboon physiology are simply too great for such a thing to occur.

Ethnographers have often noticed a similar sort of limitation on cultural evolution, in which a society fails to alter its current habits or to adopt new ones despite advantages that may seem obvious to an outsider. Monique Borgerhoff Mulder (1989) has documented such cultural inertia among the Kipsigis of western Kenya, a group of farmers and herders who place a lot of value on having many children and grandchildren. Borgerhoff Mulder can show that, thanks to the health and nutritional benefits women get from large farms, in theory the Kipsigis would be able to have more grandchildren if they let daughters as well as sons inherit land. But the idea of letting their daughters inherit land seems never to have occurred to the Kipsigis themselves. The failure of the Kipsigis to let daughters inherit land may simply be a holdover from an earlier time when conditions were different. Until a few decades ago, the Kipsigis were pastoralists, and only males inherited livestock, a pattern that Borgerhoff Mulder can show makes good reproductive sense. After they took up farming, settled down, and developed a system of property rights in land, they retained their sons-only inheritance practice. Just as winged baboons are unlikely to appear any time soon, so it seems the Kipsigis are not likely to let daughters inherit land, no matter how beneficial it might be.

Yet the Kipsigis example itself suggests why this idea is insufficient to explain cultural uniformity. Although their inheritance practices seem slow to adjust, the Kipsigis have actually been going through a period of extreme and rapid change, shifting from nomadic herding to sedentary farming, ever since the British took over Kenya late in the last century. Recent anecdotal reports also suggest that the Kipsigis have begun to pass land on to their sons-in-law, thus maintaining a patrilineal facade while actually providing their daughters with much-needed land (T.J. McMillan, personal communication).

Another Kenyan people, the Mukogodo, provide an even more striking example of how rapidly and drastically it is possible for cultures to change. Before 1925, the Mukogodo were a group of cave-dwelling hunters and gatherers, subsisting on wild animals, plants, and honey and speaking a now-forgotten language called Yaaku. In only about a decade, they completely changed their culture, leaping from one point in the ethnographic hyperspace to another. They dropped foraging and took up herding, and they lost the Yaaku language and learned Maa, an unrelated language spoken by their neighbors (Cronk 1989). Many other groups have gone through changes at least as dramatic, jumping in some cases from the Stone Age to the Silicon Age in little more than a generation. These sorts of rapid behavioral changes are precisely why culture is so useful. While baboons will never sprout wings, we, as cultural animals, already have.

Nature, Reproduction, Society, and Culture

Let's take another look at the Gethenians. Why is it that they have an approach to reproduction and family life that differs so sharply from that of any real society? The key is that Gethenian sexual physiology is quite different from our own, and thus Gethenian nature is very different from human nature. Unlike humans, Gethenians are not continuously sexually receptive. All Gethenians go through a monthly sexual cycle. During the first twenty-one days of the cycle, called *somer*, Gethenians are sexually latent: they are neither interested in sex nor physiologically capable of it. On the twenty-second day an estrus-like period called *kemmer* begins. During the few days that *kemmer* lasts, a Gethenian individual has a very strong sex drive. When a partner in *kemmer* is found, more hormones are secreted until one becomes functionally male and the other functionally female. If the temporarily female partner does not conceive, then after *kemmer* both partners will return to the sexually latent *somer* stage for another three weeks. If she does conceive, she will remain physiologically female for about eight and a half months of gestation and six to eight months of lactation, after which she, too, will return to *somer*. Normal individuals do not have any tendencies to more often become one sex or the other, and they have no control over which sex they end up with during *kemmer*. Those who have given birth do not develop any female habits, and an individual who is the mother of some children might be the father of others. Since no one has a permanent gender and since everybody on Gethen is potentially a childbearer, there can be no sexual division of labor or domination of society by one sex.

Gethenian culture and society is constrained and directed, in large part, by the way they reproduce, by Gethenian nature. But human nature and Gethenian nature are not the same, and our cultures are constrained in different but no less profound ways by how we reproduce. Thanks to the fact that all humans share a long evolutionary history together, we all inevitably have some of the same basic tendencies. Because the one imperative of natural selection is to reproduce, we ought to expect that the most fundamental commonalities among different peoples will be found in those institutions and practices that relate most closely to procreation. Those parts of the human endeavor that do not have much direct influence on reproduction—perhaps including art, music, and many aspects of religion—ought to display the greatest diversity. Although the sexual behavior of unfamiliar peoples, whether South Sea islanders or the new people down the block, may seem exotic, in fact human reproductive practices are fairly uniform.

The institution of the family, in particular, is notable both for its importance in reproduction and for its universality. Humans everywhere tend to favor the basic features of the family, including long-term mating bonds, child care mainly by parents and including significant contributions from the father, and lasting and important relationships among kin.[1] These patterns differ not only from those of the Gethenians but from those of most other mammals, as well. We can see how profoundly these tendencies are rooted in our nature by looking at instances where people have tried to pull up these roots, to create societies without families.

The most famous such experiment is the kibbutzim of Israel. The kibbutz was to be a socialist commune, abolishing all private property, inheritance, the sexual division of labor, and sexual inequality. But the kibbutzim went beyond most other socialist experiments in also trying to do away with the privacy and primacy of the family. Marriage had no official sanction, and children were to be reared communally in age-segregated "children's houses" rather than by their own parents.

Among the world's utopian socialist experiments, the kibbutzim are one of the rare success stories, but only because they have been willing to make some important concessions to human nature in order to keep the experiment alive. Although kibbutzim still give marriage little official recognition, in practice the institution of the family has become as much a part of life in kibbutzim as in any other society. Nowadays, the majority of kibbutz adults get married, and kibbutzim even finance and organize wedding parties. Although meals are eaten in common dining halls, families tend to sit together at separate tables. The attempt to house all children of kibbutz members together and to raise them collectively has also not fared well. Although parents had always visited their children daily, they quickly wanted to see more of each other. Mothers were particularly dissatisfied with the arrangement, and they began spending more and more time in the children's houses. This limited the mothers' mobility and hence their economic usefulness to the community, and it also annoyed those people, called *metaplots*, who were supposed to be supervising the children. Furthermore, almost all *metaplots* were women, and in order to avoid the problem of favoritism no mother was allowed to supervise her own child's group, making the system even more awkward. In many kibbutzim today, nuclear families have been reconstituted, and children's houses are little more than day care centers (Tiger and Shepher 1975; van den Berghe 1979, 70-4).

The utopian religious colony in nineteenth-century Oneida, New York, provides another demonstration of how difficult it can be to eliminate the human family. Oneida was the creation of John Humphrey Noyes, who preached that Christians must emulate the communism of the primitive Christian church (Mandelker 1984, 104). Noyes' communism included not only the ownership of property and other economic arrangements, but also all sexual, familial, and emotional relationships (Mandelker 1984, 105). Noyes and the Oneidans saw monogamous marriage as a form of slavery, and they replaced it with a kind of group or "complex" marriage, in which all were married to all, and in which no one was supposed to develop an exclusive relationship with or feeling for anyone else. Like the kibbutzim, the Oneidan community also communalized child care, housing and educating all of their children in one building. Children were considered to be the charges of the entire community, and parents were discouraged from developing special emotional attachments to their own children (Mandelker 1984, 122-24).

The Oneidans did not, however, trust the success of their project to the religious devotion of the community's members. In order to make sure that couples did not form, they kept a detailed record of every sexual encounter, and even stipulated the length of time that couples could spend in bed together (Mandelker 1984, 117). This sort of routine scrutiny over sexuality enabled the Oneidans to institute what may be their most remarkable innovation, a plan for systematic genetic engineering of their population that they called "stirpiculture." When stirpiculture began, Oneidan women of childbearing age, along with some of the community's young men, signed resolutions renouncing their rights to self-ownership (Mandelker 1984, 119). They gave up the right to choose their own mates, and instead proclaimed themselves to belong first to God and second to John Humphrey Noyes. Noyes, along with a small committee, then selected breeding partners for the community's members. Their goal was to produce a race of people who would be genetically predisposed to the achievement of spiritual perfection.

The bold Oneidan experiment, unlike that of the kibbutzim, did not last. After only a few years, severe strains began to show. Couples fell in love and yearned for lasting, exclusive bonds. Parents loved their own children more than those of others. And, finally, the colony was divided by an unusual political issue: Who was to have the right to initiate female virgins into the sexual life of the community? Until Noyes became elderly, he had always taken this task upon himself. Factions developed around this issue, and eventually the community dissolved and reverted to the traditional human pattern of marriage and sexuality, without genetic bookkeeping (Mandelker 1984, 143).

Although it usually seems to take an act of deliberate planning to push the family out of human society, one unplanned experiment in society without family is also known to have been performed by the Nayars of southwestern India. Before the British imposed colonial rule on their area in 1792, the Nayars were a caste of warriors serving local kings and chiefs. Men were often on the move, frequently remaining away from their home villages for several months a year. This mobility made it difficult for them to maintain exclusive sexual relations with any one woman, and true marriage did not exist. Although all Nayar girls went through a wedding-like ceremony, called the "tali-rite," before puberty, it entailed none of the legal ties of marriage. Rather, completing the tali-rite allowed a girl to begin to select lovers. A woman could have many lovers, and a man might be the lover of many women. An advantage for the men was that they could have lovers in distant places that they could visit during their military excursions. Everyone remained a member of his or her household of birth. Men were expected to provide for their sisters' children, not for those of their lovers.

When the reasons for the unusual Nayar system vanished, so did the system itself. British pacification of the area meant that Nayar men no longer had to spend so much time traveling, and it became possible to establish and maintain long-term, sexually exclusive relationships with individual women. In the two centuries since then, the tali-rite has been lost, and lover relationships are no longer standard. The panhuman standards of marriage and the family have reasserted themselves and are now the norm (Fuller 1976).

The Future of Reproduction, the Future of Society, and the Role of Speculative Fiction

If human sociality is so much a product of how we happen to reproduce, what if our techniques of procreation change? Until recently this was the realm of science fiction, but it is increasingly possible for the normal methods of human reproduction to be modified, and eventually it will be possible to circumvent them almost entirely. Breast feeding became unnecessary long ago, and sexual intercourse itself can also now be bypassed through in-vitro fertilization. Surrogate motherhood is a first step in separating a mother from her developing fetus, and artificial wombs will complete the move.

Someday soon not only intercourse but even fertilization may be avoidable as scientists invent ways to make eggs divide and develop with no sperm present. As British science writers Jeremy Chervas and John Cribben argue in their book *The Redundant Male*, eventually women may wise up to the fact that males may actually be little more than vestiges of an evolutionary history in which sexual reproduction was an advantage, of as little relevance to modern reproductive life as the appendix is to modern digestion.

But how boring such a sexless world would be! Perhaps a race of asexually reproducing females would eventually want to reinvent the practice, if for no other purpose than as an enjoyable pastime. But it seems unlikely that they would redivide the world into male and female, and this brings us back to Gethen. A month-long sexual cycle, a world of ambisexuals in which everyone has the potential to be a temporary male or temporary female, a world in which real gender is nonexistent and therefore cannot determine life history or status—this seems like the kind of world that our asexual descendants might choose to experiment with. Interestingly, our ethnographer friend O. T. Oppong speculates that Gethenian sexual physiology was the product of genetic engineering.

As we strike off into uncharted sociocultural territory, it is worth remembering the enormity of the ethnographic hyperspace. Speculative fiction has an important role to play in this endeavor as a source of ideas, inspiration, and risk-free experimentation, helping us to navigate in a realm where the only landmarks are the ones we create ourselves.2

Works Cited

Borgerhoff Mulder, M.

1989 "Reproductive Consequences of Sex-biased Inheritance." In V. Standen and R. A. Foley, eds., *Comparative Socioecology of Mammals and Man*. London: Blackwell.

Cherfas, J., and J. Cribben

1984 *The Redundant Male*. New York: Pantheon.

Cronk, L.

1989 "From Hunters to Herders: Subsistence Change as a Reproductive Strategy among the Mukogodo." *Current Anthropology* 30:224-34.

Dressler, A.

1989 "In the Grip of the Great Attractor." *The Sciences* 29 (5):28-34.

Fisher, H.E.

1989 "The Evolution of Human Serial Pairbonding." *American Journal of Physical Anthropology* 78: 331-54.

Fuller, C.J.

1976 *The Nayars Today*. Cambridge, MA: Cambridge University Press.

Kroeber, T.

1961 *Ishi in Two Worlds*. Berkeley, CA: University of California Press.

LeGuin, U.K.

1969 *The Left Hand of Darkness*. New York: Berkley.

Mandelker, I.L.

1984 *Religion, Society, and Utopia in Nineteenth-Century America*. Amherst, MA: University of Massachusetts Press.

Murdock, G.P.

1949 *Social Structure*. New York: MacMillan.

1967 *Ethnographic Atlas*. Pittsburgh, PA: University of Pittsburgh Press.

Sawyer, J., and R.A. LeVine

1966 "Cultural Dimensions: A Factor Analysis of the World Ethnographic Sample." *American Anthropologist* 68:708-31.

Tiger, L., and J. Shepher

1975 *Women in the Kibbutz*. New York: Harcourt Brace Jovanovich.

Tylor, E.B.

1889 "On a Method of Investigating the Development of Institutions: Applied to Laws of Marriage and Descent." *Journal of the Royal Anthropological Institute* 18:245-69.

Van den Berghe, P.

1979 *Human Family Systems*. New York: Elsevier.

Westfahl, G.

1990 "'A Tremendous New Force': How Science Fiction Proposes to Change the World." Paper presented to the conference on "The Fantastic Imagination in New Critical Theories," Texas A&M University, College Station, Texas.

Notes

1. Although the stability of marriages is quite variable across human cultures and throughout human history, as a species humans tend to have much longer mating bonds than do most other species, particularly most other primates. While mating bonds among many species last only long enough to ensure insemination, the typical human pattern is for mating bonds to last at least long enough for a couple to successfully rear one offspring (Fisher 1989).
2. See also Westfahl 1990.

The Dance with Darkness: The Limits of Human Interest in Science Fiction

Gary Westfahl

The fundamental hypothesis of sociobiology is that a wide variety of human activities, and many aspects of human culture, can be attributed to genetic influence resulting from the process of natural selection. Looking at literature, the sociobiologist would posit that a small number of narrative patterns repeatedly occur in different cultures because they reflect attitudes that improve human survival and improvement. As Edward O. Wilson observed in *Biophilia,*

> Certain great myths—the origin of the world, cataclysm and rebirth, the struggle between the powers of light and darkness, Earth Mother, and a few others—recur dependably in cultures around the world. Lesser, more personal myths appear in crisis poems and romantic tales, where they blend imperceptibly into legend and history. Through the deep pleasures they naturally excite, and the ease with which they are passed from one person to another, these stories invade the developing mind more readily than others, and they tend to converge to form the commonalities of human nature . . . .Continuity is essential for comprehension; the imagery chosen by the artist must draw upon common experiences and values, however tortuous the manner of presentation. (Wilson 1984, 80-81)

Thus, looking at numerous narratives from societies widely separated in space and/or time, the sociobiologist would expect to find a noteworthy degree of "convergence" and "continuity" linking all of them.

Stating this hypothesis is easy, but proving it, I believe, would be extremely difficult. Literary scholars would have to begin by adopting some critical apparatus—probably that of narratology—to identify and classify all possible patterns in narrative. Next, they would need to survey and choose examples of oral and written narratives from all known human cultures, past and present, and analyze each narrative in the context of that critical apparatus. Finally, they would need to compile statistical results clearly indicating that certain patterns and styles in narratives are repeatedly favored, while other, equally possible patterns and styles are repeatedly neglected.[1]

There is, however, another potential method of proof which would be less definitive but nevertheless highly indicative: Begin by attempting to define and encourage a new genre of literature which involved approaches and attitudes that are fundamentally nonhuman, demanding subject matter and styles that are significantly different from any previous literary forms; next, observe the evolution and development of this new genre. If the distinctive and unprecedented priorities of the genre repeatedly appear and prove popular, that would indicate that existing patterns in literature are merely a matter of cultural traditions and borrowings, not genetic influence. If the new genre resists its announced priorities and repeatedly drifts into approaches that are similar to other forms of literature, that would indicate there is an element of genetic predisposition in the ways humans create and respond to literature.

That experiment has actually begun, and it is continuing at the present time; it is called science fiction. And while the final results are not in, the history of the genre to date does seem to offer support for the sociobiological hypothesis.

When Hugo Gernsback first launched the modern genre of science fiction, he announced one major principle: "The story . . . . must contain correct scientific facts" (Gernsback 1927, 213). Of course, this requirement could simply produce thoroughly conventional stories which unproblematically incorporated some tidbits of scientific information, and Gernsback published many such works. However, the possibility emerged that in some cases, the presence of accurate scientific information might in some way distort the narrative, might force the writer into unexpected or unpleasant directions.

John W. Campbell, Jr., Gernsback's major successor, first added the principle that "Science-fiction, being largely an attempt to forecast the future, on the basis of the present, represents a type of extrapolation" (Campbell 1940, 5) —so that the genre incorporated not only the facts, but also the thought process of science, further increasing its potential for creating strange and nonhuman narratives. In addition, he explained why science fiction was different from other forms of literature. "Science-fiction is the freest, least formalized of any literary medium. . . .Because the author feels that freedom, he can let the story have its head, let it develop in any direction that the logic of the developing situation may dictate. Many times a story actually winds up entirely different from the idea with which the author started" (Campbell 1948, 5-6). Perhaps Campbell's strongest statement regarding the uniqueness of science fiction came in his 1956 essay, "Science-Fiction and the Opinion of the Universe."

> Where classical values hold that human nature is enduring, unchanging, and uniform, science-fiction holds that it is mutable, complex, and differentiated . . . . [Other personality] types are ruled by opinion: the opinion expressed in traditions, their own inner opinions, or the opinions of others. The Universe-Directed type isn't ruled by opinions—he's dominated by the facts of the Universe. . . . It doesn't matter what his opinion is, or what anybody else's opinion is, has been, or will be. The only thing that will make his device work is the Universe's "opinion." . . . The scientist will appear from the viewpoint of someone who considers opinion the dominant force in reality—rigid, cold-blooded, emotionless, and authoritarian-dogmatic. He isn't; the Universe is, and he's acting simply as the messenger of the Universe. (Campbell 1956, 10)

Then, like later critics, he discusses Tom Godwin's "The Cold Equations" to show how science fiction can indeed violate traditional expectations by adhering to scientific logic.

The value of such strange stories, in Campbell's view, was that they could help people anticipate, and cope with, unprecedented developments coming in the future; as he once explained, science fiction was "a way of considering the past, present, and future from a different viewpoint, and taking a look at how else we *might* do things. . . .a convenient analog system for thinking about new scientific, social, and economic ideas—and for re-examining old ideas" (Campbell 1962, 10, 13).[2] Of course, rehearsing possible scenarios has long been a defense of all fiction; but in Campbell's view, science fiction is uniquely valuable because its writers, governed solely by "the Opinion of the Universe," are better able to free themselves from conventional preconceptions and stereotypes.

It is also worth noting that both Gernsback and Campbell saw the emergence of science fiction as a necessary, even inevitable, stage in the development of humanity. Gernsback focused on the genre as a way to eliminate older attitudes in those who had not yet started to read it: "science fiction. . . is to be an important factor in making the world a better place to live in, through educating the public to the possibilities of science and the influence of science on life. . . . Science fiction would make people happier, give them a broader understanding of the world; make them more tolerant" (Gernsback 1930, 1061). Campbell emphasized the genre as an indication of an entirely new attitude developing in those who were reading it.

> Any form of entertainment that finds a considerable audience of patrons must grow out of some fundamental characteristic of the civilization which it serves. . . . It's not surprising, in view of this, that the recorder of happenings—the reporter—existed in Babylon and exists today. The historian, the playwright, the dancer—all existed. . . .
>
> Save for one thing. Science-fiction finds no counterpart in the entertainment of history. . . .As a form of entertainment that has attracted tens and hundreds of thousands of readers, it must represent some totally new characteristic of our civilization. . . . It arises, I think, in this: for the first time in all the history of Man's climb, he looks forward to better things, and not backward to a forgotten "Golden Age.". . .Science-fiction is not a happenstance, a fad that comes and goes by chance listing of public interest, but a characteristic symptom of this stage of evolution, a type of entertainment that would, inevitably, arise in any civilization that reached this particular level of advance. (Campbell 1939, 6)

Thus, the modern genre of science fiction is a necessary development in the history of any intelligent civilization which reaches a transitional stage between regarding the future as frightening and dreadful—which Gernsback calls the attitude of the "Middle Ages" (Gernsback 1930, 1061)—and regarding it with curiosity or even hope—the typical attitude of "this particular level of advance."

One might flesh out the scenario in this way: in the early stages of an intelligent culture, the typical focus of the desire for new things is spatial—the urge to explore unknown regions of the present environment—while the past and the future are regarded as mysterious, unknowable, and even frightening. Spatial exploration soon leads to both a steady increase in scientific knowledge and, eventually, a virtually complete examination of the available environment. The focus of the drive for the unknown then becomes *temporal*—a heightened curiosity about the past and the future—a form of exploration which demands scientific knowledge and, in areas where knowledge is not available, intelligent scientific hypotheses and extrapolation. At this time, something like science fiction appears to function as one vehicle for the imaginative exploration of the future and, to a lesser extent, the past.[4]

And how would E. O. Wilson view the possible development of a genre like science fiction? His comments suggest he would see both potential value and potential problems in such a literature. On the one hand, he appreciates the importance of a human drive for the new and unknown and makes specific reference to the inhuman visions of science fiction: in *Biophilia*, he says that "novelty and diversity are particularly esteemed; the mere mention of the word *extraterrestrial* evokes reveries about still unexplored life, displacing the old and once potent *exotic* that drew earlier generations to remote islands and jungled interiors" (Wilson 1984, 1). And in *On Human Nature*, he argues for new scientific knowledge as an important aspect of human progress.

> I hope that. . .a true sense of wonder will reinvade the broader culture. We need to speak more explicitly of the things we do not know. The epic of which natural scientists write in technical fragments still has immense gaps and absorbing mysteries, not the least of which is the physical basis of the mind. Like blank spaces on the map of a partly explored world, their near borders can be fixed but their inner magnitude only roughly guessed. Scientists and humanistic scholars can do

> far better than they have at articulating the great goals toward which literate people move as on a voyage of discovery. Unknown and surprising things await. . . . As knowledge grows science must increasingly become the stimulus to imagination. (Wilson 1978, 212)

Especially in its use of the term "wonder," often evoked as one of the genre's goals, this statement could be seen as an argument for increasing attention to science fiction.

On the other hand, Wilson seems to sense that there are certain limits in the human capacity and desire to seek out what is different and unknown. He claims that "there is in addition an optimal degree of novelty in problem-solving, difficult to measure and follow. Stick to the coast too tightly and only minor new data will follow. Venture out of sight and you risk getting lost at sea" (Wilson 1984, 66).[5]

Applying these principles to a projected genre based on scientific facts and values, then, one would expect to find a literature somewhat different in its surface features but also continually drawn back to conventional human attitudes and expectations. More often than not, that is what we find in science fiction.

Oddly enough, the very story that Campbell cites as evidence for the strangeness of science fiction—Godwin's "The Cold Equations"—actually provides evidence against that hypothesis. Certainly, the story as we see it is unconventional: everything about conventional literary patterns and human priorities leads us to expect a happy ending where a girl stowaway on a spaceship somehow survives, but the author insists that the laws of physics demand her death. However, "The Cold Equations" actually represents the triumph of an attitude exactly opposite to the one Campbell presents, because Godwin originally wrote the story so that the girl survived.[6] The happy ending naturally emerged from the story Godwin wrote; the ending we have instead was imposed by Campbell's editorial insistence and was retained by Godwin in later editions, no doubt because the story was widely acclaimed.

One can imagine what "The Cold Equations" was like in its original form. The beginning of the story was the same: a man discovers a girl stowaway and reluctantly tells her that the cold equations of motion mean that she has to die. But Godwin's original hero did not leave it at that; he kept studying those cold equations, and eventually he found a fudge factor, a loophole, and figured out a way to save the girl. That impulse—the determination to push and twist scientific reality to meet human needs—is, I submit, what actually tends to dominate in the writing of science fiction.

As another example of this process at work, consider the novel Lee Cronk offered earlier in this volume as an example of the genre's capacity for imaginative vision, Ursula K. LeGuin's *The Left Hand of Darkness*. As Cronk eloquently argues, LeGuin's novel can be viewed as an intriguing thought-experiment of exactly the sort that Campbell envisioned: what would human culture be like if all people were one sex—alternately male and female? Having established this premise, LeGuin can then employ her background in and knowledge of anthropology to develop a detailed, convincing picture of a uniquely egalitarian society and thus obtain insights into the nature of humanity which could not be drawn from an examination of any existing civilization.

However, there are some ways in which LeGuin seems to compromise this process.

One can first question the logic behind the political organization of Gethenian society. In early human culture, one sees the emergence of a power structure where members of one, physically stronger sex—men—achieve authority over members of the other, physically weaker sex—women;[7] and the institutions of absolute monarchy and its successor, totalitarianism, apparently develop as an expansion and generalization of this type of relationship: some persons—nobles, dictators—are defined as more worthy and achieve dominion over others—the common people—who are defined as less worthy. In contrast, a culture where all persons are alternately men and women would never generate, it seems, a power structure of one person absolutely dominating another, and its overall political organization would probably be based more on consensus and shared responsibility—perhaps a council of elders, each with authority at different times and in different situations. In fact, an early report on Gethen cited by LeGuin seems to explicitly rule out the development of an authoritarian political system on the planet: "There is no division of humanity into strong and weak halves, protective/protected, dominant/submissive, owner/chattel, active/passive" (LeGuin 1969, 94).

If these premises are granted, then the actual political structures of the Gethenians seem inconsistent. First there is Karhide, an absolute monarchy, with all the trappings and court intrigues of a kingdom in medieval Europe. Here, LeGuin falls back on a common assumption in science fiction which is hopelessly anthropocentric and Eurocentric—namely, that alien civilizations which are less advanced in technology than earth will invariably employ a governmental system of early earth civilization, and of early European civilization in particular. Thus, for all its apparent strangeness, her story is also one among countless science fiction works which illogically present bizarre aliens as kings, princes, and prime ministers, with costumes and functions right out of the history of earth. The other Gethenian society LeGuin depicts, Orgoreyn, is modeled on the terrestrial descendant of the medieval monarchy—the totalitarian bureaucratic state—which seems equally peculiar in the context of Gethen. Even the narrator is driven to comment on the incongruity of these political systems: "It had been entertaining and fascinating to find here on Gethen governments so similar to those in the ancient histories of Terra" (144). The fact that LeGuin's political imagination is so limited suggests that writers might face similar limitations imagining innovations in other areas.

In addition, while it is by nature a subject difficult to analyze, the typical Gethenian might view human societies, where persons are either permanently male or permanently female, as perverse, mockeries of true civilization—like a society of people who are half legless and half armless, or of people who are half blind and half deaf. In LeGuin's story, the human First Mobile, Genly Ai, is repeatedly described as a "pervert" by the Gethenians (36, 63-64, 183, 294). While Ai himself seems tolerant and open-minded, the predictable attitude most humans would have regarding Gethenians can be seen in the role that hermaphrodites now play in our culture—namely, as exhibits in freak shows. A reasonable conclusion would be that humans and Gethenians would have tremendous difficulty in finding common ground; instead, they would see each other as strange and nonhuman in fundamental ways.

LeGuin's novel goes in the opposite direction, for during a long and arduous journey, Ai and one Gethenian, Estravan, become allies and friends, with the suggestion of an unconsummated romantic attachment as well. Here, one may maintain, LeGuin is shamelessly employing some of the oldest cliches in popular literature: that persons with vastly disparate backgrounds will always come together to fight for a common cause—"Maybe we have learned to pull together. . . .Considering from what distances we have come together to share this tent a while, we do well enough" (222, 223); that a man and a woman who initially despise each other, who in fact seem like complete opposites, will invariably end up falling in love—"But it was from the difference between us, not from the affinities and likenesses, but from the difference, that that love came" (248-49); that despite apparent differences, under the skin, all men are brothers[8]—Estravan "had entirely accepted me as a human being, . . . liked me personally and given me entire personal loyalty. . . .The great and sudden assurance of friendship between us rose" (248). Estravan's death, a direct result of his decision to help Ai, might be said to illustrate that this coming together of human and Gethenian is tragically impossible. However, the fact that the Gethenians finally agree to join the Ekumen serves instead to additionally bolster and validate that spirit of conventional reconciliation, as also seen in the novel's last sentence: "Will you tell us about the other worlds out among the stars—the other kinds of men, the other lives?" (301). Thus, LeGuin implies that with increasing knowledge of and communication with each other, humans and Gethenians will achieve a true meeting of minds—a conclusion that, in light of her other demonstrations of the Gethenians' fundamental alienness, seems a bit pat.

These may be harsh judgments to make about *The Left Hand of Darkness*, and in fact there are perfectly good reasons why LeGuin chose to develop her novel in the way she did. First, as a matter of internal logic, LeGuin is careful to point out that Gethenians are related to human beings—both peoples are descendants of the ancient Hainish race—though their physiology was later transformed in some unknown way. With this noted, similarities between medieval European and Gethenian governmental systems, and the ability of the First Mobile to build a close relationship with a Gethenian, may be explained: there is a genetic and ancestral link between the two cultures. However, one may protest that there was no reason, except caution, to picture Gethenians as lost humans instead of as true aliens, and that such an explanation cannot serve to justify a limited imagination.

More broadly, there are grounds for LeGuin's choice directly related to the theory of science fiction and its usefulness as a fulfillment of some desire for new and nonhuman visions. Although LeGuin herself claims to resist the tendency to present obvious morals in her fiction,[9] one may safely say, without in any way being simplistic or reductionist, that one of her motives in writing this novel was to argue that ours is a culture which attaches far too much importance to differences between sexes; and the example of the Gethenians demonstrates that a society that lacks such differences can indeed function. She thus argues that our society might profitably pay less attention to the matter of an individual's sex. The theme emerges in Ai's comment that in human society "the most important thing, the heaviest single factor in one's life, is whether one's born male or female. In most societies it determines one's expectations, activities, outlook, ethics, manners—almost everything. Vocabulary. Semiotic usages. Clothing. Even food" (234). In the 1976 introduction to the novel, LeGuin is even more explicit. "I'm [not] predicting that in a millennium or so we will all be androgynous, or announcing that I think we damned well ought to be androgynous. I'm merely observing, in the peculiar, devious, and thought-experimental manner proper to science fiction, that if you look at us at certain odd times of day in certain weathers, we already are" (LeGuin 1976, xv).

LeGuin further indicates that the Gethenians were created as a commentary on the human race. In a strangely false note in her final chapter; when Ai sees his fellow humans for the first time in two years, he sees them as aliens: "They all looked strange to me, men and women, well as I knew them. They were like a troupe of great, strange animals, of two different species; great apes with intelligent eyes, all of them in rut, in kemmer" (296). This is not so much a believable human reaction as a direct reference to the end of Jonathan Swift's *Gulliver's Travels*, where the returned Gulliver persists in seeing humans as Yahoos and horses as Houyhnhnms—a conclusion also borrowed by H. G. Wells in *The Island of Dr. Moreau*, where the returned Prendick sees humans as beast-men. In this way, LeGuin places her novel firmly in a tradition of works which create an alternative society in order to make some statement about contemporary humanity.

With such a purpose in mind, LeGuin would surely be driven to make the Gethenians seem more human, not more alien. That is, the air of medievalism which permeates Gethenian society—especially prominent in the description of the ceremony in the first chapter—adds a necessary element of the conventional which enables readers to better identify with, and draw conclusions from, the Gethenians. The developing relationship between Ai and Estravan is another useful technique to further humanize, and to help readers see themselves in, the Gethenians. So LeGuin must make the Gethenians seem somewhat familiar in order to achieve her original goals in creating something different.

In addition, LeGuin probably felt a powerful urge to arrange her novel in this way for aesthetic reasons. To refer to Northrop Frye's *Anatomy of Criticism*, one may argue that there are two fundamental patterns in tales of transformation: strangers who become friends (comedy) and friends who become strangers (tragedy); thus, a story about strangers who remain strangers seems wrong, unnatural, and unsatisfying. After creating apparently disparate characters like humans and Gethenians, an author, almost invariably, will feel a powerful urge to reconcile, to harmonize, to bring together the opposites.

Considered as an artist, in short, LeGuin has unquestionably succeeded in producing a thought-provoking and aesthetically pleasing novel; but considered as a scientific experimenter in the manner of Campbell, she has her thumb on the scales. She is slightly fudging her data, all so that she can achieve certain prearranged—and predictable—goals. What might be concluded, then, is paradoxical: on the one hand, one of the primary values posited for science fiction is that it offers unique and strikingly different pictures and narratives; on the other hand, science fiction seems compelled to move away from the nonhuman, to familiarize instead of alienating.

One response to this judgment would be that I am describing a virtually inevitable phenomenon: human authors will always, despite intentions to the contrary, produce works which reflect human experiences and values. And yet there are texts in the genre which do suggest other possibilities. One example of a story involving contact between humans and aliens where a process of familiarization does not occur, where the aliens remain completely alien, where there is no final reconciliation or coming together, is Terry Carr's "The Dance of the Changer and the Three."[10]

In some ways, Carr's story and LeGuin's novel are similar: Both describe humans landing on another world and establishing contact with a race of aliens. Both have a protagonist whose special assignment is to communicate with and understand those aliens. Both narrators characterize their narratives in fictional terms—Ai says, "I'll make my report as if I told a story" (LeGuin 1969, 1), and Carr's hero observes, "You could take this as a piece of pure fiction" (Carr 1968, 38). And both involve not only events in the story's present but also some discussion of the aliens' past history, legends, and folklore.

However, the works are also fundamentally dissimilar. While LeGuin creates humanoid aliens on a terrestrial planet with a single physiological difference, Carr extravagantly constructs bizarre aliens called the Loarra living on a giant gaseous world. Made out of energy, the Loarra are virtually immortal, as they die and are reborn countless of times over millions of years. LeGuin's protagonist has no difficulty contacting and talking to the Gethenians, and the legends and myths included in the novel provide insight into Gethenian society and attitudes. Carr's hero, on the other hand, despite years of research and many long conversations with the aliens, remains completely puzzled by their psychology and culture. The dance of the story's title, enacting a centrally important narrative in Loarra society, seems to inexplicably celebrate a completely pointless act—three aliens struggle to create a foodbeast, then immediately eat it—and leaves the narrator completely baffled: "I always get stuck at that one point in the story, that supremely contradictory moment when the Three destroyed what they had made, when they came away with no more than they had brought with them" (50). While *The Left Hand of Darkness* ends with reconciliation and reunion, "The Dance of the Changer and the Three" stops on an uncertain note. After years of friendly contact, the aliens inexplicably attack and kill most of the humans on the planet. Instead of coming to understand and appreciate the Loarra, Carr's hero simply learns to despise them: "They were all, as far as I was concerned, totally crazy, incomprehensible, stupid, silly, and plain damn no good" (48). The story, unlike conventional narratives, lacks a true ending, as the hero is left on earth waiting for word from the authorities on whether to abandon the base or to continue efforts to coexist with the aliens. The story's last sentence—"Unicentral has been humming and clicking for ten months now, but it hasn't made a decision" (52) —contrasts most strongly with LeGuin's last sentence, since in her novel both humans and Gethenians have clearly made a decision.

"The Dance of the Changer and the Three" is thus deeply problematic to its author, to its characters, and to its readers. To make sense of it, one might characterize the story as a narrative thought-experiment in which, instead of asking, like LeGuin, What would people be like if they did not have sexual differences? Carr asks, What would people be like if they had no material existence and no fear of death? Carr's premises do not lead to any worthwhile or satisfying conclusions. On the one hand, such creatures, millions of years old, might be so bound by tradition and past experience that they would continue to repeatedly venerate, in an exactly replicated dance, a event which occurred eons ago. On the other hand, not fearing death, these beings might be totally free of any concerns for the past or future and instead might dedicate themselves to the moment at hand, to extravagant and glorious but ultimately meaningless gestures like the adventure described in the dance. Such beings might welcome the presence of human beings as a novelty in their otherwise changeless existence, but they might also regard them as an impertinence and decide, on the spur of the moment, to destroy them all. The only coherent judgment to be made about these beings is that they would be completely unfamiliar, almost incomprehensible to human beings. The suspended conclusion of the story offers no answers, but only asks the question: What can be done about aliens that humans, it seems, cannot understand?

By comparison with *The Left Hand of Darkness*, to be sure, "The Dance of the Changer and the Three" is inferior by almost every normal literary standard. It lacks the direct relevance to the human condition which LeGuin's story offers, and it lacks the structure, style, and polish which LeGuin's story displays. Yet it can hardly be denied that Carr's story better achieves a sense of the nonhuman—and that is the point. While there do, then, actually exist science fiction stories which illustrate the genre's power to move in unfamiliar directions, they tend to be neglected and regarded as minor works. In contrast, works like *The Left Hand of Darkness,* which promise strangeness and actually deliver conventionality, are more highly esteemed and imitated.

Thus, the genre of science fiction seems trapped in a tug of war. Driven by its pronounced purposes and intentions towards the unfamiliar, it also retains an attraction to the familiar patterns found in other literature. Since this latter tendency generally seems more powerful, the results of the experiment of science fiction at this time, as I previously indicated, seem to provide support for the sociobiological hypothesis.

However, biology is not necessarily destiny, and given the tremendous challenges confronting the human race at this stage in its development, one might argue that the unusual science fiction of the sort Carr offers is in fact needed to glimpse possibilities not available in other forms of literature, and in fact not available in most existing works of science fiction, including *The Left Hand of Darkness*. For these reasons, the apparent inability of human beings to create and accept truly new types of narratives might be seen as a long-term threat to our survival as a species.[11]

In earlier times, people constructed a vision of the universe which was comforting, understandable, and scaled to human needs and desires. The sky was a large bowl inverted over the surface of the earth, with lanterns called stars hanging from it; benevolent deities guided the sun and the moon across the sky and, in a more temperamental way, provided rain, fair weather, and other bounties for mankind. All aspects of nature symbolized, embodied, influenced, or otherwise matched human thoughts and experiences. Life flowed on in predictable cycles of birth and death, day and night, summer and winter, bracketed only by an origin in the distant past and, perhaps, an apocalypse in the distant future. The narratives that people read and write continue, by and large, to reflect and reinforce this vision.

But this is not the universe we live in.

Modern science, impelled by an uncompromising drive to obtain accurate data and to devise theories which fit those data, presents instead a universe that is dark, threatening, and thoroughly incommensurate with the human condition: a universe infinitely more vast and more ancient that the human lifespan; a universe which began with a few seconds of tumultuous change before settling down to billions of years of uniformity; a universe built out of superstrings with ten physical dimensions, seven of them folded in to provide the illusion of three dimensions; a universe in which humanity—or any intelligent life—seems not a product of design, or the inevitable result of a comprehensible process, but rather a result of luck, coincidence, or accident. All in all, it is an ugly, bizarre, and unsatisfactory universe.

But this is the universe we live in.

And this is the universe which our literature must prepare us to live in.

If, as some maintain, all science fiction does is to provide imaginative alternative worlds which comment on and contrast with existing reality, then the genre is merely following a literary strategy at least as old as Plato and one which promises nothing really different except for some unusual surface features. LeGuin, for one, seems perfectly content with this view of the genre.

> All fiction is metaphor. Science fiction is metaphor. What sets it apart from older forms of fiction seems to be its use of new metaphors, drawn from certain great dominants of our contemporary life—science, all the sciences, and technology, and the relativistic and historical outlook, among them. Space travel is one of these metaphors; so is an alternative society, an alternative biology; the future is another. The future, in fiction, is a metaphor. (LeGuin, 1976 xvi)

Hugo Gernsback and John W. Campbell, Jr., would reject the idea that science fiction was only offering "new metaphors," new surface details. Instead, they envisioned science fiction as a literature which would incorporate the data of science and its processes of investigation in order to produce unprecedented and nonhuman narrative visions that could be useful to modern-day humanity. Using a "scenario from science fiction," Wilson illustrates the difference between the dubious strangeness of LeGuin and the more profound sense of the alien that the science fiction might actually achieve.

> Human beings, [Robert Nozick] notes, justify the eating of meat on the grounds that the animals we kill are too far below us in sensitivity and intelligence to bear comparison. It follows that if representatives of a truly superior extraterrestrial species were to visit Earth and apply the

> same criterion, they could proceed to eat us in good conscience. By the same token, scientists among these aliens might find human beings uninteresting, our intelligence weak, our passions unsurprising, our social organization of a kind already frequently encountered on other planets. To our chagrin they might then focus on the ants, because these little creatures, with their haplodiploid form of sex determination and bizarre female caste systems, are the truly novel productions of the Earth with reference to the Galaxy. (Wilson 1978, 18)

Nozick's suggestion is a "metaphor," a smug cautionary tale with a preordained conclusion where the aliens think exactly like people and therefore judge people, as we judge animals, solely on the basis of intelligence. This analogy therefore does not evoke the truly alien. However, Wilson extends the story in a different way. He suggests that the aliens might truly think in alien terms and might judge creatures by entirely alien standards, so that humans would emerge as inferior not only to advanced aliens but to creatures that we now regard as inferior. This is a premise, like Carr's, that might be extended into a story challenging conventional assumptions and perspectives and forcing readers to ponder the unpredictable consequences of contact with alien life.

It is by including the nonhuman information and nonhuman perspective of science, then, that science fiction might become a literature which is truly nonhuman—and a literature which more truly reflects the universe as it is or as it may be. Yet science fiction seems unable to fully achieve those goals. As I have observed elsewhere,[12] science fiction, despite pretensions to the contrary, may be seen as a genre theoretically committed to the alien and practically wedded to the familiar. This may not be simply the result of the limited imaginations of particular writers but, rather, a fundamental limitation in the human imagination.

Still, even in the face of an apparent genetic inclination to the contrary, the possibility of nonhuman literature continues to exist, and the best—perhaps the only—way to achieve it is by rigorously following the procedures outlined by Gernsback and Campbell. Perhaps in this way, in defiance of their biological dictates, humans might create a literature that would truly help them accept current knowledge and prepare for future possibilities.

Because, in the universe we are now becoming aware of, human beings are going to have to dance with the darkness.

Works Cited

Benford, Gregory

1980 *Timescape.* New York: Simon and Schuster

.Campbell, John W., Jr.

1939 "Future Tense." *Astounding Science-Fiction* 23 (June):6.

1940 "The Perfect Machine." *Astounding Science Fiction* 25 (May):5.

1948 "Introduction." In John W. Campbell, Jr., *Who Goes There?* Chicago: Shasta Publishing Company, pp. 3-6.

1952 "Introduction." In John W. Campbell, Jr., ed., *The Astounding Science Fiction Anthology*. NewYork: Simon and Schuster, pp. ix-xv.

1956 "Science Fiction and the Opinion of the Universe." *Saturday Review* 39 (May 12):9-10, 42-43.

1962 "Introduction." *In Prologue to Analog*. Edited by John W. Campbell, Jr. Garden City, NJ: Doubleday and Company, pp. 9-16.

Carr, Terry

1971 "The Dance of the Changer and the Three." In Poul Anderson, ed., *Nebula Award Stories Four*. New York: Pocket Books, pp. 38-52.

Clarke, Arthur C.

1968 *2001: A Space Odyssey*. Based on a screenplay by Stanley Kubrick and Arthur C. Clarke. New York: Signet Books.

Clement, Hal

1980 *The Nitrogen Fix*. New York: Ace Books

Frye, Northrop

1971 *The Anatomy of Criticism: Four Essays*. Princeton: Princeton University Press.

Gernsback, Hugo

1927 "The $500 Cover Prize Contest." *Amazing Stories* 2 (June):213.

1930 "Science Fiction Week." *Science Wonder Stories* 1 (May):1061.

Godwin, Tom

1971 "The Cold Equations." In Robert Silverberg, ed., *The Science Fiction Hall of Fame*. New York: Avon Books, pp. 543-69.

Knight, Damon

1968 "Stranger Station." In Judith Merril, ed., *SF: The Best of the Best*. New York: Dell Books, pp. 143-68.

LeGuin, Ursula K.

1973 "Afterword" to "The Word for World Is Forest." In Harlan Ellison, ed., *Again, Dangerous Visions* I. New York: Signet Books, pp. 126.

1976 *The Left Hand of Darkness*. New York: Ace Books, pp. xi-xvi.

Lem, Stanislaw

1971 *Solaris*. Translated from the French by Joanna Kilmartin and Steve Cox. London: Faber and Faber.

Quinones, Ricardo

1972 *The Renaissance Discovery of Time*. Cambridge, MA: Harvard University Press.

Stapledon, Olaf

1968 *Last and First Men*. In *Last and First Men and Star Maker: Two Science-Fiction Novels.* New York: Dover Books.

Suvin, Darko

1979 *Metamorphoses of Science Fiction: On the Poetics and History of a Literary Genre*. New Haven: Yale University Press.

Tiptree, James P., Jr. [Alice Sheldon]

1978 "And I Awoke and Found Me Here on the Cold Hill's Side." In Brian W. Aldiss, ed., *Space Odysseys*. New York: Berkley Books, pp. 129-37.

Westfahl, Gary

1990a "'An Idea of Significant Import': Hugo Gernsback's Theory of Science Fiction." *Foundation: The Review of Science Fiction* 48 (Spring):26-50.

1990b "On *The True History of Science Fiction*." Foundation: *The Review of Science Fiction* 47(Winter/Spring):5-27.

1991 "Small Worlds and Strange Tomorrows: The Icon of the Space Station in Science Fiction." *Foundation: The Review of Science Fiction* 51 (Winter/Spring):38-63.

1992 "'A Convenient Analog System': John W. Campbell, Jr.'s Theory of Science Fiction." *Foundation: The Review of Science Fiction* 54 (Spring):52-70.

1996 *Islands in the Sky: The Space Station Theme in Science Fiction Literature*. San Bernardino, CA: Borgo Press.

Wilson, Edward O.

1979 *On Human Nature*. New York: Bantam Books, 1979.

1984 *Biophilia*. Cambridge, MA: Harvard University Press.

Notes

1. To an extent, the Stith-Thompson index has already accomplished this with regard to folklore.
2. Gernsback's and Campbell's theories of science fiction are further discussed in "An Idea of Significant Import" and "A Convenient Analog System" (Westfahl 1990a, 1992).
3. This does not mean that science fiction is necessarily optimistic about all future changes—a point clarified in a later comment from Campbell: "Science fiction. . . .unlike other literatures, assumes that change is the natural order of things"(Campbell 1952, xiii). Certainly, science fiction stories often project futures that should be feared; but the science fiction writer does not *automatically* fear the future, or future changes.
4. This formula relates to what Darko Suvin sees as a "shift" in "the location of estrangement...from space to time" (Suvin 1979, 89), although Suvin sees this as an event in a purported history of science fiction—an interpretation I dispute in "On *The True History of Science Fiction*" (1990b). Suvin argues that this change occurred around 1800, but I would maintain that the perspective originated earlier—as discussed in Ricardo Quinones's *The Renaissance Discovery of Time*—and that it was not until the twentieth century, when the earth was completely explored and when all fields of science were on solid

ground, that a major focus on temporal speculation fully developed. The notion that science fiction appears as a means of investigating other times, by the way, also explains why stories about cavemen and prehistoric peoples—who seem to lack any concern for science or scientific progress—have been accepted as "science fiction." The answer is that science fiction is not a genre of gadgets and spectacular visions, but a process of examining in a scientific matter all areas of insufficient data—such as, for example, the distant past of the human race.

5. He seems especially skeptical about the ability of humans to adapt to life in space.

> The actual colonization of space by human beings is another matter altogether. . . . Visualizations clearly reflect the designers' unconscious concession to the pull of the primitive human environment. And therein lies the problem as I see it.
>
> For tugging at the bottom of the minds of the planners is an awareness that the mental health of the colonists is as important as their physical well-being. The whole enterprise is afflicted by an unsolved problem of unknown magnitude: can the psychic thread of life on Earth be snapped without eventually fatal consequences? A stable ecosystem can probably be created from an eternal cycling of microorganisms and plants. But it would still be an island of minute dimensions desperately isolated from the home planet, and simpler and less diverse by orders of magnitude than the environment in which human beings evolved. The tedium in such a reduced world would be oppressive for highly trained people aware of the grandeur of the original biosphere.
>
> Even more painful would be the responsibility for keeping the station alive. There is a fundamental difference between the projected mental life of space colonies and ordinary mental life on Earth. . . . People cannot be expected to carry such a burden. . . . So when we dream of human populations expanding through the solar system and beyond, I believe we dream too far. (Wilson 1984, 116-17)

Thus, while there is some attractiveness in utterly unknown environments, humans would also have some natural disinclination to them—possibly leading space colonists inexorably towards unhappiness and insanity, as I discussed in "Small Worlds and Strange Tomorrows" (1991) and *Islands in the Sky* (1996).

6. As noted by James Gunn in the question-and-answer session after a talk at the Fifth Eaton Conference. At least one other commentator I recall told the same story without naming Godwin.
7. Of course, physical strength is only one possible explanation for the emergence of male dominance. The point here is that sexual differences are clearly linked to the development of authoritarian power structures, and that the elimination of those differences ought to produce different power structures.
8. While reciting these traditional cliches, I employ traditional sexist language, being aware that the proper modern expression would be, "under the skin, all persons are siblings."
9. In her "Afterword" to "The Word for World Is Forest," LeGuin, describing her writing (interestingly, in terms of Campbell's model) as "taking dictation from a boss with ulcers," in effect apologizes for the overt morality of that particular story, saying, "The boss. . . . wanted to moralize. I am not very fond of moralistic tales, for they often lack charity. I hope this one does not" (LeGuin 1972, 126).
10. Other possible examples include Stanislaw Lem's *Solaris*, Damon Knight's "Stranger Station," James P. Tiptree's "And I Awoke and Found Me Here by the Cold Hill's Side," and Arthur C. Clarke's *2001: A Space Odyssey*; but Carr's story seemed to offer the most striking parallels to *The Left Hand of Darkness*.
11. For example, science fiction writers have persistently warned about coming environmental dangers such as the loss of fossil fuels (Olaf Stapledon, *Last and First Men*), the unintended creation of dangerous lifeforms (Gregory Benford, *Timescape*), and damaging changes in the atmosphere (Hal Clement, *The Nitrogen Fix*); yet the disappointing results of the recent Rio Conference suggest that politicians and voters are resisting that message.

12. In "Small Worlds and Strange Tomorrows" (1991) and *Islands in the Sky* (1996).

Do Cognitive Predispositions Predict or Determine Literary Value Judgments? Narrativity, Plot, and Aesthetics

Nancy L. Easterlin

Within literary studies, there exists very little theory that explores either the basis or purpose of literature from an evolutionary or biological perspective. In one sense this is a curious fact, since it appears logically unassailable and even obvious to suggest that aesthetic artifacts and their functions might best be explained by a knowledge of their producers, that is, human beings. Though thinkers as removed from one another in time and as diverse in philosophical perspective as Aristotle and Shelley have suggested that art develops out of and strengthens the basic nature of human experience, only a few twentieth-century literary theorists have championed a biopsychological or evolutionary perspective—a naturalistic approach—for the study of human aesthetic behavior. Theory, like epistemology, has successfully resisted an evolutionary point of view, remaining ensconced in an outdated methodological dualism (one method for the sciences, another for the humanities) and the abstract methods of the Western philosophical tradition.

The resistance to an evolutionarily informed perspective rests on some erroneous assumptions about what such a position implies. Humanists and social scientists lacking any recent background in the relevant scientific research tend to assume automatically that discussions of biological and cognitive predispositions imply acceptance of rigid behavioral determinism. As a result of the abuses of evolutionary theory from social Darwinism onward, furthermore, many assume that a biological perspective is not only deterministic but racist and sexist in its determinations.

The answer to the moral and intellectual questions raised by these fears is best provided by scholars like Leda Cosmides and John Tooby, evolutionary psychologists who adopt an adaptationist paradigm. Differentiating their perspective from fitness maximization, which has assumed that every specific behavior in the present contributes to individual fitness in the service of reproduction, Cosmides and Tooby assert that we share a panhuman psychic architecture adapted to the regularities of the environment in which we evolved. Rather than determining behavior in contemporary environments very different from that of our evolving Pleistocene ancestors, then, domain-specific competences enable plasticity in individual response to environmental problems (Cosmides and Tooby 1992, 50-62, 113). In other words, the fact that we have universal cognitive adaptations does not mean that we always operate in the default mode, so to speak; by contrast, such paradigmatic means of construing and reacting, in providing a basic but not an inevitable orientation for all human beings, enable choice. After all, we are not machines. Our universal tendency to construe events causally, for example, does not mean that we always prefer and thus choose causal constructions, particularly when such constructions do not fit immediate circumstances and environments. In short, human behavior is the result of a dynamic relationship between organism and environment, and it makes no sense to couch discussions of human behavior in terms of the traditional binarism of nature versus nurture, which inevitably tends toward an unwarranted determinism in either case. In the interaction of organism and environment, specific behaviors result from an array of factors. This point of view is essentially that of contemporary sociobiology, which stresses the importance of *epigenesis* in understanding human behavior and mind. In Charles Lumsden's words, "Epigenesis is a term referring to the total content, and results, of the interaction between genome and environment during development" (Lumsden 1991, 259). So-called epigenetic rules, such as the universal tendency to construe events causally—a rule whose implications are vital to this essay—guide this process but do not determine outcomes.

The adaptationist approach espoused by Cosmides and Tooby currently dominates evolutionary studies and, in recommending the view that a universal psychic architecture does not prescribe or predict individual behavior, it provides the nuanced perspective necessary for social scientists and humanists who daily face the complexity of real world human behavior and an impressive diversity of aesthetic artifacts. Although, as I have pointed out, few critics are willing or ready to address art from an evolutionary view, a few have begun to do so, including Joseph Carroll, Robert Storey,

Frederick Turner, Alex Argyros, and Brett Cooke in literary studies, as well as Ellen Dissanayake in anthropology.

Because all humans share a psychological architecture, it is obvious that some of our most enduring artistic forms, modes, and techniques would bear the marks of our fundamental cognitive predispositions. Detailing the manifestations of known cognitive tendencies and aesthetic forms is not my purpose here, however; even to the extent that it is possible to pinpoint such predispositions, it would not be possible to discuss them all in a brief essay. Rather, I wish to address the question of my title—do cognitive predispositions predict or determine literary values?—by discussing one particular mode, that of fictional narrative, specifically as it is manifest in the genre of the novel. My answer to this question, a qualified "no," will be consistent with the adaptationist perspective: though aesthetic forms and modes certainly (perhaps obviously) reflect cognitive predispositions, the degree to which works express underlying predispositions does not determine or predict the literary value of any given work. In other words, works that are considered valuable or timeless are not those in which normative cognitive patterns are most closely reproduced, much less do these works simply instantiate and reinforce those patterns. In a consideration of narrative fiction specifically, the causal frame and the accompanying concept of agency which undergird the novelistic paradigm are products of our innate tendency toward narrativity; nonetheless, the strength of these features in and of themselves provides no guide to the aesthetic worth of any given novel or short story.

For the purpose of clarity, I would like to emphasize that this essay is addressing not the *popular appeal* of aesthetic artifacts, but instead the perceived worth of literary works as determined by an influential literary critical subculture, through an evaluative process extending over a significant period of time. Thus, since literary critical judgments become objectified, ultimately, with the inclusion in or exclusion from the literary canon of various works, the notion of aesthetic value assumed here is distinct from popularity, as well as from my own "subjective" value judgments. Although even those of us who are part of the critical subculture may disdain works we see promoted through canonization, such disagreements are not the issue here, for the canonical status constitutes the relevant fact for the aim of this analysis.

Across the humanistic disciplines, the little theory that exists on the relationship between aesthetic worth and human biology, psychology, and behavior tends to endorse one of two positions: (1) that artworks whose form and method are based most demonstrably on biological patterns are superior to those whose are not, and (2) that art exists to break up patterns of behavioral response (presumably biologically based), and therefore is most valuable when it deviates from cognitive or behavioral norms. For instance, writing in the 1960s and basing his analysis of visual art on Gestalt psychology, Rudolph Arnheim suggested that simplifications of form in pictorial representation are related to the ease with which humans are oriented in the environment based on shapes; following from this, Arnheim posited that a preference for relative abstraction over realism in representation can be explained by physiological research indicating that "well-organized visual form produces in the visual projection areas of the brain a correspondingly balanced organization," which explains the relationship between "well-organized form and pleasure" (1966, 14-15). At this point, Arnheim is attempting to explain visual preferences based on existing artworks; he is not deducing value judgments from a preference that seems biologically based. Later, however, he attacks the abandonment of pictorial organization by twentieth-century abstractionists such as Jackson Pollock, asserting that "a concern for unshaped matter is a melancholy surrender rather than the recovery of man's grip on reality" (1966, 191). For Arnheim, then, Pollock's aesthetics, divorced from our innate visual preference for structure and form, reinforce modern man's sense of chaos and alienation.

Also theorizing about the function of art in the 1960s, Morse Peckham suggests that the human drive to order results in the suppression of much important information, and that it is the role of art to break up behavioral orientations and create new patterns of response. Peckham's theory is based on a somewhat problematic combination of evolutionary theory, Gestalt psychology, game theory, and behaviorist psychology and is concerned with a range of aesthetic media. Whereas Arnheim values structure and form for adaptative reasons, Peckham values discontinuities in form and style for the same reasons. While Arnheim assumes that the pleasurable experience of organized form is the hallmark of true art, Peckham, suspicious of the mind's default tendencies of organization, emphasizes deviation from pattern as the sign of aesthetic superiority. Significantly, these two critics concern themselves, one exclusively and the other largely, with the visual arts, in which, in contrast to literature, the concreteness of the medium and the obvious predominance of a single sense modality (vision) simplify the assessment of experiential response—though this indeed may only lead to deceptively hasty judgments about merit, which rely too exclusively on perceptual response and ignore more complex cognitive processes. For it is one thing to say that organized form produces pleasure and another to jump to the conclusion that perceptual pleasure should be the sole or even predominant transhistorical, transcultural aesthetic criterion for visual art.

Unlike Arnheim and Peckham, Frederick Turner, in a more recent theorization of the biological basis of art, focuses on literature, asserting the value of classical literary forms and features over modernist methods because of their greater approximation of cognitive predispositions. Turner has conducted experiments indicating that traditional poetic meters stimulate a neurophysiological response responsible for the flow experience akin to that produced in ritual behavior; likewise, he asserts the value of plot, since it combines right and left hemispheric activity and connects these with the rewards of the limbic system (1985, 61-105, 21-22, 24, 50). Turner eschews free verse and antinarrative modes in favor of formalist poetics and narrative on grounds very similar to Arnheim's argument against abstractionism in painting—the excesses of modern and contemporary forms reproduce alienation and fragmentation in developed cultures already suffering from lack of unity. Indeed, Turner is forthright about his commitment to the healing and redemptive potential of formalist poetics and plot-based organizations. In Turner's words, "plot promotes and exercises the relations between cortical world construction and limbic reward. . . . Suffice it to say here that the modernist tendency to dispense with or demote plot may have been a grave mistake" (1985, 21-22). Whether artistic methods that work against the grain can erode our fundamental predispositions, as Turner here implies, is a question to which I will later return.

In asserting that art's approximation of perceptual and cognitive patterns or its divergence from these patterns provides a guide to aesthetic considerations, these analyses are perhaps not so radically opposed as they are two sides of the same coin. They all assume biologically and behaviorally based patterns have a place of high significance in value judgments, though one commentator looks on such patterns skeptically, while the other two posit that their reinforcement is the basis of an authentic art. The adaptationist view stresses that behavior arises in the interaction of organism and environment and is guided by a broad array of psychic mechanisms, and this view, combined with the insights of cognitive psychology, would tend to imply that neither is unilaterally true. First, flattering our innate cognitive modes may produce brain rewards that are in some respects psychologically healthy; on the other hand, such brain rewards were perhaps more adaptive to our Pleistocene ancestors than to modern men and women, who live in a much different, rapidly changing environment. Psychological adaptations can prove to be constraints or limitations just as surely as they are enabling mechanisms. Second, the vast array of psychological adaptations combined with developmental and environmental variations indicates that the reproduction of a single cognitive pattern is unlikely to have an overarching significance within the real complexity of human cognition. Simply put, many things, both formal and substantive, are going on in the mind of one viewing a painting or reading a poem other than responding to a visual or metrical organization. The liberative or restrictive force of any single factor is mitigated by a host of others—including, for example, color, texture, and detail in painting, and sound, semantic content, figures of speech, and the like in verse. Indeed, in contrast to theorists who wish to generalize about aesthetics from cognitive and perceptual findings, one theorist of the adaptationist school stresses the complexity of aesthetic behaviors, claiming that they are composed of "many filaments" (e.g., manipulative, perceptual, cognitive, symbolic) and constitute acts of "making special," fulfilling not a specific function but rather a general human need to elaborate beyond the everyday (Dissanayake 1988, 108, 92). Third, the creation, development, and transformation of any artistic form or mode greatly influences the reception and understanding of aesthetic artifacts, and therefore warns us against reductive statements about biological pattern. Those who have identified biologically based patterns underlying the arts make a vital contribution to our knowledge of artistic behavior and human cognition, but beyond the recognition that biological patterns and divergence from them are characteristic of artworks, such research can tell us little about aesthetic worth. In the evaluation of works of art, there are, in short, many factors that come into play.

It is worth noting that all three of the scholars discussed above focus on the significance of biologically based form rather than content. However, particularly in analyses of literature, others, like the anthropologist Robin Fox, have emphasized the biologically based content of stories and myths, such as the universally demonstrable competition between younger and older males. With respect to aesthetic considerations, the questions to be asked about this approach are similar to those about biologically based form: How greatly does this theme predominate over the full meaning of the story, and to what extent does the predominance of this theme correlate with judgments about the story's worth and value? Although such story lines and themes will not be discussed here, I would suggest that their function is similar to that of biologically based forms: while they constitute human norms which are essential to arouse audience interest—indeed, at a fundamental level, to invite audience *comprehension*—their presence does not predict or determine the value of a given work.

For the remainder of this essay, I will narrow my focus to a discussion of narrativity as a cognitive mode and, following this, its relevance to fictional narrative. This will prevent arguing in generalizations and allow me to focus on individual works; general discussions of art, assuming that this term coherent, determinate category, are most certainly doomed by their inability to address the complex and crucial differences between unlike media. Indeed, even when considering a single mode in a single medium, the issues are still imposingly complex.

In the past twenty years, research in cognitive psychology, philosophy of mind, and linguistics has significantly modified our notions of human cognition. While traditional objectivist semantics sought to explain meaning in terms of the satisfaction of truth conditions of logical propositions, contemporary research points increasingly to the fact that human thinking is *essentially* nonpropositional and nonlogical (in the formal sense of that term). For instance, schema theory, a branch of cognitive psychology, suggests that many of our generalized knowledge structures are not logical categories but Gestalt-like entities; story, script or event, and scene schemas based in experience, such as the restaurant script and the classroom script, guide our thinking and are far more easily remembered than taxonomies (Schank 1990, Mandler 1984). Consistent with this, philosophers and linguists suggest that the fundamental structure of our thought as reflected in language is not propositional but based in metaphors derived from our bodily experience which tend to concretize the abstract (Lakoff and Johnson 1980, Johnson 1987). These theorists speculate, for example, that the expression "I'm feeling down" derives from the physical drooping posture of people in the depressed state.

In all of this recent literature, narrative thinking is probably the most widely discussed, because apparently the most basic, cognitive predisposition. Although some psychologists skirt the issue of the biological basis of narrativity, language-acquisition theorists suggest that narrative thinking and the desire to share in the family's stories prompt infant language learning. Far from being produced by language and cultural ideology, as some current literary theorists, including Catherine Belsey and Anthony Easthope, assert, narrative is a primary mode of mentation that apparently *precedes* language acquisition in human development (Bruner 1990, Lloyd 1989, Carrithers 1991). Children, in short, learn to construe events in a linear fashion and thus to identify causal relationships *before* they can speak. Apparently, the role of narrative is indispensable in human mental and social life; events and mental states are not only given meaning by plot, but the construal of action and thought in narrative facilitates the retention of these phenomena in memory (Mandler 1984). Moreover, one of the single most important features of narrative is rooted the human propensity to think causally, a fact so consistently observable that E.O. Wilson identifies it as an epigenetic rule (Ruse, in Fetzer 1985, 262). Literary theorists who assert that linear organization inheres in capitalism or patriarchy notwithstanding, we are apparently biologically predisposed to look for causes and effects in the world around us, and thus construe actuality in a linear fashion.

How, then, do we define narrative? Since poststructuralist theories of narrative have been justly criticized for failing to define the term properly, those of us promoting an alternative theoretical perspective had best not fall into the same trap (Livingston 1992). The most basic feature of narrative is linearizing, a feature clearly connected to causal thinking, or to what Alexander Argyros identifies as the basic structure of narrative, the causal frame of actor-action-object (Argyros 1991, 310). Bruner's definition of narrative is consistent with this; narrativity is, in his words, the ability to organize actor, action, goal, scene, and instrument into a sequential story. But as Dan Lloyd points out, it is possible to construct narratives that do not have all the elements Bruner mentions, to wit: "'During the thaw, a sheet of ice on the roof loosened and fell. It struck a parked car, cracking the windshield.' Though hardly the stuff of great novels, this nonetheless seems to be a narrative. Yet it unfolds without human agency" (Lloyd 1989, 225). Lloyd himself argues that narratives conform to three constraints, two formal and one semantic: the representations of narrative are singular and affirmative, they give information about the temporal ordering of events, and they represent events as dependent upon one another (Lloyd 1989, 219-21). Thus, the following does not meet the normative conditions of narrative: A person not named Peter McNamara, bearing no physically precise features, did not get out of bed, did not shave, did not watch the cat sleep on the sports section of the morning paper as he did not try to read it, and did not get stuck in the flood waters not driving his car to work. Notice that in reading this antinarrative, our mental habit is to recast it in the affirmative and reconstruct a linear sequence it repeatedly denies.

Because narrative is not amenable to precise definition, Lloyd suggests that it should be referred to as a texture rather than a structure, for to make affirmative statements about specific subjects and to organize them in a linear and causal fashion hardly represents a structure. Narrativity, the ability to construe agents and actions in an extended linear sequence, is the foundation of human folk psychology—that is, of our ability to infer the desires and intentions of others, to know our own desires and intentions, and to act in the pursuit of long-term goals; at the same time, it is a cognitive mode or texture rather than a precise, rule-governed sequential structure like a sentence (Lloyd 1989, 219).

As we move from the basis of narrative thinking in cognitive science to literary theory, what we see immediately is that identifying narrative as a generalized, primary mode of mentation contributes little to our understanding of genres and forms, for it is such a basic way of thinking that it cuts across all literary categories. Since narrative is a primary means of making sense of things, logic suggests that it would be a pervasive and fundamental element of literary works, the authors of which, more than nine times out of ten, aim for coherence. This is in fact so. Even if we assume that the arts are cognitively rewarding—a point of view I share with those theorists whose work I am now questioning—we should be skeptical about our ability to pinpoint the exact cognitive rewards artworks provide. But it is another question to ask if the replication and reinforcement of our primary mode of mentation has been or should be promoted as an aesthetic value. Narrative thinking has real shortcomings, including a tendency to prefer causal reasoning when other methods are equally or more precise, and we are lucky enough to have other cognitive modes, including the analogical and the logical, to counterbalance or correct over-eager linearizing (Lloyd 1989, 216).

One conclusion we might draw from the research exploring the primacy of narrative thinking is that literature adopting the causal frame as its basis of organization will be not necessarily better but more accessible than, say, works primarily organized around extended metaphors. Those of us who teach literature know that this is certainly so; untrained students who can easily follow the sequential events of a story have no idea how to interpret a literary metaphor. If we consider the popular novel (not to mention television and film), we will be reminded that subgenres focusing fundamentally on plot, the feature of literature derived from our propensity for narrativity—a pattern or structure of events linked by chronology and causality—are the subgenres that sell: romance, science fiction, thriller, and horror novels. The manipulation of the causal chain in literature is hardly threatened with extinction. Clearly, we cannot get rid of plot in literature anymore than we can get rid of narrative thinking in life; but just as clearly, the implication that strong plotting is inherently connected with high cognitive rewards, much less with literary values, is dubious.

However, in contrast to nineteenth-century classics and to today's popular genres, twentieth-century literary works frequently eschew plot as a primary mode of organization, though narrative organization remains pervasive at some level. Virginia Woolf's *Mrs. Dalloway* and James Joyce's *Ulysses*, though concerned with the accumulations of events and distortions of time in the mind, nonetheless make affirmative statements about specific agents, unfold chronologically, and exhibit causality, though the causes of events may be more complex and less certain than in the paradigmatic realist novel. Likewise, postmodern antinarratives depend for their effects not only upon narrative thinking, but upon stereotypical patterns of cause and effect within subgenres of the novel; Thomas Pynchon and Paul Auster, in writing detective stories that go nowhere, where no number of clues ultimately adds up to a coherent sequence of events and unravels the truth behind a mystery, invoke the reader's knowledge of the complex connections and pattern of enlightenment normative to the detective novel. To appreciate having the detective novel turned on its head, we must be able to think in terms of the detective novel's strong linear progression. Similarly, Donald Barthelme, primarily a parodist, invokes fictional as well as nonfictional discursive norms to break the rules of narrativity. Thus, in "The Policeman's Ball," Barthelme shares the cabbie's thoughts about basketball as he drives the policeman and his date to the ball.

> Why do they always applaud the man who makes the shot?
> Why don't they applaud the ball?
> It is the ball that actually goes into the net.
> The man doesn't go into the net.
> Never have I seen a man going into the net. (1968, 62)

This non sequitur announces the disruption of narrative, and its humorous effects depend upon our normative expectation of narrative order, as well as upon the fact that life experience suggests the unlikeliness of such thoughts in cab drivers.

Have critics of the twentieth century judged wrongly in valuing works highly that do not have a strong narrative organization? If one thing can be said of literary genres, change and transformation are of their essence; the same is not true of biological predispositions. Because of the growing complexity of our technology, our understanding of the universe and the human mind, citizens of the twentieth century are less apt to construe the world in terms of clearcut causes and effects. Writers, in turn, do not create worlds that operate according to such rules when they no longer believe the philosophy or worldview implicit in those rules, and critics and professors do not promote works that they judge to be false or simplistic imitations of the world in which we live. Reflexive postmodern fiction, whether exuberantly decadent or actually critical of our generic and psychic norms, attests to the deeply entrenched narrativity that pervades literature; without this, such fictions would be, quite simply, nonsense. Thus, although biological predispositions such as narrative form a necessary substrate of literature, value judgments are relative not to that substrate but to the state of the culture's beliefs and the course of a genre's development. Postmodern antinarrative does not threaten to undermine narrative fiction, for parody always works against an author, style, form, or genre strong enough to be mocked trenchantly. Postmodern antinarrative mocks the conventions of literary realism, perhaps both reinforcing and transforming the mode as it does so.

What antinarrative does to our capacity for everyday *narrative thinking*, however, is a far different question. Turner suggests a direct link between the psychic results of commonsense narrativity and those of antinarrative fictional techniques:

> By narrative . . . we tell ourselves the story of ourselves and thus learn how to be a coherent and effective self. The story is the central operation by which we are able to love and to work. Certain types of mental illness might well be characterized as lesions in the narrative capacity. The inability to see other people's point of view, and the inability to string moments of time together in a valuable and meaningful way, are characteristic of a certain type of narcissistic or borderline personality which is now showing up in the therapists' waiting rooms. It also shows up in the characters and implied narrators in deconstructive postmodern fictions by the likes of Raymond Carver and Anne Beattie. (1994, 35)

I question Turner's implicit conclusion that the fictional representation of nihilism, malaise, and psychic distress is psychically and cognitively damaging to readers. A short story or a novel is a fictional world, and fictional worlds are not determinate realities. Because of this our feelings, beliefs, desires, and judgments in fictional experience are not consistent with those of real life (Currie 1990 105-6, 196-8, 207). In Gregory Currie's words, "The response to fiction is a complex product of make-believe and judgments about the work that do not occur within the work at all" (1990, 119). What Currie is saying here can, I think, be extended to our understanding of imaginative experience and commonsense cognitive modes. That is, the psychological and intellectual impact of narrative or antinarrative material on a human being depends upon the form of the experience, with the indeterminate and ambiguous range of imaginative experience allowing for greater flexibility in response over direct experience. A reader's immersion in Raymond Carver's fictional world is controlled by Carver's focus on a narrow range of experience, occupation, and socioeconomic class, as well as by the brevity, stylistic precision, and frequent satire of his technique; the stories counsel against being taken as life messages or global comments on late twentieth-century man, even if Robert Altman reduced (and inflated) them to such clichés. Similarly, if I were to believe I was Thomas Pynchon's character Oedipa Maas, following a trail of undecipherable clues to the heart, possibly, of an impenetrable conspiracy, I would doubt my own agency and the causal frame of my reality. But the world Pynchon creates is too unlike mine for me to make this mistake, and my ability to differentiate his fictional world from my reality is not the result of my specialized training. Elaborate conventions of make-believe are part of human folk psychology; those who confuse make-believe with actual life are folk psychologically insane. By contrast, if I were to go through a day where my coffee shot up in a fountain out of my cup, my husband spoke to me in gibberish, my calls to colleagues were consistently rerouted to a secret society, and my tennis balls disappeared into the backboard, I would come to doubt the causal frame of reality and the efficacy of human agency—either that, or I would lose faith in my own sanity. (I would certainly stop paying all that money for tennis lessons.) While our commonsense narrativity has a straightforward application to daily life, its relation to a fictional world is more ambiguous, shifting, and flexible.

The extent to which we expect narrative organization in a fictional world depends upon the cues an author gives, and the successful realization of that world depends greatly on how well that author follows his or her own cues. Narrative thinking serves as a vital frame of reference for our understanding of literary fiction in any case. Narrativity, in fact, makes it possible for us to understand when a weakened sense of causality and human agency is central to the value of a novel—in other words, when a weakened sense of narrativity *contributes* to novelistic aesthetics.

Nadine Gordimer's *July's People*, published in 1981, is just such a novel. The story takes place in South Africa at an unspecified time in the near future. Bam and Maureen Smales and their children have fled the city, presumably Johannesburg, where civil war has broken out, and are under the protection of their servant July in his rural tribal village. Because the Smaleses are under his protection in a community that does not really welcome them—that does not understand urban life and sees the Smaleses, understandably, as nothing more than a potential source of danger and trouble—power relations have changed utterly, but in ways no one fully understands or can adjust to. The primary drama of the novel revolves around the Smaleses' attempts to recover two stolen items—the keys to their jeep and a gun they had hidden in the thatch of the hut. The drama is carried out in arguments between Maureen and July, where mounting tensions and puzzling, angry dialogue reveal a lack of communication so great that no one comprehends the depth of misunderstanding. At the novel's conclusion, desperate and intent on her own survival, Maureen Smales runs into the bush toward what she hopes is the sound of a helicopter, leaving her husband and children behind. Such as it is, this is the plot of *July's People*.

Of course, there is a causal sequence in the novel, and we can trace human agency—July's appropriation of the keys results in an argument and thus the early signs of deterioration of (a probably illusory) mutual trust. But to focus on plot in this novel would mean overlooking Gordimer's significant psychological and technical achievement. This short novel of one hundred fifty pages is divided into numerous short sections—fragments rather than chapters, as John Cooke points out. Causal and thematic links have been left out intentionally; likewise, the lack of transitions between scenes as well as between and within points of view contributes to the realization of an utterly disorienting fictional world, in which the disintegration of language and of the norms of novelistic realism mirror the loss of a comprehensible world along with any perception of control over it.

Gordimer places the reader right in this disjunctive experience on the novel's first page by simply presenting the first scene without a narrative introduction to the fiction situation.

> You like to have some cup of tea?—
> July bent at the doorway and began that day for them as his kind has always done for their kind.
> The knock on the door. Seven o'clock. In governors' residences, commercial hotel rooms, shift bosses' company bungalows, master bedrooms *en suite*—the tea-tray in black hands smelling of Lifebuoy soap.
> The knock on the door
> no door, an aperture in thick mud walls, and the sack that hung over it looped back for air, sometime during the short night. *Bam, I'm stifling; her voice raising him from the dead, he staggering up from his exhausted sleep.*
> No knock; but July, their servant, their host, bringing two pink glass cups of tea and a small tin of condensed milk, jaggedly-opened, specially for them, with a spoon in it. (1982, 1)

Gordimer moves from July's opening question into an impersonal narrative voice that cryptically presents the situation of white to black—their kind doing for our kind—and then, without transition, moves into Maureen's fragmented thoughts. These thoughts are so disjunctive from the first page of the novel onward that they do not rightly constitute a perspective or point of view; we have glimpses of things in her head, but nothing ever so unified as a way of interpreting or understanding her situation. Maureen Smales, whose sense of self depends upon her life as a privileged urban white and on her memories of childhood as the mine shift boss's daughter, has already lost her frame of reference for selfhood at the novel's beginning. Already dehumanized, she becomes explicitly animal by the novel's close.

> She runs. She can hear the laboured muttering putter very clearly in the attentive silence of the bush around and ahead: the engine not switched off but idling, there. The real fantasies of the bush delude more

> inventively than the romantic forests of Grimm and Disney. The smell of boiled potatoes (from a vine indistinguishable to her from others) promises a kitchen, a house just the other side of the next tree. There are patches where airy knob-thorn trees stand free of undergrowth and the grass and orderly clumps of Barberton daisies and drifts of nemesia belong to the artful nature of a public park. She runs: trusting herself with all the suppressed trust of a lifetime, alert, like a solitary animal at the season when animals neither seek a mate nor take care of young, existing only for their lone survival, the enemy of all that would make claims of responsibility. She can still hear the beat, beyond those trees and those, and she runs towards it. She runs. (1982, 160)

In addition to the overt comparison with a solitary animal, Gordimer's shift into the present tense and repetition of Maureen's singleminded action (she runs . . . she runs) emphasize the frantically instinctual (though surely misguided) nature of her flight.

If Maureen Smales does not have a perspective in this novel, Nadine Gordimer does, and I have known many readers to protest the pervasive antihumanism of her view. Characters in this novel act with consistency, given their situation, but there is no sense of self-coherence or complexity of character underneath this, for very good reason—the breakdown of communication within a structure of shifting power-based relationships erodes individual agency, just as clearly as this social confusion frustrates positive courses of action. But if the purpose of this novel is to take systematic apartheid to its psychosocial conclusion, then narrative realism, with its demand for psychologically coherent characters, consistent point of view and well-ordered plot based on the development of a central conflict and its resolution, is not only a problematic but an impossible mode for telling the story at hand. Furthermore, the consistency of Gordimer's fragmentary, disjunctive style and organization of the novel forestalls the humanistic sympathy that realism typically elicits; in forcing us to confront a chaos humans have created, her method not only works, but works better than that of a novel like *Burger's Daughter*, which mixes realistic techniques and assumptions with a disjunctive style in an incompletely unified approach.

Thus, emphasizing the biological substrate of narrative, out of which we have evolved the literary concept of plot, is not crucial to the realization of a novel as a unified entity. On the other hand, *July's People* only works because of our inherent tendency to think narratively. One way to understand Gordimer's novel, in fact, is as a dramatization of the breakdown of narrativity, for, unable to comprehend one another's beliefs, desires, motives, and actions—their folk psychologies—the characters lose their own sense of agency, action, and selfhood. Whereas Donald Barthelme is primarily interested, as a parodist, in subverting literary conventions such as plot for the pleasure of disrupting *literary* expectations, Gordimer minimizes plot and dramatizes the breakdown of narrativity to depict the erosion of humanity under extreme social conditions. These two writers, then, have divergent aims in their antinarrative methods: if the pleasure of Barthelme's text inheres in the witty disruptions of convention, the pleasure, so to speak, of Gordimer's book is the result of a precise literary method that in best realizing her ruthlessly honest vision, depicts the fragmentation of experience, and demands that the reader reassemble this experience.

It could be argued that the works of Barthelme and Gordimer, representing extremes in purpose and subject matter, are exceptions that prove the rule that strong plot forms the predominant literary value for aesthetic judgments. Yet there are many novels delineating worlds both more mundane than Gordimer's and more real than Barthelme's which display a weakened sense of causality and agency. Marilynne Robinson's *Housekeeping* and the novels of Anita Brookner are not framed by the extreme social and cultural conditions that serve as the fundamental context for Gordimer's work, nor are they celebrations of the subversions of literary norms. Yet their narrators and characters generally fail to take clear and decisive action, to identify the causes of things, and to interpret the meaning of events. This is a legitimate perspective to adopt in a novel, as it is a legitimate response to life; it is also, however, as Turner rightly suggests, an outlook that often appears only trendy. Importantly, both Brookner and Robinson write self-consciously out of strong generic conventions—for Brookner, those of the novel of manners, and for Robinson, those of the nineteenth-century American novel—romance defined by the theme of man in the wilderness, and of its female counterpart, the popular domestic novel. The manipulation and transformation of these conventions, combined with an underlying conviction that the world does not organize itself according to discernible causes and effects, gives these novels substance and force.

In the middle of *Housekeeping*, Robinson's narrator, Ruthie, relates her story of being lost in the woods one night with her sister. Raised by an eccentric aunt, a sometime drifter, in a family whose history was full of unexplained ruptures, Ruthie crossed a psychological threshold at that point in her adolescence.

> I simply let the darkness in the sky become coextensive with the darkness in my skull and bowels and bones. Everything that falls upon the eye is apparition, a sheet dropped over the world's true workings. The nerves and the brain are tricked, and one is left with dreams that these specters loose their hands from ours and walk away, the curve of the back and the swing of the coat so familiar as to imply that they should be permanent fixtures of the world, when in fact nothing is more perishable. (1980, 116)

Despite the stylistic beauties here, Robinson is not asking readers to share Ruthie's epistemological skepticism, for the conditions of her upbringing are extreme and bizarre. Though we recognize the distinction between Robinson's fictional world and our everyday reality—or perhaps *because* we recognize this difference—it is possible to see this novel as a profound meditation on the unstable nature of human domesticity.

Human narrativity makes fiction possible, but the literary manifestation of narrativity in plot cannot serve as a standard for judging novelistic worth. Literary history, generic conventions, and cultural and sociopolitical realities, along with a generalized predisposition for formal organization, describe just part of the matrix in which aesthetic values and value judgments are made. Rather than proscribe an organization for fiction, narrativity makes possible the development of diverse styles and techniques for the communication of diverse experiences and themes. This is in keeping, I believe, with the view of evolutionary psychology and human sociobiology that epigenetic rules *orient* human beings rather than *determine* behavioral outcomes. A novel is the product of a human behavior, of putting pen to paper; the weakening of the causal chain in twentieth-century literature attests, perhaps, to a recognition that our primary epistemic process—and, by extension, the generic conventions built upon it—has real limitations. To know this about ourselves may force us to cope with complexities we would rather not address, but paradoxically, to know it is to gain, experientially and literarily, the measure of our freedom.

Works Cited

Argyros, Alexander

1991 *A Blessed Rage for Order: Deconstruction, Evolution, and Chaos*. Ann Arbor: University of Michigan Press.

Arnheim, Rudolph

1966 *Toward a Psychology of Art*. Berkeley: University of California Press.

Barthelme, Donald

1968 *City Life*. New York: Pocket.

Belsey, Catherine

1980 *Critical Practice*. London: Routledge.

Brown, Donald E.

1991 *Human Universals*. Philadelphia: Temple University Press.

Bruner, Jerome

1990 *Acts of Meaning*. Cambridge, MA: Harvard University Press.

Burnshaw, Stanley

1970 *The Seamless Web*. New York: Braziller.

Carrithers, Michael

1991 "Narrativity: Mindreading and Making Societies." In *Natural Theories of Mind: Evolution, Development and Simulation of Everyday Mindreading*. Oxford: Basil Blackwell.

Carver, Raymond

1974 *What We Talk about When We Talk about Love*. New York: Vintage.

Cooke, John

1985 *The Novels of Nadine Gordimer: Private Lives/Public Landscapes*. Baton Rouge: Louisiana State University Press.

Cosmides, Leda, and John Tooby

1992 "The Psychological Foundations of Culture." In Jerome H. Barkow, Leda Cosmides, and John Tooby, eds., *The Adapted Mind: Evolutionary Psychology and the Generation of Culture*. New York: Oxford University Press.

Currie, Gregory

1990 *The Nature of Fiction*. Cambridge: Cambridge University Press.

Dissanayake, Ellen

1988 *What Is Art For?* Seattle: University of Washington Press.

Easthope, Anthony

1983 *Poetry as Discourse*. London: Methuen.

Fetzer, James H., ed.

1985 *Sociobiology and Epistemology*. Dordrecht, Holland: Reidel.

Fox, Robin

1994 "Sexual Strategies and Deceit in Folklore and Epics." Literary Criticism, HBES Conference, Ann Arbor.

Gioia, Dana

1992 *Can Poetry Matter? Essays on Poetry and American Culture*. St. Paul, MN: Graywolf.

Gordimer, Nadine

1982 *July's People*. London: Penguin.

Johnson, Mark

1987 *The Body in the Mind: The Bodily Basis of Meaning, Imagination, and Reason*. Chicago: University of Chicago Press.

Lakoff, George, and Mark Johnson

1980 *Metaphors We Live By*. Chicago: University of Chicago Press.

Livingston, Paisley

1992 "Film and the New Psychology." *Poetics* 21:93-116.

Lloyd, Dan Edward

1989 *Simple Minds*. Cambridge, MA: MIT Press.

Lumsden, Charles J.

1991 "Aesthetics." In Mary Maxwell, ed., *The Sociobiological Imagination*. Albany: SUNY Press.

Mandler, Jean Matter

1984 *Stories, Scripts, and Scenes: Aspects of Schema Theory*. Hillsdale, NJ: L. Erlbaum.

Papp, James Ralph

1993 "Parodic Humor, Cognitive Scripts, and Neural Compromise." Literature and Human Nature session, MLA Convention, Toronto.

Peckham, Morse

1965 *Man's Rage for Chaos: Biology, Behavior, and the Arts*. Philadelphia: Chilton.

Pynchon, Thomas

1966 *The Crying of Lot 49*. New York: Harper and Row.

Robinson, Marilynne

1980 *Housekeeping*. New York: Bantam.

Schank, Roger C.

1990 *Tell Me a Story: A New Look at Real and Artificial Memory*. New York: Scribner's.

Storey, Robert

1996 *Mimesis and the Human Animal: On the Biogenetic Foundations of Literary Representation*. Evanston, IL: Northwestern University Press.

Turner, Frederick

1985 *Natural Classicism: Essays on Literature and Science*. New York: Paragon.

1994 *Rebirth of Value*. New York: SUNY Press.

Winnett, Susan

1990 "Coming Unstrung: Women, Men, Narrative, and Principles of Pleasure." PMLA 105.3:505-18.

Art: The Replicable Unit
An Inquiry into the Possible Origin of Art As a Social Behavior

Kathryn Coe

> Today a healthy suspicion attaches to those attempts, very popular not so long ago, to formulate grandiose theories of beginnings and of universal characteristics of 'primitive' religion or art, but although criticism can be leveled at any and every particular theory of beginnings, beginnings there were.
>
> N. Sandars, *Prehistoric Art in Europe*

Although many art scholars argue that art has no function, that it exists for its own sake, one implication of Darwin's theory is that behaviors we now regard as characteristic of our species, such as art, persisted precisely because they did have a function[1] As art is a universal and ancient cultural behavior that has persisted despite costs that can be quite high, it is quite possibly an adaptation that, at least in the past, must have been important to humans. Despite this importance, scholars do not agree on which of a variety of objects made by our early ancestors were the first art objects, and there is no widely accepted general model explaining art's origin or its persistence.

The first art objects, one scholar claimed, possibly were cupules hollowed into stone, and the first artist was a La Ferrassie stone carver who produced a gravestone (Stern 1969). Other scholars, however, who have not been so bold as to identify one object and one artist, have argued that the origin may lie even earlier in human prehistory. They point to the Acheulean handaxe (Sandars 1985) or early Upper Paleolithic intentional engravings (Marshack 1976, 1979, 1981, 1988) as examples of the first art objects. A number of scholars agree that the origin lies in the Upper Paleolithic, but they disagree on whether the first art objects were three-dimensional sculptures in the round (Collins and Onians 1978, Gamble 1982, Halverson 1987, Sandars 1985), Aurignacian blocks (Leroi-Gourhan 1967), engravings and paintings (Dulluc and Delluc 1978), line drawings on fragments of bone (Leroi-Gourhan 1967, Marshack 1976), the Solutrian laurel leaf point (Verworn 1909), or even finger paintings in soft clay (Luquet 1930). It is also claimed that the first object man decorated may well have been his own body (Brothwell 1976, Conkey 1985, Cordwell & Schwarz 1979, Gamble 1982, Halverson 1987, Roach & Eicher 1965, Mellars 1989, Vlahos 1979, Weltfish 1953, White 1982). Much of the current discussion in anthropology centers around the origin of art in representational objects and paintings, or image making (Davis 1986), arising perhaps out of trances (Lewis-Williams 1982, 1986).

Although there may be many reasons why scholars have been unable to agree upon the origin of art, primary among them is the fact that we have failed to agree upon an explicit and objective definition of art. To quote Count Leo Tolstoy, who has written insightfully on the philosophy of art, "The whole science of aesthetics fails to do what we might expect from it, being a mental activity calling itself a science, namely it does not define the qualities and laws of art" (1977, 61). Without an explicit definition we cannot even begin to search for an origin; without an objective definition our search for the origin of art must focus on cognitive phenomena, a difficult proposition in the archaeological record.

In this essay, an explicit and objective definition of art will be proposed and used to identify possible candidates for the origin of art in the works of our early ancestors and to discuss the subsequent replication of the trait through time. All objects considered as candidates for the first art will fit the definition proposed and, to the greatest extent possible, have firm radiometric dates and be found in clear association with biological elements, such as skeletal or dental remains (i.e., certain dental traits that have been used as population markers, see Turner 1983). Although these criteria limit the objects that can be considered (many of the above objects lack both firm dates and biological associations), by restricting our focus to actual evidence we should be able to increase our objective understanding of art.

Definition of Art

The following definition of art, or more precisely plastic art, focuses on the necessary elements of art and is consistent with its literal rather than its metaphorical usage.

> Art: Color and/or form used by humans in order to modify an object, body, or message solely to attract attention to that object, body, or message. The proximate or immediate effect of art is to make objects more noticeable.

This definition refers only to that art involving color and/or form. It does not refer to poetry, dance, or music, although they clearly involve form or pattern. The definition proposed does not differ substantially from that *implied* by the use of the term by some of the most influential thinkers in aesthetics.[2]

Attract is derived from the Latin word *attractus* which means to draw, or to cause to approach or adhere to (*Webster's Dictionary* 1985). "Attract" and "attractive," in their first definition and as used throughout this essay, will refer to the fact that art pulls or draws attention; they are not used in the aesthetic sense of attracting only favorable attention. The sine qua non of art is that it is noticeable.

Color has been the subject of endless discussion in the social sciences; however, it can be argued that the term refers to the characteristic ways objects have of reflecting various wavelengths of ambient light. What seems significant about color for humans, who share the ability to discriminate color with some other species, is that it makes possible the identification of subtle differences in objects and thus aids in categorization and comparison and in the identification and re-identification of objects (Hilbert 1987). Responsiveness to color, thus, can influence choices.

Form refers to the shape and structure of something (*Webster's Dictionary* 1985). Pattern is an important subcategory or type of form. Gregory Bateson (1972) wrote that "any aggregate of events or objects...shall be said to have redundancy or pattern if the aggregate can be divided in any way by a slash mark, such that an observer perceiving only what is on one side of the slash mark can guess with better than random success, what is on the other side of the slash mark" (131). Phrased more succinctly, an aggregate is a pattern when that aggregate's extension can be predicted with greater than chance success. Humans share with other species the ability to discriminate form and pattern and a tendency toward a selection of or responsiveness to them which can influence choices (Hilbert 1987).

In sum, human responsiveness to color and form can influence choices. Artists use color and form intentionally, and this use of color and form (what we call art) attracts attention. The question that must be addressed is why humans began to regularly and intentionally use color and form and why they continue to do so. In this discussion, it is argued that artists use this tendency of humans to respond to color and form in order to influence social behavior.

Defense of the Proposed Definition

Although the definition proposed omits any reference to emotion, it is acknowledged that the majority of definitions of art accepted today are based upon the assumption that the fundamental feature of art is the affective response it can arouse in the maker or viewer (Bell 1958, Boas 1955, Dissanayake 1989, Langer 1958, Plato 1977, Tolstoy 1977, and those they have influenced). One version of this, the "art for art's sake" position, claims that art is executed for the pleasure of the artist in the work and the viewer in the beholding. Another version specifies that the aesthetic response is to a feature inherent in the art, such as technique (Boas 1955). Another version, the "symbolist" position, postulates that the viewer at a "preconscious or even unconscious level" recognizes a particular animal, for example, as a symbol of his or her "deepest aesthetic feeling" (Vinnicombe 1976, 350). Collective response to the symbol, in turn, is used by functionalists to account for social cohesion and permanence.

Problems of Defining Art Affectively

The definition proposed omits the affective response because, as Anderson (1979) has pointed out, at this stage in the study of art, its inclusion may cause more methodological difficulties than analytical clarity. Anderson and others have indicted the following problems:

1. The affective response is often tautological, in that a mental state is inferred from the art and then used to explain it (Lewis-Williams 1982).
2. Subjective states are difficult to identify, particularly if they are fleeting and highly personal (Anderson 1979). There is seldom adequate vocabulary available for inquiry into such subjective states, and often we are not entirely certain of our own emotional reactions to things, much less able to articulate those feelings (Anderson 1979).
3. If we claim that there is an aesthetic emotion, a separate mechanism designed by natural selection specifically for the making and viewing of art, we must find that such an emotion exists crossculturally. However, "the number of methodologically sound accounts of art from other cultures remains small," and most do not systematically gather information on the affective aspects of art (Anderson 1979, 17).
4. By asserting that the affective state is pleasure, and by understanding pleasure as a specific emotion associated with sensuous gratification (e.g., joy, happiness), we cause problems to arise. First, many things that are clearly non-art (sunsets, for example) can evoke the same or highly similar emotions (Boas 1955). How is the so-called aesthetic emotion distinct from the emotions aroused by natural objects or non-art? Second, the claim as stated may not be true. Art, including much of religious and contemporary mainstream art, is sometimes said to arouse grave and negative feelings. If we expand the meaning of pleasure, so that an object is art if it arouses any sort of emotion, we still face problems, as a number of non-art objects can also arouse emotions. Further, art may leave the observer bewildered, confused, nonplussed, or unsure of any emotional reaction (Anderson 1979).
5. Finally, it is not clear if the presumed affective response is to the message the art may carry, the technical proficiency of the artist, the color and form, or to some other feature intrinsic to art.

The point of this discussion is not that emotion is irrelevant to the study of art. To paraphrase Munro (1949), if art were not in some way attractive (meaning that it attracts attention), people would be unlikely to notice it or would ignore it. However, does attracting our attention imply generation of an emotion? Is interest an emotion? While our being attracted to something may indeed imply an emotion, this emotion may be neither distinctive nor identifiable. Before we can progress in the study of art, these questions must be addressed; however, at this point, the concept of aesthetic emotion does not promote analytic clarity.

The Problems of Defining Art in Terms of Technique

One version of the affective explanation claims that mastery of technique triggers the aesthetic response (Boas 1955). Boas claimed that "when the control of process is such that certain typical forms are produced we call the process art" (1955, 10). He claimed that the aesthetic response was a reaction to or recognition of "virtuosity, complete control of technical processes" (20, see also Anderson 1979, Dissanayake 1989).

Although it may be true that technique is important to art (*ars* in ancient Latin meant "a craft or specialized form of skill"; Munro 1949, 26), there are still difficulties with this definition. First, it is heir to most of the problems pertaining to affective definitions. Second, it may not be valid. For example, Dubuffet's "The Fountain" (a mass-produced urinal), simple objects made and valued in other cultures, and contemporary paintings that violate all formal rules of art may not show clear evidence of virtuosity. What do we call these objects, if they are not art? Although terms like style, when used to refer to particular techniques, show that technique may be both social and important, virtuosity may not be a necessary condition of art. Finally, how would we go about using such a definition in our attempts to identify the origin of art? At what point, for example, would the application of red ochre to the body be considered to be technically well done?

The Problem of Symbols and Meaning

In anthropology, the study of symbols and meaning often is central to the study of art. Art is sometimes said to be an objective presentation of subjective reality (Langer 1958), meaning that the art object is a symbol or map of the individual artist's mind (Mills 1971). However, not only is evidence of individualism rare in the Paleolithic record, but needless to say, if this is our definition of art, it would be difficult to find evidence of its origin in the archaeological record (see Lindly and Clark 1990). Further, such idiosyncratic definitions have little to do with a discussion of the social aspects of art.

Those who discuss art as a socially meaningful phenomenon often focus on the relationship between symbols and social cohesion (Vinnicombe 1976, Lewis-Williams 1982). This "symbolist" position proposes that viewers at a "preconscious or even unconscious level" recognize a particular animal as a symbol of their "deepest aesthetic feeling" (Vinnicombe 1976, 350). Collective response to the symbol, in turn, is used by functionalists to account for social cohesion and permanence. Unless it is determined that there is a template in the mind that influences such a response, the meaning of a symbol implies an individually identified and remembered association with its referent. It is the memory of this association that is crucial to the meaning of any symbol; indeed, the association constitutes the meaning of a symbol. In other words, meaning is learned; and to the extent the meaning is shared (social), it is learned from other people presumably through their behavior (speech and actions).

To omit meaning from the definition does not imply that art is meaningless; it suggests that before we can increase our knowledge of what is fundamental to art, we must separate art from any message to which it calls attention. As Boas (1955), the "father" of American anthropology, recognized, the study of art can be "obscured" by a discussion of meaning (13). Boas argued that "significance" or meaning is "neither universal nor can it be shown that it is necessarily older than form" (13), and that "not all societies have art that is meaningful or has associative connotations" (88). In addition, within a society there can be "considerable wavering" about the particular meaning of a symbol (102). For example, "in the designs of the Californian Indians, the same form will be called by different people or even by the same people at different times, now a lizard's foot, then a mountain covered with trees, then again an owl's claw" (102).

Art and Creativity

The proposed definition omits any reference to creativity as it may be neither a universal characteristic of art nor an integral part of the origin of art. During much of human prehistory and history, evidence of creativity or rapid cultural change is rare. In many cases, culture can extend unchanged across multiple generations and far beyond the individual's lifetime (Alexander 1979). As M. G. Houston has written specifically about art, "we are confronted with an extraordinary conservation or persistence of style, not only through the centuries, but through millenniums" (1920, 2). If it also can be shown that art arose out of previously existing behaviors and endured for thousands of years with little evidence of change, creativity may be neither necessary nor sufficient for art to occur.

Advantages of the Proposed Definition

The primary value of the proposed definition is that it focuses on an objective phenomenon that is potentially testable not only among living people, but in the archaeological record. In addition, by avoiding a skill-based emphasis, this definition facilitates the crosscultural study of art, making it unnecessary to pose a dichotomy between modern and primitive art, or art and craft. Finally, this definition has the advantage of making explicit the inheritable or replicable unit, a central issue in evolutionary biology (e.g., Cavalli-Sforza and Feldman 1971, Cloak 1975, Dawkins 1976, Durham 1976, Hill 1989, Lumsden & Wilson 1981, Mundinger 1980, Pulliam & Dunford 1980, Ruyle 1973, Stuart-Fox 1986).

The Origin of Art

Humans may invent or originate many behaviors. However, only some of the behaviors will be repeated and even fewer will be repeated or copied by others. Still fewer behaviors will be copied generation after generation. Evidence of the origin of any social (or cultural) behavior will consist of evidence that the behavior has been replicated.

Methods for Identifying the Origin of Art

Although it is likely that early humans produced other, temporary forms of art that did not endure in the archaeological record, objects to be considered as candidates for the first art must be found in association with hominid or archaic *Homo sapiens* sites, have firm radiometric dates, and show continuities into the ethnographic present.

To the greatest extent possible, objects also should be found in direct association with biological traits, such as skeletal or dental remains. This last criterion makes it possible to avoid the claim that hominid bones found in association with art objects may not be those of the art makers (see McBrearty 1990). Key associations also should aid future studies attempting to identify the method of transmission (e.g., was the trait transmitted to possible descendants?) and attempting to determine whether the trait proliferates along with the population demonstrating the trait. Key associations also should aid in future studies attempting to determine if the origin of art corresponds with the transition between archaic and anatomically modern humans, a topic attracting considerable interest in archaeology today (see Chase and Dibble 1987, Klein 1974, 1990, Mellars 1989, Lindly and Clark 1990, White 1982). As parietal art (e.g., wall paintings) and portable art (e.g., Venus figurines and incised bones), with the possible exceptions of the mammoth tooth from the Hungarian site of Tata and a fossil nummulite from the same location (Vertes 1908, Mellars 1989), lack both radiometric dates and biological associations, and have been dated based on association with tool types and assemblage sequences (both of which are notoriously unreliable as temporal indicators, Lindly and Clark 1990, Mellars 1980), they will not be considered as candidates for the first art until such evidence is available.

Non-Art

Perhaps the best place to begin this search is with a discussion of objects that may not be art. To know what art is, we must know what art is not. The Acheulean handaxe, made 200,000 years ago by *Homo erectus,* has been called an aesthetic object (Sandars 1985). This axe is a symmetrical stone tool (Wynn 1985), which often is made of difficult to manage yet attractive raw materials (O'Brien 1984, Verworn 1909). To qualify as art, there must be evidence the craftsman "went beyond what was strictly necessary for utility and removed a flake or reserved a scar just for appearance, giving it an agreeable, but unnecessary symmetry" (Sandars 1985, 34).

A conclusive test remains to be made. However, if it can be empirically supported that the form of the stone axe was functional—for example, that its form increased its strength, minimized resistance while in flight or increased potential for long-distance flight, and/or allowed for more accurate impact (O'Brien 1984)—the axe is not art. The aesthetic "attractiveness," thus, may be an unintentional consequence of its use.

Art: Form

If we are looking for cultural artifacts that have firm radiometric dates and biological associations, the human body and its intentional modification is an obvious place to look. Cranial deformation and modification of the teeth, both permanent forms of body modification, cannot be discounted as possible candidates. Cranial deformation, as shown by skulls with measurements outside the normal range of variation, probably occurred incidentally early in human prehistory, as a consequence of infant cradle-board practices or sleeping habits (Rogers 1975). Incisor microwear among Australopithecines and subsequent hominids was common and quite obvious; by the approximate age of twenty, humans showed wear on all teeth (Wolpoff 1979, Smith 1976, Trinkaus 1983). This wear resulted from eating foods containing grit and from using the teeth as tools or "third hands" (Ryan and Johanson 1989, Smith 1976).

Two male crania (I and V, with possible deformation in II and IV), found at Shanidar, dated about 70,000 B.P., exhibit several of the more prominent features associated, in more recent humans, with intentional fronto-occipital head binding: frontal flattening, parietal arching, and, in cranium V, elevation of lambda (Trinkaus 1983, 146). Intentional deformation is identifiable and distinguishable from the shape of normal crania or unintentional deformation by shape outside the normal range, although it may be an exaggeration of the existing skull shape (Westermarck 1971); symmetry or near-symmetry of the form; highly similar repetition in the same social group or neighboring group; and repetition of the shape through time (see Hrdlicka 1940). The Shanidar deformations suggest an artificial process using flexible bands or head pressing, because the measurements are well outside the range of Neanderthal cranial variation and are consistent with cranial deformation in recent humans (Trinkaus 1983, but see Ivanhoe 1983).

By the Upper Paleolithic, there is clear evidence of intentional teeth filing and ablation: forcibly, intentionally, and non-curatively removing, chipping, or filing to alter tooth contours or the dental crown (Hrdlicka 1940, Romero 1970). The Minatogawa man found on the island of Okinawa (17,000 to19,000 B.P.), as one example, clearly had intentionally modified teeth (Suzuki and Hanihara 1982). Intentional tooth-wearing and -removal may be distinguished from unintentional or curative loss by the lack of evidence of disease, the symmetry or near-symmetry of the removals, the repetition of similar loss in the same social group, the breakage of the labial wall in the alveolus, signs the removal occurred in youth, and the evidence of the same practice in neighboring populations (Hrdlicka 1940).

By the late Upper Paleolithic, intentional cranial deformation and dental modification were becoming more common. By the Mesolithic and Neolithic, they were being practiced in Europe; North, South, and Central America; Africa; Australia; and Asia (Borbolla 1940, Campbell 1925, Dingwell 1931, El Najjar and Dawson 1977, Fastlicht 1971, Hrdlicka 1940, Leigh 1937, Linne 1940, MacCurdy 1923, Rogers 1975, Romero 1970). Cranial deformation was clearly intentional, and a variety of distinct cranial shapes were being produced (Rogers 1975). Dental modification was often elaborate: teeth were inlaid with precious stone, overlaid with precious metals, incised, filed into a variety of shapes, extracted in a wide range of patterns, and/or lacquered or stained.[3] These behaviors persisted in most of these geographical areas until extensive contact with other cultures occurred.

It could be argued that this early modification of the body was a by-product of another behavior (use of cradle boards, particular sleeping positions, diet, tool use); however, both behaviors persisted and intensified over time (becoming more extreme, showing a variety of forms) and, at the time of first contact with Europeans, clearly were being done intentionally. As neither cranial deformation nor dental modification have a known function other than to attract attention, they fall within the category we refer to as art.[4]

Art: Color

In the archaeological record there is a long history of the collection of what were to become coloring and painting materials (Wreschner 1980). By

120,000 B.P., seventy-five colored pigments, ranging in color from yellow to red and red brown, were collected by *Homo erectus* at Terra Amata (Howell 1966, de Lumley 1969, Wreschner 1980, but see Butzer 1980). This early reddish color consisted of hematitic or limonitic concretions (e.g., true ochre) or sesquioxide-rich clayey or sandy soils, and ferruginized shales or sandstones (Butzer 1980). Use of these early colors by hominids can be inferred from facets on the stones where they were rubbed against another object and from the fact that the color variation was due to the application of heat (see Wreschner 1980).

In approximately fifteen geographically dispersed Mousterian sites (70,000 to 45,000 B.P.) these substances are found on bodies (often of mature males), in burials (although color may have been placed on the body in funerary preparations), or strewn in occupation levels. Red coloring also was placed on the five human incisors deposited at Pinar (Jullien 1965), on the remains of a fallow-deer burial at Nahr Ibrahim (Solecki 1971, Wreschner 1980), and on mammoth bones in an oval arrangement at Molodova (Klein 1974). Possibly by 40,000 B.P., hematite was being quarried in Swaziland (Dart and Beaumont 1971).

The use of red pigments shows a dramatic increase from its appearance in only a few of the thirty-six known Eurasian Middle Paleolithic inhumations, to its more common occurrence in the ninety-six known burials of the Upper Paleolithic (Harrold 1980). Red pigment continues to be placed on the body (again, generally of mature males), often in large quantities (such as in the case of the Red "Lady" of Paviland, who was actually a male, Stern 1969). It was also placed on walls and objects and found strewn in habitation sites. Soon other colors appear.[5] It is perhaps significant that the use of red ochre increases along with evidence of modification of the body, through cranial deformation and dental decoration, and evidence of other forms of personal adornment, such as beads and pendants (Miller 1980).

Accidental Origin

Based upon the evidence presented, it is possible that the origin of art may have been accidental. Art may have arisen out of pre-existing behavior patterns. Weidenreich (1938-39, 10), writing of the deformed skull No. 102 at the Upper Cave of Zhoukoudian, argued that "this unintentional deformation or change [due to a cradle board or carrying basket] may represent a preceding stage of deliberate deforming of the skull." Similarly, intentional tooth filing and loss may have arisen out of accidental tooth wearing and loss due to such things as diet and/or tool use. Even the use of red color may have first been done accidentally, particularly as many of the colors come from clay, soft rock, and soil.

As art evolved, it became systematic. This suggests that certain techniques were developed. The implication of such careful replication is that technical aspects had become important. There were now particular methods of modifying objects, and these methods also were replicated through time. It is possible that the investment of time and energy required for the decoration of a body or object was partially correlated with the length of time it was retained, or its social importance (Guilmet 1977).

The Function of Art

Art's Costs

Why would modifying a body or object through color and form have been copied or replicated? Why would it have persisted for thousands of years? Generally a behavior is said to persist because it has a function, even though identifying the social function of that behavior may be problematic (Cohen 1968). Some scholars, however, have proposed that art, at least initially, had no function (Luquet 1930, Halverson 1987). This "art for art's sake" argument depends, at least in part, upon the costs of art being low enough. Halverson (1987) claimed that the costs of art were low because, focusing only on production, there was a great deal of free time in a traditional society.

Time, however, may not have been the only cost. Cranial deformation may alter the shape of the auditory meatus, reducing or even almost closing the ear opening (MacCurdy 1924); cause exostoses in the auditory canal, particularly in the case of fronto-occipital intentional flattening (Hrdlicka 1935); and decrease cranial volume (6 per cent in some Peruvian skulls, MacCurdy 1923). It also may affect the shape of the palate (Leigh 1937) and the orbital ridge, impeding speech and resulting in bloodshot and protruding eyes (Dingwell 1931). It also can deform the cranial base (McNeill and Newton1965), resulting in headache.

The costs of ablation, depending on the time since the removal, include considerable pain, the breakage of the labial wall of the alveolus, and the considerable approach of the remaining teeth (Hrdlicka 1940). Filing and chipping can result in alveolar abscesses and bone infections, and filed teeth are more readily subject to wear (Linne 1940). In addition, some teeth show apical pathosis caused by trauma and pulp involvement. Both filing and ablation can cause difficulty in speech and mastication (Romero 1970).

Placing color on a body also has a cost since colors attract attention not only of the desired audience but of competing conspecifics and predators of other species. Also, the procurement of pigments might have been dangerous and time-consuming. The Australian aborigines, for example, often crossed enemy territory to get at sources of red ochre (Spencer and Gillen 1939).

In sum, the cost of body coloring and shaping involved not only the actual time spent in the application of the color or modification of the form, but also time spent acquiring necessary resources. Costs also may have included facing danger, sacrificing personal comfort and even health, and learning to copy the behavior accurately. Given the potentially high costs of art, why might it have persisted? Why might it have flourished?

Art and Its Social Effects

In 1859, Darwin proposed, and others have agreed (e.g., Low 1979), that color and form were used by humans and other animals to communicate sexual interest, perhaps among other things (e.g., health, common ancestry, or species identification). If so, color and form, or art, had a social effect—it attracted the attention of potential mates. This social effect, in turn, would have influenced the replication of the trait through time.

There is tentative support for Darwin's proposal in the archaeological record. In the Middle and Upper Paleolithic burials and in the seven hundred known Mesolithic burials, a pattern is found of differential treatment according to sex (Harrold 1980). Burials of males more frequently contain grave goods, including red pigments (Harrold 1980), and by the Upper Paleolithic, the remains of males more frequently demonstrated cranial deformation and/or decorated teeth. This bias continued at least through the Mesolithic.

In the ethnographic record, there also is evidence that in kinship-based tribal societies, much (often painful) body decoration was initiated at puberty, frequently as part of rites of passage, and that it was more frequently associated with males. Although this bias may not be evident in Western, industrialized societies, as Im Thurn (1883) has argued, ornaments "among Indians as throughout almost the whole animal world, exclusive of civilized man, are far more abundantly used by the males than by the females" (195).

Not only were males more frequently decorated, but the decoration was done at puberty, and it frequently involved pain. In addition, there apparently were important social effects. In the Marquesas, tattooing was a painful process, but males who refused to be tattooed were exiled (Ebin 1979), probably to face death. Partially tattooed males, although not exiled, never married. An Australian male aborigine who failed to complete the initiation rituals (which could include ablation, keloid scarring, and circumcision) could not marry (Spencer and Gillen 1939). Marquardt (1984) reported that in Samoa men who avoided the painful operation of tattooing "never enjoyed the least respect, women despised them, chiefs refused to accept food from their hands which they called stinking" and "many a father refuses him his daughter's hand" (7-8). Among the Sebei of Uganda, sex with an uncircumcised boy was traditionally forbidden and called "dirty" (Goldschmidt 1986, 96). Among the Bavole of Northern Rhodesia, an uncircumcised male was not considered to be an adult politically or socially, and he was denied a sexually active life, ("women will not sleep with him," Ebin 1979, 44). Uncircumcised Ndemba males were called "polluted" (Ebin 1979).

Modification of the female body using color and/or form in kinship-based tribal societies is generally less pronounced than male decoration; however, it too was often involved in mate selection. In the Congo, Basongye females claim that men are so fond of their markings (keloid scars) they will refuse to have sexual intercourse with a woman who has no markings (Merriam 1971). In the Marquesas, a woman without a blue hand tattoo was not permitted to form the dough which was the dietary staple; such a woman would not be married (Eban 1979). In Uganda, a Sebei female who cried out during her circumcision had her dance regalia torn from her body in public, and she could never marry. Even if she later submitted to circumcision, she was not allowed to be a man's first wife. Her husband was not allowed to fight in wars since he would be weakened by her, she was kept away from future circumcisions as she might bring bad luck, and other women despised her (Goldschmidt 1986).

Although these descriptions support the proposition that body decoration may be related to mate selection, it still is not clear, given the high costs, why this behavior would persist. Certainly, it is not necessarily true that these individuals were in fact "stinking" or "dirty," or that uncircumcised women weakened males and, thus, were better off unmated. Talk can be, and often is, used to justify actions. Thus, it must be asked, what might be an additional, perhaps more fundamental, benefit to the individual who does decorate him/herself and to the individual attracted to the decoration? Did decoration allow for the selection of a more appropriate mate?

Although body decoration in tribal societies does communicate sexual maturity and gender, and these are of course important in selecting appropriate mates, why would humans pay such a high price to call attention to states about which there is little physiological doubt? Although art might also have intended to call attention to or exaggerate such things as health (ruddy cheeks), strength, or virility/fecundity (Low 1979), the evidence is not forthcoming. Tribal or clan decoration means that all mature males, not just strong and/or virile ones, will display similar patterns of decoration (for example, Broadbeach Cemetery in Queensland, Australia; Haglund 1976). Further, in the archaeological and ethnographic records red pigments are found to have been placed over much of the body, not just on the cheeks, and unlike cranial deformation or teeth decoration, which were done antemortem, red pigments may have been placed on the bodies of the dead.

Another possible effect, the identification of close and distant kin (Alexander 1979), may still be related to mate selection. Based upon the ethnographic evidence and the mammalian strategy of parental care, it can be assumed that early humans lived in kinship groups. Thus, the method of transmission of body decoration traditions through time would be between generations of biological kin, probably parent or other close relative to child.

To the extent the replication of the trait was conservative—and there is evidence it was (see Alexander 1979, Boas 1955, Houston 1920)—it would have the effect over time of coming to identify common descent, or what we now refer to as clans and tribes. Clans frequently are referred to as marriage categories, or exogamous groups involved in exchanging wives.

In the human remains found at Broadbeach Cemetery in Queensland, there is tentative support for the proposal that art identifies common descent. Burials at Broadbeach took place over a thousand-year period. Male burials outnumbered female burials seven to one, and most of the males over age fifteen had the right upper central incisor removed antemortem (Haglund 1976). The teeth of females were rarely removed intentionally (Haglund 1976). The amount of genetic variation in the burial population suggests inbreeding, or the regular exchange of spouses with another closely related group. A notable number of individuals were found who had a partial or complete dorsal defect of the sacral canal, a heritable trait, suggesting common descent from a common ancestor.

Ritual removal of the incisors, or other teeth, of adolescent males was a common practice in Australia at the time of first European contact and, according to Spencer and Gillen (1939), the pattern of extraction identified tribes and clans. Broadbeach thus may have been a tribal or clan burial ground. Tribes and clans were composed of individuals who shared a common ancestor and who tended to occupy a common land or at least shared a burial ground. Common descent may help explain why, as early as the Upper Paleolithic in Europe and Asia, there were clear patterns to art, with broad regions where closely similar art styles were found and corresponding boundaries where art styles abruptly changed (see Conkey 1985). Certainly, evidence of genetic affinity (e.g., genetic anomalies such as dental traits or the dorsal defect noted above) in the aforementioned population would support the common-descent explanation.

Although clan or tribal decoration and identification of common descent is of interest, it is not clear why identification of descent might be of importance in attracting mates and making a mate choice. If many generations separate the common clan ancestor from living descendants, it can be predicted that clans will include individuals who are closely related (e.g., brothers, cousins) and individuals who are not (who are more distantly related than second cousins). In other words, we cannot argue that decoration facilitates the avoidance of incest. Further, the identical nature of clan decoration is problematic. Given the widespread nature of tribal endogamy and clan exogamy, one's clan and tribal costume would not only be painful, it would have the effect, not of attracting as many mates as possible (as one would expect based upon most interpretations of Darwinian theory), but of significantly reducing the number of potential mates. It would communicate one's unavailability to females of another tribe or of the same or prohibited clan.

Alexander (1979) has proposed that similarity in dress is due to males' copying dominant males. It seems clear that individuals today do copy the body decoration of those who are famous and influential, even when that copying involves considerable discomfort. However, it is unclear why females would be so easily influenced, especially over millennia (e.g., Houston 1920), and it does not explain the persistence of the trait, particularly in new generations who had not been directly influenced by the imitated individual. Why would that form of adornment persist if each generation produces its own dominant and influential males? If decoration is copied identically through time, as continuity in the past indicates, individuals must have been copying their ancestors. Tradition, in fact, implies transmission from ancestors. Why might humans have regularly replicated the art of their ancestors? Why might they have been willing to endure pain to do so?

It is possible that the amount of time, energy, and/or discomfort that one is willing to sacrifice for a relationship is an indication of the importance of that relationship. Although some choice was involved (as the examples show, individuals could decide to forgo decoration), decorated individuals clearly had accepted the influence of the elders who encouraged the practice. The persistence of any tradition implies acceptance of ancestral influence. The Australian aborigines, for example, stated explicitly that male initiation (which could last ten to fifteen years, during which time the body was decorated) ended when boys showed signs they had learned (from the elders) the sacred secrets of the tribe, habits of self-restraint, and implicit obedience to the commands of older males (Spencer and GIllen 1938, 272). Only males who passed through initiation successfully were allowed to marry (Spencer and Gillen 1939).

Individuals need a great deal of knowledge if they are to survive in a hostile environment, especially a socially hostile one. Those who non-skeptically or voluntarily submit themselves to pain may be more amenable to the guidance of already successful elders in regard to life-saving traditions (see, however, Trivers 1974). Given the importance to humans of complex social knowledge, individuals who avoided the high costs of trial-and-error learning might well have been better survivors and reproducers.

Conclusion

This essay represents an attempt to define art empirically and to use that definition to identify art's origin and explain its persistence. It was argued that humans are constructed to respond to color and form. Artists use, and are encouraged by others to use, this tendency in order to influence social behavior. The first use of color and form, possibly placed on the human body, was perhaps accidental. However, art had social effects; it attracted attention to the decorated individual. As this decoration was transmitted to descendants it would come to be systematic, communicating or attracting attention to specific information about the decorated individual, namely ancestry or common descent. The information communicated, the message to which art attracted attention, might have been important to both sender and receiver. The social effect of decoration, thus, can be said to have influenced the replication or copying of the trait (what we mean by culture) and the persistence of the trait through time (what we mean by tradition).

Using color and form to attract attention to objects and bodies, artists have successfully influenced people for many thousands of years. In this essay, Darwin's proposal was briefly examined. However, although art apparently is used to attract the attention of mates, not all art can be explained by sexual selection. When art systematically attracts attention to a body, it may have the effect of attracting mates. Clearly art, even art used to modify the body, can have other effects. Art, by drawing attention to an object or body, makes it more noticeable and any messages more influential.

This essay raises more questions than it attempts to answer. Why was art used to call attention to nonreproductive individuals (elderly females, infants, the dead)? Why did color and pattern so frequently communicate ancestry? Why did humans so often use permanent forms of body decoration that could involve considerable discomfort? Why did elders ask for such sacrifices from their descendants? Such questions must be addressed. However, the argument has wider applicability than has been made explicit and is not confined to the visual arts: Poetry and music use patterns of sound, and dance utilizes patterns of movement in time and space. All these forms of art may draw attention to an object, making it, and any messages to which it calls attention, more attractive and influential.

Works Cited

Alexander, R.
1979 *Darwinism and Human Affairs*. Seattle: University of Washington Press.
Anderson, R.
1979 *Art in Primitive Societies*. Englewood Cliffs, NJ: Prentice-Hall, Inc.
Bateson, G.
1972 "Style, Grace and Information in Primitive Art." In G. Bateson, ed., *Steps to an Ecology of Mind*. New York: Ballantine.
Bell, C.
1958 *Art*. New York: Capricorn. (First published in 1911.)
Boas, F.
1955 *Primitive Art*. New York: W. W. Norton. (First published in 1923.)
Borbolla, D.
1940 "Types of Tooth Mutilations Found in Mexico." *American Journal of Physical Anthropology* 26:359-65.
Brothwell, D.
1976 "Visual Art, Evolution, and Environment." In D. Brothwell and C. Waddington, eds., *Beyond Aesthetics*. London: Thames and Hudson.
Butzer, K.
1980 "Reply to Ernst Wreschner's Red Ochre and Human Evolution." *Current Anthropology* 21:631-45.

Campbell, T.

1925 *Dentition and Palate of the Australian Aboriginal*. Sydney, Australia: Hassel Press.

Cavalli-Sforza, L., and M. Feldman

1981 *Cultural Transmission and Evolution: A Quantitative Approach*. Princeton: Princeton University Press.

Chase, P. & Dibble, H.

1987 "Middle Paleolithic Symbolism: A Review of Current Evidence and Interpretations." *Journal of Anthropological Archaeology* 6:262-96.

Cloak, F.

1975 "Is a Cultural Ethology Possible?" *Human Ecology* 3:161-182.

Cohen, P.

1968 *Modern Social Theory*. New York: Basic Books.

Collins, D., and J. Onians

1978 "The Origins of Art." *Art History* 1:1-25.

Conkey, M.

1985 "Ritual Communication, Social Elaboration, and the Variable Trajectories of Paleolithic Material Culture." In T. D. Price and J. Brown, eds., *Prehistoric Hunter-Gatherers: The Emergence of Cultural Complexity*. Orlando, FL: Academic Press.

Cordwell, J., and R, Schwarz, eds.

1979 *The Fabric of Culture*. The Hague: Mouton.

Dart, R., and P. Beaumont

1971 "On a Further Radiocarbon Date for Ancient Mining in Southern Africa." *South African Journal of Science* 67:10-11.

Darwin, C.

1859 *On the Origin of Species*. London: Watts and Company.

Davis, W.

1986 "The Origins of Image Making." *Current Anthropology* 27: 193-215.

Dawkins, R.

1976 *The Selfish Gene*. Oxford: Oxford University Press.

Delluc, B., and G. Delluc

1978 "Les Manifestations graphiques sur support rocheux des environs de Eyzies (Dordogne)." *Gallia Prehistorique* 21(1-2):213-438.

Dingwell, E.

1931 *Artificial Cranial Deformation: A Contribution to the Study of Ethnic Mutilations*. London: John Bale, Sons and Danielsson, Ltd.

Dissanayake, E.

1989 *What Is Art For?* Seattle: University of Washington Press.

Durham, W.

1976 "The Adaptive Significance of Cultural Behavior." *Human Ecology* 4:89-121.

Eban, V.

1979 *The Body Decorated*. London: Blacker Colmann Cooper, Ltd.

El Najjar, M., and G. Dawson

1977 "The Effect of Artificial Cranial Deformation on the Incidence of Wormian Bones in the Lambdoidal Suture." *American Journal of Physical Anthropology* 46 (1):155-60.

Fastlicht, S.

1971 *La Odontologia en Mexico Prehispanico*. Mexico, DF: Derechos Reservados S. Fastlicht.

Gamble, C.

1982 "Interaction and Alliance in Paleolithic Society." *Man* 17: 92-107.

Goldschmidt, W.

1986 *The Sebei*. New York: Holt, Rinehart and Winston.

Guilmet, G.

1977 "The Evolution of Tool Using and Tool Making Behavior." *Man* 12 (1):33-47.

Haglund, L.

1976 *An Archaeological Analysis of the Broadbeach Aboriginal Burial Ground*. St. Lucia, Queensland: University of Queensland Press.

Halverson, J.

1987 "Art for Art's Sake in the Paleolithic." *Current Anthropology* 28:63-87.

Harrold, F.
1980 "A Comparative Analysis of Eurasian Paleolithic Burials." *World Archaeology* 12:132-58.
Hilbert, D.
1987 *Color and Color Perception*. Palo Alto, CA: Center for the Study of Language and Information, Stanford University.
Hill, J.
1989 "Concepts As Units of Cultural Replication." *Journal of Social and Biological Structures* 12:343-55.
Houston, M.
1920 *Ancient Egyptian, Mesopotamian and Persian Costumes and Decoration*. London: Adams and Charles Block.
Howell, F.
1966 "Observations on the Earlier Phases of the European Lower Paleolithic." *American Anthropologist* 69:88-210.
Hrdlicka, A.
1940 *Ear Exotoses*. Washington: Smithsonian Miscellaneous Collections.
Im Thurn, E.
1883 *Among the Indians of Guiana*. New York: Dover.
Ivanhoe, F.
1983 "On Cranial Deformation in Shanidar I and V." *Current Anthropology* 24:27.
Jullien, R.
1965 *Les Hommes fossiles de la Pierre Taille*. Paris: Boubee.
Klein, R.
1974 "Ice Age Hunters of the Ukraine." *Scientific American* 30:96-105.
1990 "Human Cognitive Change at the Middle to Upper Paleolithic Transition: The Evidence at Boker Tachtit." In P. Mellars, ed., *The Human Revolution*. Edinburgh: University of Edinburgh Press.
Langer, S.
1958 *Problems of Art*. New York: Charles Scribner's Sons.
Leigh, R.
1937 "Dental Morphology and Pathology of Pre-Spanish Peru." *American Journal of Physical Anthropology* 22 (2):267-96.

Leroi Gourhan, A.

1967 *Treasures of Prehistoric Art*. New York: Abrams.

Lewis-Williams, J.

1982 "The Economic and Social Context of Southern San Rock Art." *Current Anthropology* 23(4):429-49.

Lewis-Williams, J., and J. Loubser,

1986 "Deceptive Appearances: A Critique of Southern African Rock Art Studies." *Advances in World Archaeology*, Vol. 5. Academic Press.

Lindley, J., and G. Clark

1990 "Symbolism and Modern Human Origins." *Current Anthropology* 31:233-61.

Linne, S.

1940 "Dental Decoration in Aboriginal Man." *Ethnos* 5:2-18.

Low, B.

1979 "Sexual Selection and Human Ornamentation." In N. Chagnon and W. Irons, eds., *Evolutionary Biology and Human Social Behavior*. North Scitutate, MA: Duxbury Press.

Lumley, H. de

1969 Le Paleolithique inferieur et moyen du Midi mediterraneen dan son cadre geologique. Paris: Editions du Centre National de la Recherche.

Lumsden, C, and E. O. Wilson

1981 *Genes, Mind and Culture*. Cambridge, MA: Harvard University Press.

Luquet, G.

1930 *L'art primitif*. Paris: Institut d'ethnologie.

MacCurdy, G.

1923 "Human Skeletal Remains from the Highlands of Peru." *American Journal of Physical Anthropology* 6(3):217-329.

Marshack, A.

1976 "Some Implications of the Paleolithic Symbolic Evidence for the Origin of Language." *Current Anthropology* 17(2):274-81.

1979 "Upper Paleolithic Symbol Systems of the Russian Plain: Cognitive and Comparative Analyses." *Current Anthropology* 20(2):271-311.

1981 "On Paleolithic Ochre and the Early Uses of Color and Symbol." *Current Anthropology* 22(2):188-91.

1982 "Non-Utilitarian Fragment of Bone from the Middle Palaeolithic Layer." In J. Kozlowski, ed., *Excavation in the Bacho Kiro Cave (Bulgaria): Final Report*. Warsaw: Panstowowe Wydawnictwo Naukowe.

1988 "The Neanderthals and Their Human Capacity for Symbolic Thought: Cognitive and Problem Solving Aspects of Mousterian Symbol." In O. Bar-Yosef, ed., *L'homme de Neandertal*, vol. 5. *La Pensee*. Liege: ERAUL, pp. 57-92.

Manser, J.

1946 "Prehistoric Dental Inlays in Ecuador." *El Palacio* 5: 111-15.

Marquardt, C.

1984 *The Tattooing of Both Sexes in Samoa*. Papahure: R. McMillan. (First published in 1899.)

McBrearty, S.

1990 "The Origin of Modern Humans." *Man* 25(1):131-43.

McNeill, R., and G. Newton

1965 "Cranial Base Morphology in Association with Intentional Cranial Vault Deformation." *American Journal of Physical Anthropology* 23:241-53.

Mellars, P.

1989 "Major Issues in the Emergence of Modern Humans." *Current Anthropology* 30(3):349-85.

Miller, S.

1980 "A Reply to E. Wreschner's 'Red Ochre and Human Evolution.'" *Current Anthropology* 21(5):631-44.

Mills, G.

1971 "Art: An Introduction to Qualitative Anthropology." *Journal of Aesthetics and Art Criticism* 16(1):1-17.

Mundinger, P.

1980 "Animal Cultures and a General Theory of Cultural Evolution." *Ethology and Sociobiology* 1:183-223.

Munro, T.

1949 *The Arts and Their Interrelationships*. New York: Liberal Press.

Nordenskiold, E.

1919 *The Changes in Material Culture of Two Indian Tribes under the Influence of New Surroundings*. Göteborg: Erlanders.

O'Brien, E.

1984 "What Was the Acheulean Hand Axe?" *Natural History* 93(7):20-3.

Plato

1979 "On Art," from *The Republic*. In G. Dickie and R. Sclafani, eds., *Aesthetics: A Critical Anthology*. New York: Bobbs-Merrill.

Pulliam, H., and C. Dunford

1980 *Programmed to Learn*. New York: Columbia University Press.

Roach, M., and J. Eicher

1965 *Dress, Adornment and the Social Order*. New York: John Wiley and Sons.

Rogers, S.

1975 *Artificial Deformation of the Head: New World Examples of Ethnic Mutilation and Notes on Its Consequences*. San Diego, CA: Museum of Man.

Romero, J.

1970 "Dental Mutilations, Trephination, and Cranial Deformation." In J. Wauchope, ed., *Handbook of Middle American Indians*. Austin: University of Texas Press.

Ruyle, E.

1973 "Genetic and Cultural Pools: Some Suggestions for a Unified Theory of Biocultural Evolution." *Human Ecology* 1:21-25.

Ryan, A., and D. Johanson

1989 "Anterior Dental Microwear in Australopithecus Afarensis: Comparisons with Human and Non-Human Primates Incisor Microwear." *Journal of Human Evolution* 18:235-68.

Sandars, N.

1985 *Prehistoric Art in Europe*. 2d ed. London: Penguin.

Smith, P.

1976 "Dental Pathology in Fossil Hominids: What Did Neanderthals Do with Their Teeth?" *Current Anthropology* 17:149-51.

Solecki, R.

1975 *Shanidar: The First Flower People*. New York: Knopf.

Spencer, B., and F. Gillen

1939 *Native Tribes of Central Australia*. London: MacMillan.

Stern, P. Van Doren

1969 *Pleistocene Europe*. New York: W. W. Norton.

Steward, J., ed..

1963 *Handbook of South American Indians.* Vol. 6. New York: Cooper Square Publishers.

Stuart-Fox, M.

1986 "The Unit of Replication in Socio-Cultural Evolution." *Journal of Social and Biological Structures* 9:67-97.

Suzuki, H., and K. Hanihara, K. eds.

1982 *The Minatogawa Man: The Upper Pleistocene Man from the Island of Okinawa*. Tokyo: Bulletin of the University of Tokyo Museum, no. 19.

Tolstoy, L.

1977 "Art As the Communication of Feeling." In G. Dickie and R. Sclafani, eds., *Aesthetics: A Critical Anthology*. New York: Bobbs-Merrill.

Trinkaus, E.

1983 *The Shanidar Neandertals*. New York: Academic Press.

Trivers, R.

1974 "Parent-Offspring Conflict." *American Zoologist* 14:249-64.

Turner, C.

1983 "The Dental Search for Native American Roots." In R. Kirch and E. Szathmary, eds., *Out of Asia: Peopling the Americas and the Pacific*. Canberra: Australian National University.

Venters, M.

1989 "Family-Oriented Prevention of Cardiovascular Disease: A Social Epidemiological Approach." *Journal of Social Science and Medicine* 28:309-14.

Vertes, L.

1908 *Tata eine Mittelpalaolithische Travertin-Stedlung en Ungarn*. Budapest: Akademiai Klado.

Verworn, M.

1909 *Die Angange der Kunst*. Jend: Fischer.

Vinnicombe, P.
1976 *People of the Eland*. Pietermaritzburg: Natal University Press.
Vlahos, O.
1979 *Body: The Ultimate Symbol*. New York: J. B. Lippencott.
Webster's New Collegiate Dictionary
1985 Springfield, MA: Merriam Webster, Inc. 9th ed., s.v.
Westermarck, E.
1971 *The History of Human Marriage*. 2 vols. London: Macmillan. (First published in 1891.)
Weidenreich, F.
1938-39 *The Anthropological Papers of Franz Weidenreich*. New York: Viking.
Weltfish, G.
1953 *The Origins of Art*. Indianapolis: Bobbs-Merrill.
White, R.
1982 "Rethinking the Middle-Upper Paleolithic Transition." *Current Anthropology* 23:169-93.
Wilson, E. O.
1975 *Sociobiology*. Cambridge, MA: Harvard University Press.
Wolpoff, M.
1979 "The Krapina Dental Remains." *American Journal of Physical Anthropology* 50:67-114.
Wreschner, E.
1980 "Red Ochre and Human Evolution: A Case for Discussion." *Current Anthropology* 21:631-44.
Wynne, T.
1985 "Piaget, Stone Tools and the Evolution of Human Intelligence." *World Archaeology* 17:32-43.

Notes

1. This essay was first published in the *Journal of Social and Evolutionary Systems* 15 (2):217-34. To the scholars who reviewed this manuscript at various stages of its development, the author would like

to extend her gratitude: John Alcock, Richard Alexander, Richard Anderson, Geof Clark, Jim Eder, Charles Merbs, Mary Marzke, Lyle Steadman, and Christy Turner. Any errors, of course, are solely the responsibility of the author.

2. Plato, for example, acknowledged (metaphorically) the importance of color and form when he wrote, "I think that you must know, for you have often seen what a poor appearance the tales of poets make when stripped of the colors which music puts upon them...They are like faces which were never really beautiful, but only blooming; and now the bloom of youth has passed from them" (1977, 14). Tolstoy's implicit definition of art reads similarly: "To evoke in oneself a feeling one has experienced and having evoked it in oneself then by means of movements, lines and colors, sounds or forms expressed in words, so to transmit that" (1977, 65-66). Clive Bell (1958) defined art as "significant form." He claimed that significant form, under which he included "combinations of lines and color," is the one quality common to all works of visual art (18-19; see also Suzanne Langer 1957). Social scientists, influenced by philosophers, have defined art similarly. Boas, for example, writing just twelve years after Clive Bell, although he failed to cite him, defined art similarly as "significant form" (1955, 12).

3.. Hrdlicka (1940) lists a large number of patterns of teeth extraction. These include extracting both median incisors, both right incisors, both left incisors, both median and lateral incisors, all incisors, both upper left incisors and right canine, and premolars. These patterns persist through time and were distributed in various groups in Siberia and North and South America. Needless to say, this may provide an appropriate place to test any hypotheses about art and its relationship to common descent.

4. Some types of decoration may have had more than one advantage. Blacking of the teeth, for example, might help prevent tooth decay (Bailit 1968, Borbolla 1940, Linne 1940, Manser 1946, Nordenskiold 1919, Steward 1963) and reduce periodontal disease (Bailit 1968). Generally, individuals who blackened their teeth appeared to be unaware of the benefit (Bailit 1968).

5. Lumps of white clay foreign to the site have been retrieved from an Aurignacian layer at Hayonim Cave in Israel (Wreschner 1980). In these later sites, green malachite, antimony, and cinnabar (mercury sulfide) have been found (Wreschner 1980).

Imagination and Survival: The Case of Fantastic Literature

Eric S. Rabkin

"The only thing we have to fear," Franklin Roosevelt said as America confronted the Great Depression and a world in which a little man named Adolf Hitler had just been named Chancellor of Germany, "is fear itself." Looking backward across the years of global deprivation and the horror of the Holocaust, we may be astonished at Roosevelt's ranking of the perils before the nation. Yet Roosevelt's focus, not on the dangers of the real but on the dangers of the imagined, has an important history in human affairs. Nearly a century earlier, as America groped angrily toward civil war, Henry David Thoreau wrote in his journal that "nothing is so much to be feared as fear." England's most revered modern soldier, the Duke of Wellington, admitted that "the only thing I am afraid of is fear" (Henry 1980). Francis Bacon understood this ("Nothing is terrible except fear itself"), and so did Michel de Montaigne ("The thing I fear most is fear"). Even the Bible exhorts us to "be not afraid of sudden fear" (Proverbs 3:25). "Fear" comes from an Old English word meaning "ambush" (Stein 1966). No matter how well we may in fact be prepared for the dangers around us, a sudden attack from within may be fatal. "My God, my God," Jesus cried upon the cross, "why hast thou forsaken me?" (Matthew 27:46) In *The Gospel According to Saint Matthew*, those were the last words of Jesus. Then he "yielded up the ghost" (Matthew 27:50).

In "Sophist," Plato's Socratic "Stranger" demonstrates that "an art of deception" exists which may lead us to dangerously "false judgment." His reasoning is this: Whether in silent thinking or in discourse, the mind bases judgments upon perceptions. Perceptions may be of things themselves or of images of things; those images that are "likenesses," exact copies, are true, but those that are only "semblances" are false. The possibility of semblances leads to the possibility of false perceptions and hence to both deception and self-deception (Plato 1011-12).

The problem of false images mattered a great deal to Plato. Earlier in "Sophist," the Stranger calls a likeness "a copy that conforms to the proportions of the original in all three dimensions and giving moreover the proper color to every part." Theaetetus asks, "Is not that what all imitators try to do?" No, the Stranger replies,

> Not those sculptors or painters whose works are of colossal size. If they were to reproduce the true proportions of a well-made figure, as you know, the upper parts would look too small, and the lower too large, because we see the one at a distance, the other close at hand. ... So artists, leaving the truth to take care of itself, do in fact put into the images they make, not the real proportions, but those that will appear beautiful. ... The first kind of image, then, being like the original, may fairly be called a likeness (*eikon*) [while the kind that only] seems to be a likeness, but is not really so, may we not call it a semblance (*phántasma*)?

The Stranger then gives a name to the whole process of "semblance making": *phantastike* (978-79). Our word *fantastic*, like the Greek *phantastike*, comes from the root *phantázein*, to make visible (Stein 1966). Of course, our word *imagination*, coming as it does from the Latin *imago*, or copy, also means to make visible, to produce a copy in the mind, be that copy true or false. The semantic connection between imagination and fantasy is as deep as the roots of our language, and the problem of the danger that the imagined fantastic presents for a sudden ambush of our will has been with us at least since Biblical times.

While Roosevelt may have pointed to the fearfulness of fear in part to embolden Americans against what they would understand to be, after all, a chimerical threat, Plato eschewed all fantasies, no matter how reassuring or seductive. In book 3 of *The Republic*, Socrates, in order to achieve the perfect civil state, notoriously expels the poets.

> If a man, then, it seems, who was capable by his cunning of assuming every kind of shape and imitating all things should arrive in our city, bringing with himself the poems which he wished to exhibit, we should fall down and worship him as a holy and wondrous and delightful creature, but should say to him that there is no man of that kind among

> us in our city, nor is it lawful for such a man to arise among us, and we should send him away to another city, after pouring myrrh down over his head and crowning him with fillets of wool. (642-43)

Plato's very language ("holy," "myrrh," "crown") suggests that there is something godlike in so Protean a poet, but to give to the people the ideas of a god is forbidden. In this, Plato agrees with the writer of Genesis.

Plato is not, however, against all poetry or all poets, anymore than Jehovah is against all knowledge. "We should send [that godlike poet] away," Socrates continues, "but we ourselves, for our souls' good, should continue to employ the more austere and less delightful poet and taleteller, who would imitate the diction of the good man and would tell his tale in the patterns which we prescribed in the beginning, when we set out to educate our soldiers" (643). The more "austere" poet, of course, is the one who does not create fantastic images, who incites imagination only of the true, the upright, the good. Plato does not expel poets; he expels fantasy, for the sort of imagination that fantasy represents can quite obviously and seductively undermine the state. Imagination can, after all, put ideas in people's heads.

One of the most famous imaginers of the world as it might be was Doctor Faustus. In Marlowe's version of the tale, after twenty-four years spent consorting with his dark double Mephistophilis, Faustus suddenly and fully recognizes that his fantastic knowledge imperils his place in the divine order. At that moment he turns toward Jesus, the New Adam, imploring forgiveness, absolution, and a return to Edenic ignorance: "See, see where Christ's blood streams in the firmament!/ One drop would save my soul—half a drop: ah, my Christ!" Grace does not descend, and so Faustus finally proposes to sacrifice that to which he has held most fast: "Ugly hell, gape not! come not, Lucifer!/ I'll burn my books!—Ah Mephistophilis! [Exeunt (Devils with him)]" (190). If Mephistophilis is the flesh of Faustus' fantastic knowledge, then the books are its spirit. Faustus would, finally, abjure his imagining, but it is too late.

In *The Tempest*, on the other hand, Shakespeare's Prospero both uses godlike knowledge and understands it. Perhaps most important, he understands that the place for fantastic knowledge is only in the imagined "Bermoothes." At the end of the play, as Prospero prepares to bring his plots to fruition so that he may leave the realm in which he was a god and resume his more civil authority in Milan, he addresses his minion Ariel.

> I have bedimmed
> The noontide sun, called forth the mutinous winds,
> And 'twixt the green sea and the azured vault
> Set roaring war ...But this rough magic
> I here abjure; and when I have required
> Some heavenly music (which even now I do)
> To work mine end upon their senses that
> This airy charm is for, I'll break my staff,
> Bury it certain fathoms in the earth,
> And deeper than did ever plummet sound
> I'll drown my book. (110)

Perhaps Faustus' offer is insincere; he never actually sets the fire of imagination to his books. Christ does not descend from heaven to earth, but Mephistophilis—and Faustus—descend from earth to hell. However, Prospero's offer is sincere; he extinguishes the knowledge in his book by drowning it, dissolving it, and thus impregnating the world with the possibility of a restored, regained Milan. Prospero voluntarily descends from his Bermoothean throne to resume the dukedom of earthly Milan. How many of us, given the possibility of such fantastic knowledge, could thus put it aside?

If knowledge is power, and if power corrupts, then knowledge corrupts. This is, of course, one reading of the story of the first fall from innocence. Note that knowledge in that story begins not with a direct Platonic perception but with an imagination. God has forbidden the eating of the fruit, but

> the serpent said unto the woman, Ye shall not surely die; For God doth know that in the day ye eat thereof, then your eyes shall be opened, and ye shall be as gods, knowing good and evil. And when the woman saw that the tree was good for food, and that it was pleasant to the eyes, and a tree to be desired to make one wise, she took of the fruit thereof, and

> did eat, and gave also unto her husband with her; and he did eat. And the eyes of them both were opened. (Genesis 3:4-7)

Within less than four verses, sight imagery, the language of imagination, is used four times. And that which is imagined does indeed come to be. The serpent is correct. Eating the fruit does not cause death; disobeying Jehovah causes death. "Behold, the man is become as one of us, to know good and evil: and now, lest he put forth his hand, and take also of the tree of life, and eat, and live for ever: Therefore the Lord God sent him forth from the garden of Eden, to till the ground from whence he was taken" (Genesis 3:22-23). The imagination, then, may bring about its own truth, and with this truth comes death.

The fundamental capacity of imagination to undermine must have moved the writers of the Bible deeply, for they retell this story in many ways. Almost immediately after the Fall, "there were giants in the earth." Then humanity itself became heroic. "[A]nd also after that, when the sons of God came in unto the daughters of men, and they bare children to them, the same became mighty men which were of old, men of renown" (Genesis 6:4). What happened to these wonderful "men of renown"? The very next verse explains: "And God saw that the wickedness of man was great in the earth, and that every imagination of the thoughts of his heart was only evil continually" (Genesis 6:5). Great men think great thoughts, thoughts that turn instantly to the imagination of evil. What is to be done? Just as Prospero will later drown his book, God sends the Flood.

Paul the Apostle also struggled against imagination, for to him the necessarily limited human imagination inevitably corrupted the divinity it sought to make visible. "Cast[ing] down imaginations, and every high thing that exalteth itself against the knowledge of God, and bring[ing] into captivity every thought to the obedience of Christ" (2 Corinthians 10:5). Those who made idols, Paul said, "became vain in their imaginations, and their foolish heart was darkened. Professing themselves to be wise, they became fools, And changed the glory of the uncorruptible God into an image made like to corruptible man" (Romans 1:21-23). Human imagination, in short, is capable only of deception. "For now we see through a glass, darkly;

but then [in heaven] face to face: now I know in part; but then shall I know even as also I am known" (1 Corinthians 13:12).

John Keats, in a letter to Benjamin Bailey, attempted to affirm "the authenticity of the Imagination" (1959, 257) by asserting that "the Imagination may be compared to Adam's dream—he awoke and found it truth" (258). In part Keats celebrates here what Plato feared: that imagining something may make it so. While the tone of Keats' letter suggests he is a poet who would resist Plato, the source of Keats' comparison does not suggest so wholehearted an embrace of fantasy. Adam's dream does not occur in Genesis; there the first man simply falls asleep and awakes again to find the first woman (Genesis 2:21-22). But in book 8 of *Paradise Lost*, John Milton devotes thirty magnificent lines to Adam's sleeping contemplation of a person "so lovely fair,/ That what seem'd fair in all the World, seem'd now/ Mean" (196). In his sleep "Shee disappear'd, and left me dark, I wak'd/ To find her, or for ever to deplore/ Her loss, and other pleasures all abjure" (197). Prospero "abjures" his "rough magic" to bring order to the world; Adam would abjure the world, to see again his magical image of woman. And, indeed, Adam achieved his terrible desire, a life with Eve beyond the walls of Paradise.

The tone of Adam's dream presages not the Keats of the letter but the Keats of "La Belle Dame Sans Merci." This poem begins with a question:

> O what can ail thee, knight-at-arms,
> Alone and palely loitering?
> The sedge has wither'd from the lake,
> And no birds sing. (199)

This desolation flows from a single encounter with

> a lady in the meads,
> Full beautiful—a faery's child,
> Her hair was long, her foot was light,
> And her eyes were wild. (200)

The wildness of her eyes penetrates those of the knight-at-arms. They couple in an enchantment resonant in the music of the poem:

I set her on my pacing steed,
And nothing else saw all day long,
For sidelong would she bend and sing
A faery's song.

Although "she said/ 'I love thee true,'" when he awoke on the "cold hill's side," la belle dame sans merci was gone forever. "And this is why I sojourn here ... And no birds sing" (1959, 200). As T. S. Eliot says in, also combining matters of intellectual and carnal imagination, "After such knowledge, what forgiveness?" (1962, 22).

A standard psychosexual understanding of the fear of fantasy virtually requires the conjunction of sexuality and knowledge. Aylmer, one of Nathaniel Hawthorne's scientific geniuses, is inspired by the beauty of his wife Georgiana to imagine her even more beautiful, to see her in his mind's eye with cheek unblemished by the tiny hand-shaped birthmark that some call her "fairy sign manual" (1937, 1022). He pleads that she allow him to experiment upon her. "[W]hat will be my triumph when I shall have corrected what Nature left imperfect in her fairest work!" (1024) Of course, Aylmer's attempt to "correct" Nature has a natural consequence: "You have rejected the best the earth could offer," Georgiana says. "Aylmer, dearest Aylmer, I am dying!" (1032). And so she does, a victim of her husband's imagination.

While Adam and Faustus and perhaps the knight-at-arms are the victims of their own imaginations, Georgiana, and all of us who are born with Original Sin, are victims of someone else's imagination. Evidently there are many ways to become a victim. Narrative warning against contemplation of a world too different from our own need not revolve around curiosity or even around sexuality. Jonathan Swift's Lemuel Gulliver is so sobered by his sojourn among the rational, equine Houyhnhnms, and so disgusted by the brutish, anthropomorphic Yahoos, that at his eventual return to England he finds himself trying desolately to converse with carriage horses and shuddering in the presence of humans.

> I began last week to permit my wife to sit at dinner with me, at the farthest end of a long table, and to answer (but with the utmost brevity) the few questions I ask her. Yet the smell of a yahoo continuing very offensive, I always keep my nose well stopped with rue, lavender, or tobacco leaves. And although it be hard for a man late in life to remove old habits, I am not altogether out of hopes in some time to suffer a yahoo in my company without the apprehensions I am yet under of his teeth or his claws. (1960, 238)

Edward Prendick too, returned from H. G. Wells' *Island of Dr. Moreau*, laments, "I could not persuade myself that the men and women I met were not also another, still passably human, Beast People, animals half-wrought into the outward image of human souls, and that they would presently begin to revert, to show first this bestial mark and then that" (1988, 136). Prendick hopes to overcome his mental tainting—indeed, he visits a "mental specialist" with this object—and "[m]y days I devote to reading and to experiments in chemistry, and I spend many of the clear nights in the study of astronomy" (137). In short, Prendick has not only been tainted in his view of people, but the imagination of Dr. Moreau, which created the horrible environment that marked Prendick, has now tainted Prendick's own mind. Like Moreau, he pursues a lonely science. But unlike Moreau, his science is removed from life into the study of mere matter and, resisting even more strongly in the dark night of his soul, removed from the earth altogether.

Freud would call Prendick's withdrawal into science a neurosis. "The asocial nature of neuroses," he writes in *Totem and Taboo*, "has its genetic origin in their most fundamental purpose, which is to take flight from an unsatisfying reality into a more pleasurable world of phantasy. The real world, which is avoided in this way by neurotics, is under the sway of human society and of the institutions collectively created by it. To turn away from reality is at the same time to withdraw from the community of man" (1950, 74). In his essay on "creative writers," Freud goes so far as to say that "a happy person never phantasies, only an unsatisfied one. The motive forces of phantasies are unsatisfied wishes, and every single phantasy is the fulfillment of a wish, a correlation of unsatisfying reality" (1986, 423). In other words, only someone straining at the strictures of the world would indulge his or her imagination. That very act implies psychological disability.

Although Freud's position may seem extreme because it applies to all fantasies, the danger of reimagining matters essential in one's life has always been as apparent as has the danger of fear. Paul, who presented corrupting imagination in the language of sight, himself underwent the most famous of conversions when, on the road to Damascus, "suddenly there shined upon him a light from heaven" (Acts 9:3). That this light was heavenly, one presumes, authorizes our desiring it rather than fearing it, but its immediate consequences could not have been more fearful: Paul (at that time still called Saul) was struck blind, was bereft of his identity, and was three days later reborn into a new life only by the grace of God. The Hebrew god, too, understood his own potency; kindness impelled him to reject Moses' wish to see him full face for "there may no man see me, and live" (Exodus 33:20). Semele had as her lover Jupiter, but Juno, jealous of the mortal, "insinuated doubts as to whether it was indeed Jove himself." Semele asks Jove

> a favour, without naming what it is. Jove gives his promise, and confirms it with their revocable oath, attesting the river Styx, terrible to the gods themselves. Then she made known her request. The god would have stopped her as she spake, but she was too quick for him. The words escaped, and he could neither unsay his promise nor her request. In deep distress he left her and returned to the upper regions. There he clothed himself in his splendours ... Arrayed in this, he entered the chamber of Semele. Her mortal frame could not endure the splendours of the immortal radiance. She was consumed to ashes. (Bullfinch 1942, 164)

The upper regions, of course, are the realms of the gods but also the realms of fantasy. In Hoffmann's "Ritter Gluck," the famous composer tells how he had been granted a journey into the "kingdom of dreams" (1972, 7) where he heard the ideal music of "the Euphon" (9). For having tried to write down that music, Gluck's soul is condemned to wander the earth. In each case, the access of knowledge touching on the imaginer's core destroyed the imaginer.

If one believes in Jehovah or Jesus or Jupiter, these stories represent the imagination of true knowledge, Plato's "austere" poems. But if one does not, these stories are among the many that recount simply the consequences of imagination, true or false. Just as the ancient Romans saw the true knowledge of the god as overwhelming, some observers consider false knowledge overwhelming. Iago's corruption of Othello through the imagination costs the Moor his wife, his position, and his very sense of himself. In Stanislaw Lem's *Solaris*, a sentient ocean projects into the orbiting space station of the scientists studying it simulacra of their dead loved ones: "'Certain events, which have actually happened, are horrible,'" the newly arrived protagonist is told by someone who has been occupying these "upper regions" of study, "'but what is more horrible still is what hasn't happened, what has never existed'" (1970, 80). It is the revival of his suicide wife in the form of a simulacrum that undercuts this protagonist's very sense of himself. As Gluck tells Hoffmann's narrator, "'One enters the kingdom of dreams through the ivory gate'" (1972, 7); that is, the way to essential truth may lie through the imagination of "what has never existed." In the final analysis, it does not matter whether the ghost of Hamlet's father was real or if Banquo's ghost was real; all that matters is that Hamlet and Macbeth saw those ghosts, and that they were undone.

In each of the cases we have turned to, the person of imagination has been, somehow, a person apart, touched by the gods, at odds with authority, revising reality. While some have argued, as I have myself in "The Descent of Fantasy," that the very capacity to fantasize has fundamental survival value for our species as a whole, it is clear that fantasizing is no unalloyed good for individuals. While it is true that the species may evolve through random mutation, the vast majority of all individual mutations are fatal. In the same way, one may suspect that for every marvelous imagination of a bright new future, for every inspiring *Rights of Man*, say, there are a thousand Freudian malcontents twisting in the grip of a reality made less tolerable by the futile fantasy of some better land. Better by far, for the average individual, to accept the social web in which we all live.

Interestingly, even fantastic literature underscores the danger of the imagination. Mary Shelley's *Frankenstein*, for example, not only rehearses the story of Faustus (and, for that matter, Prometheus the fire-stealer), but revises the story to define natural limits not as divine but as social. It is no accident that the novel takes an epistolary form. When Victor Frankenstein withdraws from all human contact in order to pursue his fantasy of reanimating dead flesh, he recalls a remonstrance of his father's: "'I regard any interruption in your correspondence as a proof that your other duties are equally neglected'" (1969, 55). Victor is the secret sharer of the egoistic urges of Robert Walton, the outermost frame narrator who writes the book as letters to his married sister. Just as Victor seeks the ancient dream of creating life, so Robert seeks the mythic land of Hyperborea. But while Victor forges on, only to die, Robert heeds his common crewmen and turns away from disaster. Like a more innocent Prospero, he knows when to give up the dream.

The structure of *Frankenstein* also reinforces the authority of society. Within the frame of Robert's narration is Victor's narration; within that, the creature's own lengthy exposition to his creator of the creature's awakening to life and subsequent history; and within that, the creature's narration of the love affair he observes of Felix (*fortunate*) and Safie (*wisdom*), a romance jeopardized by the unnatural perfidy of an ungrateful and prejudiced father. In short, the novel is constructed as a set of four nested narratives at the center of which is an exemplum of human community bound and betrayed. The betrayal of the creature by his creator mimics this.

Throughout the novel, there are four key terms for Victor's double: *creature, demon, miserable wretch,* and *monster.* That he is a creature, that is, a made thing existing in a world organized and regulated before his arrival, is crucial to his desire to find a world of his own. That he is a demon, from the Greek *daimon*, suggests that he is the spirit of Victor incarnate. Demon in its ancient sense means "a thing of divine spirit" (1966, Stein) while its modern sense means "evil spirit." Victor's demon, the embodiment of his fantasy of supplanting god, is clearly both. *Miserable* is a Latin-derived word that means worthy of pity, while *wretch* comes from the Old English word for exile. Together, this formula quite correctly suggests that the demon is worthy of pity precisely because he cannot find a place in society. Victor, on the other hand, could find a place in society but, led astray by his imagination, refuses it. Victor's monster, then, which brings about his death, is a warning to us all. *Monster* derives from the Latin *monere*, to warn.

Our species may advance, in the view of some, through the imagination of the few, but most of those who are set apart by their fantasies suffer. "Whom the gods would destroy they first make mad" (Longfellow 1980). In Karel Čapek's *War with the Newts*, the newts take the earth from humanity not by their inventive genius, their imaginative projection, their fantastic insights, but by relentless and common application of the tools with which humanity has provided them, for "what else is civilization but the ability to make use of things that somebody else has invented?" (1985, 241). We may—indeed, we undoubtedly do—hope for Eugene Zamyatin's D-503 to find a way out of the mechanized regularity of "the United State" in *We*, but the ultimate, tragic loss of "fancy" that leaves every citizen with the same fixed smile seems all but inevitable. As the last line so horribly reminds us, "Reason must prevail" (1952, 218).

One lesson of *We* for us as individuals is that we risk much by being too individual. Zamyatin's imagined world reverberates with fantastic truths. "Desires are tortures, aren't they?" a Guardian asks D-503. "It is clear, therefore, that happiness is when there are no longer any desires, not a single desire any more" (171). This idea is insane, of course, repulsive—and yet, on reflection, sometimes too true. How much happier would be Keats' knight-at-arms if only he could give up desire. In Zamyatin's world, the individual stands too little chance against the regulated hordes.

Although fantastic literature, by definition, presumes some taste for the fantastic, it frequently cautions against the disruptions of social reality that, as we have seen, fantasy so typically implies. In the future of C. M. Kornbluth's "The Marching Morons," the fecundity of the stupid many has overgrown the restraint of the intelligent few, so that "'the average IQ now is 45'" (1975, 127). The real work of the world is done by a clandestine minority of geniuses struggling to survive and manipulate the enormous mass of self-satisfied morons. Why do the geniuses tolerate this situation? Because there are "about three million of us. There are five billion of the others, so we are their slaves." Kurt Vonnegut laments the reality of the social desire for sameness in a story called "Harrison Bergeron." "The year was 2081, and everybody was finally equal" (1968, 7). This equality is enforced by "handicapping" those with any superior traits. Ballerinas drag leg irons, the handsome glue rubber noses to their faces, the eloquent must mumble through masks. Young Harrison Bergeron, the most gifted of all, finally decides, when he is being exhibited in fetters and mask, to proclaim his unique power and become Emperor of the world. He throws off his handicaps, commands a ballerina to be his Empress, and the two begin a heartbreakingly beautiful dance. But "Diana Moon Glampers, the Handicapper General, came into the studio with a double-barreled ten-gauge shotgun. She fired twice, and the Emperor and Empress were dead before they hit the floor" (13).

Do not imagine that fantastic powers confer true survival value. We are all caught in the social web. The Indo-European root *ueik*, meaning divination, leads both to victim, from the Latin *victima*, a sacrifice for the gods of which the entrails may be used for divination, and to *witch*, someone with secret, divine knowledge (Shipley 1984, 430). Nathaniel Hawthorne, creator of the cautionary tale of Aylmer's too-easy imagination, was a direct descendant of John Hathorne, a presiding judge at the Salem witch trials (Starkey 1969, 256), who persistently accepted the validity of witchcraft accusations based on "spectral evidence" whereby "dreams and mere fancies would be accepted in court as factual proof not of the psychological condition of the accuser but of the behaviour of the accused" (54).

The dangers of the fantastic clearly apply not only to those who imagine but to those who share the world with the imaginers. Although every so-called "slan," in A. E. van Vogt's novel of artificially—imaginatively—mutated humans, has high moral values, enormous physical strength, remarkable intelligence, and telepathy, slans are, quite naturally, not admired but despised. As one slan-hunter explains, "'If slans were allowed freedom, human beings would become nothing. It's a no-solution situation, so we keep killing them off because"—he shrugged—'there's nothing else to do'" (1968, 72). In Arthur C. Clarke's recent novel *Cradle*, aliens are about to reseed our planet with artificially improved humans built upon the stock they harvested in our dim prehistory. They mean this act as a kindness, but the current humans, who help the aliens to continue their long reseeding mission to a dozen planets, implore them not to reseed earth.

> [T]he process is more important than the end result. ... You cannot simply give us the answers. Without the benefit of the struggle to improve ourselves, without the process of overcoming our own weaknesses, there will be no fundamental change in us old humans. We will not become better. We will become second-class citizens, acolytes in a future of your vision and design. So take your perfect humans away and let us make it on our own. We deserve the chance. (1988, 407)

Inasmuch as this pretty speech is made by a talented young black man, it has obvious—and tenable—current political application. But inasmuch as it addresses the realities of species survival, it is rubbish. "We" will not learn to be better; our descendants will, in slow increments. The difference between the reseeded future and the one without the intervention of the imaginative aliens is that in the normal course of things we all change slowly and we all change together. What is really requested here is not the chance to struggle; it is the chance to remain unimaginatively safe in the midst of the herd. The aliens grant the speaker his wish. And so the novel ends with nothing having been accomplished.

In *Slan*, a different solution is found for dealing with the fantastic. Our hero comes to discover first one person and then another who is actually a crypto-slan. Indeed, although the slans are not quite yet a majority of the population, the World Governor himself is a slan, and our hero gets to marry the leader's daughter. This novel, then, indulges the imagination, displays its attendant dangers, and then assuages the fears those dangers may inspire by suggesting a reintegration of the imaginative into a whole, ready-made society. This deference to the group is a common feature of fantastic literature, even such works as have highly imaginative protagonists. In the case of Victor Frankenstein and his ilk, the supremacy of the group is made clear. Works like Shelley's and Zamyatin's, then, serve as warnings. In works engaging more juvenile fantasies, such as *Slan*, society itself is brought around. Hugo Gernsback's *Ralph124C 41+*, though only twenty-one years old, is "one of the greatest living scientists and *one of the ten men on the whole planet earth permitted to use the Plus sign after his name*" (1950, 25). In this childish, male-power fantasy, there is no conflict between godlike individual and society. For example, Ralph's "'house,'which was a round tower 650 feet high, and thirty in diameter, built entirely of crystal glass bricks and steelonium, was one of the sights of New York. A grateful city, recognizing his genius and his benefits to humanity, had erected the great tower for him on a plot where, centuries ago, Union Square had been" (40). At the explicit level, Ralph and his society function together quite well. At the symbolic level, this is because, despite his genius, he has accepted his role as child. It is never explained *how* the ten men are chosen and "permitted" (by whom?) to use the Plus. Ralph's obviously phallic "house" is an "erection" made for him by the people of the city, and placed strategically on *Union* Square. Like a gifted, obedient child for its parents, Ralph serves his society by representing a hope for the future. In due course, he will win his bride. As long as Ralph is infantilized, his genius represents no social danger.

A potentially more dangerous character is Olaf Stapledon's *Odd John*. This supernormal gathers other supernormals from around the globe and, eventually, through history. The normal humans, of course, decide to destroy John's island community. How do the supernormals react? They decide that they will kill themselves rather than impair their moral stature by warfare (1964, 149). Society is not brought around here; remarkably, the fantastic hero is.

Actually, the protagonists of fantastic fiction are often brought around. In Westerns like *Shane* it is typical for the gifted gunfighter to ride off and remove the danger that he represents or, like the Virginian, to hang up his guns. In one version of the Grimm brothers' story of "Red Riding Hood," after the child's imagination has led her astray—and clearly threatened her survival—and after the hunter has retrieved her, she vows "never [to] wander off into the forest as long as I live, if my Mother forbids it" (1972, 58). Those last five words are an interesting disclaimer. At first the girl seems to be saying that she never will indulge her imagination again, but in fact she is only bowing to present authority, granting someone else, a representative of society, the right to tell her when it may be appropriate to indulge her imagination. At the psychosexual level, Red knows she has the urgings of sensuosity, but she also knows that biology is not everything. Society, again, rules. The imagination is tamed.

Some few works of imaginative literature have not only been tamed but put to work. Edward Bellamy's blueprint for society was fostered by one hundred sixty-five "Bellamy Clubs" and strongly influenced the Populist Party, which in one election gathered nearly a million votes (1960, vi). B. F. Skinner's blueprint for a supposedly utopian community based on operant conditioning was tried with some success at Twin Oaks, Virginia (Turner 1987, 715). But perhaps these works have functioned so comparatively well in society precisely because they attempt to expunge the fantastic. Bellamy's world is supported by a highly regimented "Industrial Army" and Skinner's requires the philosophical rejection of the dangers of imagination. "'We accept our gross physical limitations without protest,'" the leader of Walden Two explains, "'and are reasonably happy in spite of them, but we may spend a lifetime trying to live up to a wholly false conception of our powers in another field, and suffer the pain of a lingering failure. Here we accept ourselves as we are'" (1962, 127). In other words, like Plato, Skinner wants fundamental social stability, and he is willing to banish the imagination to get it.

But the imagination does, after all, have some direct survival value. Spencer Holst tells the marvelous parable of "The Zebra Storyteller." It seems that an otherwise ordinary cat learned zebraic. Thereafter, whenever he hailed a zebra in his native language, the zebra was so astonished that the cat could kill him and eat him. As the cat killed more zebras, the zebras became more alarmed, some imagining that the forest was haunted, others that a new kind of lion was about. But the zebra storyteller imagined that some cat had learned zebraic and was using his language to amaze his prey. At just that moment, the zebra storyteller was hailed in zebraic by an otherwise ordinary cat, but the zebra was not amazed. "He took a good look at the cat, and he didn't know why, but there was something about his looks he didn't like, so he kicked him with a hoof and killed him." The narrator concludes: "That is the function of the storyteller" (1971, 14).

What is the function of the storyteller? Obviously one function is to provide a field for imaginative play so that when we encounter the new we are less likely to be encountering it unprepared. But notice that the result of that encounter is not, say, conversation with the cat but killing the cat, removing the fantastic element from the world of the zebras. Similarly, as

Poe's character Dupin tells us, the classic "Tale of the Great Detective" depends for its solution on an imaginative "identification of the reasoner's intellect with that of his opponent" (1973, 451). But once that imaginative leap is made, the Great Detective does the best he or she can to restore the status quo ante, thus again removing the fantastic element from the world of the narrative.

Dagobert Runes' *Dictionary of Philosophy* is clearly far from the mark, then, in defining the fantastic in art as a "product of an arbitrary imagination without any claim to reality" (1983, 123). Especially when we consider the semantic resonance between imagination and fantasy, we recognize that the seduction of the imagination, like the supposed escape of fantasy, contributes to a common family of archetypal warnings about the real social consequences of the workings of the human mind. This realistic consequence of the fantastic seems apparent in the analysis of all sorts of fantastic literature, even in fairy tales like "Red Riding Hood." The word *fairy* itself, we should note, along with *fable*, comes from one of the two principal meanings of the Indo-European root *bha*, "to speak." The other principal meaning of *bha* is "to shine," and from that, through the Greek *phantázein*, we derive fantasy (Shipley 1984, 25-26).

Imagination, then, the exercise of our capacity for fantasy, seems highly dangerous, highly attractive, and highly human. Yet this attractive danger is not so much like, say, the edge of a cliff, beckoning us simply to a thrill—or to death; rather, this attractive danger is more like a knife, offering itself to us as a weapon, as a tool, or as the basic equipment for a game like mumbletypeg, a game in which we invent new challenges, hone our skills, stretch our limits. In *We*, the United State runs an "Operation Department" to perform "the surgical removal of fancy" in an effort to stabilize the state.

> About five centuries ago, when the work of the Operation Department was only beginning, there were yet to be found some fools who compared our Operation Department with the ancient Inquisition. But this is as absurd as to compare a surgeon performing a tracheotomy with a highway cutthroat. Both use a knife, perhaps the same kind of knife, both do the same thing, viz., cut the throat of a living man; yet one is a well-doer, the other is a murderer; one is marked plus, the other

> minus.... All this becomes perfectly clear in one second, in one turn of our wheel of logic, the teeth of which engage that *minus*, turn it upward, and thus change its aspect (77).

By a change of perspective, the Operation Department goes from Inquisitor to Protector. By a change of perspective, the knife goes from weapon to tool. And by a change of perspective, the imagination itself goes from seducer to teacher. But how are we to know, in handling this dangerous capacity of ours, whether we are dealing with the weapon or with the tool? How are we to learn to change our perspective at will, to avoid the fatal dangers of imagination, and to reap both the common social benefits of shared imaginings and the precious individual discoveries of productive invention? We are to know by resisting imagination both as weapon and as tool—until we have played with it enough, until we have developed our skills, until we have stretched ourselves. That engagement and reversal of perspective that Zamyatin writes of, naturally, is precisely what fantastic literature entails. If we are not only to survive our own imaginations but to thrive with them, we need a comparatively safe field of play for their exercise. But just as we have always known of the danger of fear, we have always known this, too: that the welcome gymnasium of the human mind is fantastic literature itself. It makes us what we are, and shows us what we may be.

Works Cited

Bacon, Francis

1980 De Augmentis Scientarium. Bk 2, *Fortitudo*. In John Bartlett, ed., *Familiar Quotations*. Boston: Little, Brown.

Bellamy, Edward

1960 *Looking Backward*. Edited by Erich Fromm. New York: Signet.

Bullfinch, Thomas

1942 *The Age of Fable or the Beauties of Mythology*. Edited by Stanley William Hayter. New York: Heritage Press.

Capek, Karel

1985 *War With the Newts*. Edited by Ivan Klima. Evanston, IL: Northwestern University Press.

Clarke, Arthur C., and Gentry Lee

1988 *Cradle*. New York: Warner Books.

Eliot, T. S.

1962 "Gerontion." In *The Complete Poems and Plays 1909-1950*. New York: Harcourt, Brace and World.

Freud, Sigmund

1986 "Creative Writers and Day-Dreaming." Translated by Joan Riviere. In Charles Kaplan, ed., *Criticism: The Major Statements*. 2d ed. New York: St. Martin's.

1950 *Totem and Taboo*. Translated by James Strachey. New York: W. W. Norton.

Gernsback, Hugo

1950 *Ralph 124C 41+*. 2d ed. New York: Frederick Fell.

Grimm, Jakob, and Wilhelm

1972 "Red Riding Hood." In Margery Darrell, ed., *Once upon a Time: The Fairy Tale World of Arthur Rackham*. New York: Viking.

Hawthorne, Nathaniel

1937 "The Birthmark." In Norman Holmes Pearson, ed., *The Complete Novels and Selected Tales of Nathaniel Hawthorne*. New York: Random House.

Henry, Philip, Earl of Stanhope

1980 "Notes of Conversations with the Duke of Wellington, November 2, 1831." In John Bartlett, ed., *Familiar Quotations*. Boston: Little, Brown.

Hoffmann, E. T. A.

1972 "Ritter Gluck." In *Tales of E. T. A. Hoffmann*. Edited and translated by Leonard J. Kent and Elizabeth C. Knight. Chicago: University of Chicago Press.

Holst, Spencer

1971 "The Zebra Storyteller." In *The Language of Cats and Other Stories*. New York: Avon.

Keats, John

1959 *Selected Poems and Letters*. Edited by Douglas Bush. Boston: Houghton Mifflin.

Kornbluth, C. M.

1975 "The Marching Morons." In Dick and Lori Allen, eds., *Looking Ahead: The Vision of Science Fiction*. New York: Harcourt Brace Jovanovich.

Lem, Stanislaw

1970 *Solaris*. Translated by Joanna Kilmartin and Steve Cox. New York: Berkley Books.

Longfellow, Henry Wadsworth

1980 "The Masque of Pandora." In John Bartlett, ed., *Familiar Quotations*. Boston: Little, Brown.

Marlowe, Christopher

1933 *The Tragicall History of the Life and Death of Doctor Faustus*. In *English Drama 1580-1642*. Edited by C. F. Tucker Brooke and Nathaniel Burton Paradise. Boston: D. C. Heath.

Milton, John

1962 *Paradise Lost*. Edited by Merritt Y. Hughes. New York: Odyssey.

Montaigne, Michel de

1980 "Essays." In John Bartlett, ed., *Familiar Quotations*. Boston: Little, Brown.

Plato

1963 *The Collected Dialogues*. Edited by Edith Hamilton and Huntington Cairns. Corrected ed. Princeton, NJ: Princeton University Press.

Poe, Edgar Allan

1973 "The Purloined Letter." In Philip Van Doren Stern, ed., *The Viking Portable Poe*. New York: Viking.

Rabkin, Eric S.

1983 "The Descent of Fantasy." In George E. Slusser, Eric S. Rabkin, and Robert Scholes, eds., *Coordinates: Placing Science Fiction and Fantasy*. Carbondale, IL: Southern Illinois University Press, pp. 14-22.

Roosevelt, Franklin Delano

1980 "First Inaugural Address," March 4, 1933. In John Bartlett, ed., *Familiar Quotations*. Boston: Little, Brown.

Runes, Dagobert D.

1983 *Dictionary of Philosophy*. Rev. ed. Totowa, NJ: Rowman and Allanheld.

Shakespeare, William

1964 *The Tempest*. Edited by Robert Langbaum. New York: New American Library.

Shelley, Mary

1969 *Frankenstein*. Edited by M. K. Joseph. New York: Oxford University Press.

Shipley, Joseph T.

1984 *The Origins of English Words: A Discursive Dictionary of Indo-European Roots*. Baltimore: Johns Hopkins University Press.

Skinner, B. F.

1962 *Walden Two*. New York: Macmillan.

Stapledon, Olaf

1964 *Odd John*. In *Odd John and Sirius*. New York: Dover, 1964.

Starkey, Marion L.

1969 *The Devil in Massachusetts: A Modern Enquiry into the Salem Witch Trials*. New York: Doubleday.

Stein, Jess, ed.

1966 *The Random House Dictionary of the English Language*. Unabridged ed. New York: Random House.

Swift, Jonathan

1960 *Gulliver's Travels and Other Writings*. Edited by Louis A. Landa. Boston: Houghton Mifflin.

Thoreau, Henry David

1980 "Journal," September 7, 1851. In John Bartlett, ed., *Familiar Quotations*. Boston: Little, Brown.

Turner, Roland, ed.

1987 *Thinkers of the Twentieth Century*. 2d ed. Chicago: St. James Press.

Van Vogt, A. E.

1968 *Slan*. New York: Berkley Books.

Vonnegut, Kurt, Jr.

1968 "Harrison Bergeron." In *Welcome to the Monkey House*. New York: Dell.

Wells, H. G.

1988 *The Island of Dr. Moreau*. Edited by Brian Aldiss. New York: New American Library.

Zamyatin, Eugene

1952 *We*. Translated by Gregory Zilboorg. New York: E. P. Dutton.

The "Novel" Novel: A Sociobiological Analysis of the Novelty Drive As Expressed in Science Fiction

Joseph D. Miller

Toward a Definition of Terms

The term "sociobiology," perhaps largely due to the pugnacity of its major proponent, E.O. Wilson, tends to generate an immediate negative response on the part of "humanities"-educated academics everywhere. The very suggestion that social behavior in humans may, at least in part, be genetically determined and biologically constrained is often perceived as yet another assault on the twin bastions of free will and anthropocentrism. There has been a historical winnowing of the sphere of human action; geocentrism gives place to Copernicus, the Bible gives place to Darwin, free will gives place to the twentieth-century determinist views of Freud and Skinner. Is not sociobiology just another chapter in the erosion of the human sense of place in the universe?

No, I do not think so. To begin with, the human sense of preeminent place in the universe has always been badly exaggerated and largely illusory. Perhaps we no longer believe in the divine right of kings, but many of us still believe that Jerry Falwell has a direct line to deity. What colossal ego from a race of partly evolved monkeys on a minor planet of a second rate yellow dwarf star in a backwater spiral arm of a not particularly remarkable galaxy! I would say that any humbling produced by modern science is richly deserved, and the winnowing of the human sphere is actually the correction of a delusional state.

But is sociobiology per se a radical, new antidote to the anthropocentric delusional state? On the contrary, I believe that sociobiology, as an exclusionary specialization, is a misnomer in the same sense as neurobiology or plant biology or exobiology, for that matter. None of these disciplines exists in a vacuum (except, perhaps, exobiology); all are part and parcel of biology. And biology is inherently evolutionary. Thus sociobiology cannot produce any further erosion in the cosmic status of (or, more accurately, induction of humility in) humanity than that erosion already implicit in the Darwinian foundations of modern biology.

In the simplest expression of Darwinian biology, adaptive characters survive. Any seriously maladaptive characteristic does not allow the organism's survival to reproductive age. What natural selection selects is reproductive fitness; were this not the case, none of us would be reading this essay. (A physicist I know might call this the Weak Anthropogenic Principle)

But here is a subtlety. Evolution is conservative. Reproductively neutral characters or even mildly maladaptive characters are frequently preserved in the gene pool. Thus we all have a largely useless and sometimes even deadly appendix (and we all know that some appendixes are deadlier than others). Diseases usually acquired beyond reproductive age, like Parkinson's, Alzheimer's, most arteriosclerotic pathology, and cancer, are essentially transparent to selection pressure. How, then, does one tell whether a given character in a population is of positive adaptive value or is simply a kind of historical malingerer in the gene pool? In short-lived organisms like fruit flies or cultured cells, the answer is easy; you simply count offspring. In fast-growing cell culture, cells with too many neutral mutations will be displaced and overrun by cells with positive adaptive features—that is, any feature that contributes to the production of large numbers of viable daughter cells. (Even neutral is maladaptive in the long run) In principle, the same criterion could be applied to the analysis of adaptive features in long-lived species; in actuality the long observational spans required and the very nature of the often complex, polygenically determined anatomical, physiological, and behavioral traits involved make this approach impractical. Of course, the truly maladaptive feature is still interpretable; the appendix may be ambiguous, but there is no doubt that a condition such as anencephaly does not contribute to reproductive fitness.

Luckily, there is an indirect criterion that may be applied to the determination of the fitness of specific adaptations. The presence of the same physiological or behavioral adaptation in reproductively isolated, geographically separated populations is often taken as an index of the selective advantage of a given character. The reason for this is that presumptive neutral characters should show genetic drift. That is, in sufficiently heterogeneous environments, there should be considerable variability in neutral characters because of random mutation, recombination, and so on. In fact, this variability in a relatively neutral character may be coopted in the case of rapidly changing environmental selection pressures, ultimately resulting in a new character (or an old character at higher frequency) with positive fitness. In pre-industrial England there was considerable variability across individuals in the pigmentation of the salt and pepper moth, *Biston betularia*. With the advent of the Industrial Revolution, trees in the industrial regions became covered with soot, providing camouflage for darkly pigmented moths. In just about a hundred years the salt and pepper moth in these regions was completely replaced by a coal black variant (Alcock 1975, 32-34). Thus phyletic heterogeneity across populations may or may not indicate strong selection pressure for a specific adaptation. On the other hand, homogeneity in a character across disparate populations is often taken as strong presumptive evidence for the positive fitness of that character. Thus, one of the traditional projects of anthropology is to identify human cultural "universals." Such universals could be interpreted as characters with high reproductive fitness.

The Concept of Drive

A unifying construct of twentieth-century biology and psychology has been the drive state. Drives are thought to mediate the behavioral response to a sensory correlate, often aversive, of some tissue need. Thus thirst is largely perceived in terms of an unpleasant dehydration of the mouth and throat; hunger is perceived as an emptiness in the gut. Drive reduction is enacted through an operant behavioral response that reduces the aversive sensory correlate and satiates the underlying tissue need. In these examples it is obvious that both the indirect perception of a tissue need and the corresponding increment in some drive state, as well as the behavioral response that ultimately reduces the drive, contribute enormously to the reproductive fitness of an organism. A failure in either the perception of a tissue need or the response to that need may have lethal consequences for the organism.

An important "early warning system" for the satiation of need is the central drive state. A central drive state requires an internal representation in the central nervous system of some tissue need. Thus cells in the hypothalamus may represent, through an alteration in their electrical activity, a sensed decrease in blood glucose, tissue hydration, or body temperature, for example. This alteration in electrical activity may occur long before irreversible damage to peripheral body tissues is induced by the state of deprivation. In fact, the "early warning" may occur before, and perhaps necessarily precedes, any behavioral response to the deprivation state. This allows a very sensitive detection of small changes in important physiological parameters. The fact that such small changes may be detected and corrected by various physiological feedback mechanisms allows the organism to maintain optimal function, or physiological homeostasis. The further assumption is that associated alterations in brain electrical activity that are not immediately compensated by internal mechanisms are the physiological substrates that ultimately give rise to the subjective perception of the tissue need—e.g., hunger and thirst the central drive states. The manifestation of these central drive states are the specific behaviors that ultimately reduce the drive states through negative feedback, a process called behavioral homeostasis.

In the light of this analysis, one of the most interesting drives is sex. Here there is no underlying tissue need, the satiation of which is necessary for the survival of the individual. Sexual motivation appears to be a central drive state, extremely sensitive to both external variables—such as the availability of receptive mates, pheromonal influences, and so on—and internal variables such as hormonal state. The reduction of this central drive state through sexual behavior is of enormous adaptive significance, since it is a prerequisite for the continuation of the species. The important point here is that the sex drive operates at the species level, or more properly, the genotype, rather than the individual level, or the phenotype. To paraphrase Dawkins (1976), people are just genes' ways of making more genes.

Even more subtle drives have been envisioned. Activity drives, sensory stimulation drives, environmental manipulation drives, and even a drive for self-actualization have been suggested. In each case there is no indication of a specific tissue need corresponding to the drive state. However, it remains an open question whether these drives are of adaptive significance to the species as a whole. Can such drives increase the fitness of a population?

The Novelty Drive

Perhaps the most interesting of these more exotic drive states is the novelty drive or curiosity. Butler (1953) showed that monkeys work very hard just for the momentary opportunity to observe another monkey. A potent positive reinforcer for rodent behavior is the ability to alternate cage illumination between on and off (Kish 1955). Premack (1959) showed that a less frequent behavior may often be used to reinforce a more frequent behavior. Thus, it is well known that food pellets may be used to reinforce wheel running in rodents. It is not well known that infrequent wheel running may be used to reward the over-consumption of food! Furthermore, given a choice between freely available food pellets and pellets that are provided only after some number of operant behavioral responses such as bar pressing, rats typically choose to work for their supper (the "contra-freeloading" phenomenon, Taylor 1975).

Many of the above examples may be summarized by the statement that the exposure to novel stimuli or the opportunity to generate novel behavioral responses seems to be inherently reinforcing, whereas the repetition of a stimulus leads to the habituation or diminution of behavioral response to that stimulus. In the particular case of primates, it is very hard to work with these animals for any length of time without coming to the perhaps anthropomorphic conclusion that they are very curious animals indeed. Is it possible that curiosity per se was the primary adaptive advantage of the early hominids? How could one show that curiosity contributes to fitness, particularly when such a drive may preferentially operate at the level of the population, rather than the individual, in analogy to the sex drive?

Novelty and Drug Use

A major diagnostic feature of an adaptive character, as mentioned above, is its continuing presence in genetically isolated populations. It appears that the seeking of novel stimuli and the avoidance of boredom are universal characteristics of the human condition. Furthermore, humans in all known cultures attempt to manipulate sensory input, often through the use of drugs. The production of alcoholic beverages through the fermentation of a very large variety of substrates is ubiquitous. Similarly, a large number of psychotropic substances are routinely used in religious rites, manhood rituals, and other ceremonies. Religious experience is often associated with procedures which, while perhaps not explicitly involving the ingestion of psychotropic substances, may still be connected with the induction of hallucinatory experience—e.g., fasting, self-mutilation, and sensory deprivation.

But are such behaviors adaptive? Clearly, if they were maladaptive it would be difficult to explain their universal presence in human populations. On the other hand, the pursuit of novelty, in terms of exploration and technological innovation, undoubtedly contributed to the discovery of new food sources, the use of fire, the invention of the wheel, domestication of animals, and the utilization of tools. Perhaps the desire to manipulate individual perceptual experience, via drug use or other means, is then a kind of side-effect of the adaptive features of the novelty drive. If this is so, then Nancy Reagan's precious "Just say no" campaign was immediately doomed by a million years or so of selection for just those behavioral features that make drug ingestion initially attractive, i.e., the modification of perceptual experience. On the other hand, a rational modulation of this aspect of the novelty drive, perhaps by enlightened governmental policies (e.g., government support of research aimed at producing new psychotropic drugs without addictive potential or deleterious health consequences) and social mores ("intelligent" drug use), could contribute to the fitness of a society in analogous fashion to the constraints of ritual and ceremony on drug use in so-called primitive societies.

Even in the absence of such social pressures, there is of course a Darwinian limitation on drug use. There will always be strong selection pressure against any behavior that subtracts from reproductive fitness, including behavior that reduces longevity in individuals of reproductive age. Thus, the counter-cultural wisdom of the sixties was, "There is no such thing as an old speed freak." The assumption is that extreme vulnerability to drug addiction is not likely to be transmitted to subsequent generations. But in so far as society can rationally regulate and channel drug use, it acts as a buffer on the more direct, individual, and phenotypic effects of natural selection. The central drive state can act as a kind of early warning system in the individual for the detection and compensation of small deviations from physiological homeostasis, before the development of deprivation-induced tissue damage; perhaps rational drug regulation could act in an analogous way in the social organism to moderate patterns of drug use before the onset of major social dislocation or the probable reactionary and draconian response to such dislocation.

Novelty and Social Transmission

While the detection of novel stimuli may contribute to the reproductive fitness of the individual, it can have no effect on the composite fitness of a population unless there is some mechanism for the transmission of information concerning the novel stimulus. Thus, it is certainly adaptive for a baboon to notice the nearby presence of a lion and to subsequently vacate the premises. This behavior contributes nothing to the fitness of the baboon troop, however, unless the sentry baboon can communicate the presence of the predator to the group. Indeed, primates have developed predator-specific alarm calls to transmit exactly such information. These calls may be at least partially innate, since even infants are capable of specific behavioral responses to them. Sentry baboons transmit such alarm calls in spite of the fact that this behavior entails some risk; the "altruistic" baboon must by necessity call attention to itself in giving the alarm. Since the members of a baboon troop typically exhibit some degree of genetic interrelatedness, such "altruistic" behavior will preferentially contribute to the fitness of the shared genes involved. A corollary is that the amount of altruistic behavior should be directly related to the degree of relatedness of the individuals involved. For a highly interrelated group, the risk to the sentry is overbalanced by the benefit to the group gene pool. Genes that determine this method of "looking out for themselves" should be well represented in the population; indeed, altruistic behavior is very common in social species.

A qualitative advance in the transmission of novel information was the development of language in hominids, perhaps 200,000 years ago.[1] Language provides a flexibility of communication and density of information that far exceeds those of alarm calls or other simple signs. The universal presence of language in human populations implies a tremendous selective advantage for this character. Furthermore, the capacity for language appears to be genetically determined; the acquisition of language is simply too rapid to be explained in terms of ordinary associative learning (Chomsky 1959). However, the use of language guaranteed that information could now be transmitted between individuals and extended social groups with progressively fewer shared genes. But how does the transmission of information between genetically unrelated parties contribute to the reproductive fitness of the individual? Here we must employ the notion of reciprocal altruism. Altruism between unrelated individuals can still contribute to reproductive fitness, as long as the behavior is reciprocated—you scratch my back and I will scratch yours. In terms of language, the transmission of information must contribute to the fitness of both parties communicating. Of course, this is only possible if the language is mutually understood. Reciprocal altruism as an explanation for the adaptive value of information transfer is critically dependent on a common language among different kinship groups. The notion of differing kinship groups linked by a common mode of information transfer is a reasonable definition of nascent human culture.

Dawkins (1976) takes the meme to be the unit of transmission of cultural information as the gene is the unit of hereditary transmission. In this analysis, language is the vector of memetic transmission, as the germ cell is the vector of genetic transmission. However, the situation is further complicated by the ability of languages themselves to behave like memes or even meta-memes. As aggregates of adaptive genes can spread through a population, so languages can spread and mutate through cultures. Memes may be represented by linguistically unique morphemes, relations among morphemes, entire languages, or even the idea of language. A trivial example is a statement like "German is a particularly apt language for scientific exposition." Here the memetic unit of information is that an entire language can predispose to a particular pattern of thought. This is the essence of the Whorfian hypothesis—that language determines perception (Whorf 1956).

Approximately 10,000 years ago, a further advance in the social transmission of information occurred, the invention of writing. For the first time it became possible to keep a permanent record of information. Furthermore, the permanence of the record had a crystallizing and standardizing effect on language. Stabilizing a vector inevitably improves the efficiency of information transfer, and the permanence of the record allowed an exponential increase in the amount of transmissible information. Once again, the near universal prevalence of writing in human societies suggests a strong selection pressure for this behavior (or, more properly, the transcription of information on a more or less permanent substrate). Presumably, the reproductive fitness of individuals belonging to a literate culture is enhanced by access to the volume of useful acquired information.

Only a little over five hundred years ago, the invention of the printing press made for yet another exponential increase in both the volume and the speed of information transfer. Finally, the twentieth-century worldwide telecommunications network, in conjunction with computerized information storage, has provided an unprecedented opportunity for the storage and transfer of novel information. These historically recent behaviors are most easily conceptualized as memetic vectors (although certainly there is a meme corresponding to the idea of the printing press, the personal computer, and so on—the medium certainly can be the message). It is perhaps too early to determine whether such information vectors contribute positively to the fitness of modern humans. However, a dominant gene can completely pervade a human population in under three hundred years (Alcock 1975, 454). By analogy, it would seem that sufficient time has elapsed to demonstrate any truly maladaptive effects of efficient information transfer on the fitness of modern humans. In fact, reductions in infant mortality, increases in longevity, and the general improvement in quality of life since the onset of the "Information Revolution" argue for a net increase in fitness.

Science, Meme, and Vector

The Information Revolution itself is actually a component of an even larger-scale transformation in human thought, the Scientific Revolution. The scientific method is a systematic, institutionalized procedure for the collection and organization of novel information. The heart of the scientific method, the hypothetico-deductive method, provides both classification of information and continual-error correction by negative feedback. Hypothesis generates experiment generates data generates corrected hypothesis. Science, like language, is both meme and vector; but linguistic mutation, at least in aggregate, is random. A kind of memetic selection does operate on such mutations; "the cat's pajamas" is replaced by "rad." However, there is no guarantee that the new meme is in any way better than the old one. In contrast, science is syncretic and inclusive. The explanatory power of old hypotheses must be subsumed in the new; Kepler is a special case of Newton, Newton is a special case of Einstein. This is not so much a paradigm shift, in the Kuhnian sense (Kuhn 1962), as a paradigm sublimation. In this way, science transforms and evolves itself as memetic representation of information and as vector for acquisition and transmission of novel information. What is unique about science as a meme and as a vector is the rapidity and directedness of this autotransformation. If language is the vector for mixing the "meme pool," then science as vector functions as a kind of empirical filter on the resultant cognitive suspension. If language as meme is a slowly changing cultural bacterium, science as meme is a rapidly replicating and highly infectious virus.

Scientists are novelty junkies. But we are very specific about the nature of our fix. The knowledge that we seek to satiate our curiosity must ultimately be couched in terms of the falsifiable hypothesis. Hypothesis and theory must summarize and integrate; otherwise we have only a random compilation of unconnected data points. Furthermore, these summary statements must be testable. More trusting souls may perhaps attain to spiritual knowledge by other paths, but we scientists are all from Missouri and must be shown. Because of this constraint, science requires great patience, vast amounts of time, and considerable tolerance for frustration. Most of the time researchers are bored, but the moment of illumination, when one finally learns something new, is an epiphany. I have never found any other pursuit in life that consistently offers a comparable reward. In fact, in my own experience, most occupations ultimately become boring without even the redeeming hope of the novel experience.

Scientists tend to be less motivated by the traditional drives; certainly money is not a major factor for most of us. Fame, likewise, is rarely a concern; and power is only useful as a means to an end, getting your curiosity satisfied. The more moral of us, including me, like to think that our work in some way contributes to the improvement of the human condition, as opposed to facilitating intellectual self-gratification. Furthermore, we like to think that should we ever find that our work is actually deleterious to mankind, we would immediately burn our data books and cease our investigations. However, the strength of the novelty drive is so overwhelming that scientists are particularly prone to the temptations of the Faustian bargain, knowledge at any price. In a less sinister mode, we may simply be blind to the consequences of our actions.

Now here is the crux: Given that science is the potent vector for the acquisition and transmission of novel information that I have painted it to be, given that many thousands of curiosity addicts are constantly engaged in the pursuit of new information, and given that this new body of information is increasing exponentially, how can we know that this process is in any way adaptive for the human population, even if it has not been proven maladaptive to this point? After all, curiosity may only occasionally kill cats, but as the occasions for the satisfaction of curiosity increase, so may the probability of felicide. It has been suggested that our inability to date to detect radio transmissions from other stellar systems, in spite of considerable effort, may indicate that the temporal window for this form of communication in any civilization is very limited (Barrow and Tipler 1986). A possible corollary of this interpretation is that technological civilizations are ultimately self-destructive. Anyone with the technology for interstellar communication simply does not have it for long.

These thoughts suggest to me that science and technology badly need a kind of ethical negative feedback. Just as the psychotropic alteration of sensory input without appropriate social constraints probably reduces fitness, the unconstrained pursuit, and more particularly application, of scientific knowledge may permanently pry open Pandora's box. To some degree we provide our own feedback through editorial peer review for publication, grant-funding committees, and the informal grilling of our colleagues. But the most objective of foxes should probably not be put in charge of the local chicken house. Thus, it is completely appropriate for the wider public to have a say in how Department of Defense funds are used in the development of Star Wars technology. It is completely appropriate for the public to have an input into the decision to build new fission plants, construct space stations, develop new contraceptive agents, and implement biotechnology. At the same time, that input must be rational and informed. In other words, the decision to pursue promising avenues of medical research must not be made by individuals who believe that the life of a dog is more important than the life of a child. The decision to use tissue transplants from aborted fetuses for the treatment of Parkinson's disease and Alzheimer's disease must not be made by individuals who seriously believe that women might become pregnant for the sole purpose of producing aborted fetuses for sale to medical researchers. The decision to appoint directors of national health agencies should not be made by individuals who think that an appropriate litmus test for such a position is a candidate's personal stand on abortion.

How does one obtain informed feedback on such issues? The answer, as always, is education, particularly scientific education. If we could ever agree that a good schoolteacher is more important to society, and probably to cultural survival, than a professional football player, perhaps we could begin to redress the disparity in salaries of these professions. If teaching were a socially appreciated profession, there would certainly be more good teachers; and if there were more good teachers, surely we would have a better-educated public. Unfortunately, these are utopian sentiments. Are there any other options for feedback regulation of the scientific enterprise?

Science Fiction As the Cautionary Tale

From its very birth, as Gary Westfahl convincingly argues (1993), modern science fiction has functioned as a critic of the scientific enterprise. In Hugo Gernsback's conception, science fiction both educates the general public in science and advises the scientist as to the appropriate projected goals of science. Gernsback's view leads to a kind of egalitarian empowerment of the non-scientist, whereas John W. Campbell, Jr., believed that science fiction should be aimed at the scientifically sophisticated elite, the "practicing technicians." In either view, science fiction has a major pedagogical role for at least some segment of the population. More importantly, both editors saw science fiction as a modulating influence on scientific endeavor. Here is science fiction as *Gedankenexperiment*. Science fiction in this conception functions as a simulation or extrapolation of the effects of scientific advance. Furthermore, in the context of explosive technological advance and "future shock," science fiction is the only literature that seriously attempts to explore the social consequences of scientific innovation. While fantasy, horror, and mystery may also draw heavily on the outré, these genres are not consciously pedagogical or homeostatic in the sense I have described. In addition to its function as novelizer of novelty, science fiction determines the practical limits to the satisfaction of the curiosity drive, the point at which curiosity results in felicide. The science fiction novel is a laboratory for the study of Pandoran dynamics.

Serious extrapolation of trends is a near-ubiquitous characteristic of "hard" science fiction, exemplified in such works as Asimov's famed future history, *The Foundation Trilogy* (1948, 1949), or his *I, Robot* (1956). The Foundation novels are of particular interest because Seldon's conception of psychohistory is essentially an extrapolation of extrapolation.[2] While Asimov's Trantorian Empire owes a lot to the Romans, and the very essence of *First* and *Second Foundation* is pure Cartesian dualism, still Asimov creatively envisions the limits of extrapolation in the persona of the Mule. The Mule, as mutant dominant telepath, is a blind spot in the psychohistorical second sight of the Second Foundation. Although the Mule is defeated in the end, Asimov seems to say that even the most complete logical system must retain at least a single Goedelian inconsistency. This is the interstellar Catch 22; to paraphrase Joseph Heller (*Catch 22,* 1961), *Foundation* has a Mule in its eye, but it can not see it because it has a Mule in its eye. In the Campbellian sense, this is an epistle on humility to the scientific community. In contrast, the robot stories are positivist, and positronic, paeans to the conquest of adversity through the application of logic. Sure, there are a few glitches in the application of the Three Laws, but nothing a smart engineer could not handle with a little good work. It is only natural that the force majeure at U.S. Robots should be named Susan Calvin. At least, though, there is the implicit admission that the software/hardware bugs really are bugs, as opposed to features.

Niven and Pournelle's *The Mote in God's Eye* (1974) remains perhaps the best extrapolation of interspecific contact in the genre, but there is a sly message here on the ultimate effects of the unbridled sex drive. The idea that the Motie reproductive rate leads inevitably to a beehive-like specialization of labor can be read as thinly veiled commentary on the future of the third world. The notion that only complete quarantine of the Motie home world can prevent the eventual galactic displacement of relatively slow-reproducing *homo sapiens*—read Western Europeans—has a certain flavor of Yellow Peril ascendant. Modern mainstream social analysis in fact suggests that attainment of an advanced, Motie-comparable level of technology is probably not compatible with a high birth rate. In spite of this apparent flaw, the work can be read as an admonitory epistle to the biotechnologists on the importance of coupling Green Revolutions with birth control.

The ultimately upbeat character of the preceding works suggests that they represent studies of Pandoran dynamics in steady state, i.e., when hope has exited the box. Of course, the cautionary tale is rarely so optimistic. In Wells' *Time Machine* (1931) we are implicitly warned against the excesses of the Industrial Revolution and Capitalism. In Hoyle and Elliot's *A for Andromeda* (1962), we are shown the perils of the search for extraterrestrial intelligence. Benford's grim meditations on the downside of the evolution of desktop calculators, *Great Sky River* (1987) and *Tides of Light* (1989), exemplify the result of ignoring Herbert's injunction against artificial intelligence in *Dune* (1965). A sobering vision of what interplanetary colonization might entail is provided by Pohl's *Man Plus* (1976). The terrestrial consequences of the hybridization of biotech and cybertech are darkly portrayed in any of a large number of cyberpunk novels, notably Gibson's *Neuromancer* (1984) and Jeter's *Dr. Adder* (1984). A strong admonition concerning the consequences of self-experimentation in biotechnology is *Bear's Blood Music* (1985). The only hope is that illumination of the technosocial misstep suffices for its avoidance; *1984* (Orwell 1949) negates itself. Unfortunately, the popularity and abundance of certain forms of cautionary tale (e.g., the post-apocalyptic novel) may habituate the reader to the technological consequences that the tale cautions against or even make those consequences perversely attractive. When the "novel" novel is no longer "novel," the pedagogical function fails, with potential disastrous consequences.

In addition to this necessary novelty, perhaps the most important characteristic of successful cautionary tales is that they are reasonably plausible and consistent in their projections. For that reason the working scientist can approach them with a degree of seriousness that is impossible when considering the Luddite theme of the Grade-B science fiction movies of the fifties—"There are some things that are better off not known,"—which in turn is a dumbed-down version of the Lovecraftian forbidden knowledge of thirties pulp fiction. Few notions are more likely to alienate the true scientist.

Thus it is apparent that the cautionary tale can educate the non-scientist and inform the scientist. Of course, science fiction has far more attractions. For each of these groups science fiction depicts the novelty that is so often lacking in mundane life. If the scientist is attracted to science because of the ultimate promise of the novel finding, so much more might he be attracted to a literature whose every page may realize the bizarre and outre. Similarly, the non-scientist may find in science fiction the delights of the novel without enduring the frustrations of scientific research.

Measuring the Adaptive Value of Science Fiction

Is it possible to empirically demonstrate the adaptive value of science fiction? One might, for instance, examine the literary preferences of individuals involved in major technological accidents. I would hazard the guess that relatively few of the folks responsible for Three Mile Island or Chernobyl ever read Del Rey's Nerves (1956). Of course, a control group is needed; one should likewise examine the frequency of science fiction reading in accident-free nuclear facilities. A comparison variable would also be useful; perhaps one could determine the predilection for dark fantasy in the same groups. In addition there are a host of complicating factors, or covariates, that would need accounting. Baseline adjustment should be done within a culture to control for the availability of, and cultural differences in, science fiction. Thus, Three Mile Island and Chernobyl would first be evaluated in terms of the baseline frequencies of science fiction reading in their respective cultures before explicit comparison with each other. Additionally, it might be wise to limit such an analysis to the technocrats with sufficient power and authority to act in a crisis.

Such an analysis implicitly defines fitness in terms of individual survival and reproductive fitness. It seems to me that a legitimate question is whether science fiction contributes to fitness in a cultural sense. Cultural fitness need not be defined in terms of maximal production of offspring. In an overpopulated world, a better measure might be attainment of an optimal number of offspring relative to environmental resources. While the exact definition of optimal number may be difficult to determine, it should certainly be smaller than the population achieved by reproduction limited only by the Malthusian factors of war and famine. Certainly industrialized cultures seem to have lower birth rates. Other predictor variables might be envisioned. Per capita gross national product could be used as a measure of quality of life. The percentage of gross national product spent on pollution control and other environmental measures is certainly an indication of reciprocal altruism, and by extension contributes to fitness in a population sense. A measure of aggressive cultural tendency could be the percentage of gross national product spent on offensive weapons, a potential negative predictor of cultural fitness. Other measures could include expenditures on basic research and general education, incidence of violent crime, and so on. The point is that a multivariate predictor of cultural fitness could be constructed in analogy to predictors of reproductive fitness. High scores on such a predictor should be strongly correlated with criterial outcome variables like cultural longevity and the survival and transmission to other populations of culture-specific memes. The utility of such a predictor could be historically tested with data from extinct cultures. To my way of thinking, this problem in canonical correlation is the true project of social science. I would also like to think that the reading of science fiction might in some small way contribute to cultural fitness defined in this way.

The Future of Novelty

The science fiction novel and even the science fiction film may be only intermediate steps in the expression of the curiosity drive. A new technology is under development at VPL Research in Redwood City, California, called, charmingly, virtual reality (Flinn 1990). This technology has as its avowed purpose the construction of a perfectly convincing artificial world. Visual, auditory, and tactile information in a user-controlled, three-dimensional, animated landscape is directly fed to the participant in such a way as to give the impression of perceiving in, moving in, and being in the computer-constructed environment. Full-color eye screens and "surround sound" stereo headsets help create the illusion. The environment is completely interactive and can support multiple "explorers." Serious applications may include architectural design, remote control of deep-sea mining equipment, lunar exploration, sophisticated manipulation of waldos in radioactive environments, and, of course, role-playing games. A nascent conception of telepresence was evident in Heinlein's story "Waldo" (1950), expanded upon by Zelazny (1985) in "Home is the Hangman," and most recently employed as the basic technology in Niven and Barnes' novel *Dream Park* (1981). Already, it has been reported that "explorers" of this virtual environment have some difficulty in exiting it. When they do return to mundane reality, there seem to be relatively long-lasting perceptual distortions, described as "virtual artifacts." Perhaps this is the ultimate realization of subjective fantasy, surpassing the novelty value of drugs, science—and, dare I say—science fiction. This technology, as ever seems the case, has tremendous potential for creative use and a possibly unparalleled capacity for addictive abuse. This could be the paradigmatic case for the feedback regulation of technology by science fiction. I only hope science fiction applies such feedback before "Nancy's Naysayers."

Works Cited

Alcock, John

1975 *Animal Behavior: An Evolutionary Approach*. Sunderland, MA: Sinauer Associates.

Asimov, Isaac

1948-9 *The Foundation Trilogy*. New York: Street and Smith.

1956 *I, Robot*. New York: Signet-NAL.

Bear, Greg

1985 *Blood Music*. New York: Arbor House.

Benford, Gregory

1987 *Great Sky River*. New York: Bantam.

1989 *Tides of Light*. New York: Bantam.

Barrow, John D., and Frank Tipler

1986 *The Anthropic Cosmological Principle*. New York: Oxford University Press.

Butler, R. A.
1953 "Discrimination Learning by Rhesus Monkeys to Visual-Exploration Motivation." *Journal of Comparative and Physiological Psychology* 46: 95-98.
Chomsky, Noam
1959 Review of *Verbal Behavior*, by B.F.Skinner. *Language* 35:26-58.
Dawkins, Richard
1976 *The Selfish Gene*. New York: Oxford University Press.
del Rey, Lester
1956 *Nerves*. New York: Ballantine.
Flinn, John
1990 "Video Playground of the Mind." *San Francisco Chronicle*, February 24, morning ed., A-1.
Ann Gibbons
1992 "Mitochondrial Eve: Wounded but Not Dead Yet." *Science* 257: 873.
Gibson, William
1984 *Neuromancer*. New York: Ace-Berkeley.
Heinlein, Robert A.
1959 "The Year of the Jackpot." In *The Menace from Earth*. New York: Simon.
1950 "Waldo." In *Waldo: Genius in Orbit*. New York: Avon.
Heller, Joseph
1961 *Catch 22*. New York: Simon.
Herbert, Frank
1965 *Dune*. Philadelphia: Chilton.
Hoyle, Fred, and John Elliot
1962 *A for Andromeda*. New York: Harper.
Jeter, K. W.
1984 *Dr. Adder*. New York: St. Martin's.
Kish, G. B.
1955 "Learning When the Onset of Illumination Is Used As a Reinforcing Stimulus." *Journal of Comparative and Physiological Psychology*, 48: 261-64.

Kuhn, Thomas

1962 *The Structure of Scientific Revolutions*. Chicago: University of Chicago Press.

Elliot Marshall

1990 "Paleoanthropology Gets Physical," *Science* 247:798.

Niven, Larry, and Steven Barnes

1981 *Dream Park*. New York: Ace-Berkeley.

Niven, Larry, and Jerry Pournelle

1974 *The Mote in God's Eye*. New York: Simon.

Orwell, George

1949 *1984*. London: Seeker and Warburg.

Pohl, Fred

1976 *Man Plus*. New York: Random House.

Premack, David

1959 "Toward Empirical Behavior Laws: I. Positive Reinforcement." *Psychological Review*, 66:219-33.

Taylor, G.T.

1975 "Discriminability and the Contrafreeloading Phenomenon." *Journal of Comparative and Physiological Psychology*, 88: 104-09.

Wells, Herbert G.

1931 *The Time Machine: An Invention*. New York: Random House.

Westfahl, Gary

1994 "'Scientific Fact and Prophetic Vision': Marxism, Science Fiction, and 'The Fantastic Other.'" In Brett Cooke, George E. Slusser, and Jaume Marti-Olivella, eds., *The Fantastic Other*. Riverside: Xenos Press.

Whorf, Benjamin Lee

1956 *Language, Thought and Reality: Selected Writings*. Cambridge: MIT Press.

Zelazny, Roger

1985 "Home Is the Hangman." In Isaac Asimov, ed., *The Hugo Winners*, Vol. 4. New York: Doubleday.

Notes

1. We assume here that language and symbolic communication are at least in part characteristic of the human genotype. Recent estimates of the age of the human genome, based on the mitochondrial DNA "clock," converge on a value of about 200,000 years, although controversy continues concerning the accuracy of this estimate (Marshall 1990, 798; Gibbons 1992, 873). In contrast, the chimpanzee lineage diverged from the hominid line at least a million years ago. While there is a hint in chimpanzees of cortical lateralization, such lateralization of presumed linguistic function is much more pronounced in *Homo sapiens* (and, according to fossil cranial endocast data, perhaps in some extinct hominids). Not surprisingly, chimpanzees taught American Sign Language (ASL) never produce sentences of more than two or three words. Such utterances are more suggestive of sign than symbol, and should be considered proto-linguistic rather than linguistic in character. It can be further argued that such ASL signs should have no more adaptive value than any other signs in the chimpanzee repertory. Perhaps this explains the observation that ASL does not seem to be socially transmitted across generations in chimpanzees. Such considerations suggest that language in humans is at least 200,000 years old but considerably less than one million years old.
2. Such a second order-structure is also evident in Heinlein's classic story, "The Year of the Jackpot," 1959.

Tragedy and Chaos

Alexander Argyros

The thesis defended in this essay is that a culture that fails or refuses to acknowledge the tragic is liable to be brittle and vulnerable to internally or externally generated instabilities.

It would be impossible to offer an adequate survey here of the numerous extant definitions of the tragic. For the purposes of this discussion, I will define the tragic as the conflict felt by creatures who, because of their complex nervous systems, are capable of entertaining notions of infinity and yet who are in some way bounded by finite constraints. Simply, the tragic is the conflict between a longing for unboundedness and the awareness of the necessity to adjust to a condition that is bounded.

According to J.T. Fraser (1978), the engine for cosmic evolution is the tendency of the universe to get itself tangled up in unresolvable paradoxes. If that is indeed the case, then we might argue that the most universal of all structures is the conflict which cannot be resolved on its own grounds. Although it would be of immense interest to trace the history of such paradoxes from the most primitive stages of the universe to the present, for this discussion is focused on sexually reproducing life. As I will argue, the immense benefits of sexual reproduction are paid for by death. Furthermore, when creatures attain a certain level of neural complexity, they become aware of their mortality. At the same time, they begin to imagine the world as it will be after their demise. From this realization, although I doubt simply in reaction to the knowledge of death, intricate brains begin to project themselves into all sorts of non-real realms: the afterlife, fictional worlds, transcendental dimensions, and others. Just as sexuality itself is the irresolvable paradox between life and death, awareness of this paradox by creatures whose nervous systems have evolved to such an extent that they are able to reproduce by non-physical means (the dissemination of information) is itself a highly evolved and considerably more complex version of the original paradox. I would argue that the deep cosmic and biological roots of the tragic lie in irresolvable paradox in general and the particular form it takes in the consciousness of self-reflexive, purposive, and mortal creatures such as us.

Having outlined the general contours of my argument concerning tragedy, I will now discuss at some greater length the specific biological underpinnings of our sense of the tragic. In general, the tragic has its basis in the phenomenon of sexual reproduction insofar as it generates the unresolvable conflict between open-ended genetic innovation and death. As suggested, before the emergence of sexual reproduction, living organisms were in principle immortal. One attribute that distinguishes humans from most, if not all, other animals is that we know that we are going to die. However, although knowledge of impending death is probably a uniquely human phenomenon, death itself is not. All living things can die, though not all living things must die. Before nature "invented" sexual reproduction, death was a chance occurrence. There is no reason why, in principle, a single-cell organism cannot live forever, and, in fact, by reproducing asexually through splitting, it literally does. It is only with the introduction of sexual reproduction, with its recombination of genetic material, that death is introduced as a necessary condition of life. It is because sexual reproduction carries the tremendous evolutionary advantage of rapid genetic variation that the death of the individual is important to the robustness of the species. Arguably, death kicked evolution into a higher gear, one that eventually resulted in creatures like ourselves who are condemned to awareness of our certain demise. Therefore, tragedy is associated with the paradox that many humans feel the need to sacrifice themselves for a future or a transcendental cause that they know in all likelihood they will not be around to experience.

As Albert Camus (1970) argues, the tragic is a relation: on one side is the capacity of the human brain to imagine all kinds of transcendence; on the other side is the awareness of or desire for a range of different kinds of finitude, chief among which is physical death. To reside in the tragic requires that one inhabit these contradictory vectors simultaneously. Following Camus, I believe that human beings are wont to avoid the unresolvable paradox of the tragic by imagining that either the need for transcendence or the awareness of finitude is an illusion. There are a number of ways in which a culture can refuse to confront the tragic.

Since the tragic is here being conceptualized as a relation between two opposing human pulls—the pull of the infinite and the pull of the finite—it follows that there are two ways to deny the tragic. On the one hand, one may seek to reside exclusively in the infinite; on the other, one may seek to reduce oneself to the bounded. Among the denizens of the first camp would be mystics, religious zealots, political ideologues, idealist philosophers, and psychotics. In the second camp one might find behaviorists, scientific reductionists, analytic philosophers, alienated or displaced individuals, materialists, and psychotics. By radicalizing Cartesian dualism into two absolutely different sorts of substances—unextended spirit and extended body—and by deciding that ultimate reality resides in one side of the equation, one effectively camouflages the pathos of the irresolvable conflict that results from having a neocortex that can simultaneously envisage the infinite and its own limitations.

I wish to emphasize that the debilitating effects of refusing the tragic on a cultural level are not of equal magnitude when the finite is denied as when the infinite is denied. In general, a culture that sees itself as pure transcendence is likely to be more creative than one that reduces itself to the finite. Although neither view is as healthy as an acceptance of the tragic, idealism is likely to result in greater cultural vigor than materialism. However, and again in general, idealism, especially in the form of political and ideological idealism, is potentially far more dangerous than materialism. Materialistic cultures may atrophy, but they rarely engage in genocide.

I will now discuss eight ploys to finesse the tragic. They will be organized into two groups, according to whether the finite or the infinite is emphasized.

Among the ruses that emphasize the finite are

1. *A reduction of time to the present*

Cultures that forget their past and ignore their future by reducing time to the present or to a limited temporal horizon around the present are seldom able to understand, no less contemplate, the tragic. One of the classic forms taken by the tragic is the situation embodied in *Oedipus the King,* in which a representative of the new Athenian humanism is unable to escape the clutches of the older heroic culture. To appreciate Oedipus's dilemma it is important to see him torn between two epistemologies: the traditional view that knowledge is gained through revelation and the emergent view that a human being alone, simply through the use of reason, can attain the truth. Without a broad historical sense, it would be impossible to appreciate the irresolvable paradox between a mythic past and a humanist future that fuels *Oedipus the King*.

Among the many examples of cultures that have rejected the tragic by ignoring the future and the past are extremely materialistic cultures, such as certain aspects of modern American society, and cultures that have been forcibly removed from their traditions and ways of life, such as Native Americans and African slaves.

2. *Wallowing in indeterminacy or fragmentation*

It is a cliche of much postmodern theory that the contemporary world is so fragmented and indeterminate that an assured foundation for thought or action is no longer imaginable. Furthermore, it is taken as axiomatic that any "grand narrative "is by definition oppressive and must be abandoned or deconstructed. For those subcultures that have chosen to inhabit such postmodern paradigms, the tragic is a quaint remnant of the old patriarchy. If the tragic is a tree, its roots embedded in the ground, its branches straining toward the sky, then postmodern fragmentation leaves as much pathos in the tragic as a wood chipper leaves of a tree. In other words, without genuine confidence that the shortcomings of the present can be overcome in the future, whether this future is understood as an actual future or as a transcendental future or other world, the tragic degenerates for lack of tension. An example of such a path to the defusing of the tragic is much twentieth-century "high" art, especially literary and dramatic experimentation in open-ended or anti-narrative.

3. *Depreciation of sacrifice*

A consequence of the devaluation of grand narratives, eschatologies, and cosmologies is a kind of cynicism. In general, whenever a culture refuses to see itself as serving the interests of the future, it is very likely that a kind of nihilism will ensue. Traditionally, human beings imagine themselves as participating in a broad historical drama in which they are caretakers of the past and nurturers of the future. Frequently, the interests of the future are not identical with the present interests of the individual. Sacrifice is generally a decision to give up present advantages for either future or transcendental profits. We sacrifice for our children or for our gods because we have made a prior decision that their interests take precedence over our desires for immediate satisfaction. When we no longer believe in the importance of the future or of the transcendental realm, then we feel no compulsion to sacrifice. The very notions of sacrifice begin to be viewed cynically, and a regime of nihilism is a likely consequence. A particularly poignant contemporary example is the plight of the inner cities in the United States, where a generation of young men lives a thoroughly deconstructed life because they are convinced that the future is a luxury that is denied them.

(a) A subset of the depreciation of sacrifice is the devaluation of reproduction or of the significance of children. In the same communities that I mention above, reproduction all too frequently occurs in a mindless fashion, and children are neither honored nor brought up in a caring and loving fashion.

(b) A second subset is the devaluation of brain "children," such as scientific, philosophical, or artistic ideas and artifacts. Whenever a culture becomes blind to the value of non-material products of the human mind, what Karl Popper (1977) calls "World 3," and indifferent to their nurturing, it is in danger of losing its vitality. Many of the world's dictatorships have adopted policies that are inimical to the production of brain children for which humans are likely to sacrifice themselves. Interestingly, in contemporary American culture, it is a bromide of the now hegemonic conservative radio talk shows that government funding for the arts is a needless expenditure of money that could be better spent on more practical concerns.

The second ruse to paralyze the tragic is to focus exclusively on the infinite. Among the means to this end are

1. *A reduction of time to the past or future*

Cultures frequently see the present as insignificant in relation to the past or the future. For example, if the present is judged inferior to the past or to a projected future, then it is likely that it will be devalued. It is likely that a culture that denies the tragic by forsaking the present will see itself as either fallen from or as a propaedeutic to a golden age. In either case, cultural experimentation and creativity are likely to suffer. In cultures that drown out the present through an emphasis on past perfection, art will tend to be academic or stereotypical. Cultures that see themselves as vehicles for future glory will tend to create art that is stiffly otherworldly or mythic. Examples may be found in many traditional cultures and Ottoman Greece.

2. *A belief in an assured telos of history*

Whenever a culture conceptualizes the present as merely a step in a grand march whose conclusion has in some way already been determined, it is likely to engender a rigidly linear sense of time, one in which events occur in a logical causal chain. For societies that see themselves in light of their final cause, the telos toward which history is tending and which retroactively contextualizes and rationalizes all anomalies and contradictions, there can be no genuine tragedy. Tragedy is at most a knot in a Hegelian dialectic that will be ablated and shown to be necessary by a subsequent level jump. Examples are Marxist societies and strict Calvinist determinism.

3. *A belief in the literal immortality of the soul or of the resurrected body*

If a human society assumes that the future available to a human being is infinite, then there is no urgency to life. Of course, immortality also implies that bad decisions can haunt one forever, and if immortality were to become a reality, new higher-order kinds of finitude would probably emerge, but I suspect that the typical reaction to the fantasy of immortality is a kind of lethargy. An example would be fundamentalist theocracies whose tenets have been internalized by their citizens.

To summarize, if the tragic is seen as a relation between two opposing vectors, one pointing toward transcendence and the other pointing toward finitude, then a disavowal of either aspect is tantamount to a rejection of the tragic.

Having discussed these stratagems for deflecting the pain of the tragic, I will now suggest that chaos, or the study of nonlinear dynamics, offers a way to reinfuse culture with a healthy sense of the tragic.

Dynamical systems in a far-from-equilibrium state can begin to display chaotic characteristics. Among the hallmarks of chaos is extreme sensitivity to initial conditions. Chaotic systems are nonlinear mainly because they are generated by positive and negative feedback. Whereas negative feedback tends to damp perturbations in a system, positive feedback has the opposite effect; when the output of a nonlinear system is fed back into the system, a slight change in the input can very quickly result in massive changes in the system itself. Amplified by a geometric feedback loop, the beating of a butterfly's wings in Seoul, Korea, can, as the old saw of chaos would have it, change the weather in Dallas, Texas.

In practical terms, extreme sensitivity to initial conditions means that, whereby in linear systems small inputs tend to produce small systemic changes, in chaotic changes the most insignificant of perturbations is in a position to cascade through the system, producing significant changes. In other words, in chaos the difference between the local and the global is not as clearly delineated as it is in non-chaotic situations. The local can quickly escalate to global proportions and then, just as quickly, recede to insignificance. Furthermore, as opposed to linear systems, which allow calculations of future states, chaotic systems suffer no short cuts. In order to know the future state of a chaotic system, the researcher must set it in motion and then wait in real time to observe the evolution of the system. It is as if the price paid for the gain in agency granted by extreme sensitivity to initial conditions is a corresponding loss in long-term predictability.

One of the bromides of contemporary culture is that the world has become so complex that the individual has lost his or her potential for effective agency. The cultural and technological world now being created by the human species is, by the standards of most of our ancestors, maddeningly labyrinthine. In such a world, the individual might become increasingly marginalized and cede his or her agency to larger social units such as corporations, institutions, and governments. However, this would be the case only if the growth in complexity of the world were strictly linear. If, as it appears, the burgeoning complexity of the world is largely nonlinear, then in fact the agency of the individual might be rehabilitated. For if the individual functions in a nonlinear social environment as a minor perturbation does in a chaotic system, then there is every reason to believe that as culture and technology expand in nonlinear complexity the potential agency of the individual actually multiplies.

It appears, therefore, that contrary to expectations, a complex cultural environment might increase the potential agency of individuals. However, this gain in agency does not come without a price. To extend the economic metaphor, let us consider the fate of investments in a linear and in a nonlinear environment. In a largely linear investment vehicle, such as Certificates of Deposit, an investor sacrifices upside potential for predictability. In general, unless the entire economy were to collapse, an investment in a CD would yield a fixed amount of interest. If I know my initial investment and my rate of return, I can calculate how much money I will have accumulated at any arbitrary maturity date. However, in a highly nonlinear environment, such as the futures or options market, although a small investment could yield enormous profits, there is little assurance that the entire investment will not be lost. Furthermore, I have almost no ability to predict the status of my investment at a given point in the future. Even if I am confident that over time a given market always goes up, there is still no assurance that at some given point in the future the market will not be stuck in the nadir of an ugly bear trough and that, as a consequence, my initial investment will not have shrunk somewhat. In general, the more secure the investment, the less the potential gain; the more uncertain the investment, the higher the possibility for profit. In the language of chaos, we could translate this bit of financial wisdom as follows: linear systems sacrifice volatility for predictability while nonlinear systems sacrifice predictability for volatility. An agent in a nonlinear system could change the entire world through his or her intervention; however, this potency must be paid for by the absence of any assurance that the intervention will have any effect whatsoever, or, in the worst of circumstances, that it will not have effects that are detrimental to the robustness of the system.

The notion of extreme sensitivity to initial conditions has important consequences for the theory of tragedy. Defining the tragic as the irresolvable conflict between transcendence and finitude, it is possible to translate, *mutatis mutandis*, these terms unto the vocabulary of chaos. An agent functioning in a chaotic environment is potentially able to alter the entire system through a limited intervention. In other words, although chaos does not offer certain traditional forms of transcendence—those associated with otherworldliness, for example—it does lend itself to transcendence in the sense of the possibility of bringing about global social change.

However, there is a price paid for the potentially unearned efficacy of a single agent in a nonlinear chaotic environment. Much as in the options market, where a small investment can reap inordinate rewards for the fortunate investor but only at the cost of potentially disastrous losses, the expense of chaotic agency is an essential insecurity concerning the results of one's efforts. In other words, although the beating of a butterfly's wings could, in principle, affect weather patterns a continent away, it probably will not. One of the sacrifices that an agent in a chaotic environment must make is that, as opposed to acting in a nonlinear context—in which pushing two bodies twice as far apart as they were initially guarantees that the gravitational forces between them will be reduced by a fourth—his or her results are never predictable except in a statistical way. Furthermore, in most contexts, the odds can be extremely poor. Although it is possible that some of my ideas expressed in a class in Dallas could explode nonlinearly and result in legislation that would change the political texture of life in the United States, I would not bet the farm on it. However, the loss of certainty is not the only cost for the possibility of windfalls in chaotic systems. By locking into a complex pattern of feedback loops that he or she did not foresee, our benevolent meteorologist here in South Korea could unleash the power of a butterfly breeze only to learn that it had parlayed itself into a tornado that devastated large parts of North Texas. A second cost of chaotic agency is that the generative power of nonlinearity coupled with the extreme complexity of real-world systems creates a context in which the causal relation between intentions and effects is rendered highly problematic. Of course, this is the case in most systems. Except in highly rudimentary linear systems, it is often difficult to correlate input to output. However, when systems approach the maddening nonlinearity of human social structures, it becomes very likely that, even if we assume that it is possible to know what the good is, efforts to realize it are diverted from the agent's original intentions and end up having evil effects. The folk wisdom that imagined the material used to pave the road to hell had, perhaps, a sophisticated intuition of extreme sensitivity to initial conditions.

In conclusion, I would like to summarize the discussion so far and then suggest some possible implications for the theory of tragedy I have been developing. First, let us return to the biological foundations of aesthetics. In general, I take "foundation" to mean something like epigenetic predisposition in the sociobiological sense. The question, then, is whether it is possible to locate in the biological realm a kind of epigenetic rule for the tragic. If we define the tragic as the unresolvable conflict between transcendence and finitude, as the tendency of the human mind to project itself beyond temporal or physical constraint while periodically falling into awareness of its rootedness in the plodding rhythms of organic and inorganic matter, then the tragic can be said to be founded on the fundamental conflict that defines sexual reproduction: the conflict between the fever of creativity brought about by genetic variation and the dull thud or welcome port of death. Of course, until biological entities develop nervous systems complex enough to allow them to become aware of their own conditions, the conflict inherent in sexual reproduction is not understood as such, although it is probably felt in some species-specific way. But with the advent of the human brain, the conflict that defines sexuality has assumed a new form that is both more potent and more pernicious. Humans know that they are going to die—at the same time that they are visited by visions of permanence, eternity, and transcendence. The tragic, then, is simply the complexification of a fundamental biological conflict into tension so unbearable that most people and most societies develop elaborate ruses to disguise it.

It is a commonplace that in our postmodern era we do not have much taste for the tragic. According to J.T. Fraser,

> By its very nature, tragedy depicts a world in which final victory over evil is impossible. This is an unpopular view for a civilization that dogmatically maintains that all problems can be solved. (1987, 295)

A legacy of our ebullience over technological and scientific progress is that as a culture we prefer not to consider failure. And yet the signs of certain kinds of failure are all around us. Furthermore, those of us who grew up in the manic world of Dr. Strangelove know that lunatics with their fingers on the trigger can achieve transcendence and finitude simultaneously and nearly instantly. It is certainly true that excessive optimism and excessive pessimism can coexist in a kind of societal cognitive dissonance. It is also true that either of these two moods can be fetishized into a world view that forecloses the possibility of encountering or experiencing the tragic. Nevertheless, I would like to suggest another diagnosis of the present historical moment.

I suspect that our aversion to the tragic stems not simply from a Pollyanna-ish refusal to confront evil nor simply from fear of what madmen with a bomb can do, but from a growing, although still fairly unconscious, awareness that our world is becoming so complex that traditional forms of causality no longer describe it accurately. If, as I have been suggesting, linear forms of causality need to be replaced by nonlinear ones, and if on some level we have been aware of this shift for some time, then our resistance to the tragic might stem not from a kind of lethargy occasioned by a loss of agency per se but from a growing awareness that one kind of tragic agency—the belief that it is possible to bring about global change—being nonlinear, can no longer be trusted. In our contemporary world, agency is more like a bet than an investment, or more like an investment than a prediction. Of course, to some degree, social agency has always been largely nonlinear. Today, however, it is so understood by more and more people. That in itself should not be reason enough to disavow the tragic. After all, nonlinear agency is democratic, giving one a fighting chance to effect significant changes without a retinue of men and elephants. However, it is also more maddeningly random than most individuals are willing to countenance. We therefore retreat into fantasies of bucolic nineteenth-century American villages in our attempt to finesse the truly tragic implications of the world we have created, a world in which transcendence suffuses our lives but seems to be out of our control.

As I argued at the beginning of this essay, an index of cultural health is the capacity of a people to acknowledge and live with the paradox of the tragic. I fear that our culture has little sense of its own finitude, only a degraded sense of transcendence, and no confidence in the potency of the individual. I would suggest that one of the reasons for this state of affairs is that the tragic has itself evolved from that faced by Oedipus—for whom, although there was no good decision, the decisions available were clear, to a hazy tragic environment appropriate to a highly complex social and technological world. Today's tragic hero must live with the unresolvable conflict between transcendence and finitude without a sure sense of what transcendence or finitude means or how his or her actions can succeed or fail.

It is my hope that chaos offers a way to reinfuse culture with a healthy sense of the tragic. The idea of sensitivity to initial conditions is a double-edged sword. On the one hand, it is capable of rehabilitating the notion that an individual has agency even in a world as complex as the one we are creating. On the other hand, it also suggests that there is no real way of knowing whether an individual's actions will be inconsequential or even detrimental to the robustness of the system. The tragic uncertainty of a finite individual agent in a chaotic system requires a peculiar kind of courage. As the existentialists claimed, an individual must confront with lucidity the fact that although he or she is responsible for the future there is no guarantee that his or her actions will in fact be in the service of the right future. Such a person must be willing to work for a future he or she cannot with certainty identify as the most desirable one. Furthermore, he or she must be capable of devoting him or herself with passion and commitment to projects that are likely in the end to turn out to be either counterproductive or trivial, even if they are executed flawlessly. Finitude, which in the old dispensation was usually seen as something like death, destiny, weakness, or the will of the gods, must now be understood as all that plus the uncertainty swirling in the heart of chaos.

Works Cited

Camus, Albert

1970 "On the Future of Tragedy." In *Lyrical and Critical Essays*. New York: Vintage Books.

Fraser, J.T.

1978 *Time as Conflict*. Basel and Stuttgart: Birkhauser Verlag.

1987 *Time, the Familiar Stranger*. Amherst: the University of Massachusetts Press.

Popper, Karl R., and John C. Eccles.

1977 *The Self and Its Brain*. London: Routledge and Kegan Paul.

A Prehistory of Theatre: A Path with Six Turnings

Brian Hansen

I have taught theatre history for probably thirty years in a significant range of college and university settings—but I have yet to teach the aspect of the subject which interests me the most. Partly, I am trapped by a tradition that seems to demand that a course in theatre history spend the least amount of time on the longest portion of history. For example, at the University of New Mexico, the theatre major is expected to complete three semesters of theatre history. The ratio of class time to real time is instructive: the first roughly two thousand years of conventional theatre history is covered in the first fourteen-week semester; the next two and a half centuries take the second semester; and the last hundred years occupies the final fourteen weeks. The millennia of theatrical activity which preceded fifth-century B.C. Athens is dealt with in one or two fifty-minute lectures. Yet it is this long stretch of prehistory which interests me the most, because it was in this unimaginably long period of development that the true nature and function of theatre was revealed and refined.

Perhaps this lack of emphasis on the ancient history of theatre is the result of the very name: theatre *history* implies that we are concerned with the theatre tradition documented in the written record. But most teachers I know and respect are quite willing to consider theatre traditions in pre-industrial cultures (such as the Australian aboriginals) and to direct attention to aspects of history which are totally absent from the written record (such as the Phlyake farces of southern Italy). Perhaps, because prehistoric theatre appears to have no direct influence on the tradition which we all love best—Western high art—it is not taken seriously enough to be given equal time. There may be truth in this perspective, but many theatre history sequences (mine included) cover the Indian, Chinese, and Japanese theatres, and many would like to include the African theatre traditions.

The best explanation for ignoring prehistoric theatre is a combination of habit and innocence: theatre history courses have traditionally started with the Greeks, and we continue this pattern through simple inertia. But, equally important, until recent years there was no conceptual framework within which to explore the ancient theatre. The first barrier will fall only when the second is overcome. First we face what seems an intractable nest of questions: Was there something which we would recognize as theatre before the Greeks? How did it arise? Over what period? And—most important—why?

Biosocial theory will lead us part of the way, but there will be problems—I prefer to call them challenges or turnings—where a choice must be made and a direction taken. I have taken some pains to point them out because any reader should be very clear that conceptual choices are being made. In the large majority of cases, these leaps are made less intimidating because we have a leg up from biosocial theory, but the lack of hard evidence remains troubling. Theatrical activity is by its nature evanescent; the defining feature is, as we shall see, as fleeting as any human relationship—and yet no one thinks that early humans lacked, say, friendship, or love, or dominance simply because we cannot always detect hard evidence of them. Moreover, the external expression of elaborate theatre events—masks, scripts, costumes, makeup and other personal ornamentation, properties, effigies, and simple playing environments—are all as subject to the ravages of time as the human body itself. Therefore, it is unfair that we demand of an art form such as theatre what we do not demand from other forms of human behavior.

Challenge One: Mental Capacity

It is one thing to acknowledge that enactment and the ensuing performance contract are part of the communication potential of all humans today and quite another to believe that enactment was an option open to our forebears of, say, 200,000 years ago. Is there any information which would argue that such mental activity would have been impossible in prehistoric cultures? This subject is well beyond the scope of this essay, but it remains crucial. If the mental development of prehistoric mankind was too primitive to support imaginative leaps of the kind we seek, the question is answered once and for all.

What level of mental capacity is necessary for a performance contract to exist? At the very least, the participants must be able to recognize and hold in the mind two concepts: "self" and "not self" (Bateson). Both the performer and the audience must be able to recognize that the actor is behaving inappropriately to the current situation but appropriately to one which is not present. Furthermore, it must be clear that the behavior is intentional; somewhere in the mix of signals must be one which says, "I am only pretending." The absence of such a signal creates a situation which is at least upsetting and can be dangerous. Most animals are acutely aware of behavioral discrepancies in their fellows. If they see another member of the group behaving inappropriately, they are programmed to take action. At the very least they will avoid that specific animal; at worst, they will kill it. Such behavior has a sound biological justification: any individual interacting inappropriately with its environment is likely to be a danger to the group in the short run and a hazard to the genetic strength of the species in the long run. Such an individual is to be shunned. It may be this biological imperative which explains the extraordinary discomfort humans feel in the presence of those who are mentally disturbed; people report that "crazies" make their flesh crawl. (The symptoms reported are a clue to the biological origins of the feelings: the "crawling" flesh is the result of activation of very small, almost vestigial muscles at the base of hair follicles on the back and neck. In our primate ancestors, these same muscles would have raised much longer hairs in moments of fear or anger. The raised hairs would have increased the size of the silhouette, making the animal look larger to a potential enemy.)

The mental sophistication needed to engage in pretend play is quite high. Children above the age of two years can engage in rudimentary pretend play (Fagen 1981). However, the complexity increases with age until, by age seven, most normal children can maintain a shared imaginary world with at least one other child, peopling that world with a host of fantasy characters with special characteristics. Thus, one way of conceiving of the problem would be to trace the neurological development of our species back to that point at which experts might agree that the mental capacity of an adult human might have achieved the development of a normal contemporary seven-year-old. Most experts would place that date earlier than a million years ago.

Because the mental capacity of modern humans is closely linked to language development, this question of the evolution of human mental capacity is also related to the controversy surrounding the development of speech. There is anything but consensus on this subject. Some paleoanthropologists maintain that language is a relatively late development; some even assert that the possession of language gave Cro-Magnon man such an advantage over his mute forbear, Neanderthal man, that it alone could be the cause of Neanderthal's extinction between fifty and seventeen thousand years ago. However, there are some tantalizing pieces of evidence which suggest that language may have been developed much earlier than that. For example, work on the "handedness" of Olduvaian peoples, *Homo habilis*, from a period dating roughly 1.9 million years ago seems to show that they had about the same ratio of left- to right-handedness of contemporary humans (Toth 1987). Since handedness and footedness are related to the tendency of the brain to sort tasks into the separate lobes (lateralization), the question arises what other tasks might have become associated with particular lobes. Language is one of the tasks which evolution has assigned to different lobes of the human brain; the occurrence of lateralization in so early a hominid suggests the possibility that language existed as well. (Chimpanzees, our nearest primate neighbors, have little "handedness," but they do have the mental capacity for simple language. Experiments with chimps have shown that what prevents speech is not inadequate mental capacity but a larynx which is inappropriate for the task. When language was taught using American Sign Language or special physical symbols, the chimps did quite well.)

The question concerning the need for language may very well turn out to be a smoke screen in any case. For one thing, speech is not necessary for pretend play; many animals seem able to enter into simple pretend play. Young lions, tigers, and house cats play endless games in which they pretend to hunt one another, pretend to fight, and accept the role adopted by the other in order to extend the game. Their parents, watching their endless games while dozing, recognize the game for what it is and seldom interfere—except occasionally to join in. Chimpanzees of all ages play elaborate pretend games, complete with strategies designed to mislead other participants. Indeed, to prevent dangerous confusion, chimps adopt a "play face" which signals that even the most ferocious behavior is only "in fun" (Fagen 1981).

Thus we see that the mental acuity needed to form a performance contract may, in fact, precede the use of language. One could argue that the capacity to imagine, to combine and recombine symbols in the absence of the things themselves, an essential for symbolic communication of any kind, could only precede the development of the physiological equipment necessary for fluid speech. Otherwise, there would have been little or no benefit provided by the evolution of our distinctive vocal folds, flexible tongue, and expressive resonators.

One must recall that only half a century ago linguists were still arguing that language developed only some tens of thousands of years ago, some going so far as to declare that the cave paintings of southern France were executed by a mute species. Today, that assumption seems preposterous. The evidence is overwhelming that subtle, complex language, this most peculiarly human of evolutionary strategies, is far older than that. But how much older? Did Neanderthal man have speech? Did *Homo habilis*?

What is emerging is the possibility of expressive enactment, probably quickly incorporated into religious ritual of all kinds, at a period in mankind's phylogenetic history far earlier than anyone has yet dreamed.

Challenge Two: Diffusion Versus Independent Invention

The use of the performance contract to define theatre has many implications, none more important than the following: since the use of the performance contract seems to be universal in our species, we must decide whether its presence is the result of diffusion or independent invention. For centuries it has been a matter of faith that the practice of theatre was something which, like the use of gunpowder or steam power, was a step which any developing society would take at the appropriate time. Therefore, the development of theatre as a high art in Athens in the fifth century B.C.E. and in China in the ninth century was one of the signs of their greatness as cultures, a benchmark showing historians how ready they were to achieve the title "Golden Age." Of course, the geographical and chronological distance between these two cultures would also prove a second point: the independent invention of theatre. This means that a particular cultural aspect could develop spontaneously in two very separate cultures—given, of course, the proper cultural environment.

But this view is called into question if, as in the case of the performance contract theory, it can be shown that the crucial elements of an art form are present in all cultures, regardless of their level of development. Then the contrary view would be supported: the form of human communication which we call enactment and which lies at the center of the performance contract is a part of the general armamentarium of our species. It is responsive to cultural pressures only to the degree in which this ever-present option is supported and cultivated. In such a case, we would be dealing with, not the independent invention of an art form, but the diffusion and development of a universally available communication capacity. In this respect, the root of theatre would be less comparable to the invention of gunpowder and steam power and more like the development of language, cooking, and agriculture.

But is the performance contract a universal option? And was it such an alternative in the prehistoric period? Neither question can be definitively answered. In the first case, one would have to be familiar with every human culture that ever existed to declare that the performance contract was absent in some number of them. Even then, the mere lack of the trait in a limited number of cultures would not settle the matter; it could be argued that the absence of performance could be an anomaly resulting from active suppression of a native impulse. More useful would be some information about the presence of enactment in *prehistoric* cultures. Unfortunately, the behavior in question would leave behind no known type of hard evidence, and we are forced to discuss the issue in terms of implied capacities.

A compromise approach is to look for evidence of enactment in contemporary preindustrial cultures, arguing that the genetic capacity for a such a behavior, if present, would surface in environmental conditions similar to those of prehistoric humans.

One need look no further than a recent *National Geographic* special on a pygmy tribe in the Ituri Forest of central Africa. One could hardly find a more isolated group; few if any of them could have ever seen conventional theatre activity of any kind, especially television or motion pictures. Yet enactment of the type which we seek plays a recurring role in their lives. A single example was inadvertently captured by the videographer: a young father is seen playing with his infant son within the circle of very simple brush shelters which make up the temporary home of the band while traveling. The father is talking with the child, who is first carried on his parent's back and, later, as they play, swung around to hang onto the adult's chest. The child is somewhat concerned about this new physical relationship, and the father makes light of it, saying that this is the way monkey babies are carried. The father has an idea. He begins to walk like a great ape, making soft hooting noises as he does. At first he seems to be doing this for the benefit of his son, but a group of women sitting in front of a nearby shelter soon become an audience, laughing and shouting encouragement to the father in such a way that it is obvious that his portrayal is meant for them as well. Indeed, the cause of the appreciation is obvious: the father is doing a very good imitation of a mature ape with its young.

The whole sequence, occupying roughly two minutes of broadcast time, seems entirely improvised and undertaken completely on impulse. (What role the presence of the television camera might have played is uncertain, but the interaction appears completely unself-conscious.) Indeed, the moment seems so charming because it rings true with any viewer. It is precisely the kind of moment which any parent might create with any child and which grows appropriately in the presence of appreciative relatives. The videotape archives of most American families contain comparable footage, I am sure.

Challenge Three: Religion and Theatre

There is a recognition—a ritual bow, if you will—in the early chapters of nearly every theatre history text: the point is made that theatre probably evolved from religious ritual of some kind. The usual confusion between drama and theatre makes this connection irresistible. After all, an existing religious ritual needs only a skillful writer (or even a bardic tradition such as that of the Greek rhapsodists) to become a literary tradition of great power. But the possibility that enactment may have preceded even speech opens new options.

In ritual enactment, the performance contract is applied to matters of the greatest consequence. The "other" that the actor becomes may be a founding god of his tribe, as in the Shalako ceremony of the Zuni people. Or he or she may become some aspect of the natural world, for example, the Spirit of the Salmon for the native American tribes of the Pacific Northwest; or the physical embodiment of a redeemer figure, as in the Catholic Mass. If the previous line of argument holds, religion in each of these cases draws upon enactment just as it draws upon speech, music, dance, body adornment, or any other of countless behaviors which have the power to engage the attention of the participant and to confer special power to those who use the technique. The formal power of the expressive act becomes the most important part of the content. In some cases the ritual demands of the activity are so all-consuming that the original content is completely overwhelmed and marginalized. What remains is the behavior performed for its ritual value only, as when ritual dance has become disconnected from its original mimetic value and stands completely alone, valued entirely for its long genealogy. This is the case with Japanese Gagaku, the dance drama of the imperial household, which apparently began as depictions of battles and other contests but has long since become largely emptied of that content. Today, it exists entirely for its formal values.

The adoption of ritual enactment as religious practice presents some interesting problems. (Not the least of which is illustrated in the preceding sentence: in preindustrial societies, there is no useful separation between religion and other aspects of life; hence the imposition of any boundary between the two here is artificial.) The performance contract demands that the actor "pretend" to be something other than himself. So long as the performer really is pretending, as in the case of the Zuni people, whose Shalako no longer come themselves but send performers in their place, the issue is not overly complicated. But what of the cases where the performer disappears and is replaced by the god or spirit? In such possession, the actor's body is wholly occupied for the duration of the event—and what the audience sees in such a case would be not a representation of the god but a true epiphany. Setting aside the possibility that the god really is present, the matter becomes one of the degree of the suspension of disbelief. In the performance contract, the audience balances the desire to believe with the knowledge that the actor is acting; in ritual possession, the audience (and the actor, in most cases) believe that replacement of the actor with the god is complete. In such a case, the performance contract is voided.

Anthropologists report, however, that in practice the balance between belief and disbelief is usually much more precarious than theory would predict. Many shaman report that they hope the possession is complete, but in the absence of certainty they play their role anyway; their patients report positive results whether or not they believe the possession was complete.

In either case, it is easy to see how the simple dyadic performance contract could be incorporated into religious ritual. In such a case, it is probable that the enactment—and hence the performance contract—preceded the ritual, not the reverse.

Challenge Four: The Question of Function

It is an article of faith in evolutionary theory that any continuing somatic change must be the result of some advantage which it gives (or has given) the individual organism in a particular ecological niche. Thus, no matter how bizarre the coloring of a fish or bird species, no matter how striking the skeletal structure of a whale or how fanciful the shell of a mollusk, no matter how strange and counterproductive the antlers of some stag or inconvenient the dentation of some warthog, the reason for that configuration is clearly that it provides some competitive advantage to those who possess it.

The same article applies to the behavior of any organism. The scientific study of animal behavior—called ethology—reveals that the most amazing and seemingly random behavior patterns have a clear function for the animal that displays them. Examples abound across the whole spectrum of the animal and plant kingdoms; from the smallest and apparently simplest organisms to the largest and most complex, behavior patterns reinforce the conviction that behavior, like body shape, is sustained and reinforced to the degree that it functions to support evolutionary success.

Among human behaviors, the arts stand out. Not only are they behaviors hugely present in our species—to a degree far more striking than behaviors of any other species—but we engage in them under even the most stressful circumstances. Indeed, if one were to undertake an energy survey of all human behavior we would be amazed at the degree to which play behaviors dominate our lives. Observers have noted that play is the fourth most popular activity among humans, ranking just behind sleep, searching for and preparing food, and grooming (Jolly 1985). The only possible conclusion is that the arts comprise an evolutionary stable strategy (ESS)—theoretical jargon suggesting that, once introduced, arts behaviors will continue because of the presumed advantage they provide.

But what is the advantage? Are there multiple advantages? Or is there a single advantage which cascades into subsidiary benefits? This is the crux of the argument; if no advantage exists, there is no value to the behavior and, after a period of random appearance, it should gradually have been extinguished.

I shall suggest two different benefits for the behavior which we have defined as theatre, two possible reasons for entering into the performance contract. Neither is entirely sufficient; neither excludes the other. Nor do I believe that the ultimate benefit of theatre behaviors is either one or the other; there may be others that I have overlooked. Indeed, other benefits may be more important than either of those that follow, but what is needed here is an hypothesis: a serious claim, not only for beneficial outcomes, but for outcomes which function within the Darwinian model.

Nicholas Humphrey, in his volume of essays entitled: *Chapters in the Development of Mind Consciousness Regained* (1984), advances a theory to explain why our species has such a highly developed sense of self. Specifically, he asks why humans spend so much time concerned with their own mental processes. What possible advantage lies in our obsessive attempt to understand our own motivation? Though evidence is incomplete, it appears that no other animal spends as much time ruminating, reflecting, fantasizing, and generally dredging up mental experience. There is significant evidence that excessive self-consciousness (the American equivalent of the "consciousness" of Humphrey's title) reduces physical effectiveness and can even lead to the destruction of individuals who are too reflective. The popularity of Shakespeare's *Hamlet* suggests that humans do, in fact, believe that too much reflection is dangerous. But, if self-consciousness is dangerous in excess, what could be its value in moderation?

Humphrey argues that human self-consciousness is an effort to anticipate the actions of our most dangerous competitors—other humans. In brief, he says that self-consciousness is like a tiny organ devoted to understanding the behavior of others; by examining our own experience, we can get a better handle on what others are doing—and might do. Those who are best at understanding other people are those with a large body of information upon which to draw.

How does one gather a large body of information about human behavior? One answer is obvious: By living a long and rich life, exposed to the full range of human behavior in all its often rococo detail. Unfortunately, this is not always possible. Not all humans are fortunate enough to live such a blessed life. As important as rich experience, time is of the essence. If a twenty-year-old is competing (for a mate, say) with a forty-year-old, the odds may be equal, but if two twenty-year-olds are competing, and if one has the savvy of a forty-year-old, the odds swing in favor of experience. Likewise, in all manner of human competitions, the foolish competitor may not live long enough to become wise.

Then, how does one become wise—quickly? Our species has a huge array of general methods for undertaking this daunting task. Language is one; the elders simply tell the favored young what to do and what to avoid. Formal education has this same end, as does religious instruction. Those of us who teach for a living well know the limits of formal instruction, however. To tell someone something does not ensure that the information will be internalized and acted upon. (Indeed, the more cynical among us have come to wonder if formal instruction does not guarantee that such information will *not* be used.)

The need to find effective ways to make the experience of others our own has tested the imagination of our species at every step in our history. Humphrey suggests that the arts are one way of allowing us to expand the base of human experience, which we reference when we try to understand others. Humphrey mentions poetry, the novel, and films directly, but his argument works very well for any of the arts. It works particularly well for theatre.

The reason is the widely reported capacity for empathy—the ability to feel "into" the lives of others. Empathic involvement in the lives of others is the closest we can come to actually living their lives—and thus benefitting from their experience. Suzanne Langer first described the special power of theatre as "virtual history." I believe that it is more accurate to describe it as "virtual autobiography." In the theatre experience, the audience member is invited to live many lives for the price of one, benefitting from each accordingly.

To accord with Humphrey's theory, the value of theatre is most enhanced when the vicarious experience is largely novel to the audience member but not so bizarre as to be useless in the competitive world outside the theatre. Persons who possessed an experience vicariously would probably not be as well prepared as those who had it first-hand, but they would have an immeasurable advantage over others who had never encountered the experience in any form. Even so, the selective pressure would give the most advantage to those whose vicarious experience was most forceful, thus, there would be inevitable pressure for theatre events to be ever more involving, striking, and memorable. Each of these elements is thus valued for its ability to give the audience member a collection of mental images which would serve as well as if he had experienced the event first hand—perhaps even better. Paradoxical as it may seem, even the first-hand experience of an event may not be as forceful as the heightened portrayal on the stage (or in a novel, film, or poetry).

Thus, Humphrey's basic thesis leads us to see theatre as a method of increasing inclusive selection by providing individuals with the experience to make effective choices in the social sphere. Thus, it focuses largely on the content of the theatre experience.

An alternative view might begin in quite a different vein: by emphasizing the deceptive practices which seem inherent in theatre. Deception is an integral part of human culture and also plays an important part in all life forms: among animals camouflage and hidden hunting behaviors are obviously intended to mislead either prey or predators. The deception which counts here is not the deception practiced against other species, but against one's own species. Here, too, *Homo sapiens* is not the sole practitioner of deception.

The stag elk who attempts to appear more fearsome than he really is, practices a form of behavioral deception; and there are countless examples of non-human primate behaviors which are calculated to mislead members of the troop, potential rivals, and competitors. But the hands-down winner in the deception derby must be mankind. Only we have made the successful practice of deception an expected part of daily intercourse ("Darling, you look wonderful!") and in countless ways reward it in practice if not in theory. Indeed, the many and seemingly endless arguments against deception on the part of the world's great religions give testimony to the seniority and permanence of the practice in our culture as a whole.

With no more information than this, a human ethologist would probably be able to predict the course of history; the iron rule of evolutionary theory is that no species is allowed to use a strategy—however effective—unimpeded forever. While deception might be a successful strategy for the present, the same forces which brought it into being will demand a counter strategy. In this case, our ethologist would predict that deception detection would soon be selected for in numerous ways.

And so it is. Every human culture is so concerned about the matter that, besides inveighing against the practice of deception, each has taken measures to make sure that deception does not succeed. Children are trained, through wise saws and practical illustrations, to see through the attempts of certain nameless others who will doubtless seek to deceive them. Humphrey goes to great lengths to emphasize the role of teasing in the training of children (Humphrey1984). At first, his case seems extreme, but the central role of teasing becomes more obvious when we see it as "deception detection drill." A father playing with his son holds the child's teddy bear out the window, saying, "Well, I guess that I'm just going to have to drop Teddy out the window. Then he'll be gone and you'll never have him again." The child may answer, "Daddy, you're just kidding, aren't you?" if he uncertain, or, "No Daddy, don't do that. Teddy will break his arm and have to go to the hospital!" if he understands that a performance contract is being offered. Other examples of deception-detection training are obvious. The myths of Santa Claus and the Tooth Fairy are deceptions intended to be found out; indeed, the parents of children who are slow to grasp the nature of these deceptions are often made uncomfortable by their offspring's gullibility. And then there are the endless warnings about the intentions of people with weak chins, beady eyes, and moist palms warnings which have negatively influenced the lives of the innocent possessors of those characteristics.

There are endless betting games which simultaneously train for both successful deception and for deception detection. Card games are legendary in this regard. It is interesting how conflicted and contradictory is the praise for winners of these games when they are displaying skills which would only earn them scorn in the outside world.

As I have already hinted, the development of the performance contract could be seen as having its roots in the mix of strategies suitable for success in the deceptive environment of human life. This is especially the case since, as in many games, deception training and training for detecting deception, both essential human skills, are taking place in the same setting. It could be argued, though I think not very effectively, that this balancing of exploitative strategy with defensive strategy would inevitably lead to an escalation of both, with improvements in the deception phase of the interaction demanding increased sophistication in the response phase. This could then be advanced as the reason for the development of an art form from what had previously been little more than a social practice. Intriguing as this idea may be, it is destroyed by one simple fact: if it were true, those societies with fully developed, fine art theatre traditions would be very much better at both deception and deception detection those societies which do not have such traditions. Human history is littered with the corpses of well-educated people who thought that they could outfox members of some apparently primitive tribesmen.

Challenge Five: The Phylogenetic History of the Art Form

Even if one accepts the idea that the roots of theatre lie in a universal form of human communication, it is impossible to avoid the vexing question of how a very sophisticated art form might have grown from that rootstock. Since this question is one which must be answered by any institutionalized behavior, arguments from analogy are appropriate.

Haute cuisine and high fashion have the same relationship to eating and clothing that high art theatre has to the performance contract in a social setting. In each case there is presumably a hierarchy of behaviors which connects, say, the preparation of complex proteins for ingestion by merely throwing the body of a newly killed monkey into an open fire with the preparation of a delicate paté, or the protection and artful display of the human body by wrapping it in a bear skin with showing a new Paris line.

The step-by-step changes in these hierarchies are characterized by very different behaviors growing out of very different values; yet, at base, they maintain the same functions. Or do they? This is a parallel issue which must also be addressed: are the changed behaviors indicative of different functions? If so, how are the changed functions different?

One dimension which is immediately obvious is the aesthetic one. In the case of eating, aesthetic concerns arise by progressive degrees, and each step is easy to document or infer. Clearly there is a hierarchy of needs in matters of human nutrition; only after a specific point, once the immediate needs of the organism are met, can other values move into ascendancy. One may assume that at some point in our evolution our aesthetic interest in eating was roughly that of chimpanzees and baboons. This is not to say zero, but close to it. As with most of our fellow primates, our major daily goals were probably simply those of finding and ingesting sufficient protein, lipids, and carbohydrates to stay alive. Other aspects of nutrition such as trace elements, vitamins, and sufficient fiber were probably inconsequential. In times of plenty, other values were layered in: a proper balance of foods, restraint needed to prevent obesity, an appetizing array; and all of these second-level concerns would have overlain—or at least augmented—the primary subsistence issues. For human primates, the next level of eating behaviors might well have involved food as a bargaining chip in mate selection and expression of status: for example, hoarding of food might be one way of attracting mates; the medical dangers of obesity might be outweighed by the value of displaying fat as a token of high status—as it has been with numberless societies, such as the precolonial Hawaiian. The final step would have been the development of preparing and eating food as an art form, one in which the fine discrimination of tastes, the aesthetic value of certain colors and textures, the bravura techniques of cooking (e.g., replacing the feathered pelt on an already cooked pheasant), all become aspects of eating far more important than simply ingesting protein and calories. Before we leave this example, it should be noted that nothing prevents anyone from enjoying the full range of eating experiences. The gourmet chef may enjoy a backyard barbecue occasionally; the renowned food editor may grab a fast-food hamburger and fries while on the road.

Roughly the same process must have occurred in the phylogenetic history of theatre: a widely available communication technique must have been used in a variety of ways, some exploiting the original functions, some emphasizing later accretions. Here, for example, may lie the shared root of theatre and ritual. Enactment and the performance contract, having an already established identity in the repertoire of human communication behaviors, would have been conspicuously available as an option in ritual, especially as our ancestors sought to explain and express the mysteries of the world, particularly those aspects susceptible to anthropomorphic explanation. Hence, the portrayal of a god expresses the mystery of the divine through a familiar and accessible technique. The shift of contexts from a ritual setting to an aesthetic one has taken place in historical times in Western culture: in the early fifth century B.C. the function of theatre, especially tragedy, shifted from celebrating the gods to performing an aesthetically and philosophically important artistic act. What confuses critics today is the attempt to understand Greek tragedy of the period in the context of the older religious function rather than the newer, secular one.

Another problem in theatre history is the traditional need to see Greek theatre of the late sixth and early fifth centuries as inventing theatre from whole cloth. As a result, we have become entranced with the idea of Thespis as somehow creating tragedy rather than simply—however importantly—adapting enactment and the performance contract to the needs of the well-established dithyrambic tradition.

The idea of an hierarchical development of the art form is useful here, but it has a downside, as well. It suggests that the original function of the form has been put aside, much as the mammalian form has evolved beyond the amphibian and, therefore, lost the capacities of the predecessor. Whether this is the case in the biological realm, it is certainly not the case in theatre. The original, primitive elements of theatre have been retained in ways which make sense only when the original functions are understood. For example, if it is clearly seen that the roots of the performance contract lie in an understanding of certain social roles, it becomes imperative that the fact that a contract is in force is known to all parties. All parties to the performance contract must *know* that enactment is taking place. Therefore, we must expect that significant time and effort will be devoted to reminding everyone of the special nature of the event. Examples abound. We should expect that all theatre traditions will have conventions designed to clearly indicate the beginning and the end of the performance. Some cultures will do so with elaborate invocations and other rituals; others will use the convention of curtains, overtures, and control of the lights. The space in which the performance takes place must be changed in some way to make it detectably different from the non-performance space which surrounds it. That is what the erection of a shabby platform in the city square by a company of strolling players is about. It is also what Lincoln Center and La Scala mean. Costumes adopted by actors are not so much an attempt to convince an audience that the actor's are someone else, as a constant reminder that the actor has been invited to pretend to be someone else. In an age dominated by the conventions of stage realism, it is well to remember that the conventions of overt theatricalism are not some perverse atavism but a profoundly important reminder of the roots of the art.

Challenge Six: Comparability

To what degree are the theatrical "needs" of today also those of our phylogenetic past? If we have "evolved" past the niche within which theatre evolved, or if those needs served by theatre are being met as well by other social conventions and technological developments, the lessons of the past may not be relevant. In such a case, the facts of the prehistory of theatre are academically interesting—but largely irrelevant.

Still, a large body of compelling research and speculation suggests that, while the environment in which modern man lives may have changed greatly in the past fifty thousand years, his body and mind are roughly the same (Wilson 1978, Konner 1982). A difficulty that our species encounters is that we are forcing bodies and minds suited for one environment into a very different one. The resulting disharmony and sense of dis-ease may demand adaptive measures which are quite different from what worked thousands of years ago.

Or not. The hallmark of our species is adaptability. From our earliest beginnings we lived in places and situations so uncomfortable that other species would never have even tried to occupy them. Indeed, any phylogenetic discomfort we experience today may be no more than another example of the tension which has always marked our aggressive, curious, and adaptable species. If the arts—and theatre among them—have traditionally helped us balance stability and flexibility there is no better time to understand that function than now. Thus, this might be the very best time to understand and benefit from a thorough understanding of the roots of theatre.

Moreover, those roots, though difficult to detect and perhaps uncomfortable to recognize, are crucial to any understanding of theatre as an art form. Much of modern theatre seems to have lost its way. Confronted by the popularity of films and the ubiquitous nature of television, the theatre artist can be forgiven if he or she begins to think that the original importance of theatre has been irretrievably lost. And perhaps it has been. Just as organic species have become extinct, there is no reason for doubt that cultural institutions might do the same. Nevertheless, that judgment seems entirely premature at this point. Not until the phylogenetic history of the art form is fully understood can we understand whether it has or has not been supplanted.

I have tried to sketch here a possible evolutionary pathway, but there are at least six important decision points to be melt en route. At any of those turnings, the whole saga may take on quite a different character. What remains certain is that there is a tale to be told, one that reaches farther into the dark recesses of human evolution than current theatre history teaches us, and one which may just illuminate the art form more than current criticism does.

Works Cited

Fagen, R.

1981 *Animal Play Behavior*. Oxford: Oxford University Press.

Hansen, Brian

1991 *Theatre: The Dynamics of the Art*. 2d ed. New York: Prentice-Hall.

Humphrey, N. K.

1984 *Consciousness Regained: Chapters in the Development of Mind*. New York: Oxford University Press.

Jolly, Alison
1985 *The Evolution of Primate Behavior.* 2d ed. New York: Macmillan.
Konner, Melvin
1982 *The Tangled Wing: Biological Constraints on the Human Spirit.* New York: Holt, Rinehart and Winston.
Toth, Nicholas
1987 "The First Technology." *Scientific American* 256(4):112-21.
Wilson, Edward O.
1978 *On Human Nature*. Cambridge, MA: Harvard University Press.

Antecedents of Musical Meaning in the Mother-Infant Dyad

Ellen Dissanayake

The universality and cultural prominence of music suggest that it contributes something essential, not simply ornamental, to human existence.[1] Its mysterious and apparently unique capacity to move listeners emotionally has led people in all societies to find it profoundly meaningful, even though this meaning may be difficult if not impossible to describe. In earlier times and other places, music was assumed to be of supernatural origin; in the more rational scientific and philosophic climate following the Enlightenment, a number of naturalistic explanations have been advanced (see section I below). It remains the case, however, that there is no accepted systematic and plausible account proposed for music's evolutionary origin and function; indeed, most biological thinkers, like Darwin (1871), view music as a "mystery." Yet if one takes an evolutionary view of human behavior, it seems clear that there must have been a time in our remote past when music, like language, did not exist. Its centrality and persistence in human experience indicate that it must have been adaptive. Why then did music arise, and when, and from what antecedents? The enjoyment that people everywhere take in music; the time, energy, and material resources they often expend in making or listening to it; and its ubiquity all suggest that it has, or had, evolutionary importance.

A new look at music's evolutionary antecedents seems relevant in light of new findings and possibilities for synthesis in a number of current disciplines. Ideas in human ethology and sociobiology offer new theoretical approaches to the evolution of human behavior. Theory and information in new areas of psycholinguistics provide fertile departures for understanding human music. The field of neuroscience contributes relevant new knowledge about brain organization, function, and development in regard to music as to other branches of human mentation. Studies in ethnomusicology reveal a multiplicity of notions about and uses of music in other societies, and stimulate a widening of our concept of music as a human behavior.

In the present essay, I will synthesize ideas from the above fields in order to take a fresh look at the question of music's evolutionary origin and function. I view this as being a necessary first step toward understanding the sources and some of the reasons for its emotional power in human experience, i.e., its "meaning" as humanists and philosophers have traditionally conceived it. This discussion summarizes a larger study-in-progress and therefore is subject to the inevitable shortcomings of a complex synthesis presented in abridged and preliminary form. Additionally, it should be clear that I do not address the genesis, function, or meaning of a particular work or type, or of an individual experience, creation, or performance of music.

The essay has three parts: (I) a critical overview of earlier biological or quasi-biological accounts of music's origin and function, (II) a description and analysis of universal "musical" features in mother-infant engagement ("babytalk"), and (III) a proposal that human music, like many "derived" or ritualized behaviors of affiliation and appeasement in other animals, originated in parental behavior—specifically in mother-infant engagement.

Inadequacies of Earlier Evolutionary Views

Previous speculative accounts of the evolutionary origin and function of music are inadequate for several reasons. Explanations proposed by nonbiologists may be based on outdated or naive views of evolution, while those proposed by biologists are often ad hoc, adopted uncritically and simplistically from analogies with other animals. Moreover, what is meant by "music" is too often based on unexamined ideas that are specific to Western culture, leading to oversimplification or overgeneralization.

Although Wallaschek (1970) posited that the origin of music must be sought in a fundamental rhythmical impulse that arises from a general "appetite for exercise" (similar to the idea of "surplus vigor" suggested by Spencer (1880-82) as the origin of play and art), the most frequent suggestions about the biological origin and function of music have begun with human vocal expression and communication, e.g., emotional outcries that inherently are strongly moving or alarming—weeping, sobbing, calls for help, excited speech, shouts of joy, and so forth (North 1959, Hutcheson 1725, Lacépède 1785, Spencer 1857, Rowbotham 1893), or what today might be called "acoustical innate releasing mechanisms" (Eibl-Eibesfeldt 1975, 498-99; 1989).

Music has also been traced to other vocal sounds from human activity—e.g., hunting calls that imitate animal cries and birdcalls (Geist 1978), synchronizing sounds for rhythmic work such as pulling nets or pounding grain (Bücher 1896; Hornbostel, in Sachs 1977), lullabies, and accompaniments to dance and festal excitement (Stumpf 1911)—these sounds gradually acquiring refinement and augmented social purpose (Sachs 1977).

Other theories have looked to human speech itself—to the babbling of babies (McLaughlin 1970), to tone languages where different pitches of the same syllable are semantically significant (Kuttner 1951 and Schneider 1957, in Sachs 1977), to chanting, or even to signalling across valleys and distances—hoots and hollers (Stumpf 1911; Hall-Craggs 1969).

Charles Darwin (1871), noting that animal sounds are functional, ultimately contributing to procreative fitness, suggested that music derived from mating calls that may have preceded language in human evolution.

It appears promising to seek the origins of music in human expressive utterance, since music, like speech, alarm calls, weeping, and so forth, expresses and elicits emotion. At the same time, however, earlier suggestions in this vein do not go far enough.

To begin with, it is limiting to seek the origin of music in specific sounds with specific emotional content or purpose (e.g., calls indicating the need for attention and care, alarm, sexual desire, high spirits, or grief). While some music may be intended to express a specific emotion, it does this less with specific sounds than by organizing these into an affecting pattern. In any case, music need not, and usually does not, convey or arouse specific emotions at all. Hence, it seems more promising to look for music's origin in a human expressive vocal behavior where emotions are in some measure formalized—organized sequentially—rather than in one where emotions are simply expressed.

Additionally, the notion that music originated from emotional outcries (or anything else) requires explaining why musical treatment was given and what it added. What would be the motivation for—that is, what would be accomplished by—making music out of shouts of joy or grief? They are quite effective and communicative as is, and people who might choose to musicalize their specific emotions would not appear to receive demonstrable benefits over those who do not.

Finally, suggestions about the individual evolutionary functions or selective benefits of musicmaking are all too often commandeered from the accepted benefits of analogous or superficially similar behavior in other animals: these include signalling an individual's mood or intent, indicating recreation or enjoyment, generating contagion, regulating movement, or displaying an individual's skill or prowess. Although any of these may be accomplished by one or another specific instance of music, it seems unwise to generalize one adaptive benefit to explain the entire phenomenon. For example, once anything has evolved it can be used culturally for display or message enhancement—say, the length of one's hair or the impeccability of one's accent—but this need not imply that hair or the articulatory organs of speech evolved originally for such a purpose. Thus I suggest that although it may be that in specific instances a particular type of music may serve a specific evolutionary function or secondary function (such as synchronizing movement in work, or allowing people to show off their talent so that they are more attractive to and successful with the opposite sex), we must consider whether musical behavior in general may have initially arisen to serve a more general and overarching function.

Universal Musical Features in Mother-Infant Engagement

The Importance of Prosody in Human Speech

Prosody refers to the nonverbal or expressive features of spoken language—its intonational and rhythmic characteristics (e.g., patterns of pitch and stress, the use of pauses and timing). In human speech, prosodic features give both emotive and expressive coloring —importance of the utterance, mood of the speaker—and also may affect actual lexical meaning. "Greenhouse" is inflected differently from "green house"; moreover, I can say, "Yes, do that," and convey the ironic opposite of these words by my use of pitch, volume, elongation of vowels, tone of voice, pauses between words, and forcefulness of articulation. Such meaning is social as much as substantive, conveying who is speaking, who is to take the next turn, how the utterance is to be understood, and what the speaker's intentions toward and relationship to the listener are (Bolinger 1986, 338). Depending on one's prosody, the words "You will not go" may convey threat, challenge, taunt, or question (Beauquier 1865).

Most people would agree that spoken language usually has a not always hidden interpersonal agenda: e.g., to persuade, to dominate, to convince, to impress, to deceive, to entreat, to appease, or simply to maintain amiable association. As these aims are accomplished as much by prosody as by words and grammar, it is clear that the expressive component of speech has been of great importance to our species.

Yet this fact requires emphasis. Our neglect of the emotive components of speech is evident when we assign "language" to the left cerebral hemisphere. Granted, the left hemisphere is generally dominant for the syntactical or lexico-grammatical aspects of language: injuries to speech areas in the left hemisphere result in impaired ability to produce or understand grammatically appropriate or correct utterances.

It is less widely known or appreciated that in the right cerebral hemisphere, there are areas corresponding to those in the left that are critical for producing, processing, and responding to the affective prosodic components of speech (Ross 1983; Simonds and Scheibel 1989 in Schore 1994, 483). Thus, injuries here also interfere with correct use of "language" (Ross and Mesulam 1979, Ross 1981).[2]

In infants the two hemispheres are not as specialized as they later become, and it seems reasonable to assume that persons in preliterate societies (including our remote human ancestors) without years of schooling in sequential analytic skills of reading and writing will depend more on right hemisphere capabilities than many of us in modernized societies (see Donald 1991, ch. 8).

No matter how important lexico-grammatical meaning eventually becomes, the human brain is first organized or programmed to respond to emotional/intonational aspects of the human voice (Locke 1993,369, 416; Schore 1994). Newborns, even premature infants, will visibly take notice of a human voice and quieten to attend to gentle talking, lulling, or singing. They can respond to variations in frequency, intensity, duration, and temporal or spatial patterning of sounds (Papousek and Papousek 1981,171).

Babies only a few days old will synchronize movements of their bodies with the sounds of human speech or with adult head movements, exhibiting rudimentary entrainment (Condon and Sander 1974, Peery 1980, Condon 1984). It is of course the prosodic and emotion-conveying features of the utterances to which they respond, not to their lexical or linguistic meanings.

Babytalk

Background

In all cultures, most people, not only mothers, commonly behave differently with infants than with adults, or even with older children. The rhythms and melody of their utterances display a special clarity and appeal. They use exaggerated facial expressions, movements, and vocalizations in a way that invites a dyadic interaction, the features and patterns of which resemble dyadic ritualized behaviors in other animals. Why do they do this? What is accomplished by this striking yet commonplace communicative interaction that we tend to call, dismissively, babytalk?

Studies of the effects of maternal deprivation in nonhuman primates indicate that the mother-infant bond extends well back into our prehominid past. In the 1960s, John Bowlby, a child psychiatrist acquainted with the reactions of young children who for various reasons had been separated from their mothers, postulated that there is a positive need for infants to form what he called "attachment" with caretakers (Bowlby 1969, 1973). He described attachment as a complex of behaviors that serve to maintain proximity between the pair. He hypothesized that the evolutionary value of this proximity-seeking to the helpless hunter-gatherer's baby was that it would not wander far away, and when frightened or alone it would cry, reach out, move toward, or otherwise try to resume contact with a specific protective figure, rather than remain vulnerable to predators or accidents. We see comparable behaviors in many helpless young birds or mammals.

In the years since Bowlby's formulation, research with much younger infants has shown unexpected and quite remarkable inborn abilities and proclivities for interaction and intimacy, which suggest that attachment—concerned primarily with the infant's physical safety—should be viewed as a late-appearing consequence of a prior, equally innate and adaptive predisposition to engage in relationship and emotional communion. A few minutes after birth, for example, a neonate shows a preference for its mother's voice, which it has heard from within the womb. It can imitate facial expressions, like protruding the lips or tongue or opening the mouth, and hand opening and closing (Meltzoff and Moore 1977, Kugiumutzakis 1993). Far from being passive recipients, responding reflexively to a stimulus, babies come into the world actively ready to communicate their needs, feelings, and motives to other persons, who themselves will respond by presenting the world to the child in precisely regulated ways. In numerous papers, Trevarthen (e.g., 1974, 1977, 1979a, 1979b, 1987, 1990, 1994) has described this "with-the-other-awareness," which he calls *innate intersubjectivity* (1979a, 1992), an inherent biological foundation not only for "attaching" but for eliciting and responding to emotional communication with another.

Thus the inborn need for attachment that Bowlby described is separate from (MacDonald 1992) or built upon an even more fundamental inborn readiness of the baby to seek, respond to, and affect the mother's provision of not only physical protection and care but of *emotional* regulation and support (Dore 1983; Stern et al. 1983; Trevarthen 1984; Fernald 1984, 1985, 1989; M. Papousek et al. 1991; Schore 1994). In most cases, the pair practice and perfect their attunement of motivation and affect by engaging in a mutually improvised interaction based on innate competencies and sensitivities that are at the same time emotional and musical. Long before classically described attachment takes place, babytalk is providing enjoyment and intimacy for both participants and significant developmental benefits for the infant.

Characteristic Features

While the term "babytalk" (also called "motherese" or "infant directed speech") refers narrowly to the mother's utterances, these, and their accompanying gestures and facial expressions, are inseparable from the responses of the baby to whom they are addressed. With facial expressions, vocalizations, and movements of head, body, and limbs, infants solicit, participate in, and influence the behavior and sounds that are directed to them. Babytalk then is a sort of duet, a multimedia dialogic performance.

The typical characteristics of babytalk have been described and analyzed by many researchers (e.g., Stern 1977, 1985; Fernald 1984; Trevarthen 1984; M. Papousek et al. 1985; Beebe 1986; Greiser and Kuhl 1988; Trehub, Trainor, and Unyk 1993; Locke 1993). Such studies show a complex but describable structure and development, universal features, and demonstrable adaptive benefits.

From birth to between three and four months, a mother's babytalk utterances universally tend to be spoken in a high, soft, breathy voice. They are short and repetitive, with clear interposed pauses. They have distinctive, well-controlled pitch contours, and as one researcher has described it, are "vowel drenched," thus allowing for the contour to be sustained and emphasized. Regular stresses set up a steady rhythm that is soothing and reassuring. The subject matter comes from moment-to-moment occurrences—comments on the baby's looks, actions, on events in the vicinity, and so forth. As the weeks pass, the mother subtly adjusts her sounds and movements to what the baby seems to want (or not want), and to its changing needs and abilities. She gradually moves from gentle, cooing reassurance to trying to engage the baby in increasingly animated mutual play, as if she is assisting it to arrive at a mutually negotiated optimal level of interest and sociability. To these ends, utterances and facial expressions become even more exaggerated, both in time and space—i.e., they are formed more slowly, held longer, and punctuated with behavioral rests or silences.

What is said and how it is said also change gradually. Vocal pitch frequency remains raised, but utterances become longer, with longer pauses between them, and utilize a greater range of pitch contours. The pair interact to a "beat" set up mutually and supported by the mother's movements and vocalizations, and she will react to a baby's gesture (even a hiccup) as if it were a vocal reply. Yet there is increasing variation on the underlying rhythm in the form of dramatic crescendos, diminuendos, accelerandos, ritardandos, and glissandos. A mother will systematically modulate tempo to influence the infant's level of arousal, either increasing or decreasing it according to how she perceives the baby's state. Imitation of each other's vocalizations and facial expressions, both involuntary and deliberate, contribute to mutual enjoyment and attunement. In three- to four-month-old infants at play with their mothers, there is a remarkable simultaneity of vocalizations, which gives rise to controlled synchrony and turntaking (e.g., Beebe 1986).

As babies grow older, they desire more stimulation, and there is a gradual movement from delicate to more vigorous play. Mothers use dramatic and exciting games and songs, interspersed with excited vocalizations that induce or reinforce the baby's readiness to play. At five- to eight-months, babies respond vigorously to teasing and structured routines where their expectations are manipulated by pregnant pauses or unanticipated diversions, often building to a climax (see also Papousek et al. 1984).

Toward the end of the first year, babytalk wanes. The mother's task, led by changes in the infant's needs, becomes more instructional (i.e., more lexical). The baby finds excitement in exploring and learning about a larger world, and the mother-child interaction begins to contain more referential content and to sound more like adult conversation.

Benefits to Infants

"Babytalk" routines vary culturally, but mothers seem to find them "natural"—they do not deliberately set out to act in some outlandish way or to "teach" their babies. As far as mothers and babies are concerned, they are simply "having fun," or enjoying each other's company. Yet we can posit a number of benefits contributing to the baby's emotional, intellectual, linguistic, psychosocial, and cultural development.

(a) There is the establishment of physiological and emotional attunement and reciprocity, contributing to the bond between mother and child.[3] Both simultaneous and dialogic vocal matching and motor mimicry convey the message "I can feel as you do. I am like you" (Bavelas et al. 1987, Beebe and Lachmann 1988), and the pair provide nonverbal emotional information about each other. By negotiating shared meanings, the pair will learn to better regulate one another's stimulation and to anticipate and adjust to each other's individual natures.

(b) The baby learns emotional "coping." In the babytalk interaction, a mother offers the infant emotional regulation and support, assisting it to achieve a coherent homeostatic equilibrium (Hofer 1990) as well as to identify and discriminate different dynamic states as they are expressed vocally and gesturally. The baby gains acquaintance with its own shifting levels of excitation and positive or negative feelings, developing some degree of self-regulation of these levels and feelings.

(c) Through emotional interchange, the infant also receives cognitive and intellectual benefits. By "anticipating," the baby hypothesizes what will come next and learns how to evaluate discrepancies from the expected; based on what is given, it judges how rapidly or slowly a "climax" will occur and through experience tests and perfects these expectations or predictions.

(d) Students of language learning report how these early babytalk routines prepare the way for eventually making and being able to understand the prototypical and meaningful sounds of the language one will speak.

(e) Social (and psychosocial) benefits are enormous. The vocalizations that infants hear in babytalk help them to recognize individuals and to interpret and predict their behavior (Locke 1995). What is more, neuroscientists describe how "socioemotional interchange between an adult and a developing brain" (Schore 1994, 537) critically and indelibly shapes and influences the development of neural structures responsible for the infant's socioemotional functioning for the rest of its lifespan (Schore 1994, Trevarthen and Aitken 1995).

(f) Finally, in mother-infant interaction, what is considered appropriate in their culture is first learned and assessed. Different cultures instill their own norms of proper behavior.

Cross-cultural Variants

There is not time in a discussion of this length to address the many variations in babytalk from other societies described in the literature, although it is obvious that in order to substantiate my claim that mother-infant interaction is a plausible evolutionary origin for the behavior of music, it is necessary to take these into account. In the dozen or so societies in which mother-infant engagement has been studied (see, e.g., Leiderman et al. 1977, Field et al. 1981, Hamilton 1981, Schieffelin and Ochs 1986), the earliest phases seem most similar. Mothers and infants everywhere engage in mutual gaze, smiling, touching, holding (including rocking and patting), vocalizing (the mother in "motherese"), and the infant looking at the mother's face (Lewis and Ban 1977). These six components may vary in relative importance in different societies, but all occur. There is also a widely found "caretaker greeting" where with visual contact the caretaker makes a slight retroflexion of the head, raises the eyebrows, opens the eyes wide, slightly opens the mouth, and gives a verbal greeting and/or a smile.

In one example, young Arnhemland Aborigine infants are rocked and cuddled by their mothers, who deliberately and systematically evoke smiling responses with conventionalized noises (hisses, tongue clicks, grunts, lipsmacking) and especially by looking at the baby, moving the head toward it, and saying "Nhhhh-Nhhhh" with the tip of the tongue curled behind the lower teeth and the tongue protruded (Hamilton 1981, 30). This smile-eliciting device is frequently used by others as well, who also pinch, tickle, rock, joggle, and kiss (44) others' babies, while making nonverbal sounds and repetitive vocalizations. However, no one *says* very much to babies (41), and verbal proficiency is not encouraged. Between six and eighteen months, babies receive as many gestural messages as verbal ones (63). According to Hamilton, this culture (like cultures everywhere) makes much use of subtle nonverbal gestures of intention and emotion, and children learn to perceive these as an intrinsic part of their society's communication system.

It is in the later stages of babytalk that the most variation exists, and where individual cultural norms of appropriate social behavior are instilled and reinforced. For example, American English-speaking mothers tend to have more extreme and dramatic intonational elements than British English-, French-, Italian-, German-, and Japanese-speaking mothers (Fernald 1989). Japanese mothers use more repetitive nonsense syllables, onomatopoeia, invented words, and imitations of their infants' sounds than do American mothers (Morikawa et al. 1988, Toda et al. 1990), and they spend more time soothing and less time arousing them than do American mothers.

In some societies, mother-infant vocal and behavioral interaction is greatly subdued and might seem initially to invalidate the claim that babytalk is based on innate species-wide proclivities. For example, Navaho mothers are reported to do little to actively encourage vocalizations or smiling, although during removal from the cradleboard there is face-to-face contact, smiling, and caretaking, and the infants spend the same amount of time looking at their mothers as do infants in other societies where mothers make vocalizations (Chisholm 1983). Some researchers have reported that Mayans in Mexico had no playful mother-infant interaction at all, no elicitation by mothers of social responses (Brazelton 1977). These same infants also showed little curiosity or response to novel items shown to them by investigators. Yet Mayan villagers in Guatemala, like many mothers in traditional societies, allow infants and toddlers to sleep with them for several years, out of a reported commitment to forge a close bond with their offspring. *Mexican* Mayan mothers may well also sleep with their children, and one may imagine their interaction before falling asleep or upon waking. In other words, I take reports of *no* mother-infant interaction with a skeptical grain of salt.

Certainly, as studies of the Gusii of Kenya (Dixon et al. 1981) suggest, the "musical" components of mother-infant interaction need not be shown only or even primarily in vocalization or dramatic buildups. The Gusii have what appear to be monotonous mother-infant interactions with little eye contact or play. However, film analyses show a noticeable cyclic modulation of activity, controlled by the mother with gaze aversion (the converse of classically described mother-infant interaction, where the baby breaks contact by looking away).

Daniel Stern's (1985) notion of "attunement" indicates that the salient elements of babytalk, even among Western mothers, need not be strictly verbal. He describes how behaviors *may be matched in different modalities* rather than directly mirrored or imitated.[4] Infants can perceive such features of experience as intensity, contour, time, shape, rhythm, and duration intermodally or analogically—e.g., loudness matched by strong movement, dots on a screen matched to a rhythmic beat (Eimas 1984; Stern 1985, 153). Crown (1991) has shown mothers and six-week-old infants to interact dialogically in a cross-modal (mother vocalize/infant gaze) interaction. Microanalyses of mother-infant engagement in the United States have shown reciprocal adjustments of behavior completed within seconds or fractions of seconds with a discernible structure or "rules" of mutual regulation (Beebe 1986, 29; Beebe and Gerstman 1984). I suspect that rigorous investigation and analysis would reveal in cultures less vocal and dramatic than ours, where stimulation and intensity are not developed, or in energetic but nonverbal interactions, as in Arnhemland, that mothers and infants are nevertheless temporally and dynamically adjusting their behavior to one another, in ways that escape direct observation in real time, and achieving the individual and social benefits described by investigators in analyzing the "typical" babytalk of Western mothers.

It is interesting that when the experimenters instructed the Gusii mothers to talk and smile to their infants, the latter responded with cooing vocalizations, big kicks, and large smiles. Vocalization in babies is most effectively elicited and most joyfully produced if rewarded with parental response and turntaking (Papousek and Papousek 1979), so it is reasonable to assume that without encouragement a potential will gradually fade. The competence for the full range of behaviors seems demonstrably to be present and wanes—as in the Mayans, Gusii, and Navahos—if not reinforced. The observation that caretaker-infant association is vocally, visually, and physically stimulating in modern hunter-gatherer groups (e.g., Hamilton 1981, Konner 1977)—whose cultural behaviors are presumably closer than those in other kinds of societies to early human groups—indicates that active, arousing interaction may well be ancestral, having become subdued in some cultures.

Musical Elements

Even though semantically meaningful words are used in babytalk, they are presumably heard by the baby as combinations of sounds with particular features and relations, not as verbal messages. These combinations, features, and relations of sounds can plausibly be described as fundamentally musical (Papousek and Papousek 1981b), suggesting the possibility of an evolutionary relationship between mother-infant interaction and music as follows:

(a) The prosody of babytalk, like music, has intonational contour ("melody"), rhythmic regularity and variety, pauses or rests, and dynamic variation in intensity (stress and accent), in volume (crescendo and diminuendo), in speed (accelerando and decelerando), and in alterations of vocal timbre.

(b) Mother-infant engagement and music are temporal structures, making similar use of framed episodes, or "bouts," each with a clear beginning or introduction and final felt closure, sometimes with a refrain or coda. The utterances also appear to be organized primarily into what can be transcribed as lines (or phrases), judged either by number of words, or by timed length, generally three to four seconds, as demonstrated by Turner (1985) and Pöppel (1985) to universally characterize lines of verse—and which Lynch et al. (1995) find to characterize phrases of prelinguistic vocalization, adult speech, oral poetry, and music (see also Krumhansl 1992). Often the episodes contain a theme or themes that are varied, thereby creating, manipulating, delaying, and ultimately satisfying expectation.

(c) Of particular interest is the importance of bodily movement in mother-infant interaction, whether in eliciting interactive behavior, in sustaining intensity, in coordinating synchrony, or in recognizing each other's participation in the "beat" of the encounter. Indeed, there seem to be a number of cultures where movement takes precedence over vocalization.

As theorists have tended to neglect the importance of gesture to language and thought (McNeill 1992) and the importance of prosody to spoken language, so has the integral importance of bodily movement in musical behavior been overlooked in the way we define "music" in Western culture. Yet ethnomusicologists have pointed out that "music" in most cultures generally includes both words and movement—dancing, clapping, or otherwise marking time. Until the age of four or five, children cannot distinguish the rhythm of a piece from accompanying movements and find it difficult to sing without moving their hands and feet (Suliteanu 1979). Infants nine to thirteen months of age moved differently to a lively and to a slow recorded segment of music, indicating that they can respond appropriately to temporal patterning of complex auditory sequences (Trehub 1993). It seems clear that as a human behavior music typically includes physical movement (although in the modern "concert" context this is usually suppressed).

(d) Both mother-infant engagement and music are social behaviors, a resemblance we might overlook without the ethnomusicological observation that people generally make music for and with other people (Feld 1974, 207).

(e) And finally, the results are similar, in that

(i) Both are pleasurable and emotional, giving enjoyment through nonverbal means with much involvement of known right-hemisphere competencies—e.g., facial and intonational processing, whole-pattern recognition, and somatosensory input (Borod et al. 1983); processing prosodic contours, facial expressions, and gestures (Blonder et al. 1991); processing, expression, and regulation of emotional information (Schore 1994); and crossmodal perception or analogy (Tucker 1992).

(ii) One often hears it said that one's responses to music are inexpressible—they "cannot be put into words"—and infant experience, of course, is nonverbal.

(iii) Both attune or synchronize participants.

(iv) Both are means of social-emotional regulation and control.

(v) Attunement or synchronization leads to emotional bonding or "self-transcendence."

Music As a "Derived Activity"

The fact that the human infant is exquisitely prepared to respond to the prosodic or musical features of human speech argues for their importance to babies' subsequent development, as is borne out by the many studies that indicate the emotional, intellectual, linguistic, psychosocial, and cultural benefits attendant upon the highly musical babytalk dialogue.

Yet, any suggestion about the evolutionary origin of a behavior ultimately rests on the plausibility of the case made for the further development of that capacity. How could a complex behavior like music have evolved from anything—in the present case, babytalk? And why?

My argument uses an ethological perspective, making use of studies of both play and ritual (behaviors that exist in other animals) in order to suggest intervening "steps" between mother-infant interaction and music. Specifically, I propose that in vocal play, ancestral human children elaborated the already important and appealing "musical" elements of babytalk—keeping them going, as it were. Ancestral human adults, who of course were once children and then parents, spontaneously used and elaborated these elements as they created ritual ceremonies.

Ritualization and Ritual

Tinbergen (1952) introduced the concept of "derived" activities that during evolution arise and become emancipated from earlier functional attributes, acquiring new communicative meaning as social signals. More recently, Eibl-Eibesfeldt (1989, 439-40) has outlined the general changes that occur in this process that ethologists call ritualization. The ultimate result is to make the signal—the derived behavior in its new communicative context—prominent, unequivocal, and unmistakable to the perceiver.

These changes include the following: (a) movements (including vocalizations) are simplified, often repeated rhythmically, and their amplitude exaggerated; (b) variations in the intensity of the signal now convey information; (c) the releasing threshold is lowered, making elicitation more likely; (d) there is often a concomitant development of supporting organic structures (in animals, such things as manes, crests, tails; in humans, clothing, cosmetics, and so forth); and (e) the motivation for producing the original signal often changes as it acquires a new meaning.

Using these characteristics, I believe that it is warranted, despite cultural variations, to consider certain general features of the dyadic behavior of babytalk as composing a biologically endowed ritualized behavior, one that both partners are predisposed to elicit and respond to.

In humans, unlike other animals, culturally-created ritual ceremonies of varying degrees of complexity are also highly developed, manifesting the regularization, exaggeration, formalization, and perceptual salience of biologically evolved ritualized behaviors in animals, and concerned with similar abiding concerns of social life—display of resources, threat, defense, and (conspicuously in humans) affirmations of affiliation.

It is well known that in many mammals, birds, and insects, elements of infant or caretaking behavior are the origin of biologically endowed ritualized expressive sounds or actions ("releasers") that promote social contact, appeasement, and affiliation in adults.[5] For example, in courtship, male sparrows shake their wings like juveniles asking for food (Eibl-Eibesfeldt 1989, 146), and male ravens make a silent coughing motion of the head that resembles parental feeding behavior (Morton and Page 1992, 96). A courting male hamster utters contact calls like those of hamster babies (Eibl-Eibesfeldt 1989, 146). Even in our own species' billing and cooing, fondling of the female breast and kissing appear to derive from suckling and from parent-infant "kiss feeding" (Eibl-Eibesfeldt 1989, 138). Chimpanzees are especially likely to kiss—a signal that observably calms and reassures—during reconciliations (Trivers 1985). Mutual gaze is a feature of lovemaking in humans (Stern 1977), as it is in copulation of bonobos (Savage-Rumbaugh and Wilkerson 1978). In humans, love songs and courtship speech use childish words and refer to childish things to create and display intimacy—e.g., use of the familiar forms in language otherwise reserved for speaking to children; popular songs that express sentiments like "Cuddle up a little closer" or "You're my baby." Smiling, which is first developed ontogenetically between infant and mother, becomes in adult social interactions a universal sign of appeasement and affiliation, along with other facial expressions and movements common in mother-infant interchange—looking at the other, eyebrow raising and flashing, and bobbing the head up and down (see also the discussion in Schelde and Hertz 1994). Many adult mammals assume infantile postures and make infantile sounds to deflect aggression.

I would like to suggest that the biologically endowed temporal and other prosodic sensitivities and competencies of mother-infant interaction (described above) were found by evolving human groups to be emotionally affecting and functionally effective when used (and when further shaped and elaborated) in culturally created ceremonial rituals where they served a similar purpose—to attune or synchronize, emotionally conjoin, and enculturate the participants. These unifying and pleasurable elements of babytalk formed a sort of behavioral reservoir from which human cultures could appropriate appealing and compelling components for communal ceremonial rituals that similarly promoted affiliation and congruence in adult social life. These features were then developed, culturally codified (and, in some societies, even emancipated) as "music," as satisfactions in their own right, apart from ceremonial contexts.

Vocal Play and Imitation

There is convincing evidence in studies of infant and child development that the motivation to appropriate and elaborate prosodic (as well as lexical) features of language exists universally in humans—in children's vocal play. The earliest vocal play in infants, after eight weeks, when there is some control of respiration and the vocal tract, consists of prolonging sounds (Papousek et al. 1984). Between four and six months, there are more substantial vowel-like sounds, bilabial trills, squealing, and growling (Locke 1993,176). True babbling begins between six and ten months of age (Oller and Eilers 1988), and occurs more often when infants are alone than when they are with others.

Children spontaneously initiate speech activities—sound play, word play, distorting speech, and monologues—that are unlike any shown to them by their parents. Even Kaluli children in the southern highlands of Papua New Guinea, where parents consider such activity to interfere with proper development of language and terminate it whenever they hear it, manipulate pitch, prosody, and timing in their sound play, and invite turntaking (Schieffelin 1990, 99)—like children everywhere.

Such sound play is surely "musical." Indeed, one could argue that the differences between music and the prosody of spoken language are only in degree of elaboration (including sustaining, repeating, and patterning tones—i.e., exaggeration and regularization reminiscent of the ritualization process).

Kartomi (1991) has studied the spontaneous improvised musical phrases uttered by children while they concentrate on their play, and claims that this "play song" is distinct from the lullabies and nursery rhymes or songs created by adults for children. Rather, she says, it is created by children for use in their own adultless play world (53). Such "musical doodling" is ephemeral. The few improvised songs that are remembered and adopted into the corpus of established children's songs tend to be those whose texts express a memorable experience of pleasure, pain, fear, solidarity, or derision, and these songs are normally sung when playing games, eating together, teasing each other, and on occasions demanding solidarity with each other (62). Even these more stable songs include an element of improvisation. While rhythm and meter are usually primary and fixed, the melody and form are secondary and variable. Such a propensity in children suggests that ancestral adults could well have followed a similar course in ritualizing "natural" vocalizations at times of strong emotion and when solidarity was displayed or required.

The readiness of children to imitate adults and each other is of course well known as an attribute of sociability and, ultimately, educability (Bruner 1972). Imitation in adults also has a bonding effect (Bavelas et al. 1987); inviting a partner to imitative behavior by starting some action oneself or using imitation to express accord and thus a readiness for group play is a principle of many bonding rituals. Doing things together confirms a sense of unity (Eibl-Eibesfeldt 1989, 510).

Ceremonies, Music, and Babytalk

There are, of course, countless examples in premodern and modern societies of the use of musical means (singing, chanting, drumming, instrumental playing, rhythmic movement) in ritual ceremonies. These may be dyadic like mother-infant engagement, using alternation and imitation as a way to create or express understanding and unity, or they may be concurrent, with all individuals performing actions together and thereby creating and confirming unity (e.g., Basso 1985). I have found examples too numerous to mention here of culturally derived ceremonies whose structural and expressive elements resemble those of mother-infant engagement and which also acculturate and unify. Even societies that are poor in material culture or the visual arts still engage in musical behavior.[6]

Besides using musical elements, many human rituals of appeasement or social solidarity resemble infant-like behavior. The Bedouin ghinnawa ("little song") is an improvised poem that employs metaphorical terms evocative of childhood to reveal in a socially acceptable way sentiments that are otherwise prohibited (Abu-Lughod 1986). The song voice used in the *gisalo* ceremony of the Kaluli uses sounds associated with a child whining for food to make listeners feel sorrow and pity, and thereby reinforces cultural themes of reciprocity and obligation (Feld 1982).

The many structural and functional resemblances to be seen among babytalk, ceremonial ritual, and music are, I believe, neither accidental or spurious. They suggest not only an evolutionary relationship, as I have outlined, but argue for the existence of an underlying amodal neural propensity in the human species to respond—cognitively and emotionally—to certain kinds of dynamic temporal patterns produced by other humans in contexts of affiliation. An evolved propensity for relationship is thus at least as robust as the "self-interest" that has to date been the primary focus of sociobiological concern.

Works Cited

Abu-Lughod, L.

1986 *Veiled Sentiments: Honor and Poetry in a Bedouin Society.* Berkeley: University of California Press.

Anderson, R.

1990 *Calliope's Sisters: A Comparative Study of Philosophies of Art.* Englewood Cliffs, NJ: Prentice-Hall.

Basso, E.

1985 *A Musical View of the Universe: Kalapalo Rhythmic and Ritual Performance*. Philadelphia: University of Pennsylvania Press.

Bavelas, J. B., A. Black, C. R. Lemery and J. Mullett.

1987 "Motor Mimicry As Primitive Empathy." In N. Eisenberg and J. Strayer, eds., *Empathy and Its Development.* Cambridge: Cambridge University Press, pp. 317-38.

Beauquier, Charles

1865 *Philosophie de la musique*. Paris: Bailliere Freres.

Beebe, B.

1986 "Mother-Infant Mutual Influence and Precursors of Self- and Object-representations." In J. Masling, ed., *Empirical Studies of Psychoanalytic Theories*, Vol. 2. Hillsdale, NJ: Erlbaum, pp. 27-48.

Beebe, B. and L. Gerstman

1984 "A Method of Defining 'Packages' of Maternal Stimulation and Their Functional Significance for the Infant with Mother and Stranger." *International Journal of Behavioral Development* 7:423-40.

Beebe, B. and F. M. Lachmann

1988 "The Contribution of Mother-Infant Mutual Influence to the Origins of Self- and Object-Representations." *Psychoanalytic Psychology* 5 (4):305-37.

Blonder, L. X., D. Bowers, and K. M. Heilman

1991 "The Role of the Right Hemisphere in Emotional Communication." *Brain* 114:1115-27.

Bolinger, D.

1986 *Intonation and Its Parts: Melody in Spoken English*. Palo Alto: Stanford University Press.

Borod, J. C., Koff, E., and H. S. Caron

1983 "Right Hemisphere Specialization for the Expression and Appreciation of Emotion: A Focus on the Face." In E. Perecman, ed., *Cognitive Processing in the Right Hemisphere*. New York: Academic Press, pp. 83-110.

Bowlby, J.

1969 *Attachment and Loss*. Vol. 1. *Attachment*. London: Hogarth.

1973 *Attachment and Loss*. Vol. 2. *Separation, Anxiety and Anger*. London: Hogarth.

Brazelton, T. B.

1977 "Implications of Infant Development among the Mayan Indians of Mexico." In Leiderman, Tulken, and Rosenfeld, eds., pp. 151-87.

Bruner, J.

1972 "Nature and Uses of Immaturity." *American Psychologist* 27:687-708.

Bücher, K.

1899 *Arbeit und Rhythmus*. 2d ed. Leipzig: B. G. Teubner. (original publication 1896.)

Chisholm, J. S.

1983 *Navaho Infancy: An Ethological Study of Child Development*. New York: Aldine de Gruyter.

Condon, W. S.

1984 "Communication and Empathy." In J. Lichtenberg, M. Bernstein, and D. Silver, eds., *Empathy*, Vols. 1 and 2. Hillsdale, NJ: Erlbaum.

Condon, W. S., and L. Sander

1974 "Neonate Movement is Synchronized with Adult Speech: Interactional Participation and Language Acquisition." *Science* 183:99-101.

Crown, C.L.

1991 "Coordinated Interpersonal Timing of Vision and Voice As a Function of Interpersonal Attraction." *Journal of Language and Social Psychology* 10:29-46.

Darwin, C.

1871 *The Descent of Man, and Selection in Relation to Sex*. London: John Murray.

Dixon, S., E. Tronick, C. Keefer, and T. B. Brazelton

1981 "Mother-Infant Interaction among the Gusii of Kenya." In Field, et al., 149-68.

Donald, Merlin

1991 *Origins of the Modern Mind: Three Stages in the Evolution of Culture and Cognition*. Cambridge, MA: Harvard University Press.

Dore, J.

1983 "Feeling, Form, and Intention in the Baby's Transition to Language." In R. M. Golinkoff, ed., *The Transition from Prelinguistic to Linguistic Communication*. Hillsdale, NJ: Erlbaum.

Dubois, C.

1944 *The People of Alor*. Minneapolis: University of Minnesota Press.

Eibl-Eibesfeldt, I.

1989 *Human Ethology*. New York: Aldine de Gruyter.

1975 *Ethology: The Biology of Behavior*. 2d ed. Translated by Erich Klinghammer. New York: Holt, Rinehart and Winston.

Eimas, P. D.

1984 "Infant Competence and the Acquisition of Language." In D. Caplan, A. Roch Lecours, and A. Smith, eds., *Biological Perspectives on Language*. Cambridge, MA: MIT Press, pp. 109-29.

Feld, S.

1974 "Linguistic Models in Ethnomusicology." *Ethnomusicology* 18 (2):197-218.

1982 *Sound and Sentiment: Birds, Weeping, Poetics and Song in Kaluli Expression*. Philadelphia: University of Pennsylvania Press.

Fernald, A.

1984 "The Perceptual and Affective Salience of Mothers' Speech to Infants." In L. Feagans, C. Garvey, and R. Golinkoff, eds., *The Origins and Growth of Communication*. Norwood, NJ: Ablex, pp. 5-29.

1985 "Four-Month-Old Infants Prefer to Listen to Motherese." *Infant Behavior and Development* 8:181-95.

1989 "Intonation and Communicative Intent in Mothers' Speech to Infants: Is the Melody the Message?" *Child Development* 60:1497-1510.

Field, T.M., A.M. Sostek, P. Vietze, and P. H. Leiderman, eds.

1981 *Culture and Early Interactions*. Hillsdale, N J: Erlbaum.

Firth, R.

1973 "Tikopia Art and Society." In A. Forge, ed., *Primitive Art and Society*. London: Oxford University Press, pp. 25-48.

Geist, V.

1978 *Life Strategies, Human Evolution, Environmental Design*. New York: Springer. Greiser, D. L., and P. K. Kuhl.

1988 "Maternal Speech to Infants in a Tonal Language: Support for Universal Prosodic Features in Motherese." *Developmental Psychology* 24:14-20.

Hall-Craggs, J.

1969 "The Aesthetic Content of Bird Song." In R.A. Hinde, ed., Bird Vocalizations. Cambridge: Cambridge University Press.

Hamilton, A.

1981 *Nature and Nurture: Aboriginal Child-Rearing in North-Central Arnhem Land.* Canberra: Australian Institute of Aboriginal Studies.

Hofer, M. A.

1990 "Early Symbolic Processes: Hard Evidence from a Soft Place." In R. A. Glick and S. Bones, eds., *Pleasure beyond the Pleasure Principle*. New Haven: Yale University Press, pp. 55-78.

Hutcheson, F.

1973 *Inquiry concerning Beauty, Order, Harmony, Design*, Edited by Peter Kivy. The Hague: Martinus Nijhoff. (originally published 1725.)

Kartomi, M. J.

1991 "Musical Improvisations of Children at Play." *The World of Music* 33 (3):53-65.

Konner, M.

1977 "Infancy among the Kalahari Desert San." In Leiderman, Tulkin, and Rosenfeld, eds., pp. 287-328.

Krumhansl, C. L.

1992 "Grouping Processes in Infants' Music Perception." In J. Sundberg, L. Nord, and R. Carl, eds., *Grouping in Music*. Stockholm: Royal Swedish Academy of Music.

Kugiumutzakis, Giannis

1993 "Intersubjective Vocal Imitation in Early Mother-Infant Interaction." In J. Nadel and L. Camaioni, eds., *New Perspectives in Early Communicative Development*. London: Routledge.

Lacépède, Comte de [Bernard German Etienne de la Ville sur Illou.]

1785 *La Poétique de la musique*. 2 vols. Paris.

Leiderman, P. H., S. R. Tulkin, and A. Rosenfeld, eds.

1977 *Culture and Infancy*. New York: Academic Press.

Lewis, M., and P. Ban

1977 "Variance and Invariance in the Mother-Infant Interaction: A Cross-Cultural Study." In Leiderman, Tulkin and Rosenfeld, eds., pp. 329-55.

Locke, J. L.

1993 *The Child's Path to Spoken Language*. Cambridge, MA: Harvard University Press.

1996 "Why Do Infants Begin to Talk? Language as an unintended consequence." *Journal of Child Language* 23:251-68.

Luria, A. R.

1980 *Higher Cortical Functions*. Translated by Basil Haigh, 2d ed. New York: Basic Books.

Lynch, M. P., D. Kimbrough-Oller, M.L. Steffens, and E. H. Buder

1995 "Phrasing in Prelinguistic Vocalizations." *Developmental Psychobiology* 28 (1):3-25.

Macdonald, K.

1992 "Warmth As a Developmental Construct: an Evolutionary Analysis." *Child Development* 63 (4):753-73.

McLaughlin, T.

1970 *Music and Communication*. London: Faber and Faber.

McNeill, D.

1992 *Hand and Mind: What Gestures Reveal about the Brain*. Chicago: University of Chicago Press.

Malatesta, C. Z., and C. E. Izard.

1984 "The Ontogenesis of Human Social Signals: From Biological Imperative to Symbol Utilization." In N. A. Fox and R. J. Davidson, eds., *Affective Development: A Psychological Perspective*. Hillsdale, NJ: Erlbaum.

Meltzoff, A.N. and M. H. Moore

1977 "Imitation of Facial and Manual Gestures by Human Neonates." *Science* 219:1347-49.

Morelli, G. A.

1994 *Developmental Psychology* (July)

Morikawa, H., N. Shand, and Y. Kosawa

1988 "Maternal Speech to Prelingual Infants in Japan and the United States: Relationships Among Functions, Forms and Referent." *Journal of Child Language* 15:237-56.

Morton, E. S. and J. Page

1992 *Animal Talk: Science and the Voices of Nature*. New York: Random House.

North, R.

1959 *Roger North on Music*. Edited by John Wilson. London: Novello.

Oller, D.K. and R.E. Eilers

1988 "The Role of Audition in Infant Babbling." *Child Development* 59:441-49.

Papousek, H., and M. Papousek

1979 "Early Ontogeny of Human Social Interaction: Its Biological Roots and Social Dimensions," in L. von Cranach, L. et al., eds., *Human Ethology*. Cambridge: Cambridge University Press, pp. 456-78.

1981a "Musical Elements in the Infant's Vocalization: Their Significance for Communication, Cognition, and Creativity," in L. P. Lipsitt and C. K. Rovee-Collier, eds., *Advances in Infancy Research*. Vol. I. Norwood, N J: Ablex, pp. 163-224.

1981b "Musikalische Ausdrucks-elemente der Sprache und ihre Modifikation in der 'Ammensprache.'" *Sozialpädiatrie in Praxis und Klinik* 3:6, 294-96.

Papousek, M., H. Papousek, and B. J. Harris

1984 "The Emergence of Play in Parent-Infant Interactions." In D. Gorlitz and J. F. Wohlwill, eds., *Curiosity, Imagination, and Play: On the Development of Spontaneous Cognitive and Motivational Processes*. Hillsdale, NJ: Erlbaum, pp. 214-46.

Papousek. M., H. Papousek, and M. H. Bornstein

1985 "The Naturalistic Vocal Environment of Young Infants: On the Significance of Homogeneity and Variability in Parental Speech." In T. M. Field and N. A. Fox, eds., *Social Perception in Infants*. Norwood, NJ: Ablex, pp. 269-97.

Papousek, M., H. Papousek, and D. Symmes

1991 "The Meanings of Melodies in Motherese in Tone and Stress Languages." *Infant Behavior and Development* 14:415-40.

Peery, J.C.

1980 "Neonate-Adult Head Movement." *Developmental Psychology* 16 (4):245-50.

Pöppel, E.
1985 *Mindworks: Time and Conscious Experience*. Boston: Harcourt Brace Jovanovich.

Ross, E. D.
1981 "The Aprosodias: Functional-Anatomical Organization of the Affective Components of Language in the Right Hemisphere." *Archives of Neurology* 38:561-69.
1983 "Right Hemisphere Lesions in Disorders of Affective Language." In A. Kertesz, ed., *Localization in Neuropsychology*. New York: Academic Press, pp. 493-508.
1993 "Nonverbal Aspects of Language." *Neurologic Clinics* 11:9-23.

Ross, E. and M. M. Mesulam
1979 "Dominant Language Functions of the Right Hemisphere? Prosody and Emotional Gesturing." *Archives of Neurology* 36:144-48.

Rowbotham, J. F.
1893 *A History of Music to the Time of the Troubadours*. London: R. Bentley. (originally published 1885.)

Sachs, C.
1977 *The Wellsprings of Music*. New York: Da Capo. (Original 1962.)

Savage-Rumbaugh, S., and B.Wilkerson
1978 "Socio-Sexual Behavior in Pan paniscus and Pan troglodytes." *Journal of Human Evolution* 7:327-44.

Schelde, T., and M. Hertz
1994 "Ethology and Psychotherapy." *Ethology and Sociobiology* 15(5, 6):383-92.

Schieffelin, B.
1986 "Teasing and Shaming in Kaluli Children's Interactions." In Schieffelin and Ochs, eds., pp. 165-81.
1990 *The Give and Take of Everyday Life*. New York: Cambridge University Press.

Schieffelin, B., and E. Ochs, eds.
1986 *Language Socialization across Cultures*. Cambridge: Cambridge University Press.

Schore, A. N.

1994 *Affect Regulation and the Origin of the Self: The Neurobiology of Emotional Development*. Hillsdale, NJ: Erlbaum.

Spencer, H.

1880-2 "The Aesthetic Sentiments." Chap. 9 in *Principles of Psychology*, 2d ed. London: Williams and Norgate.

1928 "On the Origin and Function of Music," in *Essays on Education*. London: Dent, pp. 310-30. (Original 1857.)

Stern, D.

1977 *The First Relationship: Mother and Infant*. Cambridge, MA: Harvard University Press.

1985 *The Interpersonal World of the Infant*. New York: Basic Books.

Stern, D.N., S. Spieker, R. K. Barnett, and K. MacKain

1983 "The Prosody of Maternal Speech: Infant Age and Context Related Changes." *Journal of Child Language* 10:1-15.

Stumpf, C.

1911 *Die Anfänge der Musik.* Leipzig.

Suliteanu, G.

1979 "The Role of Songs for Children in the Formation of Musical Perception," in J. Blacking and J. W. Kealiinohomoku, eds., *The Performing Arts: Music and Dance*. The Hague: Mouton, pp. 205-19.

Tinbergen, N.

1952 "Derived Activities: Their Causation, Biological Significance, Origin, and Emancipation during Evolution." *Quarterly Review of Biology* 27 (1):1-32.

Toda, S., A. Fogel and M. Kawai

1990 "Maternal Speech to Three-Month-Old Infants in the United States and Japan." *Journal of Child Language* 17:279-94.

Trehub, S. E.

1993 "Temporal Auditory Processing in Infancy." In P. Tallal, A. M. Galaburda, R. R. Llinas, and C. von Euler, eds., *Temporal Information Processing in the Nervous System*. Vol. 682. New York: Annals of the New York Academy of Sciences.

Trehub, S. E., L. J. Trainor and A. M. Unyk
1993 "Music and Speech Processing in the First Year of Life." *Advances in Child Development and Behavior* 24:1-35.

Trevarthen, C.
1974 "Conversations with a Two-Month-Old." *New Scientist*, 2 May:230-5.
1977 "Descriptive Analyses of Infant Communication Behavior." In H. R. Schaffer, ed., *Studies in Mother-Infant Interaction: The Loch Lomond Symposium*. London: Academic Press, pp. 227-70.
1979a "Communication and Cooperation in Early Infancy: A Description of Primary Intersubjectivity." In M. Bullowa, ed., *Before Speech: The Beginning of Human Communication*. London: Cambridge University Press, pp. 321-47.
1979b "Instincts for Human Understanding and for Cultural Cooperation: Their Development in Infancy." In von L. Cranach, et al., pp. 530-71.
1984 "Emotions in Infancy: Regulators of Contact and Relationships with Persons." In K. Scherer and P. Ekman, eds., *Approaches to Emotion*. Hillsdale, NJ: Erlbaum, pp. 129-57.
1987 "Brain Development." In R. L. Gregory, ed., *The Oxford Companion to the Mind*. Oxford: Oxford University Press, pp. 101-10.
1990 "Growth and Education in the Hemispheres." In C. Trevarthen, ed., *Brain Circuits and Functions of the Mind*. Cambridge: Cambridge University Press, pp. 334-63.
1992 "An Infant's Motives for Speaking and Thinking in the Culture." In A. H. Wold, ed., *The Dialogical Alternatives: Towards a Theory of Language and Mind*. (Festschrift for Ragnar Rommetveit.) Oslo/Oxford: Scandinavian University Press/Oxford University Press, pp. 99-137.
1994 "The Self Born in Intersubjectivity: The Psychology of an Infant Communicating." In U. Neisser, ed., *Ecological and Interpersonal Knowledge of the Self*. New York: Cambridge University Press.

Trevarthen, C., and K. J. Aitken

1994 "Brain Development, Infant Communication and Empathy Disorders: Intrinsic Factors in Child Mental Health." *Development and Psychopathology* 6:597-633.

Trivers, R.

1985 *Social Evolution*. Menlo Park: Benjamin/Cummings.

Tucker, D. M.

1992 "Developing Emotions and Cortical Networks." In M. R. Gunnar and C. A. Nelson, eds., *Minnesota Symposia on Child Psychology*. Vol. 24, *Developmental Behavioral Neuroscience*. Hillsdale, NJ: Erlbaum, pp. 75-128.

Turner, F.

1985 "The Neural Lyre: Poetic Meter, the Brain, and Time." *In Natural Classicism: Essays on Literature and Science*. Charlottesville: University Press of Virginia, pp. 61-108.

von Cranach, M., K. Foppa, W. Lepenies, and D. Ploog, eds.

1979 *Human Ethology*. Cambridge: Cambridge University Press.

Wallaschek, R.

1970 *Primitive Music: An Inquiry into the Origin and Development of Music, Songs, Instruments, Dances and Pantomimes of Savage Races*. New York: Da Capo. (originally published 1893.)

Notes

1. This essay grew out of an earlier conference paper, "Music as a Human Behavior: An Hypothesis of Evolutionary Origin and Function," presented to the Human Behavior and Evolution Society in August 1990, and, as "The Evolutionary Origin and Significance of Music," to the European Sociobiological Society in August 1993. It was expanded for presentation to the Committee on the Biological Foundations of Aesthetics at the twentieth International Conference on the Unity of the Sciences, August 1995, and revised for publication here.
2. Interestingly, too, vowels are processed in the right hemisphere, while consonants are processed in the left (Luria 1980). Consonants, of

course, mark the semantically meaningful separations of morphemes and words; it is vowels that are sustained or otherwise elaborated dynamically (and expressively) in music.

3. Affect contagion is a basic biological tendency among highly evolved social species (Malatesta and Izard 1984), and has understandable evolutionary importance. The mother-infant bond may be viewed as the prototype for intense emotional unity.
4. Stern (1985) has refined his earlier analyses of mother-infant interaction to indicate the importance of attuning by "matching"—e.g., (a) in intensity (as when loudness of the mother's voice matches an abrupt movement of the baby's arm or leg), (b) in contour (accelerating effort by the baby is matched by accelerating vocalization by the mother), (c) in temporal beat (nodding the head in rhythm with the baby's kicking), (d) in shape (moving the head up and down as the baby moves its arms), (e) in rhythm, and (f) in duration.
5. Eibl-Eibesfeldt (1989, 144) points out that wherever brood case exists, there is also affective behavior between adults; where it does not—even where the creature is gregarious (as in iguanas)—there is no affiliative or contact behavior in adults, and communication is restricted to display.
6. E.g., the Tikopia in the South Seas have relatively undeveloped plastic arts, but their music, poetry, and dance display a range of variation and elaborate articulation with many nuances of form and expression (Firth 1973). The people of Alor pay little attention to material objects but have dances with versification; older men play gongs of different sizes in an "orchestra" where new rhythms or set patterns may be experimented with (Dubois 1944). Hunter-gatherer groups like Australian Aborigines, Kalahari Bushmen, and Ba-Benjellé Pygmies have highly developed musical traditions: song, dance, and poetry are an integral part of their lives (Anderson 1990, Sarno 1993). (The Aborigines, of course, have a rich tradition of visually elaborating artifacts and themselves.)

In Search of Texture

Koen DePryck

Questions concerning the relation between mind and body in general and between mind and brain more specifically are obviously not new. However, recent developments in neuroscience and related disciplines are now suggesting answers that are not only scientific but that also, as Patricia Churchland puts it, "are as much part of anyone's philosophical aspirations, be they ancient or modern, untutored or scholarly, as any quest there is" (Churchland 1989, 10). Nonetheless, the divide between two fundamentally different approaches very much remains. Different forms of dualism claim a more or less intimate connection between a physical brain and irreducibly mental phenomena. Monistic theories, on the other hand, have tried to dispense with either one in favor of the other.

My approach to the fundamental question raised in this volume—"does a fundamental relation exist between neurophysical and neurochemical processes on the one hand and aesthetic judgment (or preference) on the other?"—hinges on time (or, for that matter, evolution) as a complex and constitutive rather than as a purely sequential and descriptive device. A binary divide between body and brain has more to do with an essentially anthropocentric stand and with the history of our understanding of reality than with an evolving reality as a whole.

Human beings are a rather new phenomenon in this universe, even though we cannot and should not be detached from our evolutionary background, dating back as far as the Big Bang. A monistic account of our existence holds either that humans are "caused" by their past or that somehow everything that preceded humans really only existed to make humans possible (meaning that humans in a sense "caused" their past). A dualistic account claims that even though humans might not have existed without their past, they are indeed fundamentally and irreducibly new, qualitatively different from everything preceding.

If one is to take evolution seriously, it should not be confined to the arbitrary time slices that are apparently important to us. The questions relating to the body and mind are part of a much larger philosophical debate on causality and change in time. We have to establish—or so it seems—if what exists at any given point in time can be traced back through its evolutionary history or whether genuinely novel appearances have a place in an evolving reality. When asking that question, we are guided by a concept of causality that assumes that all causal processes in nature are continuous. Quantum physics, however, leaves us no option but to accept that time and space exist in "discrete packets," so that the very concept of a continuous, "smooth" causality must be abandoned in favor of a probabilistic version. Among the many far-reaching implications of this revolutionary shift in how we perceive causal relations—a shift that has not as yet penetrated our intuitions about natural processes—we must accept that evolutionary causal relations too may be of a statistical nature.

There is a sense in which not only quantum but also traditional causal relations appear discontinuous. As catastrophe theory has illustrated over and over again, a continuous change of even a single variable of a system may lead to a qualitative jump, a collapse. A catastrophe, in this context, is an event whereby a continuously varying input yields a discontinuous change when a critical point is reached. It should be noted, however, that the continuously changing input is, from a quantum perspective, discontinuous to the extent that time and space are discontinuous. Furthermore, from Einstein's theory of relativity we know that any interaction between separate entities is subject to the condition that these interactions do not exceed the velocity of light. That means that two regions of space-time may perfectly well be causally independent, whether causal is taken in a traditional or in a statistical and probabilistic sense. In other words: causal "gaps" or "barriers" are perfectly possible.

Is the mind-body dichotomy the expression of just such a gap? Before we even attempt to answer that question, it is important to note that many scientists would be highly reluctant to use these concepts outside the restricted context in which they were developed. Some would even hesitate to apply the mathematical concept of a catastrophe to the behavior of a people in revolt or to the breakdown of a person under great pressure. To those scientists, the domain of catastrophe is strictly physical and any other use could at best be illustrative. That being acknowledged, the question remains. Let us rephrase it in the terms of the subject of this volume, the (causal) relation between neurophysical and neurochemical processes on the one hand and aesthetic judgment on the other.

What would happen if we were to try to define or even just to understand aesthetic experience and aesthetic judgment not in terms of preceding causal neurophysical or neurochemical elements but in terms of our cultural accomplishments, *in casu* in terms of the contemplation of art? We would face rather difficult questions about the nature of art. Eventually, we might end up begging the question, defining art in function of the absence or presence of an aesthetic experience. In other words, the questions generated by the apparent gaps between levels of description remain essentially the same, regardless of the specificity of the levels involved. Without having to turn to institutional and other (primarily sociological) theories that make art and aesthetics subject to the whims of fashion, and without stretching the realm of aesthetic experience to include almost every single everyday experience that comes to mind, we may avoid the impasse by dramatically increasing the realm in which art and aesthetics operate. The alternative to binary and unilateral relations between levels of description that I explore and advocate here is one in which art and aesthetic judgment are intrinsic to many evolutionary changes, and not just to that part of evolution that coincides with our human existence. Obviously, this is a much stronger contention than the claim that a biological layer is required for our aesthetic judgment (or any other human feature or even humanity itself) to exist. The latter (weaker) claim is at the heart of Searle's rejection of artificial intelligence on the basis that life—in a biological sense—is a prerequisite for intelligence, even if we accept, as he most certainly does, that life itself is just a specific organization of lower-level elements. I believe Searle is basically right. But at the same time, this argument seems to indicate that some "new" life—or "artificial life," if that is what it should be called—is not in principle impossible. Even if "life" is a prerequisite for intelligence, "artificial intelligence" should not be in principle excluded—albeit, perhaps, based on "artificial life." Evolution does not follow a single path from an absolute origin in the past to an absolute objective somewhere in the future. On the biological level, too, different species have evolved simultaneously and parallel to each other, leading to similar but nevertheless distinct features. If the notion of evolution is extended beyond the realm of biology and if the notion of evolution is itself subject to evolutionary changes due to the reflexivity of the process, there is no reason why we should not acknowledge at least the possibility of similar parallel developments within non-biological systems. When looking at possible predecessors of our human aesthetic judgment throughout the history of the universe, we consider human aesthetic judgment as part of a tradition—as old as reality itself but perhaps "older" than time—of non-deterministic decision procedures.

The necessary conditions for human art and human aesthetic judgment not only to function but merely to exist are the very conditions for non-trivial existence as such. Neither in a reality that is completely deterministic nor in a reality that is completely arbitrary is there room for art or for aesthetics.

In a reality that is totally deterministic—in which everything that exists follows with necessity from an initial formula—there is no room for aesthetic judgment. In fact, in such a world, no judgment whatsoever would be called for. Judgment would at best be an illusion. But we can rest assured: We know that indeterminacy is an essential feature of reality. On the other hand, in a reality that is completely arbitrary or random, there is no room for aesthetic judgment either. In such a reality, we would not be able to make a cognitively or ontologically meaningful distinction between "normal" and "aesthetic" judgments. In such a world, the notion of judgment would be completely trivial. But this time also, we do not need to panic: Some phenomena are obviously stable (Scissors are dangerous). The search for foundations of human aesthetics only makes sense in a reality that is neither totally open nor totally closed. I will argue that not only is this a condition for aesthetic judgment to be non-trivial, it is the very essence of aesthetics. In other words, aesthetic judgment only makes sense in a reality that has aesthetics at its very core. That also means that our aesthetic judgment, rather than setting us apart from everything else in the universe, connects us to everything else. When we exercise aesthetic judgment, we add one more layer to the already complex texture of reality.

A good place to start a reflection on the biological foundations of aesthetics is Darwin's distinction between sexual and natural selection, the former being "the struggle between the males for the possession of the females," resulting not in "death to the unsuccessful competitor but few or no offspring" (Darwin 1859, 136); the latter, the "preservation of favorable variations and the rejection of injurious variations" (Darwin 1859, 131). In the same breath, Darwin excludes from the impact of natural selection those variations that are neither useful nor injurious, variations that he calls fluctuating elements. This restriction immediately opens a field of options for selections without great importance (at least not from an evolutionary biological perspective), the kind of disinterested choices and judgments that one finds in notions such as *art for art's sake* or *beauty for beauty's sake*—philosophically founded by Immanuel Kant in the eighteenth century but with traces going as far back as the Hellenistic period. Do these fluctuating elements perhaps constitute the domain in which aesthetic choices are operative? Could we possibly define the cultural level as rooted in these fluctuating elements?

A specific interpretation of sexual selection bears on the notion of good taste choice as opposed to good sense choice. It implies taste as a driving force behind selective advantages. Darwin himself insisted on calling good taste aesthetic, which he construed as a choice of beauty for beauty's sake (Darwin 1959, 371). Until late in this century, this embarrassed many Darwinians, many of whom either stressed the importance of natural over sexual selection or denied sexual selection altogether.

However, as Helena Cronin points out, looking at Darwinian theory as primarily dealing with the replication of genes dissolves the distinction between "adaptive" natural selection and "non-adaptive" sexual selection. "Adaptations," she contends, "are for the benefit of genes of which those adaptations are the phenotypic effects. Adaptations may not be prosaic or worthy; genes can further their destiny as much by apparent ostentation as by strict austerity. And they may not be of benefit to their bearers, let alone to the species as a whole" (Cronin 1992, 292). At least the kind of aesthetic elements that are implied by Darwin appear as novel elements in their own right on the level of organization or the level of complexity of the species. On previous levels, e.g., the level of the genes, aesthetic elements disappear in the pool of elements and principles operative at those levels.

The obvious result of this approach is that it ultimately incorporates the aesthetic in the utilitarian and economical views on adaptation that are at the core of standard Darwinian thought on the subject.

If one accepts the strictly utilitarian agenda of evolution, there is nothing against a utilitarian view on aesthetics. The question is whether we should accept that agenda. Even stronger: can we accept that agenda as the single driving force behind evolution? If we do, how are we to understand it in the light of the conditions for non-trivial existence indicated above?

Ultimately, the utilitarian agenda must be specified as being underdetermined: there is no way that we—or evolution—can know for sure that a specific change will indeed, on some time scale, be a solution to a problem. "Problem," in this context, refers to a situation in which some action is required—the sanction being the violation of the conditions for existence—but in which no guaranteed solution can be calculated or otherwise devised.

The hidden teleology behind the utilitarian evolutionary program—in biology as well as on the other levels of complexity but also, and perhaps even more important, in the evolution from one level of complexity to the next—is a negative one, perhaps better referred to as a drive to avoid certain states—later in this paper I will specify those as paradoxical—than as a drive to reach certain goals.

The investigation of the biological and evolutionary foundation for aesthetic judgment, while most certainly meaningful in its own right, gains its full significance against a more comprehensive background of questions related to the interaction among levels of complexity in general. This works both ways. On the one hand, the concept of evolution is no longer confined to biology. It has penetrated all the sciences as well as the arts. On the other hand, the neurobiological processes involved in the aesthetics of vision turn out to be perfect metaphors for the relations among levels of complexity in general. To quote R.L. Gregory, "'I see what you what you mean' is not a puerile pun, but indicates a connection which is very real."

In this chapter, I will focus on texture as a core metaphor, which embraces but also supersedes the hierarchy metaphor that has become since the end of the nineteenth century one of the most powerful research paradigms. The hierarchy metaphor, in order to be sufficiently sophisticated, required further specification in terms of the simultaneity of bottom-up and top-down processes. In the case of the mind-body problem, this leads to the need to integrate such apparently extremely dissimilar disciplines or programs as Freudian psychoanalysis and neurologic microgenesis—to integrate the language of id, ego, and superego with the language of limbic processes.

In a sense, the texture metaphor gets back to the surface-oriented models that the hierarchy-based approach tried to move away from. In its topological aspects, however, it preserves the dynamical aspects of hierarchies. The city no longer simply rules its surroundings but becomes part of the landscape.

I suggest that aesthetic judgment functions at the boundaries between what is stable and what leads to change. Aesthetic judgment must thus be considered as an important element in planning ahead on the topological map that is used to integrate past experience, and present experience, and to decide on paths to be followed in the future.

These three elements are essential in all planning, regardless of whom or what the planning is for, and in the anticipation of both foreseen and unforeseeable events (MacLean 1991). They are therefore also important in our teleological project, however underdetermined it may be—or precisely because it is underdetermined.

Our topological map of the past is highly selective. It is estimated that of all the information available to our consciousness (by itself a small fraction of all the sensory input) no more than one per cent is stored in long-term memory. And of that small portion, large parts are later forgotten or at least become no longer available for conscious retrieval. At the other end of the series of steps in memorization, our sensory memory can hold its enormous content for no longer than fractions of a second. The product of time and amount of information appears as relatively constant.

The same applies to our maps of the future. We foresee events on different time scales. In the immediate future, we foresee the path of a basketball as well as the path of our own body as we jump up to pluck the ball out of the air. This is quite an astonishing accomplishment, especially as we compare it to a frog that snaps directly at a fly without any kind of calculation. The cerebellar nuclei—not very developed in the case of the frog—appear essential in the corrective controls involved in these processes (MacLean, 1991).

On the long term, we plan tomorrow's lunch, our next holiday, and perhaps even our retirement. In these cases, the neurophysiological elements involved are less clearly defined. This may be a simple case of still incomplete knowledge but it may also be that the neurophysiological elements are by nature not amenable to being pinned down. The planning itself takes much longer to carry out. Details escape from our attention. Furthermore, our very plans feed back into our current situation. Either way, dreams may come true or never materialize, precisely because we had them in the first place.

The picture that emerges is the following: Around the present, a region of dense information exists, in terms of our recall of the recent past, in terms of the near future, and in terms of a few possible alternatives for our present position. The farther we move from the present, the less detail we can provide about our experienced past and our projected future. Clusters of increased detail may exist, but it is reasonable to assume that they will not constantly be in the center of our attention.

The emerging picture, in short, is one of great depth rather than extension. Its horizon is what Kant described as the *horizon of knowledge.* He said that it was "die Beurteilung und Bestimmung dessen, was der Mensch wissen kann, was er wissen darf, und was er wissen soll": The investigation and determination of what we can know, what we may know, and what we should know (Kant Logik:A54).

Contrary to popular belief, the perception of depth is not contingent upon stereoscopic vision. Monocular devices to perceive depth include relative size, interposition, linear perspective and focal depth. Binocular depth-perception relies on the convergence of the optical axes that result from the disjunctive eye movements. The closer an object, the greater the disparity between the two retinal images.

Based on research with random-dot stereograms, it has been established that stereoscopic depth-perception is independent from the recognition of objects. The computational task is enormous. Basically, every point in the left eye-matrix is scanned and compared with the corresponding point in the right eye-matrix. However, recognition facilitates stereoscopic perception, not by speeding up the scanning process but by indicating places where disparity may be relevant. This puts the emphasis on the role of local processes in the computation of global characteristics. Especially the problem of segmentation—the process of marking pixels with labels shared with neighboring pixels—is crucial.

In analyzing images, there is a high probability that regions of uniform texture indicate meaningful segments. In this respect, color vision is important.

The perception of texture—classified as either deterministic or stochastic—involves a hierarchy of resolutions, embedded characteristics, virtual visual elements, and parallel processing governed by a restricted set of rules.

Identifying objects as significant units is equally a segmentation problem, even if it can be argued that the low-level detection of boundaries based on perception of texture is, at least at first sight, less complex than high-level perception or the recognition of objects. The computational complexity of recognizing objects (function of 1-, 2-, 2.5-, 3- or 4-dimensionality, whereby 2.5D refers to David Marr's pivotal concept of visual information organized according to oriented planes) depends on the constraints imposed by the context or scene. In most contexts, for example, a 1-D analysis (based solely on length as a discriminating feature between objects) will be insufficient, if only because of the sensitivity of perception to angular alignment of objects. More sophisticated tools seem required.

The problem of segmentation is crucial not only in the context of visual perception but also in language. However, in language the tools used to recognize meaningful segments—including punctuation, capitalization, visual or auditory blanks, intonation, and morphemes—are rather obvious and pose only relatively simple computational tasks.

The *production* of meaningful segments, however, is quite another matter. First of all, at the neurophysiological level the neurons involved in the production of language are different from those involved in the comprehension of language, though the situation is somewhat more complex than a simple division of labor between Broca's area and Wernicke's area. The production of meaningful segments is especially crucial in those cases where "business as usual" no longer applies and novel elements must be introduced to maintain the stability of the system. Particularly interesting is the case where language becomes paradoxical because of self-reference. Such paradoxes—*This sentence is false*—may be solved using Tarski's notion of meta-levels. Replacing *This sentence* by "*This sentence*" eliminates the self-reference and substitutes a reference made from the level of the quotation marks. These levels are so important because they turn the potentially lethal self-reference of a system into a constructive quality (DePryck 1993). The interaction between Gödel's theorem—which basically states that consistent systems contain true statements that cannot be proven by the system—and paradoxality caused by self-reference is "responsible" for the relative uniqueness and independence of each of the levels of reality. When a system creates a next higher level to regain the consistency that it lost when one of its levels ran into semantic paradoxes, Gödel's work shows that the newly created next-higher level will contain a "true sentence" which cannot be derived from the lower levels. Biology is more than just chemistry. It produces a true expression, "life," which cannot be reduced to the level of chemistry. As a result, the levels of reality indeed cannot be equated to one another without losing the consistency gained when new levels of complexity are introduced. If it were at all possible to specify a unique formula from which all levels of reality can be generated or derived without adding something new, then such a formula would necessarily contain or lead to paradoxes. These paradoxes, then, could in principle not be avoided, because solving paradoxes is only possible by introducing novelty, by creating new levels of reality which in turn will necessitate further levels of complexity. A new level of complexity is constructed based on a selection of elements pertaining to the level on which the paradox occurred. It is not necessary to use quotation marks to indicate the new level because the increased complexity of the relations among the elements constituting the new level provides an admittedly fuzzy but nevertheless sufficient indication.

This increased complexity, I suggest, can be indicated as increased texture.

Looking at "*This sentence*" is false, a reader may easily recognize that the specific selection that was made indeed provides an adequate solution to the problem. However, it is less clear *how* that selection was made. Not every possible selection will qualify as a solution to the paradox. In fact, most selections will have destructive qualities at least equal to those of the initial problem.

This fact is at the core of the problems of a more traditionally hierarchical approach of the bottom-up type. In the case of the biological foundations of cultural phenomena—perhaps best signified by the mind-brain problem—this translates into questions concerning which selections and which types of combinations of basic biological material will indeed permit the "jump" to the cultural level. How are we to account for the uncanny accuracy of evolution, beating random trial and error by many lengths, without having to turn to a determinism that would violate the very conditions of our existence?

Caglioti uses *ambiguity* to refer to the coexistence, at a critical point, of two mutually incompatible aspects of the same reality (Caglioti 1992). Implied in his use of the term, is what I meant by *paradoxes* in my own work (DePryck 1993). From Caglioti's point of view, ambiguity assumes the existence of a symmetry, which he defines as *invariance* (the result of a transformation) or as the *indiscernibility* of the change produced by a transformation.

The symmetry, however, may be broken by an external action whereby a control parameter increases its values. The control parameter measures how far a system is from the critical point of a phase transition or the bifurcation that leads to dynamic instability. The parameter may be associated both with phase transitions between states of (thermodynamical) equilibrium in a system, and to dynamic instabilities between a state of equilibrium and a dissipative structure according to which a system may organize itself when its equilibrium is disrupted. When the symmetry is broken, correlations are established and therefore order is introduced between structural moduli that previously were indifferent to each other. Establishment of order is equivalent to the production of information and therefore the decrease of entropy. In a sense, this is similar to the perception of ambiguous figures such as urn-faces and the Necker cube, which typically alternate object and ground or position in depth. Our perception never changes the material object, the ink on paper. However, at the point of recognition, a neurophysiological event in the observer—the symmetry between the two objects is broken and information is produced: The two figures are no longer indifferent to each other but now mutually exclude one another *at the semantic level* while obviously still coexisting at the level of the material object, and even at the level of the retinal image.

This semantic process is quite similar to the formal process of *graphic condensation,* in which two gradually converging images reach a point where they cannot be seen simultaneously. As Caglioti points out, one bit is all that is needed to remove the uncertainty between the two possibilities. However, in this example, it is difficult to speak about aesthetic judgment, or about an aesthetic preference for one solution over another. In fact, the resonance between the two possibilities speaks against a choice in favor of one and against the other.

In general, however, definite choices are made. Even in the case of symmetrical equations the outcome may possess asymmetrical properties, dictated by the starting conditions of the changes and not by the equations predicting or describing the changes over time. In fact, as Barrow and Silk point out(1995), the symmetry of the initial state is completely hidden to an observer who looks only at the changes as they occur. They illustrate this with an example about a dinner where guests are seated around a circular table, with a wineglass to the left and to the right of each place. Once the first diner picks up his glass, the symmetry is broken: the party becomes either left-handed or right-handed.

As Morrison points out, modeling and forecasting require that parameters and initial conditions be optimized, which may be difficult or impossible for some systems of nonlinear equations (Morrison 1991). Except in the most straightforward and discursive cases, aesthetic judgment is at the core of the segmentation problem. Segments—the initial condition in the texture paradigm—are selected based on aesthetic criteria. In the simple but paradoxical sentence *This sentence is false*, without taking into account the grammatical and semantic constraints, 15 (namely 4 + 6 + 4 + 1) possible selections can be made. Only 1, "*This sentence*" is false, solves the paradox in a way that is consistent with the semantic and syntactic constraints of the language. In other words, solving the paradox involves an entropy of $\log_2 15 = 3.90$, a small price to pay compared to the alternative, where we get stuck with paradoxical language in which we can no longer maintain a sufficiently stable truth-notion and where we can "prove" both A and A, and thus nothing whatsoever.

Only after a selection is made can its potential be examined. The selection feeds into a non-linear dynamical system that is highly sensitive to initial conditions—i.e., the aesthetic choice.

Aesthetic choice, in this context, is a choice favoring increased texture. Recent (admittedly still controversial) research indicates that noncoding or junk DNA displays long-term correlations—meaning that the placement of one nucleotide depends to some extent on the placement of others. The fractal-like pattern that emerges (1/f noise) is consistent with the one found in many evolving physical systems. I suggest that the distinction between coding and noncoding DNA may be an aesthetic call.

In this essay, it turns out, I have reversed the expected causal order of the relation between biology and aesthetics. What has emerged is not the biological foundation of aesthetics but the aesthetic foundation of biology. The underlying hypothesis is that aesthetics is older than biology, perhaps even as old as the universe itself. This hypothesis is part of a research project that attempts to found the functioning and the necessity of aesthetic judgment in a larger onto-epistemic frame. In order to do so, I indicate the conditions under which human aesthetic judgment may function while simultaneously, from the bottom up, looking at the role of aesthetic judgment within the context of an underdetermined, dynamical (evolutionary) reality. I have referred to this as the tradition on nonlinear, dynamical decision-procedures—a tradition that is necessary in a reality that is neither totally deterministic nor totally arbitrary. The decisions involve problematic actions or events that show a certain pregnancy—they must be acted upon—without an absolute or necessary criterion for decisions.

I propose that aesthetic judgment is a universal, non-deterministic device for making (or for helping make) those decisions that must be made in order to avoid the standstill of an evolving system (for example, because of incoherence or because of internal paradoxes) but that cannot be made on the basis of deterministic, established criteria. Aesthetic judgment, as I have suggested in this essay, is especially functional at the level of segmentation—the selection of elements that will or could function as the building blocks of the next higher level of complexity.

In the context of this approach, the question about the evolution of aesthetic judgment must be asked—an evolution as a function of the specificity of the different levels of complexity that constitute the totality of reality. We might ask, for instance, if moral judgment is not a specific kind of aesthetic judgment, namely, a form adequate to at least some of our human actions. Or is moral judgment perhaps an alternative perhaps an evolutionary variation for aesthetic judgment—hence a possible conflict between the good and the beautiful?

Works Cited

Aschenbrenner, K.
1985 *The Concept of Coherence in Art*. Dordrecht: D. Reidel.
Barrow, J.D., and J. Silk.
1995 *The Left Hand of Creation*. London: Penguin.
Caglioti, G.
1992 *The Dynamics of Ambiguity*. Berlin: Springer. Translated from the 1983 Italian edition.
Churchland, P.
1989 *Neurophilosophy: Toward a Unified Science of the Mind/Brain*. Cambridge, MA: MIT Press.
Cronin, H.
1992 "Sexual Selection: Historical Perspectives." In E. Fox Keller and E.A. Lloyd, *Keywords in Evolutionary Biology*. Cambridge, MA: Harvard University Press.
Darwin, Charles
1959 *On the Origin of Species by Charles Darwin: A Variorum Text*. Edited by M. Peckham. Philadelphia: University of Pennsylvania Press.
1859 *On the Origin of Species*. London: Penguin. Reprinted in Penguin Classics 1985.
DePryck, K.
1993 *Knowledge, Evolution and Paradox: The Ontology of Language*. New York: State University of New York Press.

Fox Keller, E., and E.A. Lloyd

1992 *Keywords in Evolutionary Biology*. Cambridge, MA: Harvard University Press.

Gregory, R.L.

1994 *Eye and Brain: The Psychology of Seeing*. 4th ed. Oxford: Oxford University Press.

Leibovic, K.N., ed.

1990 *Science of Vision*. New York: Springer.

MacLean, P.D.

1991 "Fractal Aspects of Microgenesis." In R. Hanlon, ed., *Cognitive Microgenesis: A Neuropsychological Perspective*. New York: Springer.

Marr, D.

1982 *Vision: A Computational Investigation into the Human Representation and Processing of Information*. Oxford: W.H. Freeman.

Morrison, F.

1991 *The Art of Modeling Dynamical Systems*. New York: John Wiley.

Scott, P.D.

1990 "Applied Machine Vision." In K.N. Leibovic, ed., *Science of Vision*. New York: Springer.

Stephan, M.

1990 *A Transformational Theory of Aesthetics*. London: Routledge.

Wade, N.

1990 *Visual Allusions: Pictures of Perception*. London: Lawrence Erlbaum.

III Sources

Literature of Early "Scientific" and "Evolution" Aesthetics

Nancy E. Aiken

Two years before Darwin's *Origin of Species* was in the public's hands, Herbert Spencer published a little article that suggested how art might have evolved from behaviors necessary for individual survival. Darwin's thesis, which included a brief comment on how art might have evolved from courtship behaviors, spurred the development of a fair body of literature on the subject of "evolution aesthetics." The primary concern of these early Darwinians was to explain how some behaviors originally selected for survival and reproductive success evolved into aesthetic behaviors, such as art-making and art-appreciating. Ideas came from all quarters, with those in the new fields of psychology and anthropology leading the way.

Aesthetics, however, was a domain of philosophy, and the influential philosopher/aestheticians of the time found no place for "evolution aesthetics" in their view of the subject. Bernard Bosanquet, a household name among aestheticians, dismissed Spencer's idea in his *History of Aesthetic*, saying that it was "not even directed to a serious problem" (1904, 441). Bosanquet even saw fit to relegate his comment directed against the upstart "evolution aesthetics" to a footnote. Early in the twentieth century, when Social Darwinism became a synonym for racism and worse, "evolution aesthetics," to the relief of the Bosanquets of the world, died a quiet death.

The ideas of the early "evolution aestheticians" have been reborn in the last few years. A new assault has been mounted against mainstream aesthetics. Now, however, rather than emphasizing how art evolved from behaviors necessary to survival and reproduction, the emphasis is on how art itself is adaptive—how aesthetic behavior is necessary to survival and reproduction. Darwin's theory of evolution is supported by innumerable experimental reports. Ethologists have demonstrated how behavior is subject to selective forces, and the new discipline of sociobiology has a place for "evolutionary aesthetics." Modern research is based on solid footings. This time the aim is to place Bosanquet in a footnote.

Early work in evolution aesthetics fell into two basic categories. Interest in how art evolved from adaptive behaviors was the first line of inquiry and the first to be abandoned due to lack of interest or support. The second began with the work of Fechner in Germany and, with stops and starts, has enjoyed continued interest. This line of inquiry was called "scientific" or "experimental" aesthetics and evolved into research in perception. A subset of scientific or experimental aesthetics was early research in emotional response to art. Some interest in this area continued and has grown in recent years.

The following discussion is an attempt to follow these lines of inquiry in a somewhat chronological fashion, highlighting the more influential and productive work. The bibliography that follows the discussion is fairly complete for pre-1960 literature on art as evolving from adaptive behaviors (evolution aesthetics) but is not at all complete for scientific aesthetics. The pre-1970 gaps are filled in by the literature reviews and bibliographies which are covered in the discussion. Margaret Livingston's 1988 article brings the list of important works reasonably up to date. A full bibliography of scientific or experimental aesthetics from 1970 remains to be done.

Evolution Aesthetics

Herbert Spencer, a well-known philosopher of his day, based his whole "synthetic" philosophy on the theory of evolution. He may properly be called the father of Social Darwinism, which did nothing to advance the cause of evolutionary aesthetics. Evolution was a hot topic before Darwin published his famous tome in 1859. Indeed, Spencer wrote on the subject prior to that date. His 1857 essay, "The Origin and Function of Music," was perhaps the first discussion of how art might have evolved from adaptive behaviors (behaviors useful for survival and reproduction). Spencer contended that the underlying principle in all vocal phenomena is the pleasure or pain which comes from exercising muscles used in vocalization and the attachment of feeling to some passing sensation. He said that the "distinctive traits of song are simply the traits of emotional speech intensified and systematized." Darwin wrote a footnote devoted to Spencer's idea in Chapter 19 of *The Descent of Man* (1871) wherein he argued against Spencer's "interesting idea" because speech, Darwin noted, came after emotional sounds. Spencer modified his idea and later added a postscript to his article of 1857 in which he argued against the view discussed by Darwin.

> I have aimed to show that music has its germs in the sounds which the voice emits under excitement, and eventually gains this or that character according to the kind of excitement; whereas Mr. Darwin argues that music arises from those sounds which the male makes during the excitements of courtship, that they are consciously made to charm the female, and that from the resulting combinations of sounds arise not love-music only but music in general.

Spencer quite adequately summed up Darwin's view as expressed in *The Descent of Man*, but Darwin did extend his notion of music arising from sounds made in courtship to sexual selection as the basis for "ideas of beauty" in general. Recent research tends to support Spencer's more general view.[1]

Hubert Parry (1906) extended Spencer's idea about the origin of music to include the ability to share in the pleasure of a work of art created by another person. Parry suggested that art appreciation has its roots in the excitement shared by the group (perhaps in anticipation of flight) when a member of the group screams an alarm.[2]

Grant Allen (1848-1899) led the predominantly English movement in evolution aesthetics. He owed, and acknowledged, an immense debt to Spencer, and offered some interesting and at times penetrating ideas on how art might have evolved from adaptive behaviors. His book, *Physiological Aesthetics* (1877), offers a preview of what was to come in twentieth-century research. However, neuroscience was still in its formative years, and Allen was forced to speculate. Today, the book seems quaint. On the other hand, Allen's essays have import for today. In "The Origin of the Sense of Symmetry" (1879a), Allen asks why humankind seem to be universally attracted to the straight line and the circle or regular curves. He concludes that a sense of symmetry may exist throughout the animal world and traces the origin of this sense of symmetry to organized movement. He suggests that since muscles act in a rhythmical manner, we developed a "feel" for rhythm. (This idea was echoed years later by Kate Gordon in her 1909 book on scientific aesthetics, *Esthetics*.) Allen also discusses in this essay the possibility that a sense of symmetry in man has been influenced by symmetrical objects in nature, emphasizing those objects which prove useful to survival, such as a straight arrow for true flight. Many years later E. H. Gombrich discussed similar ideas about repetition, rhythm, and symmetry in great depth in his *Sense of Order* (1979), but not directly in this context.

In "Aesthetic Evolution in Man" (1880a) Allen asks what objects humans first found beautiful. Looking to other animals for his answer, he found accord with Darwin's idea that our ideas of beauty arise from the decorations and song of prospective mates. He asserts that an aesthetic sense was already inherent in the first humans and that it is completely centered around behaviors useful for attracting mates. He also notes that the face is particularly salient. In "Colour in Painting" (1878) Allen argues that "primitives" and children appreciate bright colors over subtle ones.

James Sully (1842-1923) was a professor of philosophy at University College of London who wrote on various philosophical and psychological topics. In "Poetic Imagination and Primitive Conception" (1876b) Sully suggests that poetic imagery selects qualities in objects which resemble ourselves—i.e., we see our image and feelings in nature. Aesthetic pleasure, he suggests, relies on this same process. In "Animal Music" (1879) Sully hypothesizes that lower animals derive pleasure from the same types of sound that give humans pleasure due to the nature of the auditory structure and to the songs useful for attracting mates. Many of the ideas discussed today concerning evolutionary aesthetics are not entirely unlike those of Spencer, Parry, Darwin, Allen, and Sully.

Alfred C. Haddon (1895) brings into focus the relationships among anthropology, sociology, and art of the time in his review of Grosse (1894). It was agreed that art had a practical use for "primitive peoples." Among these uses were mate attraction, social domination, and consolidation and broadening of social relationships. Grosse was the author of *Evolution in Art*, which was impossible to obtain for review but which is probably worth a search. Taine (1883), Guyau (1887), and March (1896) echoed Haddon's remarks.

Evolution aesthetics advocated that art grew from adaptive behaviors. The anthropologists saw in the art of "primitive societies" something of practical value and ventured the possibility that design was the result of "pre-existing visual impression" (March 1896). The philosophers and psychologists saw some relation between the art of children and that of primitives. They felt that this relationship might hold the key to the origin of art noting that within this relationship were behaviors which appeared to be universal—for example, the appreciation of bright colors and a fascination with representations of the human face. They also noticed a correlation of art with certain animal behaviors such as bird song and mating dances. And pointed out human behaviors which, while not necessarily aesthetic in themselves, seemed to have some relationship to aesthetic behavior, including: sensitivity to faces and to certain geometric forms such as straight lines, the "golden" rectangle, s-curves, and circles; to bright colors and sounds of excitement, such as distress or danger, and to tenderness, such as a mother's cooing to her baby; to the attractions of a prospective mate; and to internal and external rhythms, such as our own heartbeat and walking or running rhythms. Also noted was a propensity to project our human emotions onto natural objects, as exemplified by "weeping" willows and "howling" winds. The evolution aestheticians saw these behaviors as the basis for art. One hundred years later we are, again, considering these behaviors as the basis for art.

Productive ideas within evolution aesthetics began to surface again during the mid-twentieth century. Ethologists spurred interest in the idea that human behavior could be molded by evolutionary forces. Desmond Morris (1962) studied picture-making among apes and its relationship to human art, especially early childhood art, in an attempt to find some correlations. He found a striking similarity between the pre-representational stages of children's art and the stages of "art" produced by the apes. Morris's work illustrates the evolutionists' assumption that the basis for art could be found in lower animals.

In *Analyzing Children's Art* (1969) Rhoda Kellogg offers evidence to support the universality of certain graphic representations in children's art and in "primitive" art. Richard Coss suggests that "evolutionary development of human sensitivity to specific visual releasers may have influenced primitive and prehistoric cultures to select specific patterns for incorporation as decorative elements" (1968, 279). He further suggests that the reason these particular patterns were selected was the emotional power of the pattern. One such pattern suggested by both Kellogg and Coss is the zigzag pattern. Johanna Uher (1991a, 1991b) found the zigzag to be associated with agonistic adjectives, suggesting that it evokes an emotional affect of uneasiness or even fear. Both Coss and Uher suggest that the zigzag is a sign for bared, sharp teeth. Another pattern Coss suggests (1968) is used in art to evoke emotion is the eye-spot pattern. Aiken (1992) demonstrates how the eye-spot pattern can evoke emotion in natural settings and in art. Consequently, modern research provides evidence to support the evolutionists' idea that art evolved out of adaptive behaviors (in this instance, those necessary to escape predators).

Meanwhile. other modern writers were looking at ways art could have evolved from adaptive behaviors and how art itself could be adaptive. Paul Ziff (1981) concludes that art developed out of utilitarian functions. He suggests that the evolution of self-awareness may have played a role in the development of art. Ellen Dissanayake, who has published the most on the subject, contends that art has adaptive value but not as an outgrowth of useful activities such as tool-making. She suggests in her 1974 article that the actual making of art may not be adaptive but that the general behavior necessary to making art is adaptive. She wrote that those early societies which

> were not able imaginatively to see something as something else, and whose members were content to leave things as they were and not make them special, would lack the degree of social cohesion, the innovative proclivity and ultimately the potential for survival of human groups that did encourage play and art, which provide metaphorical renderings of the world about them. (215)

In her 1979 article she includes ritual as part of the general behavior from which art arose. Her later work (See "Selective Studies of the Art" elsewhere in this text) expands and amplifies these views.

Other writers have also offered ideas regarding art as a behavior shaped by evolutionary forces and as an adaptive behavior itself. Several are included in the bibliography appended here, and more are listed in the Cooke and Aiken bibliography elsewhere in this volume.

Scientific Aesthetics

Parallelling the writings of the evolution aestheticians was the work of researchers in scientific or experimental aesthetics. Fechner (1871), Wundt (1874), and Helmholtz (1875) began work in this area which continues today within the confines of psychology and neuroscience. These German researchers were interested in visual and auditory preferences and perceptions. Their work forms the basis of current studies of perception. An enormous amount of research has resulted; consequently, the following represents only examples in the lines of greatest interest in the study of the nature of art. Literature reviews and bibliographies mentioned below should fill in gaps for in-depth studies of the various areas of interest.

Music: Perception and Affect

While Helmholtz (1875) tested the limits of hearing and various sonic perceptions, Sherman (1928) asked subjects to report on the emotions they felt were conveyed by a trained singer who was asked to sing "ah" expressing surprise, fear-pain, sorrow, and anger-hate. Sorrow and anger-hate were matched by the intention of the singer and the reports of the subjects. Another study of music and affect was completed by Heinlein (1928). Heinlein found a relationship between soft chords and soothing feelings. Chords played loudly on the piano were rarely considered smooth. Chords played in the upper pitch range were described as bright, cheerful, joyful, clear, and soothing. On the other hand, chords played in the lower pitch range were described as dull, gloomy, sad, or dark. Interest in music and affect waned, but studies of perception of range and other musical elements continued. For example, Trehub et al. (1984, and 1985) found that seven-month-old infants can detect melody changes, suggesting that the ability to discern melody relies little, if at all, on learning.

Line and Feeling

Studies similar to those carried out by Sherman (1928) and Heinlein (1928) in music were done for line and affect by Lundholm (1921) and Poffenberger and Barrows (1924). These researchers were able to uncover a correspondance between the configuration of some lines and certain emotions. They especially noted an affective difference between zigzags and curves. Subjects matched affective adjectives to the lines, agonistic adjectives to the zigzags, and affiliative adjectives to the curves. In 1965 Coss tested subjects' response to zigzags and curves using pupil dilation and found the responses to the two kinds of lines were significantly different. Uher (1991a) performed a test similar to the early one of Poffenberger and Barrows (1924), with similar results.

Constraints on Perception

Work begun by Fechner (1871), Wundt (1874), and Helmholtz (1875) has established limits to our hearing and vision which are important to our understanding of the nature of art. Much of the early work in scientific aesthetics was directed at perceptual limits and preferences. Though some research was directed at affect as described above. Many studies were accomplished, and human limits and preferences gradually became known. By 1928 enough research had been done that a history of the subject was warranted. Thomas Munro's *Scientific Method in Aesthetics* (1928) provides a look at the work to that date. Munro suggested that researchers should study what happens in the nervous system when we respond to art, but the technical ability to do this was still many decades away. Chandler (1933) covers the studies in the field in *A Bibliography of Experimental Aesthetics 1865-1932*. In 1956 Munro published another update on the research in scientific aesthetics called *Toward Science in Aesthetics*. D. E. Berlyne's *Aesthetics and Psychobiology* (1971) and R.W. Pickford's *Psychology and Visual Aesthetics* (1972) are more recent surveys of the subject. Both volumes are quite useful bibliographies of scientific aesthetics. For example, Pickford discusses the problems raised and solutions formulated in regard to color perception, children's aesthetic preferences, and form perception.

Three important books in the field of perception, which predate the relevant neuroscience synopsis by Livingston (1988), are those by Yarbus

(1967) and Gregory (1966, 1970). Yarbus measured eye movements of persons viewing various objects and found, among other things, that when subjects viewed a face, most eye movements were directed at the eyes. Gregory (1966, 1970) explains the conclusions of research in perception to date and is the most influential of the modern writers on the subject.

In 1988 Margaret Livingston published her synthetic piece on neuroscience findings which answered many of the questions concerning visual perception raised and debated by psychologists for over a century. She provided the proof that the design of our visual system accounts for such peculiarities as seen in the floating colors in Ad Reinhart's *Abstract Painting* and Seurat's blending of dots of color into recognizable forms and shapes. Her essay finally answers many of the questions that Munro (1928) suggested could only be answered by tracing pathways in the brain.

In summary, the early work accomplished by philosophers, psychologists, anthropologists, biologists, and physiologists in the study of the nature of art from evolutionary and experimental viewpoints has much to offer modern students who now are searching for alternatives to philosophic aesthetics. It is humbling to note that many "new" ideas reflect propositions offered over a hundred years ago. Moreover, the main lines of inquiry remain similar to those of the early "evolution" aestheticians—the notable exception being that modern writers are looking into ways that art itself has adaptive value. This is an exciting innovation that has already provided interesting results.[3] A burden that must be borne by modern writers is the effort necessary to make their ideas heard and respected by mainstream aestheticians who are still listening to Bosanquet. A competing body of work placed in the new discipline of sociobiology may be the direction needed to accomplish being heard. The effort will need to come from solid research and clear, logical prose that effectively persuades the Bosanquets of the world.

Works Cited

Aiken, Nancy Ellen Bryan

1992 "A Biological Basis for the Emotional Impact of Art." Ph.D. diss., Ohio University.

Allen, Grant

1877 *Physiological Aesthetics*. New York: D. Appleton.

1878 "Colour in Painting." *Cornhill Magazine* 38:476-93.

1879a "The Origin of the Sense of Symmetry." *Mind* 4:301-16.

1879b "Pleased with a Feather." *Cornhill Magazine* 39:712-22.

1880a "Aesthetic Evolution in Man." *Mind* 5:445-64.

1880b "Cimabue and Coal-Scuttles." *Cornhill Magazine* 42:61-76.

1880c "The Growth of Sculpture." *Cornhill Magazine* 42:273-93.

Arnheim, R.

1965 *Art and Visual Perception: A Psychology of the Creative Eye*. Berkeley: University of California Press. Original work published 1954.

Berlyne, D. E.

1971 *Aesthetics and Psychobiology*. New York: Appleton-Century-Crofts.

Biederman, Charles

1948 *Art As the Evolution of Visual Knowledge*. Red Wing, MN: Charles Biderman.

Bosanquet, Bernard

1904 *A History of Aesthetic*. New York: Macmillan.

Chalmers, F. Graeme

1973 "The Study of Art in a Cultural Context." *Journal of Aesthetics and Art Criticism* 32:246-49.

Chandler, Albert R.

1934 *Beauty and Human Nature*. New York and London: D. Appleton-Century Company.

Cope, E. D.

1883 "Evolutionary Significance of Human Character." *American Naturalist* 17:907-19. Coss, Richard G.

1965 "Mood Provoking Visual Stimuli: Their Origins and Applications." Master's thesis, University of California, Los Angeles.

1968 "The Ethological Command in Art." *Leonardo* 1:273-87.

Critchley, MacDonald, and R. A. Henson, eds.

1978 *Music and the Brain: Studies in the Neurology of Music*. London: Wm. Heinemann Medical Books Limited.

Darwin, Charles

1871 *The Descent of Man.* See chapter 19.

Dissanayake, Ellen

1974 "A Hypothesis of the Evolution of Art from Play." *Leonardo* 7:211-17.

1979 "An Ethological View of Ritual and Art in Human Evolutionary History." *Leonardo* 12:27-31.

1980 "Art As a Human Behavior." *Journal of Aesthetics and Art Criticism* 38:397-406.

1982 "Aesthetic Experience and Human Evolution." *Journal of Aesthetics and Art Criticism* 41:145-56.

Eibl-Eibesfeldt, I.

1975 *Ethology: The Biology of Behavior*. 2d ed. New York: Holt, Rinehart and Winston.

1979 "Human Ethology: Concepts and Implications for the Sciences of Man." *The Behavioral and Brain Sciences* 2:1-57.

1991 "Four Decades of Ethology—A Personal Perspective." *Human Ethology Newsletter* 6:1-3.

Fechner, G. T.

1871 Zur Experimentalen Aesthetik.

Gayley, Charles Mills, and Fred Newton Scott

1901 *An Introduction to the Methods and Materials of Literary Criticism*. Boston: Ginn. See pp. 81-82.

Gardner, Howard

1973 *The Arts and Human Development*. New York: John Wiley and Sons.

Gombrich, E. H.

1979 *The Sense of Order: A Study in the Psychology of Decorative Art*. Ithaca: Cornell University Press.

Gordon, Kate

1909 *Esthetics*. New York: Henry Holt.

Gregory, R. L.

1966 *Eye and Brain*. New York: McGraw Hill.

1970 *The Intelligent Eye*. New York: McGraw Hill.

Griggs, Edward H.

1922 *The Philosophy of Art*. Croton-on-Hudson, NY: Orchard Hill Press.

Grosse, E.

1894 *Die Ansange der Kunst*. Freiburg: Mohr.

Guyau, Jean-Marie

1887 *Art from the Point of View of Sociology*. Paris.

Haddon, Alfred C.

1895 "The Origins of Art." *Nature* 51:241-42.

Hall, G.S.

1879 "Is Aesthetics a Science?" *The Nation* 29:380-81.

Heinlein, C. P.

1928 "The Affective Characters of the Major and Minor Modes in Music." *Journal of Comparative Psychology* 8:101-42.

Helmholtz, H. L. F.

1875 *Sensations of Tone As a Physiological Basis for the Theory of Music*.

Hirn, Yrjo

1900a *The Origins of Art, A Psychological and Sociological Inquiry*. London: Macmillan and Co.

1900b "The Psychological and Sociological Study of Art." *Mind* (new series) 9:512-22.

James, W.

1877 "Allen's *Physiological Aesthetics*." *The Nation* 25:185-86.

Kellogg, Rhoda

1969 *Analyzing Children's Art*. Palo Alto, CA: National Press Books.

Lafleur, Laurence J.

1942 "Biological Evidence in Aesthetics." *Philosophical Review* 51: 587-95.

Livingston, Margaret S.

1988 "Art, Illusion and the Visual System." *Scientific American* 258: 78-85.

Lundholm, H.

1921 "The Affective Tone of Lines: Experimental Researches." *Psychological Review* 28:43-60.

March, Colley

1896 "Evolution and Psychology in Art, " *Mind* (new series) 20:441-63.

Marshall, Henry Rutgers

1894 *Pain, Pleasure, and Aesthetics*. London and New York: Macmillan.

1905 "The Relation of Aesthetics to Psychology and Philosophy." *The Philosophical Review* 14:1-20.

Miall, David S.

1976 "Aesthetic Unity and the Role of the Brain." *Journal of Aesthetics and Art Criticism* 35:57-67.

Morris, Desmond

1962 *The Biology of Art*. New York: Knopf.

Munro, Thomas,

1928 *Scientific Method in Aesthetics*. New York: W.W. Norton.

1956 *Toward Science in Aesthetics*. New York: Liberal Arts Press. ca. 1963-68 *Evolution in the Arts*. Cleveland: Cleveland Museum of Art.

Oakley, K. P.

1981 "Emergence of Higher Thought." *Philosophical Transactions of the Royal Society of London* 292:205-11.

Parry, C. Hubert H.

1906 *The Evolution of the Art of Music*. New York: D. Appleton and Co.

Pickford, R. W.

1972 *Psychology and Visual Aesthetics*. London: Hutchinson Educational.

Poffenberger, A.T., and B.E. Barrows

1924 "The Feeling Value of Lines." *Journal of Applied Psychology* 8:187-205.

Santayana, George

1896 *The Sense of Beauty*. New York: Charles Scribner's Sons. See p. 56.

Scott, Geoffrey

ca. 1914 *The Architecture of Humanism: A Study in the History of Taste*. New York: Charles Scribner's Sons. See pp. 165-85.

Spencer, Herbert

1970 "The Origin and Function of Music." In *Literary Style and Music*. Port Washington, NY and London: Kennikat Press. Original work published in *Fraser's Magazine*, October 1857.

Sully, James

1876a “Art and Psychology.” *Mind* 1:467-578.

1876b (attributed) “Poetic Imagination and Primitive Conception.” *Cornhill Magazine* 34:294-306.

1877 “Critical Notices.” *Mind* 2:386-92.

1878 (attributed) “The Undefinable in Art.” *Cornhill Magazine* 38:559-72.

1879 “Animal Music.” *Cornhill Magazine* 40:605-21.

1888 *Illusions: A Psychological Study*. New York: D. Appleton and Co.

Symonds, John A.

1890 *Essays, Speculative and Suggestive*. 2 vols. London: Chapman and Hall.

Taine, H. A.

1883 *History of English Literature*. London. See vol. 1, pp. 1-36.

Trehub, S. E., D. Bull, and L. Thorpe

1984 “Infants’ Perception of Melodies: The Role of Melodic Contour,” *Child Development* 55:821-30.

Thorpe, L. A., and B. A. Morrongiello

1985 “Infants’ Perception of Melodies: Changes in a Single Tone.” *Infant Behavior and Development* 8:213-23.

Uher, Johanna

1991a “Die Asthetik von Zick-Zack und Welle: Ethologische Aspekte der Wirkung linearer Muster.” Ph.D. diss., Universität München, München, Germany.

1991b “On Zigzag Designs: Three Levels of Meaning.” *Current Anthropology* 32 (4):437-39.

Veron, Eugene

1879 *Aesthetics*. London: Chapman and Hall. See pp. 5-8.

Wertheim, N.

1978 “Is There an Anatomical Localization for Musical Faculties?” In MacDonald Critchley and R.A. Henson, eds., *Music and the Brain*. London: Wm. Heinemann Medical Books. Wundt, W. M.

1874 *Grundzuge der physiologischen Psychologie*. Leipzig: Engelman.

Yarbus, A. L.

1967 *Eye Movements and Vision*. New York: Plenum.

Young, J. Z.
1978 *Programs of the Brain*. Oxford: Oxford University Press.
Ziff, Paul
1981 "Art and Sociobiology." *Mind* 90:505-20.

Notes

1. See Aiken 1992 for a summary.
2. Again, see Aiken 1992 for recent research in support of this idea.
3. See the works of Dissanayake, Eibl-Eibesfeldt, Sutterlin, Pfeiffer, Aiken, and others in the Cooke and Aiken bibliography in this text.

Selectionist Studies of the Arts: An Annotated Bibliography

Brett Cooke and Nancy E. Aiken

Many scientists and critics have wondered about the natural origins of art. The mere fact that all societies practice art in some form has often elicited this by now unremarkable notion. Only recently, however, and much less often, have investigators begun to propose exactly how and why the arts are rooted in our biological heritage and to ask whether that background exerts a lingering influence.[1] What follows is a list of those rare studies which have advanced adaptive pressures for art according to tenets of Darwinian natural selection or which have discerned genetic structures in art which accord with predictions of sociobiological theory.[2] These texts vary considerably in approach, style, scope, and, most important, standards of argumentation—little of which is reflected in our notations. We have attempted to list without evaluation the adaptive functions they claim for art.

Aiken, Nancy Ellen Bryan

1992 "A Biological Basis for the Emotional Impact of Art." Ph.D. diss., Ohio University.

The proposition argued is that biologically relevant stimuli in art (ethological releasers) evoke emotion. Aesthetic appreciation is discussed from an ethological viewpoint, and examples are given of releasers used in art. The heart of the work is the description of how releasers evoke emotion in natural surroundings and in art. The mechanism is described in both neuroscience and behavioral terms and supported with research from physiology and neuroscience. In addition, original research complements the theoretical argument; the author tested American and Asian subjects for cardiovascular response to biologically relevant visual stimuli with positive results. Finally, Pfeiffers (1982) argument is supported for an adaptive use for art.

1998a *The Biological Origins of Art.* Westport, CT: Praeger Publishing.

This is the revised and updated version of the authors 1992 dissertation. Besides describing the neurological basis for how art evokes emotion, the author demonstrates how ethological releasers, used in art, can be responsible for universal appreciation of art, how certain universal visual configurations (such as circles and zigzags) might have a basis in biology, and how art can be used to obtain and maintain power.

1998b "Human Cardiovascular Response to the Eye Spot Threat Stimulus." *Evolution and Cognition*. 4: 51-62.

This is the original research from the authors 1992 dissertation. The cardiovascular responses of fifty subjects from multicultural backgrounds to the eye spot visual configuration is described. The article also discusses how, when used in art, this stimulus can evoke excitement.

Alland, Alexander Jr.,

1977 *The Artistic Animal: An Inquiry into the Biological Roots of Art*. Garden City, NY: Anchor.

Alland accounts for art as the accidental result of five unrelated adaptations which were selective in other domains but that, once they appeared, took on adaptive significance: environmental exploration, play, attention to spatial configurations, capability of fine perception, and transformative language (e. g., metaphor) and mentation, which allowed expression of stronger emotions.

1989 "Affect and Aesthetics in Human Evolution." *Journal of Aesthetics and Art Criticism* 47:1-14.

The author finds art's utility in forms of communication—both between human beings and with the environment, memory—and in education. Alland distinguishes between artistic universals driven by the constrains of materials and those pertaining to cognitive proclivities; he suggests that some of this second group may be non-genetic.

Allott, Robin

1994 "The Pythagorean Perspective: The Arts and Sociobiology." *Journal of Social and Evolutionary Systems* 17(1):71-90.

The author bases his assertion of a biological origin for the arts on their common qualities, though he raises a number of doubts. For example, looking at the number of prominent childless artists, he suggests that art is undirected altruism. Allott says that the arts, and mathematics constitute a pattern-perceiving and/or -producing activity prompted by an impulse to explore the world, both outer and inner, and to replicate it, resulting in our improved ability to act in it.

Appleton, Jay

1990 *The Symbolism of Habitat: An Interpretation of Landscape in the Arts*. Seattle and London: University of Washington Press.

The first chapter of this slim volume defends the notion that ideas about beautiful landscapes and choices of places to live are shaped by natural selection. Appleton evokes the old evolution theorists' pleasure-pain argument as the basis of art appreciation, noting that while the *criteria* for selection of habitats, for example, are different for different species, the *process* is always the same: that which affords pleasure is the situation most conducive to survival and reproductive success. The argument is extended to include all aesthetic appreciation.

Argyros, Alexander J.

1989 "Learning from the Stock Market: Literature As Cultural Investment." *Mosaic* 22 (3):101-16.

Argyros uses the relationship between literature and reality, compared to that between the stock market and the economy, to distinguish deconstruction (which denies a link between the two), from sociobiology (which depends on one). The author views literature and the arts as scenario projections which help us prepare for and shape the future. He also argues that literature individuates us, and indeed that evolution dictates the development of an increasing greater sense of identity, if only to permit a wider range of choices. In general, literature serves to shift the focus of evolution from biology and genetics to culture.

1991 *A Blessed Rage for Order: Deconstruction, Evolution, and Chaos*. Ann Arbor: University of Michigan Press.

Argyros elegantly draws profound links between sociobiology and contemporary critical theory, including deconstruction and chaos theory. He sees literature as a means for creating relatively stable and testable "world models" out of a much less comprehensible environment—one that we only delude ourselves that we understand. Indeed, the novelty of narrative serves to generate a larger number of these models for possible futures, thus affording us a greater range of choices. Literature also helps in the process of adaptation, somewhat like genetic mutation, by accentuating the greater individuality of members of a given society, thereby greatly accelerating cultural change. This greater emphasis on individual character has the effect of making us more social, in that we come to better understand each other. He also traces the great complexity of art to its linkage with the many levels of the psyche; its efficiency lies in its ability to address all brain components readily and at the same time, usually requiring little learning. As a result of this many-faceted matrix, individuals are more unpredictable, therefore more individuated, adding yet more alternatives to the positive feedback loop between literary culture and genetic heritage.

Arnheim, Rudolf
1988 "Universals in the Arts." *Journal of Social and Biological Structures* 11 (1):60-65.

Arnheim seeks the selective value of the arts in apprehending environmental conditions. He notes our ability to fathom what is significant, thanks to the "gestalt organization" of our perception. The author traces our capacity for abstract representation to food storage, our ability to grasp more than what is needed in the present—i.e., to plan for the future and the unpredictable. Art is for Arnheim an interpreter of experienced reality; like science, it tends toward simpler structures. These generally follow universal patterns, like the "golden section," and themes which are of clear adaptive value, such as the common sharp contrast of success and failure.

Barrow, John D.
1995 *The Artful Universe*. Oxford: Clarendon Press.

Barrow's book is remarkably similar in theme and theory to Turner 1991a, a source of which he is apparently unaware. Like Frederick Turner, Barrow looks at the ways in which the structure of the universe imprints itself upon our aesthetic preferences. Depending on chaos theory and citing much detailed scientific evidence, Barrow argues that the arts and sciences, however different, come from the same place. He cites the preference of young children for pictures of savannah-like landscapes and notes how architects create spaces for prospect and refuge, factors which both bore selective advantages in the Environment of Evolutionary Adaptation. He adduces our heightened sensitivity for recognizing pattern and symmetry to our ancient experience as predators and potential prey. This sensitivity causes us often to jump to unjustified conclusions and makes us vulnerable to self-deception, but it yields important positive consequences for the arts. Barrow compares our color and aural perception to other adaptive needs which, in turn, are influenced by geophysics and chemistry. He suggests that narrative both imparts a sense of understanding, hence providing self-confidence, and aids memory, which encourages non-reciprocal altruism, i.e., self-sacrifice. Noting many possible adaptive benefits to the arts, especially in his extended study of music, Barrow argues that the structure of our aesthetic response is multivalent and complex and that it may be the result of numerous factors.

Bedaux, Jan Baptist

1989 "Laatmiddeleeuwse sexuele amuletten" (Late Medieval Sexual Insignia as substitutional behavior: A sociobiological approach). In J. B. Bedaux and A. M. Koldeweij, eds., *Annus Quadriga Mundi*. Zutphen: De Walburg Pers, pp. 16-30.

Bedaux attributes the use of phallic (threat) and vulva (submission) images in European amulets to the innate ritualization of territorial defense behavior by apes. These are co-opted to guard borders and houses and ward off the evil eye and malign spirits. Indeed, similar figures defend metaphorical borders, as in the margins of texts and other objects of intellectual property.

1991 "Marino Marini's Angelo dell cittadella: Beeldhouwkunst in biologisch perspectief." ("MarinoMarini's 'Angelo dell cittadella': Sculpture in Biological Perspective"). *Jong Holland* 3:26-31.

The author traces the erect phallus of this statue to the use of phallic display by apes for territorial defense. Bedaux also notes how often religious leaders in Christian art, including Christ, are made more noticeable by bearing an erect phallus.

1995 "Comparative Iconology: A Sociobiological Approach." In K. R. van Kooij and H. van der Veere, eds., *Form and Meaning in Buddhist Art*. Groningen: Egbert Forsten, pp. 197-204.

Bedaux observes ithyphallic imagery in Asian art quite similar to what he has studied in Western European art. He suggests that the common root to these representations is biological. This iconography may be traceable to phallic display by monkeys for purposes of demonstrating hierarchical rank and to ward off alien conspecifics. Notably, such iconography performs a similar role in the human art of widely separated cultures.

Bleakney, J. Sherman

1970 "A Possible Evolutionary Basis for Aesthetic Appreciation in Men and Apes." *Evolution*, 24:477-79.

Bleakney offers a brief extrapolation of Morris 1962. He sees the preference for facial (men) and hand (ape) patterns as a form of familiarity recognition which facilitates socialization and cooperation. This is echoed in our partiality for symmetrical natural objects and is motivated by innate preadapted cognitive templates.

Boyd, Brian

1998 "Jane, Meet Charles: Literature, Evolution, and Human Nature," *Philosophy and Literature*, 22: 1-30.

Boyd issues a concise, resourceful, and in some ways original call for the application of evolutionary psychology to the study of literature. He proposes that "narrative selection" reflects the issues of natural selection. He then focuses on female sexual choice in Jane Austen's *Mansfield Park*, noting the alternative conclusions Austen offers the reader prior to settling on the best match for her heroine from an evolutionary point of view. Boyd details how this denouement is worked out in accordance with recent views on the "arms race" in the battle of the sexes between deception and its detection.

Brothwell, D.

1976 "Visual Art, Evolution, and Environment." In D. Brothwell and C. Waddington, eds., *Beyond Aesthetics*. London: Thames and Hudson, pp. 41-63.

Brothwell reviews the extant literature on the emergence of art up to the historical period. He propounds a hypothesis that art, once rooted in such biological needs as socialization and development of tool skills, became a rapidly accelerated sociocultural entity.

Brown, James Cooke, and William Greenhood
1991 "Paternity, Jokes, and Song: A Possible Evolutionary Scenario for the Origin of Language and Mind." *Journal of Social and Biological Structures* 14 (3):255-309.
Brown and Greenhood attribute the evolution of mentality, especially our ability to conceive of another person's point of view, to the development of monogamy. The adoption of roles is essential to this early form of social contract. The authors find the evidence for this in songs, intoned signals which in strings became the basis for words.
Campbell, Joseph
1959 "The Inherited Image." In *The Masks of God: Primitive Mythology.* New York: Viking, pp. 30-49.
Campbell draws a useful connection between Jung's collective unconscious and archetypes, and ethological "innate releasing mechanisms," as in the case of newly hatched chicks who flee from hawk-like images. Despite citations of Konrad Lorenz and Nikkie Tinbergen, Campbell does not make the tie-in to natural selection.

Carroll, Joseph
1994 *Evolution and Literary Theory.* St. Louis: University of Missouri Press.
Carroll argues that literary criticism should be included within evolutionary theory and argues against the deconstructionist (or poststructuralist) views which have dominated the study of literature since the 1970s. Carroll opposes idealism and its spinoffs, including poststructuralism, by pointing to verifiable tenets of individual psychology. He regards literature not as an autonomous cultural construct wholly unrelated to the environment which produced it but rather as a subjective response to the world in which we live. Carroll demonstrates how it expresses relationships which have been shaped—therefore, motivated, biased, and constrained—by natural selection. Carroll offers studies of individual texts to outline a method by which we can construct an empirical and testable Darwinian literary science.

1995 "Evolution and Literary Theory." *Human Nature* 6 (2):119-34. This article is a summary of Carroll 1994.

Clarke, I. F.

1997 "Trigger-Happy: An Evolutionary Study of the Origins and Development of Future-War Fiction, 1763-1914." *Journal of Social and Evolutionary Systems* 20 (2):117-36.

Other than the title, there is little mention of evolution in this essay, but Clarke's history of future-war fiction supports theories of art serving an adaptive role by preparing readers for possible contingencies. Early in the period covered, various authors expounded the benefits of aggression. Clarke shows how some works of fiction proved to be more effective than other forms of political education in persuading voters to take necessary defensive measures against potential external threats.

Coe, Kathryn

1992 "Art: The Replicable Unit—An Inquiry into the Possible Origin of Art As a Social Behavior." *Journal of Social and Evolutionary Systems* 15 (2):217-34. Reprinted in this volume.

Coe observes that the primary function of art is to attract attention and thereby impart a message. She produces a wide range of evidence to show that body decoration, much of it quite difficult and painful to achieve, was one of the earliest forms of art. Coe proposes that one of its purposes was to signal the bearer's conformity with social custom. Given that such traditional learning (as practiced by conformists) in most primitive contexts carried adaptive advantages over non-conformists; such ornamentation would help in mate selection, reciprocal arrangements, etc.

Collins, Desmond, and John Onians

1978 "The Origins of Art." *Art History*, 1(1):1-25.

The authors survey the earliest art, roughly from 32,000 B.C. to 23,000 B.C. They note a marked preponderance of representations of female genitalia and animals of prey in the artifacts from this period. Collins and Onians argue that heightened sensitivity to women and game animals bears selective benefits and is likely to have been genetically and environmentally programmed into the brain. Those early modern humans who were better able to discern the contours of these phenomena gained an advantage in terms of fitness—but at the cost of our propensity for jumping to projective and therefore often erroneous readings of such images. They also associate the appearance of art with the doubling of adolescence and, consequently, youthful play and fantasy.

Comfort, Alex

1962 "Darwin and Freud." and "On Laying Plato's Ghost." In his *Darwin and the Naked Lady: Discursive Essays on Biology and Art*. New York: George Brazilier, pp. 23-42, 119-35.

Comfort develops Darwin's view that art is a derivative of sexuality by linking it to Freudian insights; his call for the "marriage of psychoanalysis and biology" in this regard was only answered in 1985, by Daniel Rancour-Laferriere's *Signs of the Flesh: An Essay on Hominid Sexuality* (Berlin: Mouton de Gruyter). In drawing analogies between artistic fashions and speciation, Comfort anticipates Richard Dawkins's concept of ideas as memes (1976, *The Selfish Gene*. Oxford: Oxford University Press) which can invade the consciousness like viruses invade the body and can direct our behavior.

Constable, John

1997 "Verse Form: A Pilot Study in the Epidemiology of Representations." *Human Nature* 8 (2):171-203.

Constable scans a great mass of English verbal data to demonstrate that verse form persists virtually everywhere despite its being, in some ways, a hindrance to communication. He proposes that poetry overcomes its disadvantages by its fit with our susceptibility to verse form, irrespective of whether or not we presently have a particular need for it.

Cooke, Brett

1987 "The Human Alien: In-Groups and Out-Breeding in Enemy Mine." In George E. Slusser and Eric S. Rabkin, eds., *Aliens: The Anthropology of Science Fiction*. Carbondale: Southern Illinois University Press, pp. 179-98.

Cooke develops the common notion that space alien stories are coded narratives of inter-ethnic and -racial politics. That xenophobia and xenophilia generally are found to follow gender distinctions—it is only subdominant males who are abhorred—is advanced as evidence of a biological preadaptation for ethnic biases, one which is readily overturned for reproductive advantage.

1992 "Pushkin and the *Femme Fatale*: Jealousy in *The Gypsies*." *California Slavic Studies* 14:99-126.

The common figure of the *femme fatale* is traced to the paternal anxiety which was elicited by the process of women's liberation during the nineteenth century. Art is seen here as perniciously carrying out anachronistic biases.

1994a "Mrs. Komarovsky: Sex Abuse in Pasternak's *Doctor Zhivago*," *Russian Language Journal* 48 (159-61):103-26.

The common confusion of sexual abuse as consensual sex is repeated in Pasternak's popular novel, wherein the lawyer Komarovsky "seduces" a teenage girl about a third his age. Although Lara exhibits all the classic symptoms of a victim, she is, nevertheless, blamed for her "fall," abandoned by her husband and lover, and equated with a prostitute by the author. The sociobiology of paternal uncertainty explains why we tolerate such an immoral "double standard" in art.

1994b "Sociobiology, Science Fiction and the Future." *Foundation: The Review of Science Fiction* 60:42-51.

Cooke presents an overview of prospects for sociobiological research in science fiction and fantasy, glancing at the future on the basis of studies produced so far. He notes the particular advantages of using non-realistic literature as test material for sociobiology, given that we are better able to measure limits of interest and the prevalence of social forms in the imagination, free of empirical necessity. Like Argyros, Cooke argues that literature allows a society to try out alternative futures.

1995a "Acquaintance Rape in Kalatozov's *The Cranes Are Flying*." In Simon Karlinsky, James L. Rice, and Barry P. Scherr, eds., *O rus! Studia litteraria slavica in honorem Hugh McLean*. Berkeley: Berkeley Slavic Studies, pp. 69-80.

The article notes the poorly disguised rape scene central to this classic Soviet film and accounts for the myopia of the producers and viewers by pondering the selective advantages of self-deceit to a victim.

1995b "Microplots: The Case of *Swan Lake*." *Human Nature* 6 (2):183-96.

The author argues that art reflects and exploits patterns of differential interest shaped by natural selection. He studies how the narrative minimum of ballet's greatest classic suffices for full-length performance art because it is composed of different behavioral tendencies set into a matrix of counterpoising forces, thereby generating great plot interest.

1996a "The Biopoetics of Immortality: A Darwinist Perspective on Science Fiction." In George Slusser, Gary Westfahl, and Eric S. Rabkin, eds., *Immortal Engines: Life Extension and Immortality in Science Fiction and Fantasy*. Athens, GA: University of Georgia Press, pp. 90-101.

This article compares the writings of Richard Dawkins to space colony tales in order to show how Dawkins's postulated law of self-replication is reflected in narratives about efforts to save the human race (i. e., genes) and also its artworks (i.e., memes). Memes provide mortals with additional means to immortality.

1996b "Utopia and the Art of the Visceral Response." In Gary Westfahl, George Slusser, and Eric S. Rabkin, eds., *Foods of the Gods: Eating and the Eaten in Fantasy and Science Fiction*. Athens, GA: University of Georgia Press, pp. 188-99.

Cooke studies how modern literature exploits evolved food aversions, which have the advantage of eliciting powerful responses while bypassing rational consideration. The aim of dystopian fiction is to unsettle the reader by such recourse to the autonomic system.

1998a "Constraining the Other in Kvapil and Dvoraks *Rusalka*." In Brett Cooke, George E. Slusser, and Jaume Olivella, eds., *The Fantastic Other: An Interface of Perspectives*. Amsterdam: Editions Rodopi, pp. 121-42.

Cooke deconstructs literary treatments of the mermaid, especially Dvorak's greatest opera, to reveal their essential subtext in baronial and paternal sexual abuse of peasant girls. He notes how this narrative situation bears much repetition, as we may witness in many narratives, because of the heightened interest accorded a young woman at the peak of her reproductive value as she undergoes her highly risky transition from eligible bride to young mother.

1998b "Introduction: Deception, Self-Deception and the Other." In Brett Cooke, George E. Slusser, and Jaume Olivella, eds., *The Fantastic Other: An Interface of Perspectives*. Amsterdam: Editions Rodopi, pp. iii-viii.

The author develops Nicholas Humphrey's deduction that the selection pressure humans experience from conspecifics causes them to develop models of each others character. Cooke extends this line of thought to account for the common interest expressed in literature in unrealistic, if not contrary-to-fact, images of the unknowable Other.

Coss, Richard G.

1965 "Mood Provoking Visual Stimuli: Their Origins and Applications." Master's thesis, University of California at Los Angeles.

Psychologist Richard Coss examines visual objects with potential "releasing" qualities. His concern was how advertisers could capture customer attention, but he stumbled on the key that makes art work: biologically relevant stimuli (ethological releasers) which evoke emotional response. He enumerates and illustrates several possible visual releasers for which he tested subjects for their responses. This thesis is the basis for the Aiken and Uher dissertations and influenced the writings of Dissanayake and Eibl-Eibesfeldt.

1968 "The Ethological Command in Art." *Leonardo* 1:273-87.

Coss discusses the use in art of the "mood provoking visual stimuli" he explored in his Master's thesis (1965). This article provides the basis for works by Aiken, Dissanayake, Eibl-Eibesfeldt, Sutterlin, and Uher.

Dennett, Douglas

1990 "Memes and the Exploitation of Imagination." *Journal of Aesthetics and Art Criticism*, 48:127-35.

Dennett extrapolates Richard Dawkins's meme to support David Mandel's thesis that art contributes to human evolution. He suggests links between genes and memes, how memes may promote genes, and, especially, how memes influence genes to preserve and replicate them. The author speculates on what kind of meme-filter devices might be needed, how an "arms race" might build up between them and the memes attempting to penetrate the filters, how we are what we read, and, lastly, how our memes constitute our extended phenotype—Dawkins's notion of extensions of our bodies which influence other organisms to do our bidding.

DePryck, Koen
1993 *Knowledge, Evolution, and Paradox: The Ontology of Language*. Albany: State University of New York Press.
Although the subject of this highly interdisciplinary study goes well beyond the arts, it should be noted that DePryck examines the drawings of autistic children to conduct a virtual archaeology of the mind. No other work which touches on biopoetics so thoroughly applies concepts from chaos theory.
Diamond, Jared
1991 "Art of the Wild." *Discover*, 12 (February):78-80, 82, 84-85.
Diamond examines animal art, especially that of bower birds, to glean parallels with human behavior. He argues that art serves a sexual advantage by advertising the maker or owner's qualities and, secondly, that it serves to counterbalance environmental insufficiencies such as boredom while, thirdly, socializing men into groups, thereby promoting group survival.
1992 *The Third Chimpanzee: The Evolution and Future of the Human Animal*. New York: Harper Collins.
Diamond questions commonly assumed distinctions between human and animal art. He discusses how the art of bowerbirds serves their fitness needs via sexual selection. "Art is a quick indicator of status" and thus may attract prospective mates: "Art is a coin of sex." Diamond also argues how it contributes to group cohesion and, therefore, survival. He proposes that leisure time is actually used by humans to build up capital for reproductive needs.

Dissanayake, Ellen
1974 "An Hypothesis of the Evolution of Art from Play." *Leonardo* 7(3):211-18.

The author carefully cites the common characteristics of play (non-serious, non-functional, self-rewarding, preponderantly social, diversive, pleasure-oriented, somewhat unpredictable, and metaphorical) and compares them to the similar features of art. She uses this comparison to propose that art fosters both conservative and innovative social behavior.

1979 "An Ethological View of Ritual and Art in Human Evolutionary History." *Leonardo* 12(1):27-31.

Dissanayake compares apparent functions of animal and human ritual behavior (socialization, channeling of possibly destructive impulses, self-expression), then suggests that art hypertrophies common properties of ritual so as to make ritual, which bears selective value, more effective and likely to be performed despite its cost in terms of time, energy, and materials. This serves a vital socialization function by creating communion and a sense of meaning, as well as imparting shared information.

1980 "Art as a Human Behavior: Toward a Ethological View of Art." *Journal of Aesthetics and Art Criticism* 38(4):397-406.

This is the first and most concise presentation of Dissanayake's thesis that "making special" is a universal characteristic of art, with selective value. She emphasizes not the product so much as the experience of art's production and consumption. Whereas modern art may now be biologically irrelevant, "making special" is ancient and widespread because it makes art more effective in all of its functions.

1982 "Aesthetic Experience and Human Evolution." *Journal of Aesthetics and Art Criticism* 41(2):145-55.

Dissanayake sketches a scenario for the appearance of "making special" as a significant adaptation linked to ritual. She notes that societies tend to have elaborate and long ceremonies, rather than just brief ones. Following an analogy with infant development, she argues that once the necessary motor skills were in place, thanks to the tradition-establishing needs for ritual, primitive man produced a second "tier" of appreciation for the performance, if only to ensure that it is well done. Aesthetic pleasure would also help encourage regular performances. The author delimits the range of her ethological challenge to Kantian aesthetics by admitting that "higher-order" functions, such as detachment and innovation, probably do not apply to traditional, pre-industrial societies, creating much of our present confusion regarding what art is.

1984 "Does Art Have Selective Value?" *Empirical Studies of the Arts*. 2(1):35-49. Italian translation, 1984, "L'Arte ha un valore selettive?" *Rivista di Psichologia dell'Arte* 6(10/11):59-71.

Although "making special" is found with other activities, it is both universal to art and helps to motivate adaptive behaviors. Artistic form, for example, signals extra effort on the part of the performer, which imbues it with additional value.

1989 *What Is Art for?* Seattle: University of Washington Press.

Dissanayake builds on her theory to develop the first full-length professional demonstration of the adaptive significance of art. It is also the first truly universal perspective as Dissanayake bases her conclusions on information from a wide range of cultures. She takes care to critique our conception of art and gives special place to the feelings art elicits, further evidence of its selective value. This also promotes spontaneous performance, much as in play and ritual. The author applies "making special" to our ability to recognize what is novel; she says it co-evolved with many other typically human products, such as tools, classification, speech, and culture.

1990 "Art for Life's Sake." *The World & I*, April, pp. 571-83.

The author claims that our present dissatisfaction with art derives from our trying to adopt a "disinterested" attitude towards it, as in the case of "art for art's sake." On the other hand, as traditional societies practiced it, art was a galvanizer of social consciousness into one whole, with obvious selective benefits.

1992 *Homo Aestheticus: Where Art Comes From and Why*. New York: Free Press.

Dissanayake builds greatly on her earlier work to make this book the major statement of the selective value of artistic form. She develops her "making special" theory as a rejoinder to contemporary critical theory and aesthetics. Dissanayake cites recent findings in neuroscience and developmental psychology to describe common methods of "making special." She provides a thorough reading of previous evolutionist approaches to art and argues for considering the strength of artistic experiences as a highly significant indication of biological utility. She also cites the benefits of art and ritual as means of self-control in troubling and otherwise uncontrollable circumstances; hence, art often expresses our preference for order and manipulation. Art has a oft-noted therapeutic quality.

1995 "Chimera, Spandrel, or Adaptation: Conceptualizing Art in Human Evolution." *Human Nature* 6 (2):99-113.

The author offers an overview and analysis of conceptual issues and problems inherent in viewing art and/or aesthetics as adaptive. Dissanayake argues that art needs to be viewed as a behavior rather than as an assemblage of products, that art-making and -appreciating are universal among the human species, that the prevailing aesthetic theories fail to be applicable, and that art-making (making special) is adaptive in that it reinforces the group, promoting its strength, to the benefit of the individuals within the group.

Dutton, Denis

1994 "Fire Is Hot. Hunger Is Bad. Babies Are Good." *Philosophy and Literature* 18:199-210.

Dutton reviews among others, Dissanayake 1992, which he praises as an alternative to poststructuralist approaches to art. He complements her findings on making special with observations of his own.

Eibl-Eibesfeldt, I.

1989 "The Biological Foundation of Aesthetics." In I. Rentschler, B. Herzberger, and D. Epstein, eds., *Beauty and the Brain: Biological Aspects of Aesthetics*. Basel: Birkhauser Verlag, pp. 29-68.

The author notes how art is generally constrained by perceptual tendencies adapted for reasons not directly relevant to art but of clear selective value. These include our preferences for clarity, contrast, and the recognition of certain "gute Gestalten," such as the "golden section." Eibl-Eibesfeldt revives, for example, the idea of a man's home being his castle by noting our preference in architecture for thick walls, unobstructed views, and niches where we may sit with our backs to a wall. Art usually provides an optimal mean in terms of information flow, a balance between custom and innovation, difficulty and ease. The author concludes by arguing for the use of art as ideological indoctrination, for making object lessons of transgressions, all the better to establish shared norms and values in a given society.

Fox, Robin

1995 "Sexual Conflict in the Epics." *Human Nature* 6 (2):135-44.

Fox casts Jung's "collective unconscious" in terms of evolutionary psychology. Using literary content as the exemplar, the author explores themes of conflict between dominant and subordinate males in the classic stories of the Bible, the Arthurian cycle, the *Illiad*, and others. He sees this theme as evolving into the modern themes of incest and adultery. Fox concludes with the notion that change in literary themes could be symptomatic of change from our so-called environment of evolutionary adaption (EEA), which Fox figures stems from the Paleolithic, allowing us to glimpse future problems.

Fuller, Peter

1983 "Art and Biology." In *The Naked Artist*. London: Writers and Readers Publishing Cooperative, pp. 2-19.

Fuller offers a Marxist perspective which somewhat grudgingly acknowledges how art transcends particular social contexts; that relatively unchanging, biological processes can be the most powerful elements in art; and that we can appreciate the works of other cultures. He notes how the selection for significant post-partum cranial development, thanks to pelvic limitations, brought about our pronounced neoteny, for him a watershed in human evolution. Because of the long childhood of humans, we were able to defer apprehending reality and could indulge our imaginations more.

Gatherer, D.

1997 "The Evolution of Music: A Comparison of Darwinian and Dialectical Methods." *Journal of Social and Evolutionary Systems* 20: 75-92.

Gatherer examines the history of stylistic change in jazz according to its interpenetration with other forms of contemporary music in order to test memetics as a model of cultural evolution, comparing it to dialectical models. He argues that dialectics "is a meta-narrative rather than a scientific theory" but finds some basis to believe that memetics may meet the Popperian standard of falsifiability, noting, for example, that being particulate, they permit more complex forms of cultural evolution such as diffusion, saltation, and the partial revival of older styles. Gatherer offers objective means for measuring the pace of stylistic change, which he also applies to classical music.

Gregory, Richard, J. Harris, P. Heard, and D. Rose, eds.
1995 *The Artful Eye*. New York: Oxford University Press.
While a selectionist viewpoint is not expressly presented, the chapters in this edited collection are based on the neurophysiology of the visual system, which presumes a biological base for what is seen. Among the many excellent chapters are "The Brain of the Beholder" by Richard Latto, "Through the Eyes of Monkeys and Men" by M. S. Livingstone and D. Hubel, and "A Portrait of the Brain" by David Rose, demonstrating how the visual system is responsible for the effects we enjoy in art.

Grinde, Bjorn
1996 "The Biology of Visual Aesthetics." *Journal of Social and Evolutionary Systems* 19 (1):31-40.
Grinde outlines a theory that art itself is not adaptive, but that it is the by-product of other fitness-enhancing behaviors. He cites examples of preferred aesthetic elements which correlate with natural phenomena apparently favored by natural selection in human evolution—as in the case of yellow and red, which denote ripe fruit and which, therefore, trigger reward mechanisms in the brain. Other examples include optimum levels of visual detail, depth of field, movement, balance, symmetry, and functionality.

Hiatt, L. R.
1989 "On Cuckoldry." *Journal of Social and Biological Structures* 12:53-72.
This article compares the plots of two Restoration plays—William Wycherly's *The Country Wife* and William Shakespeare's *A Winter's Tale*—to cuckoldry behavior by various birds. Both reflect the selectionist advantage of cuckoldry deterrence and avoidance.

Humphrey, Nicholas
1983 *Consciousness Regained: Chapters in the Development of Mind.* Oxford: Oxford University Press.
Humphrey sees art as a classifying activity, by which men come to understand their environment. Since it is essential to survival, gaining cognitive control over our surroundings becomes a source of pleasure, as in the case of collectors, and responds to our drive for novel stimuli. Artistic beauty draws us to learn, thereby preparing us to cope with new situations.

Joyce, Robert
1975 *The Esthetic Animal: Man, the Art-Created Art Creator.* Hicksville, NY: Exposition Press.
In an early book in the field with many provocative ideas, Joyce insists on the role that art played in developing our cognitive abilities, such as imagination, speculation, and communication, as well as ideologies. He notes how aesthetic response requires less training than do other functions, presumable evidence of prior evolution. The author also focuses on art's contribution to social organization and points to the large proportion of early implements devoted to its production, suggesting art's high value to our forebears.

Kagan, Andrew
1983 "Some Reflections on the Biological Significance of Style." *Arts Magazine* 58 (3): 118-21.
Kagan uses sociobiology to argue that style is a survival mechanism, saying that it imparts a sense of identity and thereby helps in forming groups and diminishing conflicts regarding possession. Style also compensates for our loss of contact with nature. The author notes the close association of stylistic change with the growth of urban centers in Western society over the past few centuries.

Keil, F.C.
1981 "Constraints on Knowledge and Cognitive Development." *Psychological Review*. 88:197-227.
This article is a discussion of biologically constrained cognitive processes. Aesthetic behavior is, according to Keil, a highly biologically constrained

behavior. Although he offers no suggestions for an adaptive use for art, this solid piece of research helps to build a case in the psychological literature for a biological basis for art.

Kernan, Alvin B.

1973 "Aggression and Satire: Art Considered As a Form of Biological Adaptation." In Frank Brady, John Palmer, and Martin Price, eds., *Literary Theory and Structure: Essays in Honor of William K. Wimsatt*. New Haven: Yale University Press, pp. 115-29.

Kernan relates satire to aggression, especially to self-defense, which may be accomplished by satire without resorting to actual violence. Satire in Kernan's view is an inhibitory mechanism generated lately for us, a relatively harmless species (lacking claws and sharp teeth) which therefore needed little self-inhibition, until weapons were invented.

Knight, Chris, Camilla Power, and Ian Watts

1995 "The Human Symbolic Revolution: A Darwinian Account." *Cambridge Archaeological Journal* 5 (1):75-114.

This article provides a compelling theory of the origins of symbolization based on proto-human female reproductive strategies driven by increasing encephalization. Using menstruation as a signal for impending fertility, early female *Homo sapiens*, it is argued, elaborated the fundamental associated signal, red blood, into body painting and ritual as a collective deceptive device to force males to provision them and their children. The authors suggest this formed the basis of the elaboration of complex symbolic communication, resulting in ritual, art, religion, and language.

Koch, Walter A.

1984 "Art: Biogenesis and Semiogenesis." *Semiotica* 49:283-304.

Koch seeks a biosemiotic foundation for art in territorial behavior. According to his theory of triadic causal relationships, art plays the role of a diversionary third force which conceals and thus enables the primary forces.

1988 "Evolution of Culture As the Evolution of Stereotypes." *Canadian-American Slavic Studies* 22 (1-4):77-100.

The author insists on an innate propensity for stereotyping in nature, one based on prior images; this enables the simplification and economy of information, which becomes rigidified rituals under pathogenetic conditions. A "third-course behavior" like a represented threat obviates the issue of fight or flight and is the beginning of art, as a necessary safety valve for aggression. Hence it is adaptive. Koch also notes the similarity between animal display and human phonemic communication, suggesting profound communication analogues with animals that date back millions of years, like Turner and Poppel's three-second rule for bird song and poetry.

1993 *The Biology of Literature*. Bochum: Brockmeyer.

Koch links verbal patterns to the structures of language, information systems, and the universe itself. His enormous paradigm assumes the selective advantage of its parts. It should be noted that Koch is providing here more of a *physics* of literature, which, at a distant point of abstraction, includes biology.

Konner, Melvin

1988 "Everyman." *The Sciences* 28(6):6-8.

This article recounts an anecdote about how the Nigerian Tiv react to narration of *Hamlet*—they find it natural for Claudius to marry his brother's widow. This reminds us of the problems and the potential of seeking crosscultural behavioral universals.

Livingstone, Margaret

1988 "Art, Illusion and the Visual System." *Scientific American* 258:78-85.

Livingstone discusses optical illusions and, among other explorations, why Seurat's *pointillism* works.

Low, Bobbi

1979 "Sexual Selection and Human Ornamentation." In Napoleon A. Chagnon and William Irons, eds., *Evolutionary Biology and Human Social Behavior: An Anthropological Perspective.* North Sciutate, MA: Duxbury Press, pp. 462-87.

The author presents a massive study of 138 present-day societies to establish the relationship between ornamentation and mating systems. She posits that sexual selection motivates this very time-consuming behavior. Notably, low social status correlates with a high degree of ornamentation, which suggests that if there is a benefit to being conspicuous, then we should expect to see much innovation and fashion shift.

Lumsden, Charles

1991 "Aesthetics." in Mary Maxwell, ed., *The Sociobiological Imagination*. Albany: State University of New York Press, pp. 253-68.

An introduction to a field that barely existed at the time of writing, this article summarizes common adaptationist arguments that art (a) judges possible situations, (b) is an efficient means of indoctrination, (c) is a means of competing for resources, including mates, (d) acts as a repository for essential information, (e) serves as practice for "real life," and (f) aids in mate selection. Lumsden notes that the affective qualities of beauty motivate humans toward all of these ends. His prediction that aesthetics will be central for sociobiology in the 1990s seems to be well on its way to being fulfilled.

Mandel, David

1967 *Changing Art, Changing Man.* New York: Horizon Press.

Mandel draws on findings in neuroscience to propose that art is not only changed by man but changes man, i. e., is an active agent in our continuing evolution. That brain cells can grow with use and atrophy from neglect leads him to describe the pedagogical functions of art.

Miller, Joseph D.

1987 "Sex, Superman and Sociobiology in Science Fiction." In George E. Slusser and Eric S. Rabkin, eds, *Aliens: The Anthropology of Science Fiction*. Carbondale, IL: Southern Illinois University Press, pp. 78-87.

Miller attributes the remarkably common sexual and reproductive dysfunction of superior mutants, aliens, and supermen in fantasy and myth to a species-wide kin altruism which has the effect of our protecting our own kind: "Don't breed with aliens, lest we are destroyed." But since these wonders are male, they may be attractive to women. For reasons of genetic diversity, a few of the not-so-divergent are admitted—at about the rate of tribal exogamy.

Mithen, Steven
1996 *The Prehistory of the Mind: The Cognitive Origins of Art, Religion and Science*. London: Thames and Hudson.
Mithen notes the synchronous appearance of early modern humans, various technological innovations, art, and religion about sixty thousand years ago. He proposes that art betokens the development of cognitive fluidity which integrates older, specialized functions and thereby provides significant adaptive advantages. He examines artifacts beginning with this period as mnemonic devices for storing and imparting useful information about the natural world and early societies.
Morris, Desmond
1962 *The Biology of Art*. New York: Alfred Knopf.
This is probably the most cited book in the field. The title overstates its subject, for Morris focuses on chimpanzee painting. He discusses art as a self-rewarding activity, like play. Generally, Morris does not adduce selective pressures for this drive, other than by its links with tool-making. He notes similarities between chimpanzee proclivities and those of humans, emphasizing the art of children and leading modernists of the time, particularly rhythm and thematic variation.

Nesse, Margaret H.
1995 "Guinevere's Choice." *Human Nature* 6 (2):145-62.
Nesse studies four versions of the Arthurian legend to demonstrate that the texts (all written by men) prioritize male reproductive strategies while devaluing female reproductive strategies. The attitudes reflected by the medieval authors conformed to "courtly love," where the lord allowed his lady to flirt with his retainers in an elaborate tease, keeping the retainers placated and supportive of the Lord. From the retainers' viewpoint, "courtly love" gave subordinate males opportunities for secret matings with high-status females. Nesse shows how authors both reflect the prevailing notions of their time and remain true to evolved evolutionary strategies.

Orians, Gordon H.
1980 "Habitat Selection: General Theory and Applications to Human Behavior." In Joan S. Lockard, ed., *The Evolution of Human Social Behavior*. New York: Elsevier, pp. 49-66.

Orians proposes a "savannah theory" of human habitat selection. The savannahs of Africa offered the optimal human environment—protection from predators, abundant shelter, and plenty of resources. The savannah theory suggests that our concept of a beautiful landscape and a pleasant place to be has been molded by the environmental choices of our early ancestors. In support of his argument, Orians points out that we are emotionally drawn to savannahs; we design savannahs for our parks. We pay high prices for lots with views—of savannahs. Orians suggests that part of our idea of beauty has evolved from habitat selection during our prehistory and that our choices of habitat continue to be influenced by the same forces which molded the choices of our ancestors.

Peckham, Morse
1965 *Man's Rage for Chaos*. Philadelphia: Chilton.

Morse notes the presence of discontinuities in all forms of art and suggests the selective role of art in preparing us for analogous situations, viz. the unexpected, in real life. This takes the form of a generalized scenario preparation, as the art-experienced mind is more flexible.

Pfeiffer, John E.
1982 *The Creative Explosion: An Inquiry into the Origins of Art and Religion*. Ithaca: Cornell University Press.

Pfeiffer takes a good look at prehistoric artifacts and cave and rock art, mixes them deftly with paleontological and anthropological findings, and produces a theory for the function of art. He reaches the conclusion that art (as practiced by early and "primitive" societies) functions as the means for educating individuals and controlling the group. By implication, this thesis means that art is adaptive in the sense that it offers the knowledge necessary for individual survival and promotes a cohesive society, which is also necessary for individual survival and reproductive possibilities.

Rabkin, Eric S.

1983 "The Descent of Fantasy." In George E. Slusser, Eric S. Rabkin, and Robert Scholes, eds., *Coordinates: Placing Science Fiction and Fantasy*. Carbondale, IL: Southern Illinois University Press, pp. 14-22. Republished in this volume.

Rabkin's essay finds the survival advantage of stories in the way they socialize men, including the cautionary tales and rehearsals for various possible scenarios. He also notes the selectionist structures that make possible such narratives, if not all explanations, in that our willingness to believe derives from a social contract of trust, thereby enabling us to absorb someone else's experience and dispense with the cost of trial-and-error cognition. Rabkin also argues the social advantages of being a storyteller.

1992 "Imagination and Survival: The Case of Fantastic Literature." *Foundation* 56:84-98. Reprinted in Brett Cooke, George E.Slusser, and Jaume Olivella, eds., *The Fantastic Other: An Interface of Perspectives.* Amsterdam: Editions Rodopi, 1998, pp. 1-20. 1992 Italian translation: "Paura della fantasia." *Prometeo* 10 (38):90-102. Reprinted in this volume.

In Rabkins overview of fantastic literature, fantasy constitutes an enterprise wherein we can prepare for various contingencies by means of vicarious experience and learn to cope with our fears. Fantasy also provides a refuge for genius, which is so often oppressed by society.

1995 "Vegetable, Animal, Human: The Perils and Powers of Transgressing (Sociobiological) Boundaries in Narrative." *Human Nature* 6 (2):165-80.

Ellen Dissanayake has suggested that art has served an adaptive purpose in that it has promoted group cohesion by making individuals feel secure within their group, fueling fear of outsiders, and establishing group norms. Rabkin argues that narrative also has and does serve such a purpose. In particular, he shows that narrative has worked to set boundaries (e. g., "Thou shalt not kill") which individuals must not cross, and also has worked to push the boundaries when necessary (e.g., forbidden-fruit stories are about expanding boundaries).

Rancour-Laferriere, Daniel

1981 "Preliminary Remarks on Literary Memetics." In Karl Menges and Daniel Rancour-Laferriere, eds., *Axia: Davis Symposium on Literary Evaluation*. Stuttgart: Akademischer Verlag, pp. 77-87. Reprinted in this volume.

The author notes connections between Freudian associations and personalized memetics in the common characterization of intellectual property as the creator's self or his offspring. This attitude motivates artists and others to fight for their ideas or those of relatives and friends.

1993 "Anna's Adultery: Distal Sociobiology vs. Proximate Psychoanalysis." *Tolstoy Studies Journal* 6:33-46.

Rancour-Laferriere presents a sociobiological view of Anna's adultery, pointing out both her reasons to take a lover and why female infidelity is especially abhorred, with a Freudian/Kohutian perspective on the psychological mechanisms involved. In particular, the author traces Anna's disturbed narcissism to her childhood, which makes her all the more vulnerable to the attentive Vronsky.

Scalise Sugiyama, Michelle

1996a "On the Origins of Narrative: Storyteller Bias as a Fitness-Enhancing Strategy." *Human Nature* 7: 403-25.

Scalise Sugiyama studies how evidence of variants for folktales accords with the fitness interests of storytellers or their patrons. She demonstrates examples of narratorial bias which reflect distinctions in birth order and gender (men, for example, are more prone to aggression and self-aggrandizement, while women protect their reputations by avoiding profanity). As Scalise Sugiyama notes, this is not a one-way street. Storytellers are motivated by their own interests to better perceive and manipulate the self-interests of their audience; their fitness may depend on their ability to anticipate the fitness stratagems of their listeners. That the storyteller is often distinguished by the perception that he or she holds special knowledge may constitute the germ of fictional narrative.

1996b "What's Love Got to Do with It? An Evolutionary Analysis of 'The Short Life of Francis Macomber.'" *The Hemingway Review* 15: 15-32.

The author examines Hemingways story as a wonderful example of evolutionary psychology, which predicts that the behavior of contemporary human beings will reflect anachronistic proclivities due to their extensive history in Pleistocene environments. A man's failure in hunting sets into motion a series of moves and countermoves which expresses how the different reproductive strategies of men and women respond to each other. Scalise Sugiyama carefully demonstrates how the adulterous heroine and cuckolded hero each act in a manner remarkably consistent with a Darwinian assessment of their potential minimum reproductive investment, even as this calculation is refigured at each turn in the plot.

Storey, Robert

1996 *Mimesis and the Human Animal: On the Biogenetic Foundations of Literary Representation.* Evanston: Northwestern University Press.

Like other authors—Carroll 1994, Dissanayake 1992—Storey offers a thorough and very damning critique of deconstructionist thought. He then carefully lays the ground for a Darwinist study of the arts. The difference here is that he complements earlier studies by drawing his arguments from a number of new sources of empirical knowledge: psychology—particularly of emotions—social structures, and linguistics are prominent amongst the fields he imports into the debate. Having outlined a "biogrammar" relevant for literature and drama, the arts on which he chiefly focuses, Storey suggests a great variety of ways in which a Darwinist perspective can be applied to the arts. He scans juvenile narratives as, like child's play, rehearsals for the world they will grow into. Significantly, our interest in narrative peaks at the end of adolescence, by which time socialization should be complete in traditional societies. Adaptation to one's social norms underlines Storey's theory of comic situations. Storey also shows how tragedy induces socialization by confronting us with a universe of limitations.

Sutterlin, Christa

1987 "Mittelalterliche Kirchen-Skulptur als Beispiel universaler Abwehrsymbolik." In Johann Georg Prin von Hohenzollern and Max

Liedtke, eds., *Vom Kritzeln zur Kunst*. Bad Heilbrunn: Verlag Julius Klinkhardt, pp. 82-100.

1989 "Universals in Apotropaic Symbolism: A Behavioral and Comparative Approach to Some Medieval Sculptures." *Leonardo* 22 (1):65-74.

Sutterlin studies the ubiquity of genital-display imagery, especially in architectural sculpture, dating back into prehistory. Her analysis eliminates religious and, noting the figures' fierce grimaces, erotic interpretations. Their typical placement, near doorways, and on roof lines, suggests their atropaic use, as amulets to ward off evil. That much of this same behavior is exhibited by children leads Sutterlin to deduce that it is rooted in our biology. The 1987 German version is somewhat more detailed than the 1989 English translation.[3]

Trout, Paul A.

1993 "The Biology and Physics of Beauty." *Brock Review* 2 (2):183-200.

Trout summarizes and reviews Frederick Turner's work in biopoetics—particularly 1985 and 1991a. He also cites works of a more rigorous nature which support Turner's theories.

Turner, Frederick

1985 *Natural Classicism: Essays on Literature and Science*. New York: Paragon House.

Turner asserts that "aesthetic choice can be a determinative force in evolution"; beauty is often associated with reproductive activity. Our response to patterns is a reward for creating models of the world, hence to test predictive statements. The author notes how cultural universals parallel major themes of representational art and suggests that their number in a given work roughly correlates with its standing as a classic.

1991a *Beauty: The Value of Values*. Charlottesville: University Press of Virginia.

This is an often beautiful and inspiring essay about our preference for elegant perspectives, which Turner believes to be close to the actual order of the universe, per recent findings in chaos theory, as in the case of the "golden section." This instinct for beauty we gained via a positive feedback loop in truth-gaining. The author incorporates theories of Rene Girard regarding our unacknowledged shame at the price we have paid for human culture, often gained by the suffering of others, an inevitable result of selection processes. He sees artistic tendencies as being prefigured by "neurocharms" in the brain and correlating with Jungian archetypes.

1991b "Toward an Evolutionary Ontology of Beauty." *Oral Tradition* 6 (1):126-29.

Turner argues that neurogenetic tendencies apply to traditional as well as developed cultures, given that they are based on reproductive success in gene pools and that these rules serve to release artistic potential for both performer and audience. Making the same daring thesis as in his latest book (1991a), Turner accounts for beauty as a feedback mechanism to guide us in recognizing, harmonizing with, and contributing to the deep creative tendency of the universe itself.

1995 *The Culture of Hope: A New Birth of the Classical Spirit.* New York: Free Press.

Taking "the third side in the culture wars," this book is a cultural manifesto that concludes Turner's series of five critical prose works on "natural classicism": *Natural Classicism: Essays on Literature and Science*, 1992; *Rebirth of Value: Meditations on Beauty, Ecology, Religion and Education*, 1991; *Tempest, Flute, and Oz: Essays on the Future*, 1992; and *Beauty: The Value of Values*, 1992. Turner's highly controversial positions have been attacked by both the right and the left—the right in opposition to his foundational use of evolutionary theory, his defense of liberal freedoms, and his scientific treatment of religion; the left because Turner systematically refutes the logical and evidentiary underpinnings of much contemporary academic feminist, multiculturalist, environmentalist, and deconstructionist social theory. Though its concerns go beyond the biocultural underpinnings of the arts, much of the book is devoted to the refounding of the arts upon a biopoetic aesthetics, and the rehabilitation of traditional artistic forms and techniques such as musical melody, visual realism, storytelling, poetic meter, and dramatic mimesis. Inasmuch as modernism and postmodernism have rejected those traditions, and the emotions and morality that they imply, Turner calls for the emergence of a new cultural era of evolutionary hope. He attacks the dualisms of postmodern humanistic and social theory—order/disorder, patriarchy/matriarchy, human/animal, technology/nature, deterministic/random, and Western/non-Western—exposes the fallacies of cultural relativism and static pluralism, and argues for a reconsideration of the value of dynamic hierarchy as the indispensable tool of understanding. Turner extends his theory of beauty as the universal principle of evolutionary emergence through chaotic self-organization and feedback, and concludes with an avowedly speculative metaphysics of nonlinear time as the basis for cultural renewal.

1996 "An Evolutionary/Chaotic Theory of Beauty and Meaning." *Journal of Social and Evolutionary Systems* 19 (2):103-24.

Much of this essay is a condensed version of Turner 1991a. Turner presents an aesthetic theory encompassing biocultural coevolution, in which the evolution of our sense of beauty works by non-linear feedback loops so as to give us a greater preference for the fundamental generative processes of the universe. This sense probably yields adaptive benefits. He outlines panhuman "natural classical neurocharms" which accelerate our response to such "emegence promising systems."

Uher, Johanna

1991a "Die Asthetik von Zick-Zack und Welle: Ethologische Aspekte der Wirkung linearer Muster." Ph.D. diss., Universität München, München, Germany.

The thesis is that zigzag and wave motifs as seen in art have universal meaning and, thus, a biological basis. After a discussion of the appearance of these patterns in art (examples are offered from body decoration, architecture, weapon decoration, ritual items, and utensils for everyday use), Uher presents the results of a questionnaire-study she conducted using 1,100 central European subjects. The questionnaire consisted of one motif, twenty-four polar adjectives (such as "scary" vs. "comforting"), and a seven-scale rating. She found a statistically significant difference between the adjectives paired with the zigzag and the adjectives paired with the wave pattern. The zigzag pattern was associated with agonistic adjectives and the wave pattern with affiliative adjectives. Another questionnaire using these patterns in combination with eye motifs was presented to the subjects, who again chose adjectives which they felt corresponded to the combinations. The results of this study were less clear although the eye combined with the wave tended to be associated with agonistic adjectives in contrast to the affiliative effect of the wave alone.

1991b "On Zigzag Designs: Three Levels of Meaning." *Current Anthropology* 32 4):437- 39.

This brief article provides a social context for the findings in Uher's dissertation (1991a). Because zigzags normally appear together with eyes and threatening motifs in amulets, masks, etc., it is assumed that the zigzag pattern has a similar function, i.e., threat. The zigzag may be compared to the bite threat, a facial display showing the canines, thus hinting that the zigzag is used in social signaling.

Washburn, S. L.

1970 Comment on "A Possible Evolutionary Basis for Aesthetic Appreciation in Men and Apes." *Evolution*, 24 (4):824-25.

In a response to Bleakney 1970, Washburn offers the ability to evaluate tools and hand skills as a selection pressure for artistic judgment. This brief note reminds us that in the past and at this level of activity virtually all humans were artists, if we assume that most had to make their own tools. A second source of adaptation benefit comes from the social esteem one might gain by being a master in making tools.

Wilson, Edward O.

1985 "The Poetic Species" and "The Serpent." In *Biophilia*. Cambridge MA: Harvard University Press, pp. 57-102. Reprinted in this volume.

For a discussion of these chapters, see Brett Cooke's "Edward O. Wilson on Art" in this volume, pages 104-112.

1998 "The Arts and Their Interpretation." In *Consilience: The Unity of Knowledge*. New York: Alfred A. Knopf, pp. 210-37.

This chapter is discussed in this volume in Brett Cooke's "Edward O. Wilson on Art," pages 113-115.

Ziff, Paul

1981 "Art and Sociobiology." *Mind* 90 (October):505-20.

This is an early article which considers how sociobiology and aesthetics might come together. Philosopher Ziff ruminates on aesthetic response, discussing what biological value it might have.

Notes

1. A number of essays have made this assertion. Although they do not advance any hard evidence or likely rationale, they are frequently cited. Among the better-known sources of this kind are
   Gregory Bateson. *Steps to an Ecology of the Mind: Collected Essays in Anthropology, Psychiatry, Evolution, and Epistemology*. New York: Ballantine, 1972.
   Stanley Burnshaw. *The Seamless Web: Language-Thinking, Creature-Knowledge, Art-Experience*. New York: George Braziller, 1970.
   Suzanne K. Langer. *Feeling and Form: A Theory of Art*. New York: Scribner's, 1953.
2. Besides vague arguments for the biology of art, I have also excluded studies which use the arts largely as a convenient database and say little about art per se. These include
   Gonzalo Alvarez. "Child-Holding Patterns and Hemispheric Bias: Evidence from Pre-Columbian American Art." *Ethology and Sociobiology* 11 (1990): 75-82.
   Bruce J. Ellis and Donald Symons. "Sex Differences in Sexual Fantasy: An Evolutionary Psychological Approach." *Journal of Sex Research*, 27 (1990): 527-55.
   Otto-Joachim Grusser. "Mother-Child Holding Patterns in Western Art: A Developmental Study." *Ethology and Sociobiology*, 4 (1983): 89-94.
3. We have not been able to examine what seems to be a book-length study of the same subject: Ireneaus Eibl-Eibesfeldt and Christa Sutterlin. *Im Banne der Angst: Zur Natur- und Kunstgechichte menschlicher Abwehrsymbolik*. Munich: Piper, 1992.

Author's Page

Nancy Aiken
Independent Scholar, Guysville, Ohio

Wayne E. Allen
Executive Director, Treaty Site History Center, Saint Peter, Minnesota.

Alexander Argyros
Professor of Arts and Humanities, University of Texas at Dallas, Richardson, Texas.

Joseph Carroll
Professor of English, University of Missouri, St. Louis, Missouri.

Kathryn Coe
Assistant Professor of Anthropology, University of Missouri, Columbus, Missouri.

Brett Cooke
Associate Professor of Russian, Texas A&M University, College Station, Texas.

Lee Cronk
Associate Professor of Anthropology, Texas A&M University, College Station, Texas.

Koen Depryck
Institute of Knowledge Management, University of Ghent, Dilbeek, Belgium.

Ellen Dissanayake
Independent Scholar, Seattle, Washington.

Nancy Easterlin
Associate Professor of English, University of New Orleans, New Orleans, Louisiana.

Brian K. Hansen
Professor Emeritus of Theater and Dance, University of New Mexico, Albuquerque, New Mexico.

Joseph D. Miller
Associate Professor of Pharmacology, Texas Tech University Health Sciences Center, Lubbock, Texas.

Eric S. Rabkin
Professor of English, University of Michigan, Ann Arbor, Michigan.

Daniel Rancour-Laferriere
Professor of Russian, University of California, Davis, California.

Frederick Turner
Founders Professor of Arts and Humanities, University of Texas at Dallas, Richardson, Texas.

Gary Westfahl
Learning Center, University of California, Riverside, California.